" "

Bruce is a passionate Christian and an extraordinary street-evangelist. For many years he journalled his experiences on the streets and this book is the fruit of that long loving labour. It is chock full of smiles and tears and testimony. If you enjoy a homely yarn and you want to see the inside of a beautiful life, Bruce's winsome musings will delight you.

Rev Dr Allan Demond, *Senior Pastor, NewHope Baptist Church, Blackburn Vic.*

It is not often that I have known a person of deeply committed Christian faith whose total life has been an example of selfless service to other people and the Lord Jesus Christ. Bruce Kelly, who I have known for nearly 50 years is one of those people. I met him when we were both junior members of the Victoria Police stationed at metropolitan police stations. Bruce was a genuine, dedicated Christian police member with high integrity and I thought he should be striving for promotion. However, he was dedicated to performing the valuable daily operational tasks of policing on the ground. After early retirement, he served as a Baptist Pastor in several churches followed by years of voluntary service sharing his deep and genuine Christian faith and supportive Christian material with people on the streets of Melbourne. I am sure readers will experience an inspiring insight into the life-long commitment of this Christian policeman and evangelist.

Bob Boucher, *Retired Assistant Commissioner, Victoria Police.*

From farmer to policeman to street evangelist, this book tracks the ordinary yet extraordinary life of Bruce Kelly. Bruce's account of his life's journey is an example of simple obedience to the Great Commission with a simple strategy: seizing every available opportunity to plant a gospel seed by engaging people from all walks of life in conversation, asking them the 'Big Question' and distributing literature, all the while expecting God to do an unseen work in the lives of those with whom he shares.

Sharon Rodrick, *Board Member, One Mission Society*

In Front Of Them All

Bruce R Kelly

Ark House Press
arkhousepress.com

© 2023 Bruce R Kelly

All rights reserved. Apart from any fair dealing for the purpose of study, research, criticism, or review, as permitted under the Copyright Act, no part may be reproduced by any process without written permission.

Scripture taken from the New King James Version®. Copyright © 1982 by Thomas Nelson. Used by permission. All rights reserved.

Some names and identifying details have been changed to protect the privacy of individuals.

Cataloguing in Publication Data:
Title: In Front Of Them All
ISBN: 978-0-6457741-1-5 (pbk)
Subjects: Biography; Christian Inspiration;
Other Authors/Contributors: Kelly, Bruce R,

Design by initiateagency.com

Foreword

This book is dedicated to the memory of the pioneers and original members of the Light Community Baptist Church (LCBC), East Ringwood Vic, founded on 8th February 1925 and constituted by the Baptist Union of Victoria on 17th February 1929. Gratitude is extended also to the Godly mentors at NewHope Baptist Church (North Blackburn Vic) who in earlier days laid in my life a sound Christian foundation and supported us in various ways on a continuing spiritual basis. Thanks also to the Pastors, members and friends at LCBC where we currently encounter many expressions of Tender Loving Care and practical assistance.

Special thanks to my wife, Jan, for her faithful years of assistance in compiling and circulating the monthly reports from which much of the material for this book was gleaned, and for her computer skills, spiritual advice, and editorial work. To Lesley Cole, Shirley Carlson, and Emily Trueong, sincere appreciation for your help in proof reading some of the manuscripts.

The book title **'In Front Of Them All'** is borrowed from signage above the entrance to the United Nations Head Quarters village on the South Korean side of the 38th parallel dividing North and South Korea. It was here that the rampaging North Korean military were repelled by United Nations Forces in their intended invasion of South Korea. The title 'In Front Of Them All' neatly describes my city evangelism ministry.

My goal was to evangelise three days a week, sharing testimony and literature with ten contacts per day. Most times this goal was achieved. I tried hard to keep this ministry based on scriptural principles. Contained herein are references to some of my contacts. A few became Christians. Many remain friends. Most contributed in some way to my spiritual growth.

Construction of the underground city rail loop had eventually closed down many city cafes and fast-food outlets in Swanston Street and Federation Square. COVID-19 lockdowns reduced overseas students and tourists in the city, and commuters on the public transport system to a trickle. A significantly broken ankle sustained on 18th December 2020 further limited mobility to our local street, park, and shopping centre. Ministry in closer proximity to a local church appealed to us. Our membership of forty-five years at NewHope Baptist Church, was transferred to the LCBC.

During the lengthy and difficult aftermath of this injury our Pastor said, "Bruce you need a challenge to occupy your mind during the recovery process. Write a book!" I had never dreamed of writing a book. Becoming an author had never crossed my mind. My immediate reaction was: "What on earth would I write about, and who would read it anyway?"

Selwyn Hughes, in an edition of his 'Every Day with Jesus' study notes in commenting on the Parable of the Lost Coin (Luke 15:8*) said, "God sweeps the universe with the broom of His redemptive grace until He finds the coin on which His image is stamped." Searching for 'God's Lost Coins' is an uplifting experience well worth writing about. The only Bible some people will read are the lives of Christians. We are a letter anyone can read just by looking at us. Christ Himself wrote it, not with ink but with His living Spirit, not chiselled into stone, but carved into our hearts and we publish it (2 Corinthians 3:2-3).

Reflection on entries from an almost lifelong obsession with journal writing conjured up memories of wonderful people I have met and marvellous experiences I treasure. I am privileged to share a few of these moments and events with you.

The caricature reproduced on the front cover, was drawn by Manish Kumar Gamir, an Indian art student, in a remarkably brief moment of time while the Gospel was shared with him and his two mates in Federation Square.

Throughout this book some titles, events and locations are changed for security reasons, and to alleviate repetition.

To facilitate your reading convenience the glossary below contains abbreviations of terms you will meet as you read through the book.

Glossary:

BQ – Big Question - 'What is the most important question in all the world for you?' (Perhaps you may ponder on this question as you read).
BC – Blessing Cards
TPTL NT - The Pocket Testament League New Testament.
WW1G - the replica World War 1 Gospel of John produced by Life Words.
NWT – New World Translation produced by the Watchtower organisation.
FS - Federation Square, Melbourne CBD
FSRSP - Flinders Street Railway Station Platform.
LCBC - Light Community Baptist Church.
ERRP - East Ringwood Railway Platform.
CBD – Central Business District.

References:

Luke 15:8 -Or what woman having ten silver coins, if she loses one coin, does not light a lamp, sweep the house, and search carefully until she finds it?

Contents

Foreword v
Introduction xi

Chapter 1: Sheep Farmer's Journey to Multi-Cultural City
Streets Ministry 1
Chapter 2: Birth of the Street Ministry 14
Chapter 3: Overview of Street Evangelism 24
Chapter 4: Significant Christian Influence Among Africans 39
Chapter 5: Asian Background Associations 47
Chapter 6: Brazilian Experiences 72
Chapter 7: Conversations with Buddhists 78
Chapter 8: Friendly Burmese 90
Chapter 9: Dutch Backpackers and Tourists 98
Chapter 10: Egyptian Encounters 103
Chapter 11: French Backpackers and Tourists 107
Chapter 12: German Responses 112
Chapter 13: Garrulous Greeks 120
Chapter 14: Numerous Indian Contacts 131
Chapter 15: Challenging Discussions with Israelis 165

Chapter 16:	Italian Outreach	171
Chapter 17:	Japanese Students and Travellers	175
Chapter 18:	Encounters with Koreans in Australia and South Korea	187
Chapter 19:	Characters Encountered in McDonalds and Hungry Jacks	208
Chapter 20:	Interactions With Muslims	227
Chapter 21:	Nepalese Students and Tourists	255
Chapter 22:	Persian (Iranian) Visitors	271
Chapter 23:	Seeking Sikhs	286
Chapter 24:	Sri Lankan Experiences	311
Chapter 25:	Three Sectarian Influences	322
Chapter 26:	Endless Opportunities in Melbourne Business District (CBD)	358
Chapter 27:	Melbourne's Maze of Laneways	382
Chapter 28:	Public Transport Evangelism	390
Chapter 29:	A New Direction - Local and East Ringwood Outreach	403
Chapter 30:	Church Planting and Interims	424
Chapter 31:	Overseas Adventures	464
Chapter 32:	Interstate Journeys	488
Chapter 33:	Medical Procedures and Birthday Celebrations	506
Chapter 34:	Legendary Mentors	520
Chapter 35:	Sacrificial Service – 'Wars, Wounds & Wisdom'	538
Chapter 36:	COVID-19 Lockdown (2020-2021)	553
Chapter 37:	Conclusion	556

Timeline...565

Introduction

Occasionally, I wondered why I continued with my 'In Front Of Them All' ministry. However, my farming background of ploughing fields, sowing seed, and harvesting, reminds me of our Lord's parable in which He said, **"So, is the Kingdom of God**, as if a man should cast seed <u>into the ground</u> and during his sleep, the seed springs up and grows but he knows not how" (Mark 4:26-27 KJV). The work goes on secretly and silently for weeks or months. God reveals only a fraction of His working to our sight. Sometimes I prepared the ground, sometimes I planted, sometimes I watered, but praise God, He gives the increase in accord with His timing.

Prayer the Turning Point

Jan and I once travelled across Canada with Dr Wesley Duewel, a former One Mission Society (OMS) missionary in India and OMS International President. Dr Duewel authored several classics on the Spirit filled Christian life. On March 5, 2016, Dr Duewel graduated to glory. It felt like I had lost an old friend.

In one of his books entitled 'Touch the World through Prayer', Duewel wrote, "OMS began its work in India in 1941. The first twenty-five years of hard labour, sweat, tears, prayer and fasting produced an average of one or two local churches per year. As I flew across the Pacific for furlough in 1964, God led me to ask for a thousand prayer partners to spend fifteen minutes per day in prayer for India and our work. Some years later, churches in India numbered 300 with 25,000 believers, and with twenty-five or more new churches established every year. As of December 2015, the numbers had increased to 5,276 churches and 11,620 house churches" (page 112). One thousand prayer warriors uniting in praying for the harvest was the key.

A key question that often arose was, 'How does the Spirit guide you to contacts for evangelistic purposes in street ministry?' Prayer is invaluable! A team of four or five Christians frequently accompanied me to the city, and prayed for guidance. Additionally, many readers of my monthly newsletters regularly assured me of prayer support. In response to these prayers the Lord lead me into contact with thousands over the years. Occasionally, the Spirit specifically led me, but mainly I shared with anyone within reach and encountered very little hostility. As I see it, 2,000 years ago Christ lined up all Christians on the starting blocks, turned them loose in the world and with a loud voice said, "GO YE! I am with you always."

Genesis 12:1-3 – The Key that Unlocked my Ministry

Though I had been around the church scene for several years, a two-year intensive Bethel Bible study course under the guidance of Rev Dr Graeme Smith, a former Pastor at the North Blackburn Baptist Church, taught me how to love, treasure and navigate the Old Testament. The first three chapters of Genesis includes references to God's awesome creation. The remainder of the Bible reveals what God is doing to restore His creation to its original glory. This simple overview proved both revelatory and fascinating to both me and later to many contacts on the street.

My Launching Pad for Ministry

From Genesis 12:1-3, I caught a glimpse of God's unfolding drama of redemption beginning before time and stretching beyond eternity. It led me into an understanding in broad terms, where I fitted into God's divine intentions for reclaiming His lost heritage.

> "The Lord had said to Abram, leave your native country,
> your relatives, and your father's family and
> Go to the land that I will show you. I will make you into a
> great nation. I will bless you and make you famous,
> and you will be a blessing to others. I will bless those who
> bless you and curse those who treat you with contempt.
> All the families on earth will be blessed through you"
> (Genesis 12:1-3 NLT).

Abram set sail into the wide blue yonder not knowing where he was headed, nor how to perform, but He trusted God to supply the giftedness, guidance, and resources along the way.

Go For It!

Abram's (later Abraham) calling became my benchmark. Through it I understood (somewhat dimly I think) that God was launching me into a twenty plus year street ministry of evangelism. My calling through Abram's vision included a progressive revelation of God's giftedness, guidance, and bounteous provision in ministry. I now believe that most, if not all ministry gifts i.e., apostles, prophets, evangelists, pastors, and teachers (Ephesians

4:11), are discovered in the pursuit of opportunities. Evangelism is an exciting journey of discovery. Abraham's calling became my second blessing.

The Biblical doctrines in the first three chapters of Genesis, stamps Christianity as totally different to all other philosophies and religions. These three chapters are the seedbed from which most, if not all, Biblical doctrines grow. Explaining my relationship with the Creator through faith and trust in the risen Saviour, the entire cosmos of God's glory, and human beings as the only creature made in God's image, is essential to ministry. Other faiths insist their religion has much in common with ours, but you better believe it - Christianity is a standout. My weak faith is valid because the object of my faith is a powerful Saviour.

In Front of Them All

In 2005 Jan and I visited the famous 38th Parallel, the narrow de-militarised zone dividing North and South Korea. The UN Command Security Battalion HQ was established on the south side of this parallel in 1952 after successfully securing the South Korean Peninsula against advancing communist hordes. Across the archway above the entrance to their UN HQ command village at Pan Mun Jom is suspended a sign written in large words 'In Front of Them All'.

In June 1950, the North Korean army had crossed the 38th Parallel and massively invaded South Korea. Within months, General Douglas MacArthur cut the North Korean army in half with his swift Inchon landing and the United Nations forces captured 150,000 North Korean prisoners. Harold Voelkel, an American Presbyterian evangelist, recognised them as unparalleled evangelistic opportunities. Voelkel organised more and more meetings within prison camps. Events were attended by up to 10,000 North Korean prisoners singing hymns, listening to messages, praying. It is estimated that some 15,000 men found Christ during the three years they were prisoners.

This phrase, '**In Front of Them All**' became my personal mantra, and title for this book. A.W. Tozer, a famous preacher of yesteryear, once said, "It has been the history of the world that the masses are never right. The masses were wrong at the time of Noah's flood. It was only Noah and his family who were right. The masses always go the wrong way." One man standing is God's order.

Bruises and Blessings

When New Testament Christians preached 'repentance and remission of sins', sinners realised the consequences of breaking God's law was judgement and eternal punishment. We do not hear enough of these principles being taught today. Sinners will flee from wrath to come if they believe there is wrath to come. God's Law brings them to this realisation. The Spurgeons, Wesleys, Moodys and Finneys of yesteryear followed this pattern with great results. To suggest to my contacts that they are liars, thieves, blasphemers, adulterers, and murderers and that God's anger burns against their sin, is not the way to win friends in the ordinary sense of the word. It is an experience not to be undertaken lightly, but it is scriptural. Awakening sinners to their need of repentance and remission of sins is a task for which I am unequal, however through prayer and Holy Spirit guidance, I plant and water, but God gives the increase. I praise God that sometimes I was there when salvation occurred. Praying that new Christians would become crucial witnesses in towns and villages in their homeland was always a priority in street evangelism.

A member of a radical political group in the Bourke Mall said, "I remember you. You talk to us from time to time. You are fixed in your thinking. All you do is waste our time. Goodbye!" I shook their dust off my shoes. "Go ye.........." (Mark 16:15) is one of Christ's imperatives. Being pushed into the outer perimeter of insignificance is not part of God's plan.

Jesus entered, possessed, and inherited by way of example. Paul entered, possessed, and inherited as a condition of the Great Commission. It hasn't changed. The church still enters, possesses, and inherits. Redemptions, sanctifications, and divine healings currently abound often in most difficult of anti-Christian climates.

Spiritual Growth

A book entitled 'In Search of Persons of Peace' by Carolyn L. Knight, contains up-to-date illustrations, narratives and evidence-based suggestions for multiplying evangelism and long-term discipleship. Another Christian and I have conducted prayer ministry in dozens of local streets for some four years (at the time of writing). We discussed one chapter from this and other books as a preamble to our weekly prayer ministry. Dr Knight's book continues fueling my prayer. By putting the 'persons of peace' concept to work we can multiply opportunities for people to know Christ.

> "But whatever house you enter, first say, "Peace to this house."
> And if a son of peace is there, your peace will rest on it;
> if not, it will return to you"(Luke 10:5-6).

God strengthens His people through His Word in times of plenty and need. 'Bruises and Blessings' work together for good to them that love God and are called according to His purpose. When uncertainty grips cling to Him who is steadfast.

Learning to share the Gospel is a process not an event. Nothing beats physically standing 'in front of them all' in a ministry area. Face to face with the hordes, walking amongst them, watching expressions, looking into their eyes, and experiencing different cultures is challenging. Sharing the Gospel, even if only with one lost soul, is heart lifting and exhilarating. It inspires worship and praise in ways I seldom otherwise experience.

Chapter 1

Sheep Farmer's Journey to Multi-Cultural City Streets Ministry

The Journey Begins

Let's go back to 1936. A baby boy arrived at the Kyabram Bush Nursing Hospital. He lived his first twenty-five years on a dairy and sheep farm at Wyuna in the Goulburn Valley district of Northern Victoria. In his teenage years, he saw Divinity in the blue sky and beautiful country sunsets but couldn't understand how he fitted into the overall pattern. This dilemma combined with personal issues, niggled for years. In despair, he looked up into a night sky with zero pollution, punctuated with millions of tiny twinkling stars and said, "God, I do not know who you are. I don't even know if you exist. But if you are there, please help me." Soon enough his prayer was answered.

Devoutly active evangelical Christian neighbours operated a small local country post office in their home near where we lived. They were raised in the old-fashioned Methodist tradition and had graduated years before from the former Melbourne Bible Institute. Soon after my prayer, I walked across to the Post Office to collect our mail. A travelling evangelist in an ancient van with scripture verses painted along the side panels, 'happened' to be overnighting with these neighbours. Equipped with portable loudspeakers and a demountable platform, he could set up on a street corner and be preaching in five minutes.

Starting Somewhere

In the early hours of that morning, the evangelist led me to Christ. This was the starting point of my Christian experience. I got out of bed next morning feeling like I'd had a spiritual bath inside. The sky was bluer. Grass was greener and birds sang more sweetly in the trees.

My mother was born Florence Ross in Carnoustie, Scotland. Her parents, four siblings and a boarder lived together in the same three roomed house. Three slept in the same bed to keep warm on cold winter nights. They embarked in London on the S.S. Borda and disembarked in Melbourne in November 1914. The Ross family eventually settled in Wyuna South (Vic) on land which they developed into orchards. My father, Keith Sydney Kelly, who lived on a nearby dairy farm and Florence were married in the Presbyterian Church at Kyabram on 31st October 1934.

Blessings and Bruises

The great Welsh preacher, Dr Martyn Lloyd-Jones, once said, "There is no grosser or greater misrepresentation of the Christian message than that which depicts it as offering a life of ease with no battle and struggle at all. Sooner or later every believer discovers that the Christian life is a battleground, not a playground."

Disappointment, failure, temptation, disillusionment, and opposition followed hot on the heels of my first encounter with Jesus. My decision for Christ was vehemently opposed by my parents. The level of mother's anger shocked me. Shaking with rage she shouted, "Why get mixed up in this crazy religious rubbish! You're a good law-abiding boy! It'll send you mad! What's wrong with you?" She burned Christian literature sent in the mail, banned me from visiting our neighbours and from attending church. Her ferocity hit me with the force of an unexpected howling gale. Cowed into silence, I survived as a Christian for the next ten years by listening secretly to Christian radio programmes with my bedside radio turned low late at night.

My older brother's death, as a babe in mother's arms before I was born, must have impacted her deeply. In hindsight I believe his death may have been the bitter blow which flavoured her philosophy on life. I doubt she ever fully recovered. I always knew her as a driven woman burying herself in hard work. In more recent years, I surmised that she unrealistically projected all her hopes and dreams for my older brother on to me. I look forward to meeting my brother one day.

Old age and ill health eventually caught up with my mother. My sister and I took turns in sitting at her bedside in the week preceding her death in a Brisbane hospital. I talked with Mum about her spiritual destiny. Although she could no longer articulate, the old hostility quickly and loudly resurfaced. She was suffering, had no quality of life and would never recover. She died early next morning at age eighty-eight. Mum had proudly shown photographs of me in uniform, referring to me as her son the Policeman, but never once as her son the Pastor. Later she was heard to say, "I've lost two sons. One to illness and one to religion." Regrets? I have a few.

That mother bitterly refused to acknowledge my Christian faith even in her last moments, is a big one. I have spent far too much time trying to forget things I don't want to remember. I became trapped in a prison of resentment for years. Resentment can too easily develop into hatred. The best answer I know is the one Jesus offered on the Cross: "Father, forgive them, for they know not what they do." John Wesley said, "Freedom is a word that best sums up the Christian life. Therefore, refuse to be trapped by your past."

However, flashbacks regarding aspects of my family history occur at unexpected moments. Notwithstanding, I am grateful to God for His gift of forgiveness; to my parents for their long years of labour and toil and the financial wizardry of my wonderful wife, who carefully grew our inheritance into a comfortable lifestyle:

> "Through the Lord's mercies we are not consumed, because
> His compassions fail not. They are new every morning; great
> is Your faithfulness; the Lord is my portion, says my soul.
> Therefore, I hope in Him." (Lamentations 3:22-24)

My parents had set their hearts on me, their only son, taking over the family farming enterprise. How could I leave them? My dilemma was real. The extrication process was painful, daunting and ten years in the making. But suffering does not always have the final say. The Crucifixion demonstrates God's love for us. Resurrection is God's power to live life triumphantly. The secret is trusting Jesus on a daily basis. Blessings are sweeter when God delivers from bruises. 'Burdens are lifted at Calvary.'

> "Blessed be the God and Father of our Lord Jesus Christ,
> the Father of mercies and God of all comfort,
> who comforts us in all our tribulation,
> that we may be able to comfort those who are in any trouble,
> with the comfort with which we ourselves are comforted by God."
> (2 Corinthians 1:3-4)

Time to Move On

My farming exit came to a head one day as I was shearing our flock. I was a fairly good shearer, but it took fifteen minutes between sheep to straighten my aching back - besides I hated sheep with a passion. I think sheep are close to being the dumbest of animals. One day, as I walked from the shearing shed to the house for lunch, my mother suggested I attend a Police recruiting campaign in the old Echuca courthouse that afternoon. She had seen the advertisement in a locally circulating newspaper. She must have realised I would never make it on the land, and that a successful application would signal the end of her hopes and dreams.

Several high-ranking Police Officers comprised the selection panel - one of whom was eventually promoted to Chief Commissioner. They were lined up behind the 'Bench' from where justice was meted out. I was ushered to the defendant's stand. I didn't realise its significance then. They looked down at me with an imperious glare from their high and lofty vantage point and overwhelmed me with almost impossible questions. One of those officers was a devout Presbyterian. Their spelling list included the word 'Presbyterian'. I was the only one of fourteen applicants who spelt it correctly. That little achievement may have been the key that unlocked the door to my twenty-five-year Police career.

A Rooky Copper in Action

Joining the Victoria Police was not even a faint blip on my radar screen. The recruiting campaign simply amounted to an escape from that cursed shearing shed for a couple of hours. I walked into that courthouse with light step and out bothered and bewildered. Being selected was a reality shock. What on earth had I got myself into? I understand now that God alone led me through that courthouse venue with its imposing inner décor and magisterial inquisition into a Police career, the fellowship of the redeemed, a wonderful marriage, a stint of church planting and an enjoyable, rewarding twenty-year street ministry.

A never to be forgotten lesson occurred during one of my first rostered shifts at the Russell Street Police HQ reception desk. A couple, old enough to be my parents shouting expletives at each other, appeared at the counter. This single, innocent, raw, inexperienced and naïve young country copper did his bumbling best, but they walked out still shouting. After they departed my ageing, fidgety, supervisor with florid face, red nose, watery blue eyes, and quivering beer gut called me across to his desk and sternly barked, "Son! Be like the Wailing Wall of Jerusalem. Stand still. Listen. Say nothing. And they'll walk out thinking you're the best copper they ever met."

Will Durant, an American historian, and philosopher put it this way, "Nothing is often a good thing to do and always a good thing to say." An ancient writer said, "Even fools are thought wise when they keep silent; with their mouth shut they seem intelligent" (Proverbs 17:28 NLT). In years to come, adhering to these principles smoothed my way through many a difficult situation!

Here Comes the Bride

As a trainee Constable, I endured the abusive shouts of a loud gravelly voiced drill sergeant for marching round the old St Kilda Road Police training complex parade ground with two left feet. Upon graduation I resided in barracks for twelve months at Russell Street Police HQ. Around this time, a fellow recruit (Ken) introduced me to Scots Presbyterian Church in Collins Street. This marked the beginning of my church going career. One Sunday evening after the service, at a young adults' meeting, I was smitten by a beautiful young lady. I would have married her on the spot, but soon enough she became the wife for whom I longed and for whom

I am eternally grateful. The years rolled on. Due to my absence on duty, too much responsibility of raising three kids fell on her shoulders, but she worked wonders faithfully supporting and upholding our family through thick and thin. Fifty-eight years (at the time of writing) of blissful marriage has well and truly dulled the impact of that gravelly parade ground voice. I am forever grateful to Ken for his significant contribution to my life.

Some Shades of Grey

Permit me to reflect on the lives of some who attended our wedding but are no longer with us. Senior Sergeant Viv Hancock and I were instructors together at the Police Training Academy. One day, we were conducting a training exercise when he was thrown to the ground by an over-zealous recruit. The resulting bruise on his thigh developed into cancer. He died younger than me at age fifty. Senior Constable Ced Foulds, a unique but competent officer, was bitten by a drunken lout while quelling a bar room brawl. As a result, Ced contracted hepatitis, which turned into terminal liver cancer. Senior Sergeant Harold (Smokey) Dawson, the best man at our wedding, was killed in a car accident early one morning on his way to work. He was popular and hugely capable. His untimely death shook the Police Department to its core. Over 1,000, including the Chief Commissioner, attended his funeral. Beverley, Jan's younger sister died at forty-nine-years of cancer leaving a bereft husband and three teenage daughters. In later years, Roslyn, Jan's sole remaining youngest sister, succumbed in August 2022 after battling many years with cancer. It was a sobering moment for Jan to realise she no longer had any sisters. All were close friends and contributed to my life at various times.

Many Arresting Sermons

This transition from farming brought me into contact with life on the other side of the fence. I saw the best and worst of people both inside and outside the Police Department. I spent twenty-five years attending accidents, crime scenes and training Police recruits. My policing experience taught me much about God, others, and myself. This was good preparation for a church planting career where I tried (not always successfully) to preach many 'arresting' sermons and later a career of street evangelism.

When I approached my Officer in Charge at West Heidelberg Police Station early in my career with a request for a new uniform, he surprised me by asking, "So you've decided to stay!" "Huh!!!" So, I had, and so it was. I subsequently served at several police stations and branches including Geelong, Doncaster, and the Training Academy.

Years later a member of Squad 9/77 which I had trained, called with an invitation to attend a reunion at the Rydges Hotel, Exhibition Street, Melbourne. Cost $50 for the meal and BYO drinks. Whew! But I felt constrained to attend. All but three of the original members were present and only seven still served. Some bald. Some grey. Some rotund. Most recognisable. I intended leaving about 9:30 but the night was enjoyable and the food good. Alcohol consumption was minimal. The war stories clean - well most times! Each member recounted something of his life since graduation. Stories ranged between hilarious to tragic. Marriages had disintegrated. Cancer terminated careers. Another who had worked with me at Doncaster Police Station and with whom I had shared my faith, had left the department to pursue an acting career. He has since played leading roles in major TV dramas and stage productions. Another, then a Chief Inspector, in his speech called me a trainer of compassion who left his mark on the squad. The respect I was given and the esteem in which I was held was surprising, touching and generous. To my astonishment they gave me a presentation. They didn't need to. I was sufficiently honoured to be invited.

Prior to becoming a Police Officer, I was traumatised by the thought of speaking in public. During my tenure as a Law Instructor at the Police Academy, I learned to speak loud enough for a student in the far corner of the classroom to hear, and clear enough for the most intellectually deficient student to understand. These valuable lessons learned at taxpayer's expense, assisted in the art of future sermon presentations. Resignation from the Police Service was a reality check. No more fortnightly pay packets! No more police camaraderie!

My Evangelistic Passion

Those who led me to Christ were passionate evangelists. Maybe, it was they who inspired my evangelistic passion. I pictured myself fearlessly trotting along jungle trails in far off equatorial Africa, a pith helmet on my head, Bible in one hand, rifle in the other warding off marauding lions, followed by a line of half-naked tribesmen toting loads of Bibles. Thankfully it never happened! I would have been woefully underprepared for missionary service.

My earlier church experiences, beginning soon after I left home, were filled with a diet of seminars, Christian books, and videos on evangelism. With the unfolding of time, came the realisation that I could die attending seminars, reading books, and watching videos without ever once having evangelised. Now the mission field is outside our front door. Multicultural Melbourne presents opportunities galore to share testimonies. 'The fields are white unto harvest.' Paul said, "In Him all the fullness of Deity dwells in bodily form, and in Him you have been made complete" (Colossians 2:9-10). The 'all sufficiency of Christ' equalises Christians (including me) to the task of evangelism.

Included in this learning process were snippets of wisdom shared by senior Christians. An excellent one sentence counselling session occurred when, as secretary of the Blackburn North Baptist Church missionary committee, I was in discussion with J Oswald Sanders, proposed guest speaker at our forthcoming missionary convention. He was a world-famous missionary statesman and author of note. I shared my difficult experiences as a new Christian. I was looking for sympathy, but all he said was, "You've had a good education, haven't you?" How unsympathetic!!! But on reflection, his remark helped me understand that blessings and bruises work together for good to them that love God and are called according to His purposes.

Mature Christians assured us that prayer is excellent and necessary, but praying of itself always seemed an inadequate reflection of our Lord's Great Commission of 'Go ye'. Praying and going are inextricably entwined. Paul exhorts all believers to do the work of evangelism (2 Timothy 4:5). Evangelising is not necessarily a specialist area. God grows what we plant and water. What was I planting that God could grow and increase?

On the Job Training

Seminars, videos, and books have their place, but the approach of the early disciples was more direct and practical. "They went out and preached everywhere, and the Lord worked with them, confirming His word through their prayers and accompanying signs" (Mark 16:20). God is not working near the church, for the church or around the church, but 'with' the church. 'With' is the language of partnership and co-labouring. I resolved to take the Gospel outside the four walls of the church onto the streets but had no idea how or where to start.

I began by placing 100's of tracts in a local phone box. I never found one scrunched up in the gutter or blowing in the wind. I progressed to chalking texts on local park footpaths. Outreach in Box Hill Shopping

Plaza found businesspeople and shoppers too busy to talk. All these efforts proved unsatisfactory.

One day, as a last resort, I caught the train to Flinders Street railway station (FSRS) adjacent to Federation Square (FS) in the Melbourne CBD. In FS I found 100's of tourists and overseas students killing time, eating lunch, or waiting for friends. Most willingly listened to a Gospel promotion and accepted literature in their own language. FSRS and its proximity quickly became a prime stamping ground for evangelism. Public transport also proved fruitful. Trial and error in evangelistic outreach methods proved to be the best and most fruitful seminar on evangelism I ever attended, enormously educational, rewarding, enjoyable and satisfying.

Making the initial contact was often a personal battle. Fears crowded in as I approached my contact. They might punch my nose, make me look a fool, ask questions I couldn't answer. But God invited me to jump into stormy lives with the Gospel, and Jesus by His grace, oftentimes astonishingly kept me afloat. Gospel presentations are spiritual battles won through prayer and praise. "I am alive. They are alive. I have a tongue. They have ears. Preach therefore and preach with all your might. Exhort them privately and personally with all the seriousness that you have. Quickly or it will be too late. Prudently or Satan will overreach you. Fervently or your words will be disregarded." (Richard Baxter's booklet 'Now or Never' published 1689).

> "Cry aloud, spare not; Lift up your voice like a trumpet;
> Tell my people their transgressions,
> And the house of Jacob their sins."
> (Isaiah 58:1)

Reading Matthew 28:18* alone risks trivialising the text into a lullaby or a cuddly little teddy bear soothing away feverish, restless bedtime anxieties. But blending verses 18 with verses 19 and 20 enlarges the meaning to include: "Go therefore and make disciples of all the nations baptising them in the name of the Father, Son and Holy Spirit and teaching them to observe all things that I have commanded and lo I am with you always." Verse 19 could also be rightly translated: 'As you are going' instead of just 'Go!' So, whether you are going on the train, to the shops, or work, search for opportunities to share your testimony, which can have a powerful impact. Each time we share we sow a seed into someone's life. The Holy Spirit will one day use that precious seed to harvest more souls for the Kingdom. Faith in the Saviour transforms lullabies into rousing anthems of sacred praise.

Melbourne is a multi-cultural community of pluralistic religions, and philosophies threatening to engulf our society as never before. This global mix is changing the face of our land. Media, politics, and pressure groups are jumping on the bandwagon with their brand of loud confusing demands, foreign to our Christian heritage. Many genuinely seek truth within this 'Great Commotion' but struggle to make sense of the 'Great Commission.' Christians are called into this garrison of the uncircumcised to boldly demonstrate the uniqueness of Christ. One small act of love in Christ's name may spark the revival for which devout Christians long and pray. Never underestimate the value of that first small step. Risky and uncomfortable perhaps but exhilarating and rewarding.

Some will happily accept Jesus as 'one of many'. Others may admit to the possibility of a power out there beyond. Some understand Jesus as a first century Jewish teacher, a perfect man, a moral exemplar rather than a divine Saviour, but in all these cases the uniqueness of Jesus is their stumbling block. While we may meet exceptional people, there is no one like Jesus. He is the one and only universal Saviour. The battle in every generation is this, 'Is Jesus the universal Saviour?'

References:

Matthew 28:18 - And Jesus said, "All authority is given to Me in heaven and on earth."

Chapter 2

Birth of the Street Ministry

Paul's Three-Point Testimony

Testimonies are the cutting edge of the church. Following a greeting, I begin with the Big Question: "What is the most important question in all the world for you?" Often my contacts replied, "I haven't thought of that. What's it mean for you?" A good opening for my testimony. Paul's perfect three-point strategy in Acts 26 sets out: 'What his life was like before becoming a Christian', 'How he became a Christian' and 'What his life was like since.' Paul's structure for a testimony was short, sharp, and shiny. My testimony was often framed along Paul's lines.

(before) 'As a teenager I had problems' (vs9-11).
(how) 'Someone led me into a relationship with the Creator' (vs12-13).
(since) 'Life is better now' (vs22-23).

It's that simple. Keeping it down to three or four minutes, is critical but as time or circumstances permit, each or all of the above points can be amplified according to circumstances. Often-times short testimonies extended into half hour conversations. Never be afraid to ask good questions and listen.

Rev Richard Johnson – a Hero of the Faith

It so happened that while Jan and I were staying at a harbour-front apartment in Manly NSW a memorial service to celebrate the construction of the first church erected in Australia in 1793 at the corner of Bligh and Hunter Streets, Sydney, came to our attention. Search as we could, we were unable to locate the memorial of that opening. The Sofitel Hotel concierge in Phillip Street, said, "Wait a minute! Did you say you were Christian? I know who can help you! He's a Christian. He tells me about his faith. I listen to him." A devout Pentecostal Sri Lankan limousine driver detailed the Richard Johnson story and directed us to the memorial. The concierge accepted Christian literature.

Rev Richard Johnson arrived in NSW with the first fleet in 1788 with some 760 convicts, women, and children. He was also responsible for the spiritual wellbeing of four companies of marines and government officials, taking the total number in his parish to just over 1,000 people. He was the only Christian preacher in Australia for a while.

The Rev Johnson, regarded by many as the father of the Australian Christian Church, preached the first sermon on Australian soil at 10am on Sunday, February 3, 1788, under a great tree growing close to the harbour. His key text was:

> "What shall I render to the Lord, for all His benefits toward me?
> I will take up the cup of salvation, and call upon the name of the Lord.
> I will pay my vows to the Lord, now in the presence of all His people."
> (Psalm 116:12-14)

This memorial marks the beginning point of Australia's Christian heritage. At the service an excellent youth choir sang a range of beautiful old hymns to commemorate Johnson's ministry. The Governor of NSW addressed the issue admirably. I was personally challenged to extend this Christian heritage, even if only in a small way, in my home city of Melbourne.

One Person at a Time?

At a church service we sang a chorus entitled: 'It's a lovely, lovely name'. The following Tuesday whilst travelling on a train from Flinders Street, my lips silently moved to its words and toes tapped to its rhythm. People sat stiffly in the carriage seemingly locked in their private world and stared pensively out windows. I had prayed for an opportunity to speak for Jesus in that carriage. A woman three rows up complained loudly, "The swaying train is making me sleepy. I am scared of overshooting my station." Then she loudly added, "Why don't you sing the song on your lips so we can all hear it?" I briefly considered whispering the words in her ear, but God said, "No! Stay where you are, yell it out."

I replied to her, "I cannot sing but will quote it if you like?"

She said, "Ok!" So, I focused on a passenger at the other end of the carriage and shouted the following lines:

> "It is a lovely, lovely name, the name of Jesus,
> It is a lovely name from heaven above,
> Dispelling the clouds of doubt and fear,
> Filling the saddened heart with cheer."

Even the train rattles seemed to stop. A passenger froze above his crossword. A young woman's jaw dropped open. The astonished woman who asked the question exclaimed, "That's beautiful!"

If you want to witness, the opposition will put barriers in your way. My barrier on that occasion was fear of ridicule. I regard myself as a conservative middle-class Baptist not normally given to yelling chorus lyrics in noisy train carriages. But Jesus dispels doubts and fear and fills saddened hearts with cheer, light, guidance, hope, forgiveness, and cleansing. '**One Man Standing**' by the grace of God can make a difference.

Occasionally, I have been asked, "How can you expect to make a difference with your evangelism?" I don't think it's necessarily my right to see any differences made. A small seed planted for God could yield a multitude of fruit we may never see. Our job is simply to do the job God calls us to do, to continue praying over our obedient acts, and let God take care of the harvest.

I am sometimes asked, "How do I identify the person with whom to share the Gospel?" Mother Teresa is reputed to have said, "Never worry about numbers. Help one person at a time, and always start with the person nearest you." Basically, that's my system. A switched-on home group member in our church recently accepted a World War One (WW1) Gospel replica. She passed it on to her Christian friend who was praying for the salvation of her father. Though not a soldier, he is a WW1 enthusiast who attended a recent Gallipoli dawn service. His acceptance of the abovementioned Gospel triggered good conversations between father and daughter. Our Gospel is the story of God's action in Christ to bring redemption to all creation, one at a time. Christians are commissioned for this purpose. It's a huge task, but believers have much to offer if we trust God and love others.

Many times, I hear Christians saying, "I'm still looking for God's will." I believe much of God's will is located between our ears. It's called sanctified common sense. I use a simple formula for service: 'Opportunity plus relentless intensity multiplied by God equals Kingdom victory.' Every believer has service opportunities. It's the nature of the Spirit filled life. Opportunities sit right under our noses. They may be so small we overlook them, but our responsibility is identification and pursuit. We safely leave the saving bit to God. Jesus went about doing good (Acts 10:38b). Paul said, "Do good to all, especially to those of the household of faith," (Galatians 6:10) and "Do not grow weary in doing good" (2 Thessalonians 3:13). Each day is another opportunity to show practical love and kindness in the name of our Lord Jesus.

Treasure or Trinkets?

On Friday, April 29, 2011, the authority, power, and clarity with which James Middleton (Kate's brother) read the scriptures (Romans 12:1-2, 9, 18) to a worldwide viewing audience at the royal wedding of William and Kate was impressive. Who didn't watch the event? I suspect not many, but on Sunday morning two young women at the bus stop sniggered, "Young people don't watch that stuff now."

I said, "Where are you going?"

They replied, "Camberwell market to buy some trinkets. Where are you going?"

I told them, "Church. It's an anchor for my soul in a crazy world." Strident, confused materialistic philosophy would consign the church to the outer perimeter of insignificance, dishonour, scorn, and derision but our treasure is a victorious risen Saviour.

The courts of our land determine the outcome of cases based on clear, honest, and accurate testimony. Our legal system is built round the power of a firsthand report. In much the same way, God's system for reclaiming His lost world depends largely on the power of Christian testimony.

Sometimes witnesses in law courts think they must persuade or convince the judge and jury of the truth and their need to accept it. This is not the role of a witness. In a court room, a witness simply states what he has seen and heard as accurately as he can. The rest is up to the court. State what God has done in your life as clearly as possible. The Holy Spirit alone convicts men of sin and judgement but uses straight forward accounts of believers in the process.

Picture Jesus walking resolutely along Swanston Street. Behind Him are twelve disciples, amazed. Beyond are followers, afraid. Lining the route are street kids, shoppers, students, tourists, the curious. It's not the Shrine in St Kilda Road we're heading for. It's our last journey with Jesus before His Crucifixion. We're astonished by His courage and fear for our safety. Today, we have Bibles to guide us, and the Holy Spirit to strengthen and defend us as we journey through the office, classroom, construction site, hospital, factory, armed services. Though amazed by the bravery of Jesus, we still suffer the same crippling fears of following Him as did His first disciples. Resurrection is the great proof of the Gospel. It may not prove the truth of God to every non-believer; however, it certainly empowers Christians to speak of the mighty changes He made in their lives.

Such was the case with the woman at the well who immediately following her conversion, aroused the curiosity of Samaritan friends by saying, "Come see a man" (John 4:29*). But it was only when they came to Jesus that they said, "Now, we believe." (John 4:42a) Several thousand testimonies later, I can truly report that a good story arouses curiosity, but it's only God who raises to new life.

Trusting God in Trying Times

Mephibosheth, Jonathan's lame son (2 Samuel 9) had fallen on tough times, but David showed him kindness for his father's sake, and Mephibosheth ate at David's table as a king's son. Herein, David pictured Christ who would enter the house of a chief Pharisee and eat bread with sinners on the Sabbath, but religionists were (Luke 14:1*) ready to pounce. Living on the edge for Jesus may attract self-righteous disapproval (Luke 14:13-14*) but deepens prayer life.

In 2006 Jan and I visited 'Soweto', an iconic slum city in South Africa, the home of President Nelson Mandela, whose death at an advanced age was mourned by a nation. His capacity for forgiveness and humility was learned in the 'trough' of despondency during twenty-seven painful years of unjust imprisonment. For the Christian, nothing is as divine as experience and the deeper the experience, the more divine it can be. The claim accepted by generations of Christians, stands true for us today.

> "No condemnation now I dread, Jesus, and all in Him, is mine!
> Alive in Him, my living Head, And clothed in righteousness divine,
> Bold I approach the eternal throne, And claim the crown,
> through Christ my own." (Charles Wesley)

"No condemnation now I dread" (Romans 8:1). Struggles offer opportunities to experience God's grace and mercy. The years ahead may challenge but always there is victory.

How do I prevent the negatives out-muscling the positives? Pastor Smith told us how 'not to lose hope' in a sermon based on 2 Corinthians 4:17-18:

> "For our light affliction, which is but for a moment,
> is working for us a far more exceeding and eternal weight of glory,
> while we do not look at the things which are seen,
> but at the things which are not seen."

God often energised this earthen vessel with a word fitly spoken at a point of need. Someone said, "When written in Chinese, the word 'crisis' is composed of two characters. One represents opportunities. The other danger." Dangers are opportunities to extend God's kingdom. Pressing on with loads of unresolved defeat and guilt puts Christians at a disadvantage but Jesus is our starting point. We press on from victory to victory. Our Saviour is the victor, and we take our place in Him.

Challenging Times in a Dangerous World

Terrorism, pandemics, earthquakes are the radical edges into which Jesus calls us. 'Go, teach all nations, baptising them in the name of the Father, Son and Holy Spirit', 'Lift up your eyes and look on the fields that are white already unto harvest'. There is explosive church growth in Latin America, Africa, China, Persia and India today. There are more people ready to listen to a testimony than there are Christians willing to share the message.

A.W. Tozer said, "No Mary, No Buddha, No Allah, No saints can save us. Only Jesus does and He is always enough." And again, "Christ will be Lord, or He will be judge. Every man must decide whether he will take Him as Lord now, or face Him as judge then."

Jesus said, "Truly! Truly! I say to you, he that hears My word, and believes on Him that sent Me, has everlasting life; and shall not come into condemnation, but is passed from death to life" (John 5:24 - ESV).

Encouragements

It was a privilege to baptise three new Christians. One from the Middle East, one from India and the other from Asia. All were keen to share the good news. One returned to her previous country with several multi language Bibles to hand out to friends of long standing. They understood the Great Commission and the need to establish new Christians in small groups and to multiply these groups.

Overall, encouragements far outnumbered discouraging experiences in street evangelism. Most contacts have contributed in some way to my own spiritual growth. I am privileged to have had such an exciting role to play in God's plan for world redemption.

The Bible says, "Work out your own salvation with fear and trembling." Take responsibility for your own Bible study. Comply with each revelation to the best of your ability. Occupy your mind with Godly things, and ungodly distractions will less likely consume you. God's grace works out what God works in you. Do all things without murmuring or disputing. Encourage your leaders. Be cheerfully obedient, peaceful, and loving. God's commands should be obeyed, not disputed. God has abolished death and brought life and immortality to life through the Gospel.

Prayer: "Father, help us to love You more than anything else and to share our faith in Jesus with everyone we can. Amen." (Prayer by Warren Hardig, Men for Missions Global Ambassador).

Taking it to Heart:

1. How do sanitised testimonies impact the world?
2. Describe some ways the Gospel is sanitised?
3. What impact do sanitised testimonies make on those of other religions (or none at all)?

References:

Luke 14:1 – Now it happened as He went into the house of one of the rulers of the Pharisees to eat bread on the Sabbath, that they watched Him closely.

Luke 14:13-14 – But when you give a feast, invite the poor, the maimed, the lame, the blind. And you will be blessed, because they cannot repay you; for you shall be repaid at the resurrection of the just.

John 4:29 – Come see a man who told me all things that I ever did. Could this be the Christ?

Chapter 3

Overview of Street Evangelism

You Can Do It!

Selwyn Hughes, in his Every Day With Jesus (EDWJ) notes, defined an evangelist as 'a person with the gift of reaching large numbers of people with the message of salvation.' A light switched on. His empowering thought inspired greater confidence, purpose, and direction in my ministry - notwithstanding, my call may be vigorously tested by those who will delight to do so.

Maybe my confidence in introducing the Big Question (BQ) was probably developed through contacting a wide variety of people during my times as a serving Police Officer. Mostly I could build a relationship with someone in five minutes. You can do this too! The friendliest people ask sincere questions and listen. Learn to ask questions. Try not to be nervous. but memorising formulas or copying others may not work for you. Beginning with a simple greeting like, "Hi. How are you?" might trigger the response upon which you can build a gospel presentation.

Literature distribution, the Big Question and Blessing Cards were helpful tools in street evangelism. With these three tools any Christian can do evangelism. Care to join me? Read on and learn how you can play an important role in the Lord's worldwide evangelism team today.

Literature Distribution

The following edited email was received from NewHope Baptist Church friends: "Our tour group was passing through a small town in Finland, where we stopped for lunch. While there, a man gave a couple on our bus a tract in English and talked about salvation. They told him they were Christians from Sydney. There was much rejoicing. So, Bruce, in Porvoo, Finland, someone is handing out leaflets to tourists. Great isn't it!"

Fantastic!" The Fin and I are members together in a worldwide literature distribution network headed by our Lord Jesus Christ. Ordinary believers like you and me are God's ambassadors with authority to spread His blessings. Strange creeds, denominational affiliations, religious rituals save no one, but God said, "This is my beloved Son, who brings me great joy. Listen to Him" (Matthew 17:5*).

There are views that Christian literature distribution is a thing of the past. I beg to differ! It is cost effective and simple. It need not impose financial burdens on the church. Committees maybe useful but not necessarily required. A friend sent a lady in hospital the tract and a New Testament I gave her in the Bourke Mall. The friend asked, "Do you have a suitable Christian CD for her?" Arrangements were made to assist with her request.

On arrival at the Wood Workers Expo in Jeff's Shed, Southbank, a female listened to a brief testimony and responded with evangelical language. Sensing that she was pretending, I sternly asked, "You are not attending church, are you?" Her eyes dropped. Her face coloured.

I suggested to her, "Find a good church."

She said "Yes."

I said, "Read your Bible." She accepted scriptures. As we parted, I said again to her, "What have I just asked you to do?"

She repeated, "Find a good church and read my Bible."

A beaten-up old car with interior silver sunshades lining all windows was parked in the NewHope Baptist Church car park. Strewn on the bitumen all round this vehicle were screwed up McDonalds' brown paper bags, food scraps and rubbish. I knocked on the window. The car rocked with movement. I knocked again, and again, each time more loudly on the roof. Two beady eyes peered suspiciously through sun slats inside the rear window.

I indicated to the occupant to open the window. His driver's side rear window lowered a fraction. To a pair of bloodshot eyes framed with tousled hair in a pasty, pimply face I said, "Clean up your rubbish. People use this car park, and we need it clean and tidy." The male with track marks on his arms said, "Yes.". The stench from within was strong. I threw a tract through the window and said, "Read this! Get right with God. Without Him your future is bleak!" He said, "Yes. I know." The window closed.

The Big Question (BQ)

Frequently, throughout this book, mention is made of the 'Big Question' – 'What is the most important question in all the world for you?' The BQ quickly became a sharp point for which I had long been searching. It paved the way for many testimonies, Gospel presentations and literature distribution.

Some years ago, the BQ was brought to my attention by Warren Hardig, now retired Executive Director of Men for Missions Int., the layman's arm of OMS. He used it one morning as his key point in a Bible study he was leading in our home. At the very moment Warren shared it, an Indian telephone salesman pressed our front doorbell. In a rare burst of inspiration,

I asked the salesman the BQ. I said, "The most important question in the world for me is knowing what happens to me when I die. Here's my second question. What brings you the most joy in your life?"

He replied, "Enjoying each day as it comes."

I stated, "What brings me the most joy is answering your question as to what happens when you die." He accepted a Gospel of John, and beat a hasty retreat.

How does it work for me? An example: In Hungry Jacks a man put aside his newspaper and gazed into space. After greeting him, I asked, "Do you mind if I read your paper?" "Not at all," he answered.

I was not interested in the newspaper other than that it may provide an entrance into his life for the Gospel. After a one-sided conversation, my contact must have decided I was OK, and so I asked the BQ.

He replied, "How to manage my daily problems and not worry too much."

"The Bible contains God's answer to the BQ*. Would you like a copy?" I responded.

He jumped at the offer saying, "My parents were Christian. I was brought up in the Christian faith. This is awesome. I'll read it on the train."

A lady in a crowded local shopping centre, offered me a flier. I asked the BQ. She said, "That's hard."

I answered, "The most important question for me is knowing what happens to me when I die."

She replied, "I don't want to go there."

I asked her, "What brings you the most joy in life?"

She said to me, "Relieving the suffering in the world."

I declared, "The thing that brings me most joy is telling you the answer to my first question."

She reacted with a smile saying, "That's a new approach" and accepted a scripture tract entitled 'Four Things God Wants You to Know'.

Blessing Card

Another helpful innovation was the Blessing Card (BC), based on the Aaronic Blessing in Numbers 6:24-27. It was produced in more recent times by an elder in our Light Community Baptist Church (LCBC) for distribution at significant events such as Christmas, Easter, birthdays, and pandemics, etc. In Numbers 6:27 God said, "Whenever Aaron and His sons bless the people of Israel in my name, I myself will bless them." The Jesus rendition of the 'Aaronic Blessing' in Luke 10:8 says, "If you enter a town and it welcomes you, eat whatever is set before you. Heal the sick, and tell them the Kingdom of God is near you now." The Blessing Card may be a pathway to salvation for some lost and desperately needy soul.

Based on God's Word, I may confidently state to my contact, "I have authority from God to pronounce His blessing on you." Christians proclaim! God blesses! Opportunities to proclaim the Aaronic Blessing occur in a thousand conversations. You may think, as Aaron probably did, that speaking out the 'Blessing' is not easy. But we are pronouncing the blessing with God's authority in Jesus' name. I am not praying, though the whole process is bathed in prayer. I am not explaining, interpreting, theorising, philosophising, or spiritualising. I am simply blessing my contact as printed on the BC. Complimenting Hungry Jacks' staff by name for their professionalism often created openings for the gift of a BC. The following procedure arising out of practical experience with hundreds of contacts is suggested:

1. I introduce myself as a Christian,
2. Pronounce the blessing (Numbers 6:24-27),

3. Offer the Blessing Card,
4. Share testimony,
5. Pray for continuing opportunities with your contact,
6. Trust God to actuate the blessing.

The BC went viral. A country church contact printed 100 BCs. Several churches requested cards for outreach purposes. One lady enclosed a BC with each COVID-19 face mask she made and sold. Another enclosed a BC with each food hamper her church distributed. A ninety-eight-year-old Christian from interstate had circulated over 400 (and counting) in his letter writing ministry. You are encouraged to reproduce these cards. They look good on stiff paper with colored edging. Printed on the back are the words of Isaiah 40:29*. Feel free to replace with your choice of texts if required. Copies are available from the LCBC. There is no copyright or fee.

The audiologist who repaired my defective hearing device, accepted a BC. An ancient male customer grumbled, "I can't understand this new-fangled technology."

I stated, "Here's a blessing for you."

He accepted the BC, glanced at it, smiled with delight, and said, "Wonderful! I am a Christian. We need more of this. Thank you!"

The Apostle Paul writes

> "Knowing this, that our old man was crucified with Him,
> that the body of sin might be done away with
> that we should no longer be slaves of sin." (Romans 6:6)

If you are crucified with Christ and Jesus lives in you by faith, the way is open for you to **go** anywhere God wants you to go. **Do** anything God wants you to do. And **give** anything God wants you to give (Romans

12:1*). God will never ask you to be a blessing without providing resources for you to do so.

A Youth With A Mission (YWAM) group invited me to observe at a mobile soup kitchen on Friday evenings in St Kilda (Melbourne). Englishmen, Americans, Asians, and Aussies manned the transit van. We set up shop in Fitzroy Street outside a private hotel. Folding chairs provided seating for patrons. A portable generator created power and witch hats diverted traffic. Some forty disadvantaged folks with battle scarred saddened faces surged round the trailer. Paper plates were quickly filled and recipients scurried with eyes downcast into darkness.

One man lost his wife eighteen weeks ago with cancer. His three children had abandoned him. He had been recently discharged from a twelve-day stint in hospital.

An attractive female, maybe twenty-years-old with lacerated, sutured, blood caked lips, lent against the hotel corner. Tears coursed down her cheeks. Her words were slurred. Her reddened blue eyes bored into mine with the peculiar hopeless intensity of a deeply disturbed life spiraling out of control.

An introverted little old man from Northern Victoria, near where I grew up, listened to my testimony. Opposite were two buskers. One, a didgeridoo (aboriginal musical instrument) player. The other, an acrobat on a bicycle. The didgeridoo player flung the bike in the gutter and roughed up its rider. The old man shrugged and said, "Life is tough." Indicating the nearby private hotel where he lived, he said "Terrible things happen in there!"

Some stayed and talked, and occasionally listened to a testimony. A team member played guitar and sang Christian songs. A frail old man clutching his doggie bag, tottered feebly across Fitzroy Street coming within a whisker of adding his name to the statistics. This event is mentioned in so far as it gives colours to my world of city evangelism.

Melbourne Mind, Body and Spirit (BMS) Festival

Exodus 15:11: "Who is like You O Lord among the gods? Who is like You, glorious in holiness, fearful in praises, doing wonders?" But New Agers at the BMS Festival in the Exhibition Centre usurped godlike status for themselves. With others from the Christian Eternity Stand, I represented the Lord God among these pseudo gods. But the whisperer said, "You have no right to intrude in their privacy."

Thousands of restless, hopeless, people on a ceaseless quest for spiritual meaning filed past these stands. Jan and I had signed up for a four-hour stint with the 'Eternity' team under the leadership of Julia Pope of NewHope Church to present the Gospel to some of these multitudes. Deliberate and intentional interaction with pedestrians often commenced with, "Excuse me! Are you interested in spiritual issues?" A dumb question? I think not. They wouldn't be there otherwise.

The story of Peter walking from the boat to Jesus on the stormy sea, inspired me. When I looked into the eyes of the needy, I heard Jesus say, "No matter what happens, follow me into this person's stormy life and share the Good News."

This festival was an eye opener. The frontal blurb above the entrance at the Exhibition Centre ran: 'For every mind searching. For every body craving. For every spirit awakening'. Numerous stands offered amazing secrets to create unstoppable self-confidence, break free of fears and find the most satisfying relationships ever dreamed of.

- An unhappy lady with an American accent, searching unsuccessfully for her pot of gold at the end of the rainbow, listened to my

testimony. Her cynical smile faded. She wistfully said, "I'm glad you found your pot of gold."
- Weeks previously I had given a tract to a cleaning lady. At the festival she recognised me. That would be more than coincidence!
- A lapsed Christian girl made a recommitment. Ministering to her was a team effort.
- The natural products salesman asked why I was here.
- A tall lady was a genuine seeker and a young lady was interested.
- A farmer from the Grampians didn't know what to believe but leant to Buddhism.
- A non-Christian lady married to a Christian husband, didn't need a Saviour.
- A practicing Catholic lady was unconvincing regarding her relationship with God.
- An Asian girl with a Christian background was living life her way.
- A Greek girl baptised in a Baptist Church, was burnt and now goes nowhere.
- A Sri Lankan Buddhist and his Asian girlfriend were almost persuaded.

A well-dressed man and his wife challenged me along the following lines, "Do you suffer heart disease, cancer, diabetes, chronic fatigue, lupus (and a host of other health issues)? They are relieved through the medium of angels, auras, astro travel, energy medicine, past life regression, spirit guides, hypnotherapy, the power of the talking stick, tantra to enrich sexuality, clairvoyance, and massage issues. Would you like to learn more about the missing link to optimal health? Do you realise the body can heal itself given the proper tools? Did you know there is an unprecedented business opportunity with low-cost startup and a global income opportunity? Did you know that business success can be combined with a beautiful lifestyle?"

During our hour-long conversation, I shared my testimony and Christian literature, but they insisted on firing one last futile shot at involving me in their 'magnificent' business obsession.

Melbourne Docks

At Melbourne Docks the P.O. Nedloyd Barossa Valley container vessel, with capacity to carry 2,600 containers, was birthed. I accompanied a European Christian Mission (ECM) Port Missionary up a high wobbly and steep gangplank and was introduced to the ship's impressive captain - very much in control and respected by his crew. He had two grandkids the same age as ours. The captain and some crew accepted literature.

Another container vessel included a crew of Filipinos, Indians, Yugoslavs, Bulgarians, Turks, Lithuanians, and Romanians. An Indian responded well to the Christmas story. We prayed with a stressed Filipino steward. He was grateful. The Turk appreciated a brief opportunity to improve his limited English language skills. The missionary followed up with email communications and Bible correspondence courses. Pray for this valuable ministry.

Some say the crucifixion was the worst defeat in history and the resurrection was the greatest victory. I believe the crucifixion was the greatest victory in history and the resurrection was the proclamation of that victory. These treasures of Gospel light and grace are now contained in earthen vessels. Every contact represents opportunities to demonstrate crucifixion and resurrection power in Jesus.

Folks sometimes ask how the Spirit guides me as I identify contacts for evangelism. Frankly, I am not always aware of much guidance. Maybe I am not that spiritual. I simply share my faith anywhere and with anyone within reach. As I see it, some 2,000 years ago Christ lined up all Christians on the starting blocks and turned them loose with a loud 'GO YE!' This race is still in progress. I am one of the runners, along with a team of prayer supporters cheering me on.

The Frozen Fox

An illustration from my farming experience years ago helped focus my ministry on many occasions. On our farm, a burgeoning fox population played havoc with newborn lambs. To reduce this problem, I would chase foxes from the undergrowth, in which they sheltered in the bends of the nearby Goulburn River. Dad would blow them into oblivion as they escaped along the river edge with his trusty old double barreled twelve-gauge shotgun. One day Dad drew a bead and pulled the trigger with a deafening report. For a split second that old fox froze, his neck hair stood on end, he leapt six foot in the air, hit the ground running and disappeared in a cloud of dust, never to be seen again - wiser and harder to catch next time. The bang of the gun had its effect, but the pellets missed their mark. Am I evangelising like a report from a shotgun, making much noise but missing the target?

Am I inoculating my contacts against Christianity with a 'sub-scriptural' approach? Does my approach allow for the reshaping of the incorruptible God into an image made like corruptible man, sometimes with grotesque, ugly results. Most contacts will decide which is acceptable and unacceptable behaviour, accusing or excusing (Romans 2:15*) themselves according to their worldly value system. 'The perfect Law of the Lord, which converts the soul' (Psalm 19:7) has little or no place in their psyche.

Earlier New Testament Christians ripped away mistranslations with an exposition of the Perfect Law, i.e., the Ten Commandments. Hearts were stirred when, sinner's realised the consequences of breaking God's Law. The finality of judgement and eternal punishment is still taught in God's Word, though we do not hear enough about it today. Sinners will flee from wrath to come only if they believe there is a wrath to come. The Law is the schoolmaster that brings them to this realisation. The Spurgeons, Wesleys, Moodys and Finneys of yesteryear followed this pattern with great success. Modern day evangelism would do well to emulate them.

Methods of presenting Christ's message will change but the Mission continues unchanged. Christ commissioned His Apostles to carry on His work (John 20:21-28) after the Ascension, but Thomas's deep-seated doubts of resurrection over-shadowed his future involvement in this mission. His doubts were addressed by Jesus tenderly and with compassion. This event is one of the loftiest encounters with the Lord recorded in scriptures. Thomas' instant confession represented a magnificent victory won from doubt. There may not be a more dramatic change in attitudes than that demonstrated by Thomas. There is no more encouraging example for doubting Christians. According to tradition, Thomas afterward laboured in Parthia, Persia, and India.

To suggest to my contacts that they are liars, thieves, blasphemers, adulterers, and murderers and that God's anger burns against their sin is not the way to win friends in the ordinary sense of the word. I do not relish the idea of confronting sinners with the perfect Law. It is an experience not to be undertaken lightly, but it is scriptural. I have lost count of those I have met who were disenchanted by 'religious' Christianity. 'Banging' on with a sanitised Gospel often converts contacts into hardliners. May God raise up fiery, urgent, earnest, available, humble, loving, Spirit filled evangelists to preach an un-sanitised Gospel. Prayer support is constantly needed for discernment, wisdom, love, grace, and the anointing of the Holy Spirit. A Christian lady known to us said, "I am evangelising everywhere I go, exactly as you taught me."

An Evangelist is Never Off Duty!

One evening, I invited Jan to Shoppingtown to purchase stationery for the office. I shared my testimony with a salesman. He bumped me off course with a mixture of Greek Orthodox theology and gritty determination. During our conversation Jan dematerialised. I located her just as we were about to become the proud owners of an expensive queen size bed. I enquired, "Did you intend buying that bed tonight?" She replied, "No, I was really interested in a nice big TV!"

Jan and I drove to the nearby Dandenong Ranges. We stopped for coffee and cakes in Olinda. I was seated on a planter waiting for Jan to finish browsing. A shiny red MG sports car with roll bars pulled into the curb. An older man with stylish grey hair, fashionable clothes and expensive sunglasses, stepped onto the footpath. He was escorting a tall, slim, much younger brunette. A smiling Indonesian man and his wife walked past. He said, "It's beautiful!" He was referring to the car.

"Do you mean me?", I said.

He laughed and replied, "You have a good aura."

I asked him, "Where do you get auras?"

He told me, "From nature, the sun, birds, everything that's beautiful. When you absorb good things from nature you give them out in the form of an aura, which influences people around you."

I replied, "Let me tell you where my aura comes from."

He accepted my testimony and changed direction, saying, "I'm a Christian."

I asked him, "How did you became a Christian?"

He said, "My mother brought me up in the Catholic Church." I quoted John 14:1-6 and gave him a Gospel of John. He said to me, "I have a Bible."

I explained, "But this one includes the steps of salvation." He reluctantly accepted. Jan and I enjoyed coffee with a vanilla slice.

In John chapter 11 the death of Martha's brother uncovered her deficient understanding of resurrection. She spoke of the gift of eternal life as a future event, but Christ brought the promise into the present. He said, "I AM the resurrection. I AM the way. I AM the truth. I AM the life." Many Christians are likewise deficient in their understanding of the Gospel, but Jesus' interaction with Martha was instructive. He gently transformed her deficiency into an understanding of the Gospel in the present sense. Think about it! If you agree that a soul is of the greatest value and the only investment you can make in this life that pays dividends for all eternity, why wouldn't you share the Gospel with your friend, relative, or neighbour.

Importance of Prayer

We might make the following prayer of an eighty-nine-year-old inspirational American ours.

"Lord, I give up all my own plans and purposes, all my own desires and hopes, and accept Your will for my life. I give myself, my life, my all utterly to You to be yours forever. Fill me and seal me with Your Holy Spirit. Use me as You will. Send me where You will. Work out Your whole will in my life at any cost now and forever." ('Still Sharpening', page 52 – Warren Hardig).

I can only imagine how much further, and faster the Gospel would travel if more Christians prayed like that. Hardig asked, "Do you mind if John McLaughlin and I send out your prayer letter to other Men For Missions (MFM) Ambassadors as an example and encouragement to witness for Christ?"

Taking it to Heart:

1. How many ways may the Gospel be presented?
2. Describe ways the Gospel may be sanitised.

3. What Gospel presentation is God most likely to bless?
4. Share your brief testimony with another Christian.

References:

Isaiah 40:29 – He gives power to the weak, and to those who have no might He increases strength.

Matthew 7:5 – Hypocrite! First remove the plank from your own eye and then you will see clearly to remove the speck from your brother's eye.

Romans 2:15 – The work of the law is written in their hearts, their conscience also bearing witness, and between themselves their thoughts accusing or else excusing them.

Romans 12:1 – I beseech you therefore brethren, by the mercies of God, that you present your bodies as a living sacrifice, holy, acceptable to God which is your reasonable service.

BQ – Big Question - What is the most important question in all the world for you?

Chapter 4

Significant Christian Influence Among Africans

Lunchtime and Coffee Encounters in Hungry Jacks and McDonalds

Countless times scriptures brought to my attention during devotions were useful later among contacts many of whom appreciated my story and accepted literature. A high proportion of Africans contacted were either Christian or familiar with Christianity.

In Hungry Jacks
- Deng, a Christian Sudanese refugee, has thrown in the towel.
- Emmanuel, an unemployed black African Christian, owed his family money and exited his church in Melbourne due to relational difficulties. He shared in testimony, in song and he prayed.

- An African from Darfur converted from Islam to Christianity in a Somalian refugee camp. He said, "I am an evangelist and lead a small group in a Baptist Church." He prayed for me.
- A Sudanese Christian from Khartoum offered me half his lunch but excused himself for an appointment.
- An obese African male accepted silver coins from a Caucasian female. He followed that with, "Do you have any gold ones?" She gave him more. He systematically harvested money from other customers. He approached me as I was about to sink my teeth into a bacon wrap - I replied, "You can have this." Without a word of thanks, the African took one mouthful, threw the remainder on a nearby table and continued begging.
- One evening, at 11:10pm a voice on the phone said, "John here. We met in Hungry Jacks in the city in March 2016. I found the book you gave me. I promised to call but never got round to it. I'm ringing to see how you are."
- I asked, "What was the verse I gave you?" He replied, "John 8:12. Could you give me some more verses?" He lives with his brother on a farm in Gippsland Vic.

In McDonalds

To a black Zimbabwean model, I commented, "I saw your photo in the paper." She replied, "That's right, the Herald Sun." Her mobile phone rang. She said, "I'll be back in twenty minutes." True to her word, she returned and impressed me by the honour and respect with which she accorded me. Another Sudanese model read aloud John 8:12*.

A happy young Zimbabwean Christian student asked, "Do you have any more John's Gospels?" A nearby Samoan student informed me that he reads his Bible and prays every day."

Another African has "Never been better." I asked, "Why?" He replied, "Jesus is the way, the truth and the life. I follow Jesus."

A Sudanese lass with excellent English, tearfully outlined issues in a home conflicted with her Christian faith versus her family's religious views. She quoted Psalm 23 by heart.

Two Sudanese females arrived. The infant child of one accidentally dropped his hamburger in a nearby Chinese man's lap. The embarrassed Asian unhappily departed. To the mother I said, "They will give you a replacement." The other lady commented, "In our culture we are promised in marriage as babies. When we reach puberty, we are sent off to our husband. My mother had me when she was fifteen. I came to Australia when I was five. My promised husband in the Sudan wanted to come and get me, but I refused and linked with my partner when I was nineteen." She attends a church.

George from Johannesburg, South Africa, cited horrific life experiences as his reason for recently emigrating. I replied, "You really need to link up with a church."

Owura, a Ghanaian born Canadian, left a lucrative job in Ottawa and arrived in Melbourne two weeks ago to 'find himself'. He accepted a John's Gospel which provides direction and purpose for life."

A Christian Eritrean Melbourne radio program manager accepted Tigrinya literature.

A back-slidden Zimbabwean student remembered the old hymn 'What a friend we have in Jesus'. He accepted a hard copy of the hymn and a reading from 1 Samuel 7:3*.

A young African male unknown to me, approached saying, "Hello, I'm ... What's your name?" This Pastor's son born in Australia, was taking the opportunity during his lunch break for prayer and Bible study. He said, "But I wasn't expecting a talk with an evangelist."

A Nigerian sitting nearby asserted, "All religions lead to the same place." He angrily added "Find out how many other religions talk about Jesus?"

A tall devout South Sudanese Christian university student, who attends an Arabic speaking church in the western suburbs of Melbourne, accepted Arabic and English literature.

Another Sudanese youth with a Christian praying mother, has strayed from the straight and narrow. We discussed. He promised , "I'll start going to church again next Sunday." I replied "Call me after you attend."

An African lady evangelist accepted Tigrinya literature and commented. "I know the man who wrote this." That this Eritrean lady accepted literature in Melbourne, printed in America, in her own language by an author she knows surprised us all. .

Adrian, from Zimbabwe, who converted to Christ from Catholicism five years ago prayed he would meet a Christian that morning. That I was the second Christian he had bumped into that day amazed him. He asked for my number saying, "I am interested in evangelising like you."

Monique, a Kenyan student of journalism, recalled John 3:16*, John 8:12* and John 14:6*. I commended her, "God loves you. You are His special person. Never let anyone tell you otherwise." She said, "I'm inspired." Later I saw her reading the Gospel as she walked along Swanston Street.

Federation Square (FS)

- Some African teenagers allowed me into their group. Sam is trying to reform himself.
- I asked the girls, "How should Sam reform himself?"
- Lucy, a Pastor's daughter asserted, "Dump his friends."
- Sue, a Christian, added "Go back to school."
- Dora, visibly moved, said, "Give up the ice." The girls are forthright indeed. They accepted my story, a Gospel message and literature.

SIGNIFICANT CHRISTIAN INFLUENCE AMONG AFRICANS

- A Swahili speaking Kenyan student and his Arabic speaking Sudanese girlfriend accepted English literature. He claimed to be a Christian.
- She stated, "I am a Christian – born again. I knew you would give me literature when you approached."
- A twenty-two-year-old South Sudanese refugee rapper and song writer invited me to listen via his earphones to his music. I asked, "Are you a Christian?"
- He replied, "I don't know."
- I said, "Do you have a Bible at home?"
- He replied, "Yes." I drew his attention to Matthew 7:13-14* and suggested, "You have been on a long journey. Why not write about your life on the wide and narrow roads?" He replied, "Good idea!" He noted my contact details, accepted literature, and promised to contact me in due course, but never did.
- To a man of African appearance I asked, "Where do you come from?"
- He sarcastically replied, "Outer space."
- I tried the BQ*. He replied, "Life is a shadow."
- I explained, "But there are no shadows without light?"
- He retorted, "Let's put it another way. Life is a reflection in a mirror."
- I said, "If the mirror smashes, what next?"
- "Nothing! Have a good day," and off he walked.
- A jovial South African living in Perth was interested to learn that "My grandfather fought for the English in the Boer War. My wife and I travelled through the Drakensburg Mountains in South Africa and saw 'Long Tom' (a long-range howitzer used by the Boers to harass the English). Why my grandfather, an Australian, fought for the English in South Africa mystifies me. What is the greatest mystery in all the world for you?"
- He said, "I hadn't thought of it like that." He accepted literature.

East Ringwood Streets and Railway Platform

In the main street a schizophrenic male African refugee is worried about lack of finances. When he's off medication, he hears voices and thinks he's God. "It goes back to my childhood in the Sudan."

"Can I pray for you?" I asked.

He said, "Yes! I'm a Christian when I get down, I read my Bible." He accepted prayer and literature and occasionally attends Light Community Baptist Church.

Millie, a Catholic Nigerian student, spoke excellent English. When asked the Big Question (BQ*) she replied, "Do the best I can at studies. The biggest issue for her in Nigeria is Boko Haran terrorism." She listened attentively to my testimony and comments based on Psalm 23 and John 8:12* both of which she knew by heart. She accepted a Gospel of John.

Omot, a very tall young Sudanese male is a Christian who believes in all religions." He accepted testimony and a Gospel of John. I referred him to John 8:12* and added, "There are hundreds of beliefs, but only Jesus said, 'Whoever follows me, will never walk in darkness but have the light of life'." I prayed with him.

A black African Kenyan youth politely listened to my testimony. It occurred to me he is the son of a lady who recently attended our church. He said, "I'm off to the city to meet with mates." His troubling comment prompted counsel against bad company, alcohol, drugs, and crime.

A young woman from Morocco listened to the BQ* and testimony. She replied, "It's wonderful you have come to faith, but I am converting to Judaism. I already have my faith."

My response - "I became a Christian as a young teenager. Now I am over eighty years old. My Lord has never let me down."

Trains and Buses

On a train, Abraham, a Sudanese baker, seduced from Christ by the pull of the world, has a devout mother who prays for him daily. We adjourned to a Lilydale coffee shop where he made a profession of faith. He asked, "Where do I go from here?" He accepted counsel, a Gospel of John, an invitation to our church and prayer. Unfortunately, he never attended.

A Zimbabwean lass has been a Christian for a long time. Four years ago, I came to grips with the Lordship of Jesus. Listening to Joyce Meyer was my turning point."

In the bus, on the way to NewHope Baptist Church, Chiedza, a Zimbabwean lady passenger volunteered, "I like the way you smile at the passengers. You must be a Christian."

At the railway station, a shy West African lady is reading a learner driver's book in preparation for her licence test later in the day. I had no idea what religion, if any, she followed but asked, "Can I pray for you?"

She responded, "Yes." After I prayed, she said, "Amen," and smiled and waved through the carriage window as I walked along the platform.

Two Nigerians, Isaac, and Morrison, attending a Christian youth conference in Melbourne, clearly articulated details of their government, economics, and corruption at every level in their mineral resource rich country. I prayed with them along the lines of Habakkuk 3:2 – "Lord God, revive through your powerful Holy Spirit the work begun by the crucified, resurrected Lord Jesus Christ in Nigeria generations ago." The impact these young men could make through the Gospel in Nigeria is huge. Their gratitude knows no ends.

Solomon from Ghana, a committed Christian, listened intently to my testimony and accepted literature. I read to him from Isaiah 45:2-3 -

> "I will go before you and make the crooked places straight;

> I will break in pieces the gates of bronze and cut the bars of iron.
> I will give you the treasures of darkness and hidden riches of secret places,
> That you may know that I, the Lord, who call you
> by your name, am the God of Israel."

Taking it to Heart:

1. Discuss methods religious people (Including atheists) might rely on to confuse or divert Christians
2. How may these crooked places be straightened for those who have lost their way?
3. What might your suggestions look like in real life?

References:

Matthew 7:13-14 – Enter by the narrow gate; for wide is the gate and broad is the way that leads to destruction, and there are many who go in by it. Because narrow is the gate and difficult is the way which leads to life, and there are few that find it.

John 3:16 – For God so loved the world that He gave His only begotten Son, that whoever believes in Him should not perish but have everlasting life.

John 8:12 – I am the light of the world. He who follows me shall not walk in darkness but have the light of life.

John 14:6 – Jesus said to him, 'I the way, the truth and the life. No one comes to the Father except through Me.

BQ - Big Question – What is the most important question in all the world for you?

Chapter 5

Asian Background Associations

The following references regarding 'Asians' includes those from a variety of countries. Most accepted the Big Question (BQ*), literature in relevant languages and testimony. In an age where absolutes are lacking and everything is relative or a matter of degrees, it is all too easy to sugar-coat a Gospel presentation to make it more palatable to those of different faiths or none at all. But all believers are ambassadors for Christ and now more than ever we should, as a matter of urgency, present the unadulterated Gospel as God's sure solution for a broken world.

'I Walk the Line'

Johnny Cash, a devout Christian, wrote his famous song entitled 'I walk the line', which has always been a favourite of mine. It was written as a proclamation of fidelity to his first wife during his heroic struggles in 'walking the line' with personal issues. His title caught my attention. Somehow, it reminded me of the choice most Christians must face - a world gone mad with a 'me first' attitude, or the wisdom, guidance, and grace of the Holy Spirit. One of the Cash stanzas in his famous song runs thus -

> "I keep a close watch on this heart of mine,
> I keep my eyes wide open all the time,
> I keep the ends out for the tie that binds,
> Because you're mine, I walk the line."

A friendship with an elderly Chinese gentleman at the local bus stop was a case in point. He had previously accepted literature. During one of our contacts, I indicated a line in the concrete footpath by the bus stop and demonstrated by walking up to this line and turning back, up to it and returning, up and back saying, "This line represents the truth of God. Those who are convicted by the Spirit of God will walk across this line into a faith relationship with God through Jesus. Too many walk up to the line or even along it, but foolishly turn back." When they cross the line, they live. If they don't cross the line, they merely exist. The paralysis of refusing to act on God's Word leads nowhere.

With a brief flashing smile, the Chinese gentleman replied, "That is good word for me." The line I drew for my Asian contact included testimony and a Gospel message. Many church goers are likewise one simple prayer away from totally yielding to God. They hesitate to utter this one simple prayer: "Lord, I yield everything to you. I want a whole new level of relationship with You."

> "We will not turn away from you;
> **Revive** us and we will call upon your name.
> **Restore** us, O LORD GOD of hosts;
> Cause your face to shine upon us, and we will be saved."
> (Psalm 80:18-19)

Public Transport to and from the City
At the Bus Stop

It's 10am at the bus stop. A car stopped. A rear door burst open. An Asian teenager with tousled bleached blond hair tumbled out the back seat, rubbing sleep from his eyes. The door slammed. The car with its glum faced occupants accelerated into the distance. The teen buckled up his trouser belt on his way to the bus shelter, whipped off his shoes, pulled on a pair of socks, replaced his shoes, then inspected the timetable. I explained, "It's a Sunday timetable. We've got a three-quarter hour wait." After a brief conversation he said, "I've been to some churches." I referred him to an Asian friend at our church for follow up.

A middle-aged Chinese friend proudly articulated two words: "Left, and Right" but forgot which was which. Inscribing 'Right' on his right hand and 'Left' on the other clarified his confusion. Then with the aid of his electronic dictionary it became clear that he was headed for the fish shop in Box Hill. He actually communicated. Proud as punch he was.

Jack, an Asian student of human sciences, stated, "I am preparing myself to help people." I said, "Excellent, but I'm talking about a personal relationship with your Creator." He replied, "I didn't expect a lesson on the issues of life. This day I'll never forget."

A diminutive young Asian lady, with two well behaved infants, a heavy pusher and loads of groceries, bravely battled the odds as she struggled to board the bus. This tiny human dynamo said, "I remember! You gave me a card. I have it in my shoulder bag." She looked so young and frail, but no doubt about it, she was cheerfully and competently in complete control. She's had a busy day but said, "Now I go home and cook dinner."

Fay tearfully disputed on her cell phone regarding rental payments. I said, "Roll your burdens onto God and He will provide all your needs according to His riches in Christ."

A Chinese male said, "I have degrees in accountancy. I am a good man but cannot get work. My father was a good man, but he died a dreadful death from cancer. I went a few times to a Mormon Church and prayed to God. but God did not help us. I do not believe in God or Buddha."

I exclaimed, "This booklet (Gospel of John) answers your questions."

David, an Asian student, listened to my Psalm 23 testimony then asked, "What happens when we die?"

I answered, "What you do with Jesus now determines what he does with you in the next life." He accepted literature but did not respond to an invitation to our youth group.

Six Asians waited at the bus stop. One was my English 'pupil' from a week previously. We reviewed his precious lesson. Another Asian had an umbrella. We discussed the word 'umbrella'. Other Asians chipped in to help. My friend got it and repeated, "Umbrella for rain." The audience clapped and cheered. For this brief interlude we became community.

An Asian couple, resident in Australia for twenty-one years asked, "Where do I catch the train to Box Hill?" His wife is a devout Christian. He continued, saying, "If God is a God of love why does he allow war?" She presented the Chinese literature to her husband desperately hoping he becomes a believer.

On the Train

An Asian friend and I rode the train to the city. During lengthy conversation, he produced the Gospel of John, which he had previously received. I marked out John 3:16*, 8:12*, and 8:31-32* in his Gospel to read. He said, "You are my best friend."

An overseas student, who arrived in Melbourne one month previously, smiled when offered Chinese literature. His aunty in China had given him a Bible. Upon reading it he became a Jesus follower. He is praying his parents will become Christians and intends to enrol in a Bible College. He will not return to China because the Government there is 'no good for Christianity'.

A Vietnamese masseuse frankly discussed her duties with male and female clients. She is earning money to visit her ageing father in Ho Chi Min City. An Asian lady said, "Remember me?" I couldn't. She said, "I would like to go to a Bible study"' She accepted suggestions.

An Asian male informed me, "I have no religion."

I said, "I am a Christian. May I bless you?"

"Yes," He replied.

"I bless you in the name of Jesus Christ in your workplace today and in your future with happiness and security."

His response - "Thank you. I hope we meet again."

A male accepted Chinese literature and remarked, "Some friends took me to church in Sydney. I have just moved to Melbourne - I'm looking for a church." He was to meet his wife and child arriving from China at the airport that evening. He lived nearby and was referred to our Chinese Pastor.

An Asian lady lost her Australian husband three months ago with cancer. She said, "You can sit with me. You look a good man."

I replied, "Apples look nice and red and juicy outside, but worms turn them rotten inside. I was a rotten apple. On December 25th I will celebrate the birth of Jesus Christ who changed me inside."

A pleasant young Chinese bio-medical student said, "Newton's Law of Physics causes me to wonder about origins. I have concluded there must be a God with a middleman between us but my thinking is not clear."

An Asian airlines captain on holidays stated, "I am a paid-up member of the Communist Party and do not believe in God." His little daughter grabbed the Chinese booklet from his hand and read avidly.

I said to him, "May the God you do not believe in richly bless you." He laughed.

A mother and mature aged son invited me to sit with them. She spoke no English. He lamented the fact that Chinese culture was giving way to materialism, he analogised that: "Water represents women and wood represents man. The male earns the money, and the softness of the wife upholds him and the kids at home. He is the big strong tree; she is the water that keeps him going. But now women go to work, earn big money and drive flash cars." He accepted Chinese literature.

A Chinese youth, with dyed blonde hair and ear studs stated, "Mondays are not good for me. I work all weekend and party all night."

I said, "Early to bed, early to rise makes young men healthy, wealthy and wise."

He answered, "Yeah, I know, an old Chinese proverb."

I said, "Here's a Christian proverb" (I read Proverbs 3:5-6).

An Asian cookery student said, "Everyone has a god and devil inside him."

I said, "True! We all have a black dog and a white dog fighting for control of our lives. Which one will win?"

He said, "That's a hard question."

I said, "Feed the black dog with bad thoughts and he'll win every time."

An elderly gentleman returned the Chinese literature, extracted a harmonica from his shoulder bag and beautifully rendered a selection of well-known Christian hymns, including Beethoven's 9th symphony in 'D' minor (He told me). I was surprised!

A Singaporean cook with Japanese parents said, "Many things in my life were not good. I became a Christian late last year."

"What are the main issues you now face?" I asked him.

He replied, "Loneliness and financial insecurity." He allowed me to pray for him.

On the Railway Platform

An eloquent Taiwanese student believed in taking the best from all religions. He remarked, "I volunteered in a geriatric hospital."

I said, "The whole world is a hospital with eight billion patients. Jesus as God in human flesh came to cure them all."

He exclaimed, "You have no right to force religion on others."

I answered, "If you have cancer, and I have the cure, wouldn't you want me to share the cure?"

A fourteen-year-old Asian student accepted Chinese literature. She said, "My family are still in China. We don't have religion there, but my mother asked me to find out about Christianity in Australia."

An Asian declared, "I like tennis."

I stated, "A player at one end of the court yells AHHH! A player at the other end screams OOOH! An umpire in the middle shouts OUT. It's like marriage. A husband shouts AHHH! A wife shouts OOOH! But the man in the middle shouts OUT, that's no way to conduct marriage."

The Asian said, "Who is the man in the middle?"

I said, "God."

Nancy, and her husband Hollis were warm hearted, receptive Asian born Canadian residents visiting his mother in Melbourne. I asked, "Are you Christians?"

Nancy replied, "I have two Bibles – Chinese and English. I read them every day and pray. My husband is sympathetic."

He said, "I'd like to believe but don't know how." He was trying to understand God before he made a decision.

I suggested, "Accepting the event of salvation is the first step. Understanding Christ is the process which follows the event."

He said, "It's a miracle! We come all the way from Canada and meet you in Melbourne." I prayed with them on the Croydon railway platform and parted with handshakes and a hearty hug from mother-in-law!!

Some Delightful Filipino Contacts

Joshua and Joy, a delightful Filipino Christian couple, accepted a Gospel of John months ago at the Box Hill railway station. They embraced me and conducted a public prayer meeting on the landing at the top of the escalator. Their loud fiery prayers, clearly audible to the surging throng, were inspiring. She said, "We depend on older Christians like you, to light the fire in young Australians."

Months later, a friendly voice at the above-mentioned station platform called, "Hello Bruce." To my surprise Joshua reached into his shoulder bag, grabbed a Gospel of John, and offered it to me with twinkling eyes, saying, "Do you love Jesus?" He further stated, "Every Sunday we go to Federation Square, hand out literature and pray with people. I have given out over 200 booklets. You inspired me to do this. I am copying your ministry." They attend a well-known church nearby.

A Filipino businessman from Brunei was migrating soon to New Zealand. He listened to my testimony but said, "I'm a Christian too. I say my rosary every day."

I asked him, "If you were to die today, how would you respond if God said, 'Why should I let you into my Kingdom'?"

He answered, "I would tell Him I obey the Ten Commandments. Keep the Golden Rule. Attend church." I used Bill Newman's Eternity brochure to explain God's plan of salvation. He said, "I will accept Christ. What's my next step?"

I said, "Link up with a Bible believing church in NZ as soon as you arrive."

He stated, "I will let you know how I go." I never heard from him.

A Filipino physics teacher residing in NZ was here for job interviews re an overseas posting. He explained, "I know what will happen when I die. I base my belief on John 3:16*, Ephesians 2:8-9* and John 14:6*. I am applying for this job so I can take the Gospel to the Middle East. Your ministry is encouraging. I have learned a lot today." We prayed together.

At the NewHope Church, North Blackburn Vic

Some months ago, a cheerful, non-Christian Chinese national with good business qualifications and infant child entered our NewHope café to improve her English-speaking skills. She quickly mastered the dishwasher and serving (as distinct from surviving) patrons. She accepted a Chinese/English Bible.

Upon return from a visit to her homeland she associated with the 'Mainly Music' church ministry group for infant children and presented Jan with an exquisitely ornate carton of sweets and a canister of Chinese tea in gratitude for our friendship. At 'Dinner Tonight' a free meal was provided to some 150 disadvantaged every Saturday night at our church. I sat with Asian visitors, including an old man I previously met on the bus. He explained, "Mao left us with empty hearts. If we said anything against the Government, we disappeared, but it's getting better. The Chinese nation needs something to fill the gap. I'm going into the Chinese Church now to see how it works."

To another Asian lady I said, "Have you worked out your nationality yet?" She laughingly replied, "I am a citizen of the world, and a pilgrim on the highway of life, heading to the eternal city."

My devotional life had been interrupted by new routines, but prior to attending the morning service at NewHope, I read through Romans 5. At church, an Asian walked off the street and said, "I have big problems. I can't kick the drug habit and want to commit suicide."

I asked, "Why did you come here?"

He said, "I have deep guilt. Should I turn myself in to Police?" He listed some serious crimes he had committed.

I told him, "By all means turn yourself in! That might satisfy the law, but it won't fix your guilt." We examined Romans 5:8*.

He said, "God would never save me. I am too bad." I spoke strongly from this verse against his comment. He accepted a New Testament, salvation literature and promised in front of witnesses to attend church next Sunday, but never did.

'Billy' from Beijing lamented, "We have all we need in China - food, clothes, house, job and money, but who fills the hunger in my heart? China is materialistic. We have no spiritual dimensions." Discussion followed on science, creation, evolution, and a Bible overview. Billy was excited to discover for the first time that faith not science, was the ingredient that made the Gospel live. He accepted a New Testament. He subsequently attended an Alpha Course.

A lady arrived after the 11am service at the NewHope Church and tearfully explained that her best friend died in China last night. Two Christian ladies comforted her. Arrangements are made to get her a bi-lingual Chinese/English Bible with follow up.

One evening, as I was securing our NewHope Church on lockup duties, I strolled across to McDonalds. The Edinburgh Military Tattoo (EMT) in Australia was broadcasting on TV. An Asian couple smiled. He said, "What does EMT mean" This led to my testimony.

I said to her, "Are you a Christian?"

She answered, "No."

He informed me, "My grandparents in China were Christians. My parents were Christians. I am a Christian. When I was little, they took me to a house church after dark. They carried little torches in their coat pockets to read the Bible. Turning lights on risked getting caught by the authorities. Being a Christian was hard then. I have a Bible, but I don't attend church because of shift work."

I said, "Your grandparents and parents prayed for you."

She said with feeling, "Yes. I know."

I said, "You should go to church."

He said, "We should."

A few years ago, Matt, one of our younger church members, acted as a lead tenant to several Asian students in the old NewHope manse. My wife and I attended weekly Bible studies in situ. One of those students since married, with two infant children enrolled in the Mainly Music ministry in our church. Another young Asian who boarded with Matt, attended the group. I prayed silently for an opportunity to introduce the Gospel to him. Quotes from a secular book he was reading provided this opening. I cupped my hands protectively round his flickering spiritual interest and spoke words of redemption into his tiny flame. The Asian's focus changed. It registered in his eyes. We think he made a genuine decision to surrender to Jesus, but concealed below that an inscrutable surface may lay snags of cultism, culture, or language. It is too easy to slip presumptuously into the role of a self-contained evangelist, only to be jolted by the reality that God alone brings sinners through to repentance.

Melbourne CBD Café Ministries
McDonalds

To a young Asian lady, I said, "I'm a Christian. May I bless you?" (Godwin's book 'The Way of Blessing' is insightful).

She said, "Yes!"

I stated, "In the name of Jesus I bless you in your office duties with enjoyment and satisfaction and in your life every spiritual blessing for your relationship with God."

She smiled and said, "Enjoy your coffee."

An Asian lady explained, "I was only interested in business and a good time, but when I turned thirty, I realised I wanted a husband and family. Now I am thirty-five and have no one." She grew up under a communist regime and did not believe in heaven and hell. I shared the Gospel from Genesis 1–3.

Sodnomsambuu, a tall, well-built, good-looking Russian speaking Mongolian of Asian appearance arrived in Melbourne at 8am this day to study. His English was good, but he declined literature saying, "No thanks! I'm normal." No offence meant. None taken.

An Asian student said, "I am not interested, but my grandmother in China was a Christian and gave me a Bible."

Remembering that ancestors are venerated in Chinese culture, I told her, "Your grandmother would have prayed for you. She and I are brother and sister in Jesus. I will pray for you too." She accepted Chinese literature.

A bare-footed Asian youth, in black eastern garb, insisted on carrying my bag. He exclaimed, "I feel the anger of earth through my feet and express love to the world through my hands." He followed Taoism, an ancient Chinese belief system. He accepted literature.

An English literature student from Hong Kong related this analogy: "God said to his angels I have a word. What will I do with it? Will I put it above the sky or under the sea? An angel replied, 'Put it in the minds of people where it can be used. It's up to them to uncover it'."

I replied, "You will filter God's truth through the framework of your prejudices and misconception. Jesus Christ is the only one who died and now lives to guide you."

A tall nineteen-year-old Asian student, with good English, candidly discussed the attributes of his Chinese Government. I asked, "Would I be accepted in China as a Christian?"

His response - "I am Christian."

I said, "How did you become a Christian?"

He replied, "I read books on freedom, democracy and Christianity in a public library in Melbourne last year. I also attended church in Melbourne but returned to China for holidays over Christmas and changed to Christianity." He accepted a Chinese Bible and asked, "Can I have an English version too?"

Lei, a recently arrived Chinese student, patiently listened to my testimony and some teaching on Psalm 23. His English comprehension was low. He accepted literature and explained, "I tried reading the Bible but couldn't understand it."

Lei was replaced by Wang Wei, a student who arrived in Australia three weeks previously with no English and a broad smile. How some of these students understand classroom English beats me. He accepted Chinese literature and said in surprise, "You Christian? I go to church in China."

To a pleasant young Chinese student, I asked, "What are you studying?"

He said somewhat cynically, "Accounting. All I will do for the rest of my life is make money."

I asked the BQ*. He shrugged and said, "I don't know."

I explained to him, "The most important question for me is what will happen when I die? What brings you the most joy?"

He said, "Being with family I suppose?"

I told him, "The thing that brings me the most joy is giving you the answer to what happens when you die."

Swanston Street and Bourke Mall

An old Indian tourist tripped and fell beside me in Swanston Street. Asians rushed to his aid. He regained his feet. His wife said, "Parkinsons!"

An older lady in the Asian group asked, "Is he alright?"

I said, "Getting old is not funny, is it?"

She answered, "No. It isn't!"

I asked her, "Can you answer a question?"

She said, "If I can."

I said, "What happens when I die?"

She said, "You will go to your god I suppose."

I asked her, "Do you have a god?"

She said to me, "We won't go into that," but accepted Vietnamese literature.

Victor, a Thai Karen Christian security officer, was studying Isaiah 40:29-31* from his bi-lingual Bible as he worked. His grandfather was a shaman but got saved. Grandfather led his family to Christ but was murdered whilst conducting an evangelistic campaign. I had heard this well-known story in the annals of Burmese Christian history previously.

I had forgotten my pen. I said to the Chinese cash register attendant, "Do you sell pens?"

With a blank look she said, "Pants?"

I said again, "No! Pens! Pens! Pens! Teach me English so you can understand."

She laughed. I returned with a pen from the shelf. I said to her Chinese boss, "I want to make a complaint. I asked for a pen, and she tried to sell me pants." He gave her a make-believe clip on the ear. I paid for my purchase and gave her the little red Chinese Gospel booklet. Later I returned and said to her, "Excuse me, do you sell pants?"

Quick as a flash, she walked to the lingerie section, held up a pair of lady's unmentionables and said, "Yes" and laughed. Checkmate!

A young Asian was seated on a bench in the Mall. I said, "You look worried." Wordlessly he handed me his sheaf of papers. He had been fined $3,500 in default imprisonment. I asked him, "Have you told your family?"

"No!" he explained,

I asked, "Have you obtained legal advice?"

"No!"

I explained, "You have three very important things to do. Tell your family. Get legal advice. Pack spare underpants and a toothbrush, because tonight the sheriff will call at your house and lock you up." He disappeared like a streak of greased lightning. I had no opportunity to share my faith. Wonder why?

A Chinese student studying tourist literature in the Mall said, "Australians velly hostile." My puzzled expression prompted him to consult his Chinese English electronic dictionary whereupon he nervously giggled saying, "I velly solly, I mean hospitable." He accepted the Four Spiritual Laws tract, Chinese literature and asked, "Do you believe in God?" I replied, "What stops people becoming a Christian?" He said to me, "I need to think."

Degraves Street

I was in Degraves Street for coffee and donuts. A dishevelled male approached. I expected him to ask for money. I tried to get in first by saying, "No! No! No!" Quick as a flash, he grabbed my donut, wolfed it, and walked, without so much as a backward glance.

Two startled Chinese students sitting nearby were disgusted. These nice young girls from a part of China we had visited asked, "What do you think of China?"

I replied, "China is very materialistic."

One said, "Yes. It is not good. We are so busy; we have no time to ourselves." They accepted a Gospel presentation and Chinese/English literature. Each week they attended a Christian discussion group.

A pretty young Asian student asked, "What are you writing?"

I explained, "My journal."

She said, "Why?"

I answered, "Maybe to make a book for my family."

She said, "What will the title be?"

I said to her, "In front of them all."

A druggie pointed at me and said to her, "Watch him! He chats up young girls like you and rapes them."

Undaunted, she continued, "What does 'In front of them all' mean?"

I recounted the story behind the 'In Front of Them All' signage mounted above the UN HQ village in Pan Mun Jon, then gestured toward the crowds in Degraves Street saying, "I stand, 'in front of them all', not with bullets and bombs but a message of peace."

With mouth agape she said, "Huh!" I shared my Psalm 23 testimony. She accepted Chinese/English literature.

A Chinese student with limited English wondered what the words 'Merry Christmas' meant. This was an ideal opportunity to introduce testimony and bi-lingual Chinese/English literature.

As his understanding opened, I said, "What stops you from giving your life to Christ right now?"

He said "Nothing!" He prayed the sinner's prayer and gave his life to Christ. His decision seemed genuine. He said, "Thank you my brother." He was referred to a Chinese church.

Federation Square

A practitioner of Zen Buddhism said, "We focus on self-emptying of our minds, rejecting the bad things and filling it with good things. I can learn from you and you from me. Our lives must be held in this balance. We all worship the same God. The earth is god. You are God." I put the Christian position to him and left.

To a Catholic widowed Chinese grandfather from East Timor, I asked, "Will you ever remarry?"

He informed me, "I have eight kids and seventeen grandkids. A new wife would be a headache." He accepted literature and offered a small medallion as a parting gift.

To Jimmy, a Chinese student with PR, I said, "What is the most important question in all the world for you?"

He said, "I'm forty years old and never married. I want a wife." He listened to my testimony but stated, "I won't believe what you can't prove."

I explained to him, "Your only options are evolution or creation. Which is it?"

He answered, "Neither, we are extra-terrestrials."

I said, "And you can't prove that either! What about the historical Jesus Christ?"

He exclaimed, "He's only an invention to make people feel good. Why do we kill the animals your God created? God should stop that killing. I don't want to live with a cruel Jesus. What about all the other religions? They are just as valid as yours."

I said, "Let's meet again soon."

He replied unenthusiastically, "Yes. Let's do that" and accepted Chinese literature. He never responded.

A couple from Beijing listened to a Gospel presentation based on Genesis 1:1-3. During our lengthy conversation he asserted, "I am a scientist. Biology teaches me that life ends at death."

She gestured heavenward, laughed derisively, and said, "I will go to Hell rather than accept your Jesus." They accepted Chinese literature and a Gospel of John.

A female Chinese student, who arrived in Australia fifteen days previously with permanent residency in mind. He spoke with cultured, fluent English. I showed her the plan of salvation. She caught on quickly. Her friend appeared. We discussed the Shepherd Psalm. They permitted me to give their contact numbers to a member of our church small group. The late arrival said, "Can we meet again?" We arranged to meet at 4pm next Thursday but it never happened.

Kevin, an Asian student who attended a house church in China, had a Christian grandmother who prayed for him daily. This impressive young gentleman accepted Chinese literature. I said, "Tell your grandmother an old Australian Christian sends her Christian greetings? She will be encouraged."

He said, "I will!"

A Chinese student accepted my testimony but said, "I lead a good life. I don't need God." To my surprise he began weeping.

I explained, "The universe is undeniably upheld by natural laws. Just so, God gives spiritual laws to guide us, but we can't keep them. Christ paid the penalty for our sin with his death on the Cross and gives us new life through the Resurrection."

He said, "I can't make this decision in a few minutes, I need time."

A Chinese student from the University of Wollongong, was reading a National Geographic magazine article containing graphic photographs of hundreds of terra cotta warriors placed in his tomb by an ancient despotic

Chinese emperor for protection in his afterlife. This was a perfect opportunity to present the claims of the perfect living emperor whose Crucifixion was a magnificent victory over our sin and whose bodily resurrection was the proclamation of that victory and our introduction to eternal life. I said, "Do you understand?" He said, "Clearly." He prayed the sinner's prayer and gave his life to Christ. Enquiries through the Melbourne Chinese Christian Fellowship and a Sydney based Christian FM radio station produced an email from an enthusiastic young interstate Christian worker who linked my contact to the Wollongong Baptist Church and it's Mandarin Language Fellowship.

Box Hill Centro

A Melbourne based magazine included an article on the Chinese lunar New Year with the title 'Kung Hei Fat Choi', which I'm told roughly translated to, 'Have a happy and prosperous new year.' To an Asian husband I said, "KHFC."

He replied, "I got it."

I said, "I am a rat."

He answered, "I am a tiger."

I stated, "Tigers eat rats. Where does that leave me?"

His wife, chipped in said, "I am a dragon. If he can survive me, you're safe." They accepted a KHFC tract.

Indonesians

I visited a St Kilda Road cafeteria, managed by a competent Indonesian born Christian lady known to me, for lunch. The service, food and fellowship were excellent. I left her with Habakkuk 3:2: "O Lord, revive thy work in the midst of the years; in the midst of the years make known; in wrath remember mercy."

An Asian Muslim lady said, "All religions are the same."

I replied, "The Jesus of Islam and the Jesus of the Bible are hugely different. The Bible says all men will die. All men will be raised. All will be judged. Jesus will be that judge. He'll divide all men into two groups, the positive and the negative. That division will be permanent. Say, Yes to Him now and He'll say, yes to you then. Say No to him now, and your eternal destiny will be terrible." She accepted Indonesian literature.

Amy, an Indonesian, said, "Which is your church?"

After some explanation she informed me,

"I am unhappily married with an Australian! I was a Muslim, a Catholic, Mormon and now Salvation Army. I support World Vision and gave my granddaughter a set of rosaries blessed by the church to put under her pillow, but she gave it back."

I said, "It's not about rosaries, Baptists, Salvoes, Mormons, Muslims, Hindus, or Buddhists. It's about Jesus, Jesus, Jesus."

Jan and I headed to Warrnambool (Vic.) for a break. At Kennett River Caravan Park, along with 100's of Asian tourists, we searched for koalas. Fortunately, one climbed to the ground near our feet. Pang and Tan, two young Malaysians stood fascinated beside us. This delightful young couple listened to my story and accepted a Gospel of John. Later, in Port Campbell they took selfies of the four of us.

Encouraging Baptisms

Jan and I attended the Kew Baptist Church for the baptism of a Chinese student who became a Christian at the conclusion of an evening service in the NewHope Church one Sunday. In her moving testimony she paid tribute to those who helped her come into the Christian faith. I am honoured to be one little link in that long chain and to be invited to witness her baptism.

I was invited to speak at the baptism of an elated Asian lady in a local home. She testified after her baptism by putting her hand on a Bible and saying among other things, "This is my birth certificate. I searched twenty years for peace and found it when I read this, and my burdens went." Testimonies are the cutting edge of the church.

Jan and I had met a young Asian couple at a function in NewHope. They wanted practice in conversational English. Over several weeks we studied English through the 'Christianity Explained' course, with a Chinese Bible, (which we can't read) and an English Bible as our textbooks. They became Christians and were baptised in the Chinese Baptist Church. Their subsequent text message from Queensland where they now live, was reassuring.

House Church Reflections

On a trip to China, our English-speaking guide took us on a tour of the beautifully manicured Yun Tai Gardens. In the evening, we weaved our clandestine way through dingy city back streets to a well-known unregistered house church in a poorer part of town. Along the way we passed displays of snails, water beetles, fish, crabs, oysters, and newly hatched chickens on offer for sale as food. There was no signage to guide us. We depended on handwritten instructions. A non-English speaking local guessed the purpose of our visit and pointed us in the right direction. We entered an unmarked single fronted three storey building divided into six chapels.

Three thousand people worshipped there during weekends with the aid of speaker systems. We were ushered into one of those chapels, sat on rough wooden seats and awaited the arrival of the Pastor. I had heard about him for years. Suddenly he breezed in - an aged, frail little man (recently deceased) with cheerful grin and excellent English. He, who fearlessly stood in front of them all with the Gospel had many battle scars, imprisoned twenty years for his faith, and fifteen years hard labour in a coal mine, escaped death many times, suffered extreme hardship, but shared a joyful victorious testimony with a humbling request for prayer. His business card bore the biblical text: 'Be thou faithful unto death (Revelation 2:10c*).' We departed prior to the service for security reasons.

A female student said, "My grandmother in China took me to a house church in China when I was little. I am a Christian."

I drew on a brown paper bag the Christ-centred and the self-centred circles and asked, "Which represents your life?"

She answered, "I am a mixture." She accepted testimony.

An Asian in Federation Square said in surprise, "I am a Christian." He was Han Chinese from an autonomous Muslim region of Northwest China and attended a house church there.

I asked him, "Have you ever been persecuted for your faith?"

He replied, "Yes. I was interviewed by Police, but I just told them I believed in God. About 200 years ago English missionaries brought the Gospel to China, now there are too many Christians for Police to control." He accepted Chinese literature saying, "I've been looking for Chinese literature for my Mongolian friend." This friend arrived at that moment. I sensed a deep, gentle Christian spirit in this contact. Communication was difficult but his company was warm.

A friendly Asian student asked, "Can you teach me about God? My government does not believe in God. My aunty told me about God." He later attended our 9am service. It was his first church service ever, anywhere. He signed up for a six-week Tuesday evening Bible course and attended.

An Asian student said, "I am Christian. I go to a house church in China. Your literature is very good." His attention was drawn to Proverbs 3:5-6:

> "Trust in the Lord with all your heart, and lean
> not on your own understanding.

In all your ways acknowledge Him, and
He shall direct your paths."

I was greeted on the bus with a chorus of hellos, and smiles from friendly Chinese passengers. A Taiwanese lass proudly showed me the Gospel of John I had given her months ago. A friendly Asian female voice at the bus stop called, "Hello Bruce" and offered me a lift to the Box Hill transit station. I prayed quietly as we drove. I had an inkling God was about to do something special today.

An Asian young man accepted Jesus as his Saviour over a cup of coffee in Box Hill Plaza and was referred to a special group in the NewHope Baptist Church for follow up.

A Chinese lady majored in English literature in Melbourne University fourteen years previously and later taught in a prestigious education institution in her home city in China. During her earlier stay in Melbourne, she found Bible references contained within her study material, which led to a deeper search and subsequent conversion to the Christian faith. Healing from a lengthy serious illness switched her on to become a fearless 'on fire' evangelical Christian. She invited me to Hungry Jacks for coffee and showed me photos of her large home church and several baptisms. We were amazed to discover that her long standing friend, and I attended the same NewHope Baptist Church. She departed for China soon after. Subsequently, her friend later sent me the following email:

"Thank you for what you did for that Asian lady on the train last week. Over a decade ago, my wife and I were asked if we would host a mature age student from China whilst she studied English at Latrobe University. She stayed with us several weeks and as part of the family attended NewHope each Sunday. In due course she returned to China, and we had occasional contact. She returned to Australia to visit her son who is studying at the

National University. She spent the weekend with us. Over a cup of tea and Anzac biscuits she told us her story since we last met." She said:

"By 2008, I was exhausted and at the end of my tether. I told my school where I was teaching, that I had to take twelve months off to recover my health. Then I remembered that there was a God and if I had no more strength, I could turn to him. I began attending a Christian Church and I started to believe in Jesus in my heart. I recovered but knew that my pattern of hard work for others was not sustainable. I prayed to God to allow my husband and me to start a business.

"God answered my prayers. A friend and I agreed to introduce our husbands to discuss the business plan. We visited in each other's homes and our husbands got to know each other. The men agreed on a plan to manufacture oil filters for cars. Some investors were introduced and we made an agreement with an international company to market our product. All the time I prayed to God for the business. The business is now established, and we are independent of hard work for others. I have had the opportunity to travel to South Korea to worship in the world's largest church and to attend a Christian teaching conference in Singapore. We now have a growing church in our neighbourhood and a Christian couple from Singapore are our Pastors. We now see new baptisms as people believe in Jesus. I wish to come to NewHope Church where I heard about Jesus many years ago."

Could it be that our churches are controlled by fear - they won't like us, the music isn't right, they won't come, it's not politically correct? Is culture consigning our churches to the outer perimeter of insignificance rather than the church changing culture? Are we preaching a sugar-coated Gospel rather than a message of repentance and surrender? What do you think?

Taking it to heart:

1. What are some blockages that stop Christians sharing the Gospel?

2. Are there church people you know who walk up to the line but do not cross?
3. In what ways can Christians make crooked paths straight for their contacts?
4. Share ways you might address this matter personally.

References:

Romans 5:8 – But God demonstrated His own love toward us, in that while we were still sinners, Christ died for us.

Revelation 2:10c – Be faithful unto death and I will give you the keys of life.

Isaiah 40:29-31 – He gives power to the weak, and to those who have no might He increasers strength. Even the youths shall faint and be weary, and the young men shall utterly fall. But those who wait upon the Lord shall renew their strength: they shall mount up with wings like eagles, they shall run and not be weary, they shall walk and not faint.

John 3:16 - For God so loved the world that He gave His only begotten Son, that whoever believes in Him should not perish but have eternal life.

BQ – Big Question – What is the most important question in all the world for you?

Chapter 6

Brazilian Experiences

A Brazilian Immigrant, a Ceremonial Event, and a Graduation

My Brazilian experience began with a recently arrived, tall, lean, bearded, dark and handsome guy sitting with eyes closed opposite in a train carriage. I seriously pondered the wisdom of disturbing him, but he readily accepted Portuguese literature. When Leiser was invited to NewHope Baptist Church, North Blackburn, he said, "I will be there next Sunday." I'd heard many such promises, but true to his word, he appeared the following Sunday at a morning service with wife Laura and child. They quickly made themselves at home. Later, he surprised me by saying, "At the very moment you spoke to me on the train that day, I was praying that God would lead me to a good church." They were welcomed into a church home group and admitted with stirring testimonies into church membership.

God prompted Leiser and Laura them to set up a Face Book (FB) entry advertising a 'Community of Hope' in their own home especially for

Brazilian contacts. Leiser ministered the Gospel dynamically in Portuguese (His mother tongue) to Brazilians living in Melbourne for travel, study, or work opportunities. He and Laura pastorally supported numbers of Brazilian families. Group attendance quickly built up to thirty-five at weekly Sunday lunch gatherings in their own home. Numbers outgrew space so they transferred meetings to the YWAM HQ in Surrey Hills. This happy, friendly, and vibrant lot encouraged me as I addressed them (with translation) on one occasion on Psalm 40:1-4, using the words 'Trust and Obey'. Following one such discussion a student said, "What you said makes me think about my life." Several returned to Brazil at the end of the year as new Christians. They were replaced with a newly arrived batch of Brazilians.

Melbourne Town Hall Ceremonial Event and Leiser's Graduation

On 31 May 1976, the then Lord Mayor, Ronald Walker, hosted a civic reception in recognition of the service Victoria Police Officers were providing to the community. As part of the event the then Chief Commissioner, Reginald Jackson, headed a parade of 200 Police Sergeants marching with the Police Pipe Band accompaniment from Russell Street Police Complex to the Melbourne City Town Hall. Mr Jackson, many years previously, was a member of the panel which selected me for a Police career. Marching with this contingent was a proud moment for me and for Jan, who proudly participated with spectators in the enjoyment of this occasion. A Police Ensign was presented to Mr Jackson at this event. The Lord Mayor in his speech, said among other things, "We are fortunate that the enforcement of laws in this state of Victoria lies in the hands of the very highly acclaimed and efficient Police service, which are today being commended by the City of Melbourne for their devotion to duty, their loyalty and their unceasing and tireless service to the whole community at large." So, say I! Proudly I might add! Praise God for our wonderful Police.

In 2015 Jan and I attended Leiser's graduation as a Protective Services Officer (PSO) at the Police Training Academy in Glen Waverley. He looked every inch a policeman – tall, dark and handsome.

In conjunction with Leiser's graduation, the Police Ensign presented to Mr Jackson all those years ago was retired and replaced with an updated version acknowledging the recently formed PSO's, symbolising unity within the Victoria Police. I was privileged to meet the then current Chief Commissioner, Mr Graham Ashton, at this function. He was interested in my story. My function program is endorsed by Mr Ashton with the following comment, "Great to see you here today. Thanks for being part of the original ceremony thirty-nine years ago," signed Graham Ashton, Chief Commissioner.

My involvement with the marching party all those years ago, my attendance at Leiser's graduation, and the totally unexpected (for me) ceremonial exchange of the ensign on November 27, 2015, triggered off many memories. It was significance bordering on astonishment.

While at our church, Leiser and Laura juggled ministry with work commitments whilst caring for small children, but good things came to an end. Leiser trained a successor to lead his Brazilian group, resigned his commission as a PSO and pursued ministry opportunities amongst the Brazilian community on the Sunshine Coast, Queensland. Laura, a highly qualified university-trained language specialist was last heard of undertaking further studies.

More Brazilian Contacts

A female media student working with a laptop in the City Library in Flinders Lane (FL), was unaware of my presence. Later, she sat opposite me in McDonalds. My testimony triggered a flood of tears. She said, "I am Catholic. You tell a story beautifully." Melbourne is about as far from Brazil as one can get. Her family, culture, and friends are a long way away. Homesickness and loneliness may have contributed to her tears. She was on a journey of discovery and hoped to return home a better person, but for now reality was utter perplexity. Worldwide injustice and the disparity she saw between Brazilians, who die of starvation and Australians, who she considered lucky, was difficult for her to process. We discussed John 3:16* at length. She accepted a New Testament and a Dixon booklet entitled 'God's Plan for Your Life'.

A Brazilian student said, "I am a Christian. I attended a Pentecostal Church in Brazil and now the AOG Church in Richmond. What do you do?" I related some stories of my evangelism activities. He commented, "What a marvelous job you are doing."

I replied, "'God forbid that I should glory except in the Cross of our Lord Jesus Christ by whom the world is crucified to me and I to the world'(Galatians 6:14).

In Federation Square (FS), Abigail, a hospitality student from Brazil attended a local Planet Shakers Church. She accepted testimony, a Dixon booklet 'God's Plan for Your Life' and Christmas literature. Her mother died in Brazil and her father intended remarrying. She no longer felt Brazil was home and added, "I've been in Australia two years and eight months and you are the first Australian to speak to me about the Lord. I am encouraged."

Cabral, from Brazil, accepted the BQ* and Portuguese literature, and said, "How do I help the poor?" He readily accepted a TPTL NT* with John 8:12* underlined.

I asked him to read the verse aloud and said, "As you read through John and come to a part you understand, FOLLOW."

In FS, Djalma Melo (Wilton is his adopted Aussie name), a friendly Brazilian, recently arrived in Australia. After several futile attempts at crossing the language barrier electronically, I put him in phone contact with a Brazilian friend. Their lengthy and obviously enjoyable conversation produced many smiles. Wilton later reappeared at FS for his next English conversation. We discussed in Hungry Jacks John 1:12*, 8:12* and 1 John 1:8-9* with the aid of his electronic Portuguese/English dictionary. Never did I dream of ministering the Gospel electronically to a Portuguese speaking Brazilian with practically no English in Hungry Jacks.

In Hungry Jacks, Michelle, was the second Brazilian requesting help with English language learning. She later arrived for her third lesson in conversational English. She had made a big effort to mingle with English speakers and her language skills had improved noticeably. I enjoyed conversational English with two other Portuguese speaking Brazilian young women in Hungry Jacks.

Our church Communications Director later alerted me to the following Facebook entry from Wilton. "I talked a bit with this Pastor, was very nice, because I went to Melbourne to learn English and in the same place, I met Pastor that with few words gave me a nice message, it's a shame because as soon as I returned and I had the pleasure to go to your church, move'm back next year and hope to meet you to thank you." (Signed Djalma Melo).

References:

John 3:16 – God so loved the world that He gave His only begotten Son, that whoever believes in Him should not perish but have everlasting life.

John 8:12 – I am the light of the world. He who follows me shall not walk in darkness, but have the light of life.

John 1:12 – But as many as received Him, to them He gave the right to become children of God, to those who believe in His name.

1 John 1:8-9 – If we say that we have no sin, we deceive ourselves, and the truth is not in us. If we confess our sins, He is faithful and just to forgive us our sins and to cleanse us from all unrighteousness.

BQ – What is the greatest question in all the world for you?

TPTL NT – The Pocket Testament League New Testament.

Chapter 7

Conversations with Buddhists

Many non-Buddhists have little understanding of Buddhist culture, family structure and lifestyle. My discussions with numerous Buddhists led me to believe that few, if any, know little about Christianity or the Bible. A way of investigating this deficiency was by asking well thought-out questions.

My mentor and Pastor, Rev. Dr. Graeme Smith, excelled at leading congregations from the familiar to unfamiliar in his teaching. Missionary, Don Richardson, defined this principle as 'Redemptive Analogies' in his book 'Peace Child'. Sharing the Gospel with Buddhists as with most faiths, is simply finding ways of taking people from their understanding or belief into a clear understanding of Christian theology. Paul's address to the men of Athens in Acts 17:23* re the unknown God, is instructive.

I introduced myself as a Christian. The man replied. "I'm Buddhist." End of story? Not so! I think. "Great!" Opening conversation with the phrase 'God loves you' may well be a conversation stopper for the Buddhist. Beginning with a conventional, but unfamiliar Christian approach can be confusing. Rather begin with, "No matter how hard I try, I can't seem to keep the Ten Commandments of the Christian faith which are similar to the five commands of Buddha - killing, theft, adultery, alcohol, or lying. Do you have problems keeping your Five Commands?" "What's been your experience?" Vulnerability and empathy often open a door for honest sharing. The Buddhist concept of karma springs from Hinduism.

A Hindu student from North India sat at one end of a parapet in Federation Square (FS) reading a book written by a famous Indian author named Khushwant Singh.

An Asian Buddhist sat at the other end of the parapet. I sat between them and said to the reader, "May I see your book?" One short story in this book related to a learned Indian holy man who attended a funeral and gave the dead man's wife a Hindu Holy Book. Some words in this book read: 'Like a man who casts off old garments and puts on new ones, so does the soul.' As the holy man contemplated this saying, he was disturbed by the movement of a little fluffy white dog between his feet. It licked his trousers and when the author patted its head, it licked his hand. The holy man looked uneasily from the corpse to the dog and back again. He pondered, "Could the soul of the dead man already be reincarnated into this little dog?" This thought triggered three possibilities concerning his own death:

1. Submit to the searing flames of cremation and go to paradise or be extinguished into nothingness,
2. Find your way to an evil city and live a life of debauchery and self-indulgence, or
3. Return from where you came.

Which one to choose? He decided on a coin toss. If it came down heads, he will be cremated. If it fell down tails, he would live a life of debauchery. If it fell on its edge, he would return from whence he came. The Asian

Buddhist, who had been edging toward the epi-centre of our conversation, said, "Buddhism is a philosophy. It has no God."

The Hindu student said, "All religions say the same thing and lead to the same place."

I said to them, "Let's look at John 14:6* and John 3:16*." They accepted Gospels of John.

Thousands of Australians are embracing Buddhism. An event arising out of 'Come Celebrate' Christmas carols at the Whitehorse Soundshell in Nunawading illustrated how suffering often paves the way for Christian outreach. We received the following written prayer request:

"My fiancée (John) is dying from terminal pancreatic cancer at the age of thirty-five years. He is a Buddhist and believes his cancer is punishment via karma. I just want him to know Jesus, that healing is possible, and he doesn't have to face death as punishment."

John's sad plight and his fiancée's deep concern stimulated my thinking. If opportunity arose, I might respond to John as follows: "Your illness is of deep concern to both your fiancée and me. Be assured of our prayers. Suffering is part of life. Most of us, regardless of faith, suffer in some way. The issue is not so much whether we suffer, but rather how we respond when it happens."

Buddhism responds to impending death by declaring that deeds and misdeeds on earth determine the number of reincarnations you endure before escaping into the infinite - but nobody knows how many reincarnations are enough. One Buddhist lady I met thinks eight. A learned Hindu guru was recently reported as suggesting: '2,700 should suffice'. Some say the cycles are endless. These torturous thoughts offer no eternal security and may even produce harmful emotional health consequences. On the other hand, the Jesus I follow and to whom I have given allegiance, said, "Let not your heart be troubled. You believe in God, believe also in me.

In my Father's house are many mansions. If it were not so I would have told you. Behold I go to prepare a place for you that where I am you may be also" (John 14:1-3). The lady was invited to make further contact with NewHope Church, but no response was received.

To a male Thai Buddhist on the train, I asked, "Do you have problems keeping Buddha's Five Commands?"

He replied, "Yes! I do!"

I said, "How do you escape karma?"

He replied, "I don't know. Do you?"

I said to him, "I'm a Christian. I think following the Buddha Five Commands and the Christian Ten Commandments are similar. We all fall short, but John 14:1-6 takes us beyond karma. Jesus said, 'I am the light of the world. He who follows me shall not walk in darkness but have the light of life'" (John 8:12). He accepted a Gospel of John.

To a holidaying Sri Lankan Buddhist couple, I asked, "Can you explain Buddhism?"

Among other things he replied, "Rebirth is tedious."

I said, "How many rebirths have you had?" But he didn't want to go down that path. I tried again, "How many rebirths are enough to get you to Nirvana?"

He avoided answering by asking, "What is your story?" They listened as I read John 14:1-6. I suggested they might like to compare Christian scriptures with their own sacred writings. They accepted a Gospel of John.

I was reading a book on Buddhism at a Blackburn Square bookstall. A lady glanced briefly at the book. I asked her, "Are you interested in Buddhism?"

She said, "Very!"

I asked, "Why does it appeal to you?"

She answered, "I like its truth."

I stated, "Could I show you some inconsistencies in Buddhism as revealed in this book."

She read the section, then replied, "I'm not familiar with the fine points."

I said, "According to Buddhist doctrines, there is nothing to stop me reincarnating as a cockroach in South America in the next life."

She replied, "I believe we reincarnate progressively as better humans."

I explained to her, "Did you know that is not the teaching of Buddha?" I shared my story, then quoted John 14:6*.

"Fascinating!" she responded. She accepted a Gospel of John.

In response to a Gospel presentation, an Asian said, "I am torn by loyalty to Buddhism in my home country and a desire to settle permanently in Australia."

I said, "Buddhism came into the world as a word and stayed a word. Jesus Christ as the Word of God became flesh and dwelt among us. You are responsible to Jesus Christ the Judge of the world." She accepted an Alpha Bible study outreach programme invitation.

At the Centro shops in Box Hill, an Asian Buddhist lass answered the BQ* saying, "I am returning to China soon. How can I enjoy my family and friends better?" I said to her, "We visited a large house church in China a few years ago. They enjoyed each other's company wonderfully."

She replied, "I met many house church Christians when I lived in China. They were kind and beautiful."

In FS, Prakash, a Bhutanese Buddhist accepted the BQ*. Even though I had no Dzongkha literature (his mother tongue), he understood my English literature. He read John 8:12 from a John's Gospel aloud. He said, "Impressive! I deeply appreciate you speaking to me. I'll treasure this book. Thank you."

A demonstration for Eritrean peace was in progress in FS. An older Scottish lady with Buddhist leanings asked, "Do you think there will ever be peace in the world?" Part way through my testimony, she began crying saying, "What a beautiful story. I wish I had an experience like that." She accepted a Gospel of John and a salvation tract and rushed off to join the march.

An Asian lady with a baby in a pram said, "I have a sixteen-year-old son under the China one child policy. I took advantage of my Australian Permanent Residency to have another child before it is too late for me." She and her husband run a worldwide chain of franchised restaurants. She accepted a Gospel of John and a Chinese tract, and replied, "I'm Buddhist. Buddhism and Christianity are the same."

I replied to her, "Read these booklets. They outline major differences between the two faiths."

To a friendly Tibetan Buddhist refugee on the bus, I enquired, "How many lives have you had?"

She replied, "Don't know."

I said, "What level of life will you have after you die?"

She declared, "Don't know."

Following further conversations I said, "I am a Christian. All people will die. All will be raised. All will be judged. Jesus will be that judge. He will divide all people into two groups, the positive and the negative. What you do with Jesus in this life determines what He does with you in the next." She accepted a Gospel of John.

At the Box Hill transit station, an Asian youth in shorts and 'T' shirt, one freezing cold winters day said, "I am a Thai National kick boxing champion."

I asked him, "Do you have problems keeping Buddha's Five Commands?"

"I don't get angry," he replied.

I said, "Christ helps me keep the Ten Commandments." He accepted a Gospel of John with emphasis on John 8:12 and the word 'follow'.

An Asian Buddhist, on holidays from Hong Kong, listened to my testimony and accepted a Gospel of John in the Box Hill Centro. He said, "That is fascinating!" Seeing Chinese literature peeping out of my breast pocket he said, 'Can I have those too? My wife is a Christian, but we argue about it." We discussed how to become a Christian. He promised to commit to Christ in faith with his wife when he got home. I counselled him to speak to a Pastor, attend a Bible study and not go back on his promises. He declared, "I will! I will!" What a beautiful providence: a Buddhist lecturer of Information Technology, in a Thai university, together with his Asian wife on holidays in Melbourne, accepted my story and a Gospel.

A student listened to my testimony and said, "I am Buddhist. We have the same things in our religion."

I replied, "A Thai National Christian recently commented, 'Suppose you are adrift in a small boat on a stormy ocean. Buddha will send you instructions on how to swim. Jesus Christ will put you on solid ground'."

Heat and thirst made a thick shake at McDonalds irresistible. A Chinese lady from Penang invited me to sit at the only available seat with her. This petite, uninhibited little Buddhist jokingly said, "Maybe it's your grey hair."

I asked, "How many incarnations will get you to Nirvana?"

She replied, "About eight."

I said, "How long does it take?"

"No one knows," She replied,

I asked her, "What do you reincarnate as?"

She replied, "A bird maybe."

I suggested, "There is no end to karma. It follows you forever!" I quoted John 14:6*, which clearly contradicted reincarnation.

She readily accepted Chinese literature and surprisingly said, "My son wants to go to church. Do you know a church we could attend?"

I gave her a Chinese Pastor's business card and suggested, "Do please call him. He'll help you find a good church."

On the Box Hill railway platform, an Asian male Buddhist accepted my testimony and literature. Later that week I met him again on the platform. He waved the booklet at me with excitement saying, "I was looking for you yesterday. I am reading your literature. My wife and twelve-year old son are also interested. Where is your church?" They attended NewHope next Sunday and were referred to our Chinese fellowship.

A Sri Lankan born nominal Buddhist, delivering fliers for a local estate agent in East Ringwood, walked by saying, "I believe in all religions."

I said to him, "A belief system is only as valid as the object of its belief." He accepted a Gospel and read aloud John chapter 8:12. I drew attention to the word 'follow' and asked, "What do you think?"

He exclaimed, "Profound!"

On the train, Jan and I discussed culture with a friendly Asian Buddhist lady. When we mentioned we had visited her home city in China she readily accepted Chinese Christian literature.

On the bus, I entered into conversation with Kim, a South Korean Buddhist lass sitting across the aisle from me. I enquired, "Do you have trouble keeping the five commands of Buddha?"

She replied, "I can't remember what they are." and accepted a Gospel with reference to 8:12 'follow'.

Huge pennants fluttering above the Melbourne Town Hall advertised Buddha's Day, an event to be held in FS on May 19-20. Our Chinese Buddhist Lord Mayor probably played a part in organising this event.

An Aussie male on the train, said, "I was brought up a Catholic but not anymore. Twenty years ago, I became a Buddhist".

I said to him, "How do you go keeping the five commands of Buddha?"

He sidestepped the question saying, "I'm on my way to a Buddhist leadership conference. What do you think about the identity of the Holy Spirit?" He was introducing a diversion designed to confuse the issue.

I replied, "I will be attending the Franklin Graham Crusade in Melbourne this Saturday; would you like to attend with me?" On reflection, a better reply might have been, "I know nothing among you save Jesus Christ and Him crucified (1 Corinthians 2:2). If you want to see true love, look at the Crucifixion of Jesus on the Cross. If you want to see real power, look at the Resurrection of Jesus from the dead. The Holy Spirit holds love and power in balance in accordance with Scriptural principles," and then leave him to it.

A Cambodian student at the Mitcham railway station said, "I am Buddhist".

I said, "A Buddhist girl who converted to Christianity recently said, 'Buddha will send you written instructions on how to swim if you are sinking in a stormy sea. Jesus Christ will pick you up and take you safely to shore'." She accepted a Gospel and listened to the story of Jesus walking on the stormy sea: -

> "But the boat was now in the middle of the sea, tossed
> by the waves, for the wind was contrary.
> Now in the fourth watch of the night Jesus
> went to them, walking on the sea.
> And when the disciples saw Him walking on the sea,
> they were troubled, saying, "It is a ghost!"
> And they cried out for fear. But immediately Jesus spoke to them, saying,
> "Be of good cheer! It is I; do not be afraid."
> And Peter answered Him and said, "Lord, if it is You,
> command me to come to you on the water."

> So, He said, "Come."
> And when Peter had come down out of the boat,
> he walked on the water to go to Jesus.
> But when he saw the wind was boisterous, he was afraid;
> and beginning to sink he cried out, saying,
> "Lord, save me!" And immediately Jesus stretched
> lout His hand and caught him."
> (Matthew 14:24-31)

Some time ago I financially supported a young evangelist in the Buddhist kingdom of Bhutan in the Himalayas. In a letter he said among other things, "In recent months, I distributed a good number of Gospel literature pieces and New Testaments. Through my ministry, many people came to a saving knowledge of Jesus Christ. At present fifty people regularly attend our worship services." It was a privilege indeed to play a small part in contributing to the Lord's work in this way.

A Brief Understanding of Karma

Similarities and contrasts between the five laws of Buddhism and Ten Commandments may lead to your Buddhist friend to consider the utter futility of the karmic reincarnation system and launch into a journey of discovery regarding the Biblical teaching of Ephesians 2:8-9:

> "It is by grace you have been saved through
> faith, and that not of yourselves;
> it is the gift of God, not of works lest you should boast."

This strategy opened the door to conversations, testimonies, Gospel messages and gifts of literature with Buddhists. Slowly my understanding of Buddhism is increasing but in reality, I have only scratched the surface.

A book entitled: 'From Buddha to Jesus' by Steve Cioccolanti, contains a wealth of helpful information in sharing with Buddhists. Some teachings from his book are reflected throughout these pages.

Karma is a continuing cycle of cause and effect. A person's thoughts, words or actions will affect him/her for good or bad at some future time. A good deed leads to future benefits while bad deeds lead to harmful effects. Wrapped up with karma is reincarnation - being reborn in a new human body or a non-human body according to actions performed in a past life. Buddhists believe all their sins must be paid for and it's not enough to suffer in one lifetime, however, the Bible teaches that sins can never be erased by good deeds. Jesus is the only person who can break the cycle of suffering. The Bible plainly says, "It is appointed unto men once to die and after that the judgement (Hebrews 9:27)." Paul has good news for the Buddhist:

"Therefore, if anyone is in Christ, he is a new creature,
Old things have passed away; behold all things have become new."
(2 Corinthians 5:17)

Taking it to heart:

1. Share ways of building up your knowledge of Buddhism.
2. How might you respond when your contact says, 'I am Buddhist.'
3. Think of ways to introduce your testimony.

References:

John 3:16 – For God so loved the world that He gave His only begotten Son, that whoever believes in Him should not perish but have everlasting life.

A Significant Contact with a Retired Burmese University Lecturer

This retired university lecturer (then in his 70's), had travelled to Melbourne to visit his daughter in Box Hill North. Upon arrival, he was seized by a strong desire for Bible study to enable him to encourage the Chin Burmese Baptist denomination through a special project he had in mind. It was a privilege to supply him with an English Bible and some documented accounts of early Christian outreach in Burma donated from the library of a retired Baptist minister.

The Burmese retiree with good English, with a request for help to study the Bible, was assigned to me. We completed several studies on the call of Abraham (Genesis 12:1-2*) in his daughter's home and also at the NewHope Baptist Church. He deeply desired to extend his new-found knowledge to Pastors in Burma where Christians are reverting to Buddhism through lack of teaching. We discussed the implications of faith and good works from Genesis, Romans, Galatians, and Hebrews. He said, "Very important! I get it now. It is by faith not works that we come to God." He lamented never having studied the Bible.

I told him, "God will restore to you the years the locust has eaten" (Joel 2:25). "He will complete that which is begun in you on the day of Jesus Christ" (Philippians 1:6).

He was conflicted by the apparent contradiction as he saw it between the 'everlasting' Old Testament (OT) covenant of circumcision in Genesis 17:10* and Paul's supposed cancellation thereof in the New Testament (NT). I said, "The Old Testament reference to circumcision of the flesh points forward to the New Testament circumcision made without hands:

> "In Him you were also circumcised with the
> circumcision made without hands,

> by putting off the body of the sins of the flesh,
> by the circumcision of Christ,
> buried with Him in baptism, in which you also were raised with Him
> through faith in the working of God, who raised Him from the dead.
> And you, being dead in your trespasses and
> the uncircumcision of your flesh,
> He has made alive together with Him, having forgiven you all trespasses,
> and the uncircumcision of your flesh, He has
> made alive together with Him,
> having forgiven you all trespasses."
> (Colossians 2:11-13)

When he returned from guest lecturing and research at the Australian National University in Canberra he said, "If you are a butcher, everyone regards you as a butcher. If you are a baker everyone looks on you as a baker. As a lecturer in Burma, I was given menial duties and resigned in frustration after twenty years. Frequent statements including: 'Owing it to his godly mother' etc, made me wonder if he still thought good works and karma were pre-requisite for salvation. He attended 'Dinner Tonight', our church outreach to the disadvantaged, with his granddaughter. While granddaughter and my wife attended Chapel, grandfather and I spent more time in Bible study.

He became troubled by Genesis 6:5-6*, wondering if he would be judged for backsliding, but verse 8 explains that God's grace to Noah through the provision of the Ark foreshadowed the NT message of the Cross. The professor responded, "Ahh! A very important verse." He may have understood then what it meant to become beneficiary through faith, not works, to the righteousness and peace which kissed each other at the Cross (Psalm 85:10*).

But this is not all! It was discovered that his granddaughter had been mentored for three years in the local school mentorship program by a member from our church. The following week, pupil and mentor were happily reunited, which resulted in his granddaughter attending Kid's Church.

Why did this retired professional gentleman arrive here in such a timely way? (Aspects of his journey are not disclosed by request). Could it be that God wanted our church involved in supporting his proposed ministry to the struggling Chin Burmese Churches begun by Judson so long ago?

On the morning of his return to Burma he invited several of his contacts to the church cafe for a farewell coffee. Soon after an email received from Rangoon, Burma, included the following comments: "I was relieved to learn that you are now free from the exhausting work (referring to our babysitting duties in Brisbane last month) and back in Melbourne enjoying coffee at NewHope Church. Your email message reminds me that I am not lost but remembered by good friends of NewHope. It is indeed delightful and encouraging news for me. Allow me to convey my heartfelt thanks to you, Mr. Trevor (Farmilo), Dr. Phillip (Lind), Rev Chris (Pittendrigh). Please convey my special regards also to Rev. Dr. Allan (Demond). I missed the peaceful days under the shelter of NewHope Baptist Church in Box Hill. I wish I could spend the final days of my life under such shelter of peace, love, and benevolence."

On the train, Pone, a diminutive Buddhist Burmese student, was intrigued by the story of the retired Burmese professor. I asked her the BQ*. She was at a loss to answer. I said, "Let me tell you the answer." She listened to a Gospel presentation and accepted a TPTL NT*. She continued reading the New Testament as Jan and I disembarked at Box Hill.

East Ringwood Encounters

Most of the following contacts occurred on the East Ringwood railway station platform (ERRP).

Bik, a Burmese refugee student, listened to my testimony, accepted English literature, with reference to John 8:12* 'Follow' and said, "We have a Burmese bible at home."

Van, another Burmese in answer to the BQ* said, "What will happen to me when I die?" He answered his own question. "Jesus will take me to be with Him!" This Christian musician in his church band, was one of a few I've encountered to answer the BQ* this way.

A Christian Burmese Chin speaking refugee with limited English, arrived in Australia recently. He happily accepted English literature. To a physically limited Asian male I said, "Let me pray for you. 'Father, give this man a new birth in Christ. Fill him with your Holy Spirit and grant him victory in life'."

On the ERRP a Burmese male with a heavy smell of alcohol on his breath and a loud slurred voice slept under trees in a local park and was moved on by Police. His Bible knowledge was surprisingly good. I prayed with him as the train arrived.

John, a Burmese 'Zomi' speaker, who I had previously met, said, "I've read your booklet (Gospel of John). I am Roman Catholic and believe what it says, Jesus saves me. I have no vision in one eye and weakening vision in the other."

I replied, "Would you like me to pray for you?"

He answered, "Yes!" and accepted more literature.

To a friendly trainee nurse with Burmese heritage walking by, I asked, "Can I offer you some reading material?" She accepted church literature and a Gospel of John and read aloud John chapter 8:12*.

She asked, "Are you a Pastor? Do you pray? I had an accident with my car and didn't know what to do. Could I ring if I need prayer?" She was encouraged to call but never did.

A female Burmese Christian secondary student became a Christian while reading her Bible under the guidance of parents in her homeland. She attends church on Friday and Sunday evenings in Mooroolbark and accepted a Gospel of John with reference to 'follow' in John 8:12. When asked if she would like prayer, she said, "Yes please."

An impressive Christian Hakha Chin speaking family arrived as refugees two months previously and attends the Burmese fellowship in Croydon. They caught a train for their first shopping excursion to Box Hill and invited me to sit with them on the way. Problems with their invalid ticket with Railway Inspectors at Box Hill were awaiting them. I suspected these problems arose from their innocent failure to tap on (electronic ticketing wizardry, so called) at East Ringwood. The inspectors were tolerant. All is well that ends well.

Bourke Mall, Melbourne CBD

An adult Burmese male sat brooding and alone. Will I intrude on his privacy? Being spoken to by a total stranger may be the last thing he wants. But looking beyond his posture to his real needs motivated me to cross the street. He responded warmly. He and his family recently arrived in Australia. He was searching unsuccessfully for employment. He walked with me to the railway station chatting along the way and subsequently dined with us at home. He enrolled his child in our church preschool. His wife attended our 9am service. Evangelism is one of the simplest gifts. Many fears in sharing the Gospel never eventuate. Why does evangelism present such mountainous problems to so many Christians? Try it. Just walk across the road. The rewards may surprise you.

In conclusion I acknowledge with gratitude my association with and encouragement from several young Burmese Christians in our church. They are excellent citizens in our local community, and personal friends.

Taking it to Heart:

1. In what ways will you discern God's plan for your life?
2. How might God's plans and purposes for your life pan out specifically?
3. In what ways will you rely on God's provision for ministry?
4. How will you present these thoughts to others?

References:

Genesis 6:5 – Then the Lord saw that the wickedness of man was great in the earth, and that every intent of the thoughts of his heart was only evil continually. And the Lord was sorry that He had made man on the earth, and He was grieved in His heart.

Genesis 12:1-2 – Now the Lord had said to Abram (Abraham): 'Get out of your country, from your family, and from your father's house, to a land that I will show you. I will make you a great nation; I will bless you and make your name great; and you shall be a blessing.'

Genesis 17:10 – This is My covenant which you shall keep, between Me and you and your descendants after you: Every male child among you shall be circumcised.

Psalm 85:10 – Mercy and truth have met together; righteousness and peace have kissed.

BQ – Big Question – What is the most important question in all the world for you?

TPTL NT - The Pocket Testament League New Testament

Chapter 9

Dutch Backpackers and Tourists

This chapter relates solely to Dutch backpackers and tourists.

In reply to my testimony, a young tourist in Federation Square (FS) said, "You need to know that I do not believe in the existence of God and will probably die that way."

I answered, "I respect your right not to believe and would even defend it."

He stated, "I believe in evolution."

I said, "Neither the existence of God nor evolution can be proved scientifically. You and I come to our respective belief position by faith." He accepted a booklet entitled 'Is there really a God?'

To a forty-two-year-old Dutch Policeman who once lived four years on an Israeli Kibbutz searching for answers to life, I asked, "Did you find them?"

He said, "No!"

I asked the Big Question (BQ*), "What is the greatest question in all the world for you?"

He replied, "Being surrounded by family and friends who are healthy. I recently lost some close friends through cancer. It shook me up."

I explained, "The most important question in all of life for me is what happens to me when I die?" He listened to my testimony and received a Gospel of John.

A tourist stated, "I don't believe in God or churches. They are full of hypocrites." He allowed me to share my story but said, "I don't believe in what you said, but I like the way you said it. If you want to believe that stuff, it's OK by me."

I said to him, "God bless."

He replied, "Good luck."

A Dutchman and his Kiwi girlfriend listened to my story. He told me, "I still believe, but you'll never get me inside a church. I spent the first twenty-five-years of my life there, but it is full of hypocrites. I even learned the catechism when I was young, but I do like your low-key approach."

She said, "What a wonderful story. Thank you." I offered them a Gospel of John and wrote John 3:16 on the flyleaf.

He exclaimed, "That must be the most quoted verse in the bible."

I said to him, "Quote it." He did.

I asked a backpacker the BQ*. She replied, "How to find happiness and care for my friends." She listened to my testimony, accepted a Gospel message, and a TPTL NT* and said, "You've really given me something to think about."

I asked another backpacker the BQ*. He replied, "When I was young, I destroyed my faith. How to find happiness I suppose." He accepted Dutch literature and a Christmas booklet.

A backpacker on his way to work at a cattle station (ranch) near Broken Hill NSW, answered the BQ* saying, "To find my purpose in life." He listened to my testimony and accepted a Gospel of John with reference to John 8:12*. A tourist smiled with surprise as she accepted Dutch literature.

A blonde blue-eyed young lady who said, "That's a hard question" listened to my testimony with misty eyes.

Turning Points for Dutch Backpackers

A backpacker intently listened to my testimony and accepted a tract. He smiled and said, "I am a Christian. I can see where you are heading" and excused himself. His three Dutch fellow travellers appeared. I repeated my testimony and gave them Gospels of John. Tessa said, "Excuse me. I need the toilet." She did not return.

Gustavo, a short, nuggety boxer and long-distance runner with olive complexion had migrated to Holland with his Brazilian parents as an infant. He said, regarding my story, "That touches questions I've had all my life." His mate, Toine, tall, slim, blond, and blue-eyed had university degrees in chemistry. It is hard to imagine two more unlikely travelling companions. I took them through the plan of salvation. Toine said, "We had better change our plans. We will see you tomorrow." No thought was given to **my** plans for tomorrow!

A man sitting quietly within ear shot said, "Inspirational!"

Next day it was raining in Federation Square. The two backpackers and I therefore rendezvoused upstairs in McDonalds. I have rarely (if ever) met two young men so driven to settle their eternal destiny. A Bible lay opened on our table. A Gospel message is interwoven through a study based on Genesis 1, 2 and 3. The passion, intensity and volume of our voices increased. Nearby patrons looked curiously in our direction. Sometime, during the course of our discussions, these two young men slipped into the Kingdom. Somehow, they were transformed into eager young Christians excited for their future. It was a miracle of God's grace. Each said, "Everything has fallen into place. We will follow Jesus." Their smiles said it all. They still carried grave clothes, but God will complete that which He began in their lives. That afternoon, they began a journey to inland Australia. Ours was an emotion charged farewell.

Later, in a panic-stricken phone call from a holiday park in the remote outback town of Jerilderie NSW, Gustavo said, "My caravan is rocking up and down. There is no wind. The door is banging open and shut. There is a terrible smell." It had the hallmarks of a satanic attack. I suggested Bible verses, prayed with him over the phone and assured him that intercessors in Melbourne were praying and that he should try to locate a local church and speak to the Pastor. He was currently casually employed in a local vineyard where temperatures reached 40 degrees.

Later, again Gustavo called saying, "I've been in contact with Toine. It worked out good. We took your advice and we're getting stronger. We worked out a prayer and wrote it down. We prayed that prayer several times. The evil spirit came back last night but did not have the strength to break through."

I asked, "Tell me how you prayed?" What followed is repeated as accurately as I can recall from his quotation over the phone.

He said, "Dear God, thanks for the message we needed. The way and the word was very clear. We confess we have sinned. We truly say we are sorry. We are on our way. We'll follow and not fear. Please give us the protection we need. Amen."

I said, "Where did you get that prayer?"

He answered, "It just came to me." I gave him more scriptures and encouraged him.

Toine, who was pruning grape vines elsewhere in remote NSW, also called and exclaimed, "It all came clear to me when we spoke with you in

Melbourne. I was alone working in the vineyard yesterday. I was so happy; I was almost crying. I am now on the good way. It is beautiful."

I said, "You and Gustavo are brothers in Christ. Take care of each other."

In a later related phone call, Emily uttered, "You don't know me, but I was at a church service in the York Peninsula, South Australia. Gustavo gave his testimony and through that testimony I became a Christian. He asked me to tell you." It seemed Gustavo's faith was strengthening. He is reading his Bible and other Christian books voraciously. He is sharing his testimony (she called it preaching) with all and sundry. He is currently unemployed in Alice Springs, Northern Territory and living in a Salvation Army hostel. The next day he was required to vacate and unless he found alternative accommodation, he would sleep on the street. He was going through hard times but said, "The Lord is testing me." Emily made it very clear that Gustavo was trusting the Lord and not asking for money. Presumably Toine and Gustavo have returned to Holland.

Taking it to Heart:

1. What steps have you taken to prepare your testimony?
2. Think of methods/ways/styles that may support your testimony in the street?
3. How will you gain the ear of a potential contact for the Gospel?

References:

John 8:12 – I am the light of the world. He who follows me shall not walk in darkness but have the light of life.

BQ – What is the most important question in all the world for you?

TPTL NT – The Pocket Testament League New Testament.

Chapter 10

Egyptian Encounters

On a bus tour of Egypt under the auspices of MECO our Egyptian hostess said, "A long time ago Egypt was a Christian country. There's a lot of Muslims around now who would not like to hear me say that." At the conclusion of our tour, she graciously accepted a Bible from our tour leader.

In October 2010, my wife and I visited the famous 'Cave Church' located in the Mokattam Mountains in South Cairo, Egypt. Removal of materials for construction of the historic Egyptian pyramids eons ago created space for this vast cathedral like auditorium currently seating some 20,000 worshippers at weekly services. This largest Christian Church in the Middle East is centered in a local population of about 30,000 'Rag Pickers' mostly Coptic Christians. Thousands leave early in the morning with horse or donkey drawn carts and return in the afternoon with loads of trash produced by Cairo's millions. The waste is processed and sold for profit.

Back in Melbourne, a derelict Egyptian said, "Your original inhabitants are not Aboriginal. They are Egyptian and Colombian. In fact, there goes a member of the Colombian royal family now (indicating a person of Aboriginal appearance riding his bicycle)." He accepted literature.

On a local bus, a burdened Egyptian Christian lady, who I had previously met, discussed raising teenage sons in the non-Christian climate of same sex marriage, gender identity and living together before marriage etc. She inferred these are worse dangers than living in war torn Middle East.

In Hungry Jacks an Egyptian youth said, "What do you do?"

I said, "I am a retired Police Officer."

He replied, "I hate coppers. They harass me. They are never there for me. They are always against me. If they get into trouble, I laugh at them. Once a cop always a cop." But he stuck out his hand saying, "You are the first copper I've ever shaken hands with. I hope you won't report me," and ducked quickly out the door.

Muhammad was raised in Cairo in a family with a heavy emphasis on Islam - a good solid Muslim boy who knew the Quran by heart. But during years of travel, he became disillusioned with the faith of his fathers, made a cleancut conversion to Christ and was baptised. His family planned his murder. He fled and now attends a church in Melbourne.

A nineteen-year-old Egyptian student journalist and I enjoyed a stimulating and challenging discussion on Islamic and Christian culture. He asked, "Would you mind sharing your experience of how you came to God?" He attended my testimony with moistened eyes.

I said, "What would you say to an offer of an Arabic Injil?"

He said to me, "If it is written in Arabic, the door is wide open." He accepted his Arabic Injil and said, "I feel bad about receiving something and having nothing to give in return."

I answered, "You have given me half an hour of your time. That is the most precious gift any one can give another."

I asked an Egyptian to explain the difference between Christianity and Islam. He claimed, "Christian scriptures are superseded by Muhammad. The Old Testament prophets all point to Muhammad. God did not have sex with Mary as Christians believe. The Bible is polluted. We do not need priests like Christians." He listened to my testimony and accepted a Gospel of John.

He took umbrage when I added, "Salvation is found in no other name than Jesus."

An ex-tour guide, who had conducted groups through the ancient temple city of Luxor, Egypt and I discussed places Jan and I had visited. I said, "I am so glad my eternal destiny is not dependent on law keeping but, on the grace, and mercy of God through faith in the crucified and resurrected living Saviour who loves me." 1 Peter 3:18 says it all:

> "For Christ also suffered once for sins,
> the just for the unjust,
> that He might bring us to God,
> being put to death in the flesh but made alive by the Spirit."

I received the following text message from Michael, a Coptic Christian Egyptian, who I met previously in the Bourke Mall. "Hi, Mr Bruce. This is Michael J. I just wanna know you're alright? Also, I wanna tell you that I've been practising my faith in the last four months and I succeed to bring some people to Christianity. I hope to hear from you soon."

An Egyptian cyclist in the Melbourne CBD said to me, "The hate and anger of Islam disturbed me deeply. I found no answers in the Koran. That started me on a journey to convert to Christianity in the Coptic Church (he didn't say which Coptic Church). My family threatened to kill me. The church in the Middle East is growing rapidly."

I personally returned from Egypt with greater sensitivity, compassion and understanding for my Egyptian contacts in Melbourne.

Taking it to Heart:

1. Why is it necessary to develop understanding and compassion to Islamic culture and religion in evangelism?
2. Why should we evangelise Muslims?
3. How would you approach your Middle-Eastern Muslim contact with the Gospel?

Chapter 11

French Backpackers and Tourists

Somehow, a French backpacker located our church website and as a result, attended our free Sunday morning English as a second language classes (ESL). From there someone invited him to 'Dinner Tonight' at NewHope Baptist Church where he enjoyed a good meal, listened to the testimony of an Iranian Christian, asked questions about the Christian faith, and accepted testimony and a TPTL NT*. He believed religion was like God on a mountain top and the pathway up is through anyone of multitudes of religions. The Frenchman attended the Persian New Year celebrations enjoyed by some 250 mainly Iranians, both from our church and visitors. He was impressed by the life and activities in our church.

In Hungry Jacks, a friendly French tourist seemed unaffected by recent terrorist activities in his homeland. This agricultural scientist from Normandy happily accepted French literature and spiritual counsel based on Genesis 2:15: "Then the LORD God took the man and put him in the Garden of Eden to dress, till and keep it."

A French lass, handing out brochures in Swanston Street, was searching for a pot of gold at the end of her rainbow. She said, "I was in a bad accident and nearly died, but some church people prayed for me, and I'm still here. There's someone up there, but why does God allow suffering?" She accepted the answer in a Gospel presentation based on Genesis 1-3 and a gift of French literature.

In Federation Square (FS) a French touring couple attended a Catholic Church in France. In response to the Big Question (BQ*) he said, "How to be happy."

She said, "What will the world be like in ten years?"

I explained, "Jesus is the answer to your biggest questions." They politely listened to my testimony and accepted French literature.

Ronny, from France, was in Melbourne to improve his English. He listened to my testimony and accepted the 'Silent Night' booklet asking, "Is this about WW1?"

I said, "Yes!"

He replied, "I'm interested in WW1 history."

A younger French woman with flawless English said, "Hello! I'm with the ABC (Radio Australia), I'm doing a training video. Would you assist?" Her video included an interview during which she asked, among other things, "How long have you been married?" When I told her she commented with surprise, "What kept you together so long?" An open doorway for a testimony! My case of literature was open to view. Readily accepting French literature, she asked, "Why all those languages? Can I retake you with St Paul's in the background and your range of literature open?" She seemed genuinely surprised and promised to send me a copy of her video clip. Trusting she was genuine, I pursued this opportunity with intensity, believing God for a Kingdom victory in due course, but the promised clip never arrived.

A French-Canadian tourist In Hungry Jacks provided an opportunity for the BQ*. He craftily responded, "What about you?"

I said to him, "The most important question for me is what happens when I die?"

He listened carefully to my testimony and said, "I don't have a story like that."

I stated, "If you died tonight and God said, 'Why should I let you into my Kingdom?' What would you say?"

He replied, "That confirms to me that I am not a Christian." He quickly departed. A young French speaking New Caledonian couple with broken English, accepted a tract and an invitation to visit our church.

A French tourist in FS was catching the plane for France that night. I said, "My first twenty-five years was on a farm looking after sheep. My second twenty-five years was in the Police department looking after two-legged sheep. My third fifteen years was in church looking after two-legged sheep. I am a shepherd, but I am not THE Shepherd. The Lord is my Shepherd."

He said to me, "My father is a farmer. There are no churches in France now, but I believe God." He accepted a Gospel of John. We discussed the difference between religion and relationships. He undertook to find a Bible believing church in France.

In Federation Square a French tourist said, "I have not found my pot of gold yet." He broke into my testimony saying, "I have been to churches. People ask me to give my life to God, but I prefer to worship God, whoever He is in nature, without religious ritualism and tradition."

I explained, "Religion is not my point. I am discussing a personal relationship with the Creator. There is a general revelation of God in nature, but the specific revelation of God is found in the Bible. Without that specific revelation your general revelation could easily take you down the wrong road." He read with me from John 1:1-5*. I declared, "The Bible contains everything you need to know about Jesus." The tourist accepted the booklet but was distracted by an approaching vision of loveliness in a tight fitting bright red dress. They embraced, kissed, looked tenderly into each other's eyes and suddenly I was out of the picture!

Pierre, a tourist, had arrived from France three days ago. With the aid of a large map, he plied me with questions about his proposed Australian adventure. He said, "I might find a wife."

I said to him, "Be careful of girls and crocodiles!"

He asked, "Why?"

I declared, "They both bite." He laughed and accepted French literature and TPTL NT*.

French flags were flown at half-mast in Federation Square in honour of victims of the deadly terrorist attack in Paris. Two more prayer team members joined us for devotions and coffee. Through devotions, Jan said to the French waiter, who also served us last month, "Do your flags bring you comfort?"

He replied, "Yes. Very much!" The Parisienne carnage, including murder by gunfire of his close friend, deeply impacted him. He was also moved by many public expressions of support. Providentially, Jan had found a platform for evangelism. The Holy Spirit orchestrated devotions and evangelism to occur simultaneously in Federation Square. By God's grace we brightened the waiter's day with a glimpse of someone far above the circumstances of our world.

Conclusion

Focusing on Apostolic Doctrines is essential in Gospel sharing. Novelties, opinions, and controversies are a waste of time. A famous old church father of long ago bluntly said, "Essentials are common and obvious. It is the superfluities over which we waste time."

Augustine, another church father, said, "I would rather have speeches that are true than those which contain nice distinctives. Just as I would rather have my friends who are wise than merely those who are handsome." Avoid non-essentials or novel ideas. Stick to the essential truths balanced with gentleness, according to the context of the character of each person and situation we encounter. Learning how comes with experience.

References:

John 1:1-5 – In the beginning was the Word, and the Word was with God, and the Word was God. He was in the beginning with God. All things were made through Him, and without Him nothing was made that was made. In Him was life and the life was the light of men. And the light shines in the darkness, and the darkness did not comprehend it.

TPTL NT – The Pocket Testament League New Testament

BQ – Big Question – What is the most important question in all the world for you?

Chapter 12

German Responses

A story I recently read tells of a young man who was ashamed of his Dad, who had such old-fashioned ideas. Dad was a real square. The son never saw him for two years. When the lad finally caught up with Dad, he was absolutely amazed to see how much Dad had learned in that two-year interval. A lot of young people find out after they themselves have been out in the school of hard knocks a while, that their Dads have learned a great deal. (1 Peter 5:5*).

Reflection on two separate encounters in Federation Square (FS) with German Pastors reminded me of the Lutheran influence still alive in some evangelical churches. The story of Luther, famous German church reformer, born November 10, 1483, in Saxony, then part of East Germany, was relevant. He studied law, became a monk, was ordained as a priest, and in the course of time was appointed a professor in a theological college. After years of fruitless wrestling to attain righteousness by works, he came across Romans 1:17: "The Just shall live by faith." Through reading this verse Luther suddenly understood that the righteousness of Christ is a gift and that faith in Christ alone justifies.

Becoming concerned about excesses of the Catholic Church, Luther registered his protest by posting his famous ninety-five theses on the church door in Wittenberg. This event triggered the stiff resistance he encountered in his lifelong ministry of reform. His verse also underpinned my sharing with German tourists.

German Tourists Contacted in Melbourne CBD

A pleasantly sociable German patriarch and his tourist family sat beside me in Federation Square (CBD). His English was good. His uncle was an evangelical Pastor in East Germany prior to the infamous Berlin wall crashing down. He accepted German literature with interest.

Most of the following German tourist contacts accepted the BQ*, testimony, a Gospel challenge, German literature and TPTL NT*.

- Nicolas, a young man asked, "Why are we here?"
- Lars, from Kassel, had arrived twenty-four hours ago, and presented me with a small fossil stone collected by his grandfather years ago from the island of Hiddensee in the Northern Sea.
- Two German tourists had just returned from tomato picking in Toolamba (Vic). The cheque from their Turkish employer bounced. The logistics of recovering this money would be difficult and costly. Departing soon for Germany, they might have to put their loss down to experience! She said, "Thanks for an interesting story."
- Timor believed in all gods. "Do enough good and you will be OK." He kept his gift of German literature with his passport, girlfriend's photo, and tobacco, all the 'important things'.

- Fabian once lived two doors from the then current Pope. "But," he lamented, "He is a hardliner. I prefer the Protestant position."
- Twenty-four-year-old Christophe, with an evangelical background, clearly betrayed his evolutionary bias, but admitted "You have covered all the points. I don't want your literature, but your presentation was professional."
- Nadine's questions included: "If God is a God of love why does he allow suffering?" She was teetering on the brink of a decision but was preoccupied by her forthcoming working holiday interstate.
- A German tourist left his farm labouring job in Germany, his family and girlfriend to find meaning for life." I said, "Do you consider yourself a good man?" When walked through the Ten Commandments. He exclaimed, "I know I do wrong and will never get to Heaven." I replied, "Would you consider inviting Christ into your life now?" He said, "I don't know what to do, but I don't want follow up."
- A pleasant tourist from Stuttgart, puzzling over his itinerary said, "If I get into trouble, I dig myself out. I don't think Christians should try to convert atheists like me." I replied, "I cannot convert you. Your only hope is for the Holy Spirit to bring you under heavy conviction of sin. Then you will ask God's forgiveness. I pray God will do that for you. When the Holy Spirit brings you to Christ, telephone me." He smiled and replied, "I will."
- Comparison of cultures led to a discussion on religions. The backpacker disclosed, "I tried eastern meditation in Asia. I got sick and felt life was terribly empty." After hearing my testimony, he said, "That happened twice to me, but each time I ran away." I answered, "Don't run. Trust is a gift from God. Accept it!"

- An elderly tourist was a Lutheran Pastor in Germany. He and his wife saw me bird watching. He smiled, "I am a bird watcher too." He was reading his Bible. He said, "My favourite verse is 1 Peter 5:5*."
- Jenny (a German) doesn't know here to find peace in the world. Andreas, her ex-Polish boyfriend from Dortmund, complained, "The world is full of problems." I said, "Are you a Christian?" He stated, "I was christened as a child." This receptive, delightful couple departed for Germany the following day.

In a Cowra holiday caravan park (NSW) three German tourists – Robin, Tim and Jacob, accepted testimony and literature. Their English was good. They showed utmost respect. Jan and I were impressed.

Andre was a good conversationalist and excellent listener. He headed for Mildura that evening to work in the vineyards for three months. If he fulfilled his obligations to the Immigration Department, they would allow him to stay in Australia for twelve months.

After listening to my testimony, a tourist said, "This is a bit overwhelming. You've only been here seven minutes and told me your life story."

I replied, "I am giving you something to think about. No one can make you a Christian, but I hope my comments will be a link in a chain of events which might result in you deciding to become a Christian in due course."

A waitress accepted German literature with surprise, saying with an impish smile, "Quick, let me hide it." Slipping it into her apron pocket. She explained, "I am promoting McDonalds. We are not allowed to accept religious literature."

A German female asked, "Which platform do I use for Flinders Street?"

I replied, "Follow me." We sat with a female Asian student in the carriage. The German and the Asian accepted literature in their respective languages.

The Asian said, "You gave me one of these, last time. Don't you remember? I felt much better when I read it." She accepted a different tract. Her brief testimony surprised the German who took greater interest.

The German said, "Which church do you attend?"

I replied, "Baptist. Have you heard of them?"

She answered, "Yes, but they are not common in my country." The girls walked along the Flinders Street platform amiably chatting.

A traveller with his head on his backpack, was relaxed along a parapet like a sleepy lizard on a post top in warm sunshine. Will I wake him or leave him? I gave him a try. He sat bolt upright and seemed glad to talk. He had arrived in Australia three days previously and was looking for work. As he listened to my testimony, he punched the air with enthusiasm. I took him through the plan of salvation. He accepted a Gospel of John and said, "My parents took me to church, taught me how to become a Christian and I read my Bible."

A sports scientist recently split with his partner of eight years. Loneliness was real for him. He said, "I am a Christian. My parents attend church in Germany."

I explained, "If you died tonight, why should God let you into His Kingdom?" After moments of deep thought, he replied, "That's a hard question." Then with triumphant smile he elaborated, "I have done many good things. Excuse me I have to meet my friend."

A German born Australian noticed me reading a book. She said, "I read 1000's of books. What are you reading?"

I replied, "It's a Christian book."

She immediately dogmatically asserted, "If God is a God of love, why does he allow suffering? I gave away church years ago. I'll never talk religion again."

I said to her, "That sounds like a declaration of war." Taken aback, she smiled and was drip-fed with my testimony for the duration of our train journey home. We parted good friends.

A German lass collecting donations for Care Australia, listened to my testimony. She replied, "I followed the drug trail across India, and had a near fatal car accident. I should have died. Jesus took away my drug dependency and healed my injuries. I am now looking for a church." Her's was a wonderful testimony! Over coffee I supplied a list of churches and explained the importance of fellowship. She asked, "But how do I work in the church?"

I replied, "You have an amazing story. Share it. That's a good start."

She said, "I have a boyfriend."

I asked, "Is he Christian?"

She replied, "I think so."

I said, "Make sure! Marriage with an unbeliever will draw you away from God."

A Catholic Indian lady from the city of Sundern, Germany, was born and raised in India and married a German. She said with perfect English, "There's no joy in the mass. It's too impersonal. In Melbourne I attended many churches to make up the deficiency. I wanted to serve God but didn't know how. I know of no-good churches in Sundern."

I said to her, "Take one tiny facet of the Great Commission and pursue it with relentless intensity and God will lead you on. You could make an excellent personal worker." She was returning to Germany shortly.

A German Backpacker Accepts Christ

A German backpacker commented, "You are not head-hunting, are you?"

I replied, "I cannot make anybody a Christian, but I do have a story." I shared with him over coffee.

He smiled, "I have just graduated with a medical degree. I thought I had my future all mapped out, but now I am confused. I started reading the Bible at Genesis but found it hard to understand."

I asked him, "Would you like to be a Christian?"

He replied, "Yes!" and prayed the sinner's prayer. He was counselled to seek fellowship in a Bible believing church upon his soon coming return to Germany, to read his Bible and pray daily. He said, "You have been a big help." His decision seemed real.

'Here I stand. I can do no other.'

On TV I watched an episode of Roadside Breath Testing (RBT). I am prone to watching police shows – it's called nostalgia. One intercepted driver said, "Basically I'm not a bad bloke. If you do enough good, it'll come back to you. It's called karma." This contagious philosophy underpins the logic of a hugely significant proportion of our local and visiting population. It is therefore essential to promote the Good News accurately.

Martin Luther (1483 – 1546) whose conversion through reading Romans 1:17 (*'The just shall live by faith'*) sparked the 'Reformation', initiating the rise of the evangelical church. You could say that Luther is our exemplar, defender of the faith and a spiritual father. When challenged by the legalistic authoritarian church establishment of his day, he defended - "Here I stand. I can do no other." The essence of Luther's teaching is a timely reminder that faith in the promises of Christ alone justifies. Only faith in the crucified, resurrected Christ who removes our sin and imputes His righteousness saves us. 'Here I stand. I can do no other'.

References:

1 Peter 5:5 – Likewise you younger people, submit yourselves to your elders. Yes, all of you be submissive to one another, and be clothed with humility, for God resists the proud, but gives grace to the humble.

TPTL NT – The Pocket Testament League New Testament.

BQ – Big Question – What is the most important question in all the world for you?

Chapter 13

Garrulous Greeks

I sometimes reflect on my frequent encounters with an ancient Greek in Hungry Jacks in Swanston Street, Melbourne CBD. His argumentative, but cunningly devious philosophies made him a standout. Though difficult, I came to understand that interactions with him and others like him are beneficial. He forced me to examine more closely some of our treasured Biblical doctrines and taught me heaps about patience and persistence in dealing with difficult contacts. We eventually became friendly in a funny sort of way. I occasionally catch myself wondering what happened to my garrulous friend. Abbreviated comments arising from some of our numerous discussions are included in this chapter. But firstly, let me introduce you to some other Greeks I met along the way. Then we'll return to my ancient garrulous Greek friend.

A Greek tourist said, "I'm lost. I have many temptations." We discussed Creation and the Fall.

A male sitting beside us said, "I'm interested in your conversation. Do you mind if I join you?"

I said, "It depends on your angle."

He moved in anyway and stated, "You cannot differentiate between science and faith. They are the same." But this guy was a troublemaker. The Greek quickly declined literature and just as quickly departed.

I said to the intruder, "I refuse to discuss this!" and moved off. The interloper caught up with my Greek contact and engaged him in an animated discussion as they walked down Swanston Street.

An Orthodox Greek studied theology in Greece for four years. He believed only the Orthodox Church was true, that "Protestant churches are of Satan, but some Protestants may get to Heaven."

I asked, "What impact does your faith have on your life?"

He exclaimed, "It guides my behaviour. I might get to Heaven."

I said, "I'll be waiting for you."

An unknown female, walking along our street, crossed over to talk with me. She had Greek/Persian background, spoke both languages and was Orthodox by belief. Her husband and family were in New Zealand. She was here caring for her daughter with heart problems and an eight-year-old grandchild. She was shedding tears. I read to her from 2 Corinthians 12:9 in my Gideon's New Testament: "My grace is sufficient for you. For my strength is made perfect in weakness." She accepted the NT, (she had a Greek Bible), my name, and phone number and departed with a smile.

In McDonalds, a retired Greek tourist, with poor English stated, "I am Orthodox, but all religions lead to the same place."

I said, "Why does God say, "You shall have no other gods but me?"

He replied, "I read my Bible every night but it's OK to tell white lies. I get angry. Everyone does. If I am away from home for a long time, I play up, but for one month each year I attend a monastery in Greece. It feels like being in heaven. I'll send you some photos. You must come to the monastery." He later forwarded in the mail an expensive photographic inventory of Greek monasteries.

In Federation Square, George, a friendly Orthodox Greek national on holidays said, "We love to sit and philosophise." After some discussion I read to him from Acts 17:22-34 with emphasis on v23: "As I passed by, and beheld your devotions, I found an altar with this inscription, To the unknown God whom you worship ignorantly, Him I declare to you." Then I referred him to v32 and said, "You either mock the Lord, put Him on the back shelf or follow Him. Which is it?" He accepted literature.

My Garrulous Greek Friend

During my Melbourne ministry I had continuing dialogue with a weirdly notable ancient Greek for about four years. Mostly, these conversations occurred in Hungry Jacks in Swanston Street. I eventually enjoyed our verbal jousts. Some of his many responses over about four years are touched upon herewith:

He said, "I have read the Bible. It is a fairy tale. When you die you fade into nothingness."

I said, "Explain the Crucifixion."

He answered, "Don't worry about that. All you do is out-weigh bad with good."

I declared, "You have completely misunderstood the Bible. Your views are discouraging. You have no hope, but if you must criticise the Bible get your facts right."

He caught me trying to elude him in Hungry Jacks and triumphantly slapped Von Daniken's book 'Refuting Scriptures' on the table in front of me. "What do you think of that?" he crowed.

I answered, "Thousands of books have been written by ratbags like him. Why read that rubbish? Trust the Bible."

He said, "I believe the Bible, and quoted Ezekiel from Daniken's book and added, "That's from the Bible."

I said to him, "That's Daniken's commentary on the Bible. Throw it out."

He asked, "What does the Bible say?"

I explained to him, "All men will die. All will be raised. All will be judged. Jesus will be the judge. He will divide all people into two groups, the positive and the negative. That division will be permanent. What you do with Jesus in this life determines what He does with you in the next. Say no to him now and your future is bleak indeed."

His elderly Greek friend nodded sagely saying, "Come back again."

The ancient Greek fired the opening message saying, "You're always talking about Genesis. I've got books which explain all that. Explain the apple. I can buy them in computer shops." His ancient mate was on my side.

I said, "Don't talk to me about books, read your Bible." Our good-natured discussion was interrupted by an excited teenage lass from our church who said, "I've just bought a man some drinks and a hamburger."

The old Greek said in surprise, "Does she go to your church?"

In between the same old arguments, he said, "When I was five my mother attended church twice each day in Italy. In the morning it was a 5am service. The stress of her church involvement killed her."

I replied, "We've been through all that many times but let me read from 1 Corinthians 15:1-8." To my amazement he actually listened. I continued, "Blow the dust off your Bible. Read the verses and we'll discuss them next week."

He smiled wryly saying, "I look forward to the lesson."

Later, he raised another 'pet' subject, namely animal cruelty. I replied, "I don't keep pets."

He said, "Anybody who has no pets has something wrong with him. If God is so good, why does he allow animals to suffer?"

I replied, "We've been through all that too. We could sit here all day going round in circles. I don't intend to do that. Go home, like I said, blow the dust of your Bible and read Genesis 3."

He said, "I must ask you to stop that. It's too upsetting."

Again, he said, "According to the Mayan calendar May 2012 would be the end." I quote Galatians 2:20*. He said, "I am searching for truth."

I replied, "You are looking in the wrong places."

He stated, "I believe in nothing, but I believe in everything. Truth is even found in lies."

He was recently hospitalised due to a heart attack. I said, "You should give your heart to Jesus as soon as possible."

He said, "It's all words." Strangely and unexpectedly he tearfully continued saying, "My parents entered into an arranged marriage. My fifty-five-year-old father died four months after I was born. My twenty-two-year-old mother was committed to an institution for the insane. I was brutally treated in an orphanage and suffered years of psychiatric treatment (including shock treatment). I am alone in this world." He accepted literature. Knowing a little of his dysfunctional family background enabled me to respond to his weird philosophies with more sympathy and understanding.

Among other things I said, "Your mind is full of confusing philosophies. It is difficult for you to believe in the crucified resurrected Christ."

He wistfully said, "I wish I could believe."

I quoted my testimony. He replied with quotes from his horoscope. I said, "Read your Bible. Back up your statements with references."

He answered, "The Bible is baloney. Ezekiel even talked about helicopters."

I said, "Give me a reference and I'll chase it up."

He proclaimed again, "The Bible is a fairy tale. What about the five million children who die each year of starvation?"

I asked him, "What have you done to help just one of those kids?" He went through his usual routine. I said, "How many times do I have to tell you. The answer is in Genesis."

He said, "The world is not working. If I had my say, I'd never have been born."

His ancient mate said, "He is so sad. Make him glad."

The old Greek continued, "Earth is hell!"

I said, "There are three locations, Heaven, Earth and Hell."

He responded scornfully, "What has earth to do with Heaven and Hell?"

I said, "Earth is where we finalise our eternal destiny. Depending on what we do with Christ here determines whether we finish up in Heaven or Hell for eternity. Every person is a sinner and has fallen short of God's glory. Forget your philosophies. Your only hope is Jesus." He produced a book containing what he claimed approximates to Bible quotes but quickly lapsed into philosophical speculations.

He carried the remnants of his once powerful physique with limping difficulty. As far as I know, he is unmarried but often reflected unabashedly on his sexual exploits in times past. He was blissfully unaware of my nasal discomfort arising from odour emanating from incontinence, due to removal of his cancerous prostate. He said, "We live in a good country. Why do people get sick? I know," he continued in good humoured but mocking fashion, "the answer is in Genesis 3."

I mentioned my 4pm appointment with my urologist. The old Greek and his two henchmen responded with ribald suggestions, and an invitation to attend their reunion and a free senior's train trip to Shepparton Vic. That they moderated their language in Jan's presence, was appreciated. The ancient Greek was reminded, as always, that he must make peace with his Creator before he leaves this earth.

The old Greek and his two mates argued that the Bible cannot be proved scientifically and proposed alternative philosophical theories. They said, "The historicity of Jesus is questionable. Everyone is biased somehow. You are biased. One philosophy is as good as another." I read aloud Colossians 1:12-14*and repeated 1 Corinthians 15:5-8* listing over five hundred witnesses who saw Jesus alive post Crucifixion.

One Greek said, "Come back next Thursday."

My ancient friend listened to a reading from 1 Corinthians 1:24* regarding Christ, the power and wisdom of God. I said, "There's no point in going round in philosophical circles. This is where I stand. I rest my case." He seemed content to leave it at that. He and his two mates always seemed glad to see me.

The old Greek solemnly proclaimed in reference to the recent American floods, "The world is fighting back." His (and his cronies) frequent modus operandi was to greet me as a long-lost friend, soften me up with ribald comments, followed with philosophical statements, which contradicted the Bible, then sit back with a crafty glint in their eyes and listen to my response.

I said, "Butting your head against brick walls only gives you headaches. Give your life to Christ. What you do with Jesus in this life determines what He'll do with you in the next."

The old Greek asked, "Where will you spend Christmas?"

I said, "With family. Where will you spend it?"

He said, "Here in Hungry Jacks. We have nowhere else. How can I escape my terrible past?" He read yet another philosophical extract. His equally ancient friend fell asleep during his monologue.

I said, "It's rubbish! Read the Bible." He listened for the twenty-fifth (approx.) time to a Gospel presentation, but why did I bother?

Later in Hungry Jacks, he loudly stated, for the benefit of many patrons, "Here comes the messiah. What will he teach us today?"

I said, "All men are sinners and fall short of God's glory." He trotted out his usual philosophical rubbish. I declared, "I've heard all this a thousand times. I keep telling you the answer is in the first three chapters of Genesis."

He exclaimed, "I believe there is something out there, but I don't know what." That's a good step. I was glad, by the grace of God that we could speak with candour on such widely divergent views and remain friends.

He squared up like an aged bare-knuckle pugilist in a fight to the end. The wheelchair evangelist next to me counter-punched beautifully. Thank God for genuine competent defenders of the Christian faith. I said, "Your philosophy gets you nowhere."

He broke in sarcastically saying, "Yes, I know, believe the first three chapters of Genesis."

I wondered why my friendly old foe was absent for some weeks. I knew he did not enjoy good health. It transpired he was hospitalised following surgery, but suddenly he was there, blaming God as usual for cruelty and suffering. As always, I responded with the Gospel. He said, "I get more value from Pinocchio than the Bible." His equally ageing but slightly more sympathetic orthodox friend had noticeably deteriorated physically in recent weeks.

The old Greek adopted a fierce scowl and with a deep throaty voice bated me with his argumentative views. Such are the vicissitudes of life for an evangelist. However, both the old Greek and his ageing and an even frailer Greek friend, seemed glad to see me. The old Greeks orthodox mate sighed, "Another argument?" But I think he's on my side. Another atheistic book critical of the Christian faith was offered.

I repeated, "There are 100's of books like that. Throw it in the rubbish. Read the Bible." We parted good friends.

The ever-stirring ancient Greek asked, "Still clawing more into paradise? Do they get an ice cream when they arrive? How's heaven today? When's Armageddon?"

I said, "You are more interested in your next hamburger."

His ancient friend said, "You are a man of the cloth, buy that cold and hungry girl (referring to a sleeping female under dirty blankets on the footpath) a hamburger."

I said to him, "You say, you are a Christian, why not practise what you preach?"

The old Greek's long standing, fruitless search for meaning to life in the world of philosophy and weird speculations regarding life's dilemmas, was, by his own confession, a road to nowhere. I could only continue to invite him to embrace the Lord Jesus who carried our griefs and sorrows to the Cross; and assure him that Christ accepts full responsibility for his personality, characteristics, weaknesses, sins, burdens, bruises, and circumstances. Another 'religious' friend, so called, was pushing weird and wonderful 'Christian' teachings down the old man's throat. As far as I know I'll never see my antagonistic old friend again. I released him into the mercy and judgement of the righteous Saviour. In conclusion I cheerfully mention two elderly Greek evangelists -

Two Elderly Greek Evangelists

At our local shopping centre, a man was offering brochures to pedestrians. His compelling riveting gaze grabbed my attention. I asked, "What are you handing out?" Wordlessly, he offered a brochure entitled 'The Good News April 2007'. I said, "Which church do you attend?" He indicated the website address on his brochure of the Greek Free Church, 161 Peel St, North

Melbourne. I doubt he spoke English. Further along, his compatriot also offered literature. His English was marginal.

These clean but poorly dressed elderly men reminded me of photos I had seen somewhere of illiterate peasant farmers in remote mountainside villages of Northern Greece handing out Christian literature in bygone times.

Somewhere along their journey of life, these two evangelists had been captured by the Lord Jesus. They bravely crossed, what for them, must have been formidable cultural barriers with the Gospel. Much of the Gospel had probably marched across centuries and continents in the shoes of such humble unlearned simple Christians. My encouragement resulted in joyful gap-toothed smiles, a loving arm around my shoulders and loud heavily accented, "Praise the Lord!"

Taking it to heart:

1. Have you ever been confronted with stringent criticism of the Christian faith?
2. How might you prepare yourself for such criticism?
3. What action might you undertake in this regard?

References:

Galatians 2:20 – I have been crucified with Christ; it is no longer I who live, but Christ lives in me; and the life which I now live in the flesh I live by faith in the Son of God, who loved me and gave Himself for me.

Colossians 1:12-14 – Giving thanks to the Father who has qualified us to be partakers of the inheritance of the saints in the light. He has delivered us from the power of darkness and conveyed us into the kingdom of the

Son of His love, in whom we have redemption through His blood, the forgiveness of sins.

1 Corinthians 15:5-8 – That he appeared to Cephas, and then to the Twelve. After that, he appeared to more than five hundred of the brothers and sisters at the same time, most of whom are still living, though some have fallen asleep. Then he appeared to James, then to all the apostles, and last of all he appeared to me also, as to one abnormally born.

1 Corinthians 1:24 – Christ the power of God and the wisdom of God.

Chapter 14

Numerous Indian Contacts

In 1987 my daughter and I travelled to India for four weeks with a New Zealand One Mission Society (OMS) team under the leadership of Evan Carr from New Zealand. During this journey I began to understand India as a smorgasbord of language, culture, food, socio-economic diversity, and rich cultural heritage.

I had cut my evangelistic eye teeth on evangelising in the western Christian belief world view. More recently, my focus expanded bit by bit to include a deeper understanding of how to approach those with different faiths and world view backgrounds, including those who drifted back and forth along the continuum between belief in the Biblical Christian God and other forms of philosophy. My Indian contacts taught me much in this regard.

I never cease to be amazed by those of different faiths who claim Christian doctrine, including Crucifixion and Resurrection, has no conflict with their religious or philosophical beliefs. I was frequently told, "We all worship the same God, there is simply nothing to argue about." I do not hold that opinion.

One Sunday evening I watched an illuminating TV documentary highlighting the difficulties Indians entrenched in life-long Hinduism, could experience should they attempt to convert to Christianity. The documentary claimed that the Hindu god is monotheistic, that healing miracles occur within Hinduism, that Hindus are free to choose which manifestation suits their personality and the Bible unfairly states that all are sinners in danger of judgement if they do not convert to Christianity. However, the love and power of the Gospel, kept in balance by The Holy Spirit in accordance with scriptural principles, answers this confusion. Paul, in grappling with these issues said:

> "Woe is me if I do not preach the Gospel." (1 Corinthians 9:16b)
> "A great and effective door has opened to me,
> but there are many adversaries." (1 Corinthians 16:9)

The Australian Diamond Company (ADC) in the Bourke Street Mall, Melbourne, hired Indian students to hand out promotional fliers to passing pedestrians. These students, Hindus and Muslims, were a guaranteed audience. They were paid to stand there. Sharing the Gospel through storytelling, and literature distribution to such a 'captive' audience offered ongoing opportunities for Christian outreach. The field was 'white unto harvest'. Some became Christians. Many remained good friends. A small selection of their stories is listed herewith.

Samuel*

Samuel, a part time employee of the ADC, was miraculously converted, and subsequently began attending church. His Christian friends unwrapped years of spiritual bandages of misunderstanding that blinded him to the Gospel truth. But it was Jesus, and only Jesus, who raised him into newness of life.

He became a key figure in my Indian student outreach. My basic discipling method included face-to-face discussion, literature distribution in different languages, and electronic texting. The first three chapters of Genesis were always good conversation starters. From there we explored the relationship between Old and New Testaments. Samuel was intrigued by related passages in John, Romans, and Corinthians etc. He later said, "I have read all of Genesis. When I get time, I'll study the other references." He followed through on his promise while juggling college assignments and part time employment priorities,

Samuel understood the need to unwrap his religious bandages. He told me, "I was born a Hindu, but since I left home I have seen the way Christians live. I am more open now. I understand the missing part is Jesus." He learned first-hand the truth of Ecclesiastes: "Though one may be over-powered by another two can withstand him and a threefold cord is not quickly broken." His relationship with God deepened as we prayed together about problems that surfaced in his life. He wanted to travel to India but was not sure he could re-enter Australia due to an ongoing health issue.

I stated, "Acknowledge the Lord in all your ways and He shall direct your paths" and suggested he read Proverbs 2-3. Samuel recorded every verse I gave him on his device. He was happy for his Christian 'brothers and sisters' to join him in his prayer requests.

Samuel said, "The Beatitudes are very good, but how do I live up to them?"

I answered, "Do not be unequally yoked together with unbelievers. For what fellowship has righteousness with lawlessness? And what communion has light with darkness" (2 Corinthians 6:14*). Carefully consider who your marriage partner will be. Marriage to an unbeliever, may draw you away from the truth."

He responded, "This will not be easy. In my culture parents choose the bride, and she won't be Christian."

Another twenty-four-year-old Indian recently returned from Mumbai where his family had arranged for him to meet five young ladies from which to choose a bride. In a state of total confusion and anxiety, he chose the first cab on the rank, packed his bags, and fled to Melbourne!

Samuel asked, "Can I be a Christian without baptism?"

I replied, "What do you mean by Christian?"

He said, "I believe Christ died for me and rose the third day to give me victory over death."

I explained, "Baptism doesn't make a person a Christian. It's what Christians do. Baptism is an outward sign of an inward work of God's grace."

He thought through the implications and replied, "If I were to be baptised my decision would be difficult for my Hindu family in India."

I too weighed my words, "If you are serious about following Christ you should get baptised." Christian Indian friends, Sujin and Vishnu (both referred to below) and an Indian Pastor, visited Samuel and prayed with him.

Samuel excitedly informed me one day, "My mother has given me the all clear to attend church. Our problem is that she believes in Jesus Christ as well as all gods, but Christianity believes only in one God." He asked my opinion on which church he should attend while in Melbourne. I suggested he try Sujin's and Vishnu's churches, or our church, and attend where he felt most comfortable. Samuel said, "How shall I respond when my family want me to go with them to the Temple?"

I said, "Go with them. Do not pray to their gods, but demonstrate the fruit of the Spirit - love, joy and peace" (Galatians 5:22).

Samuel was now mentoring a new believer, Suren. Sujin, a Christian, greeted me with his usual cheerful grin, saying, "Samuel is really coming on with his Bible Study and his understanding of Christianity. Thanks for all your help. You really encourage us."

Samuel had just returned from a trip to Inia. He mentioned, "I read my Bible and prayed all the time I was away. I told my family and friends that I'm now a born-again Christian. I told them I would go to the Temple with them, but I will never pray to their gods. I prayed they would accept my belief. Can you believe it? They want to become Christians too!" He was so grateful to God for answering his prayers and had no problems with the Immigration Department getting back into Australia. He greeted me on one occasion with the words, "I want to get baptised." Great news! Samuel and I had worked together in Bourke Street Mall for over three years. God is good!

Throughout my contacts with Samuel, I watched him transition with more than his fair share of trials and doubts from devout Hinduism to born-again Christianity. On Sunday November 10, 2010, at the NewHope Church evening service, Samuel was baptised upon confession of his faith and at his request by immersion. His strong testimony delivered at his baptism closely matched his life.

Samuel's Testimony

"I was brought up with strict Hinduism customs and values, often visiting Temples and offering prayers. I came to Australia in 2006 to pursue a post graduate degree. Fortunately, I met Mr. Bruce in Bourke Street Mall. He is the one who introduced me to Jesus Christ and the Bible.

He gave me Bible verses to read whenever I met him. I listened only because I was taught to respect my elders. I began reading the scriptures and found no difficulty in accepting 'Jesus Christ' as one of the gods. But Mr. Bruce insisted 'Jesus Christ' is the *only* God and we are all sinners, and our salvation is only through Christ. Sometimes I was offended because I couldn't accept myself as a sinner. Whatever he said went into the deaf ears.

"After graduating from university in 2008, I started searching the Bible for answers. I was encouraged by Mr. Bruce, my housemate, and my colleague. Two verses (Isaiah 49:15* and Jeremiah 1:5*) stirred me deeply and in May 2009, I decided to give my life to Christ. I repented of my sins and prayed to Jesus Christ, to come into my life, transform and free me. Amazingly my family accepted my decision to believe in Jesus Christ and to be baptised!"

While still in India, Samuel had emailed me a video of his sister's elaborate betrothal ceremony. This marriage had been organised by a marriage broker. Neither parties, nor their families had previously met. The broker assured the families that it would be a good marriage. that the horoscopes and astrology charts matched. Another Indian student laughed when he recounted to me that his friend had fallen in love with a girl who worked in the family business. Their elopement and marriage in a registry office caused huge family ructions. He wondered with a smile, "What would happen if I married an Australian girl in a registry office without telling her parents?"

I responded, "Don't even think about it."

Watching the proceedings of Samuel's sister's ceremony, so different from western weddings, helped me understand his heroic step of faith. He was stepping away from his closely knit, extended Hindu family belief system, so ingrained in cultural tradition, and stepping into monotheistic Christianity.

Upon returning from his extended holiday, Samuel shared with me some observations of his home country. "I noticed a big change in India. Billboards advertising Bible texts had sprung up everywhere." He shared many stories regarding his Hindu family's attitude to his newly acquired Christian faith. We concluded our time of sharing and Bible study with prayer. He was learning how to pray about everything, including employment and permanent residency. He brought presents for my wife, Jan – some delicious Indian sweets - and for me, Indian language Christian literature to help with evangelising Indian Hindus.

Samuel said, "I am reading the book of Acts. If I read daily for the next thirty days, then I will increase my chances that Bible reading will become an ingrained habit. I don't want to avoid struggling with the hard questions in the Bible. I want to stick with it because then the truths will be imbedded deep into my heart. If I have questions, I know I can always email you."

When he finished reading Acts, I encouraged him by saying, "You realise Acts is an unfinished book. Your name is in the chapter now being written."

Samuel returned to India to be married to an arranged bride. She is almost certainly Hindu. I last heard he was living in Singapore with his wife and family. I suspect he may be struggling with complex spiritual and cultural priorities.

Felix

Felix, a devout Catholic, had difficulty finding employment in Melbourne in his chosen field, post-graduation. So, he found temporary employment interstate. Moving on to Perth, he worked night shift at bakeries and all-night cafes. He eventually completed further studies and found suitable employment in Perth. His company transferred him back to their Melbourne HQ where he installs and maintains electrical wiring in cherry pickers.

Felix's marriage was also arranged in India through a broker. One Sunday afternoon Felix and his new wife invited us to dine in their rented unit. Their tablecloth consisted of newspaper pages spread across their dining room floor. I suspected they couldn't afford furniture. Time moved on. His intelligent, lovely young Indian wife and he are now in their own home and are proud parents of a beautiful curly-headed, brown-eyed, happy kid. They followed a daily Bible reading plan without fail. She sings in her local church choir. That night I led Felix, his wife and Manny, another Indian from ADC in a devotion based on Isaiah 40:29*. I have occasional continuing contact with them.

Manny

Manny, an Indian of Catholic by heritage, asked, "If you have an event at your church I'd like to come." He accepted an Alpha invitation. Nearly 100 attended an Alpha introduction at NewHope Baptist Church. He thoroughly enjoyed the evening and signed up for the course. His Christian grandmother in India prayed for him daily but the pull of the world was strong. A serious setback re Manny's application for Permanent Residency (PR) cost him dearly to finance his appeal. The ensuing uncertainty was painful for him and his family overseas. I mailed him a booklet entitled: 'How to Face a Crisis' written by Rev. Francis Dixon, a prominent

British Baptist Pastor, who preached many years ago at Belgrave Heights Convention. Later, Manny won on appeal a lengthy, difficult, frustrating PR application. We celebrated with friends his much prayed for new Aussie status over dinner in our home. He volunteered as a helper at the next Alpha Course. He is intelligent and articulate and could contribute well to our society and should make a good Aussie citizen.

Vishnu

One of the many notable young Indians I met was Vishnu, who became like a son to me. This good-looking young athlete of above average cricketing ability made centuries for his club in Melbourne. He was a delight to interact with. Vishnu, who had survived some fairly intense spiritual struggles of his own, said, "The cleaner where I work has breast cancer and wants to know about Christ." He gave her a John's Gospel and a Gideon New Testament.

Vishnu said, "I now pray."

I said, "If you are simply adopting a certain aspect of Christian culture forget it. You must totally commit yourself to Jesus. What would your family in India say if you became a Christian?"

He said, "They'd be upset." Notwithstanding, he is returning to India for holidays soon. Before departure he said, "I need a Tamil Bible for my mother, one for my friend, Surenda, and three English New Testaments."

Unable to find suitable employment upon return to Australia, Vishnu returned to his homeland where he struggled with two significant established religious systems within his close family circle. Sometime after his departure from Australian shores Vishnu married and when last heard of was living in Denmark with his wife and two infant kids. I sent him a biography on C.T. Stud, a famous English test cricketer turned missionary statesman in Africa, along with a supply of Christian literature. His emails reproduced below unfold something of the story of his journeys.

"Dear Bruce, how are you doing? Hope you are excellent. I'm now with my parents in Bangalore. My prayer life is good and missing you so much. Hope you and your family are doing well. My prayers are always there for you and Jane. Wish you a merry Christmas! I'm still looking for a job and learning many things about Christ's love for us through many disappointments and failures. Pray for me and my family that JESUS needs to guide us according to HIS plans. With lots of luv, Vishnuvardhan.R."

In another email he included the following encouraging news: "How are you? I got a job in Chennai as a System Integration Engineer. All glory to GOD, He was with me all the time."

And again: "Hello Bruce, it has been long time since I email you. How are you doing? How is life? Hope your health is good now. My life is good, and job is interesting too. Once I was without a job and now am enjoying it. I'm going to church on Sundays, but not frequently. I am still lacking that consistency. Hope I will catch up the lessons in the Bible and use them in my life. I miss you sometimes and your preaching, which I enjoyed. I would like to see you again in my life. You are a good man! Hope Jane and your family are doing good. Awaiting your reply :) :) With loads of love, Vishnuvardhan.R."

In another text he said: "Am very happy to see your message after a long time. Am blessed to have you in my life as well. Happy birthday to you & hope Jane is doing great as well. Please send my warm wishes to her. I always miss talking to you about the Word of God. I am doing great by the grace of God. I am happy growing in the knowledge and understanding of Christ. Am married and I have a two-year-old daughter, her name is Vidha and my wife's name is Danu. Living in Europe Denmark, Aarhus, for the past three years and God has been good with me all the time for the sake of his love in all my ups and down. My wife also got baptised few months ago. I always thank God for you in my prayers and have told many people about our conversation in Bourke Street Mall. Now I am having the same conversation with my wife about the Word of God during our family prayer time. It is too good to share the Gospel to anyone around you. I hope I will again see you one day soon :)"

"Hi Bruce, how are you doing? I miss you a lot whenever I think about you! How is Jane doing. Convey my regards to Jane!!! How is Australia? I always keep you in my prayers!! My life is well in the LORD. I would like you to write few lines about how you met me and how did I respond to you? So that I can share it in my blog. Keep in touch always! Let the risen LORD be glorified." It was a pleasure to comply with his request.

Sujai

Sujai reckoned, "I must be getting old. My parents want me to marry soon. I wrote an essay about you for my exams last week. You are like a father to us." It was heart-warming to see Sujai, Samuel, Suren, and Vishnu supporting each other and discussing Romans 13:13-14*.

Siva

An email received from Siva on holidays in India: "Dear Bruce, how are you. I am fine here. My family members are good here. How about your family members? Are you getting ready for the Christmas? What is special up there? I am reading the Bible whenever I am getting time."

Samson

The following text message said, "Hi Bruce, I am Samson. Hope you are doing good. We first met in 2012 outside the ADC where I gave out fliers.

I now live in Tasmania. I will surely catch up once the borders open!" (COVID lockdowns). I enjoyed many interesting chats with Samson, a devout Christian, during my city ministry. He regularly sends me high quality Christian music recorded in his homeland via What's App.

Suren

Suren invited me to lunch at a nearby Indian restaurant. I first met him at a Christmas dinner in Hawthorn with other Indian students last year. Suren accepted a Bible from Vishnu at this function. He said, "I believed in no gods. But something is changing in me." We continued our discussion over coffee. He asked, "How would my conversion impact my Hindu family in India? Why are there so many different churches? How many good works must I do to be a Christian? Why am I so unhappy? Why do I do silly things?" He listened to a Gospel presentation based on Genesis 1, 2 and 3, and said, "This conversation has helped me. I would like to become a Christian now." We prayed through a prayer of commitment. He suddenly looked different and accepted a study booklet on Genesis.

In a subsequent meeting, Suren said, "Vishnu took me to church on Sunday."

I said, "What did you learn?"

He replied, "God gave me mercy. I must give mercy to others." But concern at the effect his baptism might have on his family in India weighed heavily. Samuel, who had also struggled with the same issue, tried to encourage Suren.

Suren said, "Before I left India, I believed in no gods, but in Melbourne I lost my self-assurance. You and Samuel kept talking about Christianity. Now I worship one God and attend church regularly. I'm lucky to have you and Vishnu to support me. Samuel is my mentor." He accepted Tamil literature. He later left his job with ADC for a more secure job in aged care.

Aneesh

A new brand of fruit juice was being promoted in the Bourke Street Mall. Sample bottles were collected for Aneesh, Sujai, George, and the Indian nut seller nearby. Aneesh, a devout Catholic with high intellect with English - better than mine, asked, "I have free time. Can I sit with you while you have lunch?" Aneesh and I found a shady seat in Swanston Street. He said, "Last week I read Psalm 23 and found it helpful. I'm reading from Acts 17 about idols and the unknown god. I don't often open up to people, but I trust you. Would you help me write an order of service for my church youth group meeting? I'd like to use some of your illustrations."

He also accepted literature. I said, "God saves us, but expects us to form habits and character by adding to our faith virtue, to virtue knowledge, to knowledge, self-control, to self-control, perseverance, to perseverance Godliness, and to Godliness brotherly kindness and to brotherly kindness, love" (2 Peter 1:5-7*). Your obedience to this verse will attract all the omnipotent power and superb grace of the Godhead through the atonement. This being the case, you should never be unfruitful or barren in the knowledge of Jesus Christ."

Aneesh later moved to Alice Springs (Northern Territory) and was employed by a government social service agency among local Aboriginal communities. I took him to lunch in Degraves Street as a farewell gesture. He said, "Have you anything to say for me?"

I said, "Genesis 1, 2, and 3 is the foundation for biblical knowledge and Christian living. Chapter 1 tells of God's creation, Chapter 2 reveals God's plans for mankind. Chapter 3 tells us what went wrong. The remainder of the Bible tells how God is restoring our lost destiny." Aneesh carefully inserted my drawings into his wallet. I said, "My prayer for you is from Philippians 1:9-10: "And this I pray, that your love may abound, still more and more, in knowledge and all discernment, that you may approve the things that are excellent, that you may be sincere and without offence, till the day of Christ."

Who knows when we will meet again? This hour passed too quickly. Years later a cheery, "Hello Bruce!" surprised me on the East Ringwood railway station platform ramp. Aneesh is now employed with a local government agency in Melbourne assisting among others, the needy son of a church attender. It was good to catch up with him briefly after all these years.

Sujin

Sujin and I were talking in Bourke Street Mall. Venomous glittering dark brown eyes glared at me. To my astonishment from the midst of the crowd, an Aboriginal yelled, "F... idiot!" He further shouted, "You are a f ... idiot" and spat on me. Sujin wiped the saliva off my shirt front with tender care and deep concern. Ibrahim the Muslim was angry.

My initial thoughts were, "I'm glad he spat on me and not Sujin" and "This bloke can sure spit straight." I have never seen this guy previously. He could not know about my ministry. Sujin later commented regarding the spitting incident. I responded, "It's a badge of honour to be spat upon for Jesus." Sujin was leaving soon for holidays in India. I asked, "What can I give you to remember me by in India?"

He said, "A good Scripture." I suggested Psalm 23. He rattled off the Psalm by memory in Tamil.

Three of my Indian contacts, including Sujin, read 2 Peter 1:5-7* from my Gideon NT and listened to a short presentation on character and habits based on these verses. Sujin said, "This morning I am empty. Now I am full." He recently accepted the role of worship leader in his church.

Along with representatives from Matt Adam's group, Jan and I were invited to Sahni's restaurant in Hawthorn by our Indian Bourke Street Mall contacts for a Christmas get together. They were excellent hosts and organised a delicious menu (not too spicy).

Two courteous Hindu students invited us to another Indian restaurant to attend a farewell dinner in Sydney Road, Coburg. We enjoyed eating Indian cuisine without cutlery. Washing hands between courses in a foot operated hand basin in the corner of the restaurant is a new cultural experience. Each was presented with a gift-wrapped Tamil Bible.

Conversational Snippets from Other Indian Contacts in or near the Bourke Street Mall

- "What do you think of the house fire in which three Indians recently lost their lives?" I said, "Those who died could easily be you, or me. What you do with Jesus in this life determines what he does with you in the next. If these three guys had believed in Christ they'd be in Paradise."
- Churning over his failed permanent PR application an Indian student sadly said, "This door is closed." He accepted a John's Gospel.
- Sanjeed, a mature aged Indian, in answer to the Big Question (BQ*) said, "I measure the success of my family and work performance against my conscience." He accepted testimony and a TPTL NT*.
- To an Indian, who said, "My family is fine, but I am having a hard time." I replied, "An oak tree was blown about by storms, gnarled, and twisted, but its roots were deep, and it never fell. You may be going through rough times but if you believe in God, you will never die but have eternal life. Be an oak tree for Jesus. Find strength by sending your roots deep into God's Word."
- A smiling Indian Christian said, "My Pastor preached on the raising of Lazarus on Sunday. You told me to put Christ first in everything.

I've done that with my studies. I have been blessed since. Thank you."
- A student said, "I have been studying late and I'm tired." I replied, "You've been watching too many Bollywood movies." He replied, "Yeah that's what mother in India tells me."
- An Indian friend returned for holidays, and I warned him, "Watch out, your family might send you back to Australia with a wife. Ever thought about finding your own wife?" He said, "If I did that mother would suicide. It's emotional blackmail."
- An Indian complained, "The world is hard, dangerous, cruel and unforgiving." After discussions, he understood his core values were little more than survival techniques. I said, "Love God with all your heart and soul and mind and your neighbour as yourself." He accepted literature.
- An angry Hindu student blurted "I will not stay in Australia one day longer than I have to." I asked, "Why?" He replied, "Australians are not to be trusted." I stated, "What about Indians?" He said, "They are liars." I answered, "Can you trust yourself?" He said, "What do you mean?" I asked,, "Have you ever told a lie?" He replied, "Sometimes, but only if it is justified." I mentioned, "It only takes one little lie to make you a liar." He accepted literature. I said, "My God came to earth in human flesh and died a terrible death on a cross to forgive your sin, and rose the third day to give eternal life is Jesus Christ. This is why I am a Christian."
- A nineteen-year-old Hindu Pakistani student had a parting of the ways with his Muslim girlfriend. He said, "I can't stop thinking about her. My studies are affected. I've thought of suicide." He accepted literature.

- A Punjabi student couple decried loose morals in our city streets. I said, "In the jungle, lions eat zebras, leopards eat gazelles, and eagles eat rabbits. It is a natural law. Something must die that something will live. This principle extends to our daily walk with God. In the jungles of our heart our worldly deeds must die that Christ will live in us" (Romans 8:13*). He accepted Punjabi literature.

The Kumbla Mela Festival

The Kumbla Mela Festival at a major River site near Hyderabad in India, is held regularly at auspicious times. It is reputedly the world's largest religious festival. One mythical Hinduism I heard of relates to two gods fighting over a container of holy nectar in heaven. In the ensuing struggle four drops of this nectar fell to earth. Where they fell rivers formed. One such river is the Ganges. Bathing in this river is said to wash away sins. One sip of its water leads to eternal bliss.

I spoke to Praveen, an Indian student, "Have you bathed in the Ganges?"
Praveen said "Yes."
I asked, "Are you without sin?"
He replied, "No one knows." His attention was drawn to John 4:14:

"Whosoever drinks of the water that I shall give him will never thirst. But the water that I shall give him will become in him a fountain of water, Springing up into everlasting life."

Watching the 'Rising Sun' Whilst Floating Down the Ganges

The following comments are typical of responses offered by Indian students to the 'Rising Sun' analogy over the years. To a student I said, "I am a

Christian. I floated down the Ganges in a boat with a man who worshipped the rising sun. Why did he do that?"

The student said, "The sun gives light and heat."

I said, "True! But the sun has no eyes, ears, mouth, or intelligence. Why not worship the Creator of the sun?"

He replied, "It depends on your belief."

I explained, "Your faith is only as valid as the object of your belief. If you cross a chasm on a weak plank with strong faith, you will crash. If you walk on a strong plank with weak faith, you may safely cross."

To an Indian from Hyderabad I said, "Have you washed away your sins in the Ganges?"

He replied, "No, if I wash now, I'll have to go again - it's better to go later and get the lot done in one hit."

A fiery little female Indian Christian convert from Hinduism fearlessly proclaimed the Gospel. She scornfully asked, "How does bathing in the Ganges wash away sin?"

- "I have bathed in the Ganges. Its 'medicinal' qualities cleansed me from sin."
- "Sunlight reflecting off the holy waters of Ganges into our eyes gives us spiritual life."
- "The sun gives us light and warmth. We thank him for his provision."
- "There are 1000's of gods living in the sun, including Jesus Christ. They are all subordinate to the main God."
- "We have 1000's of gods. I would never upset another religion."
- "33,000 gods are contained in each cow. That's why we cannot eat beef."
- "There is one major difference from Christianity - Karma!"
- "There are nine reincarnations."

NUMEROUS INDIAN CONTACTS

- "We could be facing up to 50 million reincarnations."
- "Karma breaks the cycles of reincarnations."
- "We will include your booklet in my Temple."
- "Eight reincarnations should get you to Nirvana.
- "Count the number of animal species, birds, and fish on earth. Reincarnation as each could take a millennium."
- "An Indian holy man is reputed to have said eight thousand should suffice."
- "The truth is no-one knows.

An Indian student, whose home is near the Golden Temple of Amritsar, in the Punjab sat with me. I said, "I am a Christian. Could you explain how many reincarnations Hindus go through please?"

He said, "As many as there are animal and bird species in the world. That's about 8.4 million. The good and bad things you do in this life determine the number of reincarnations."

"That troubles me deeply", I commented.

He replied, "The cycles are endless but don't worry, there is nothing you can do about it."

"Do you have a Bible?," I asked.

He said, "No." I opened a New Testament to John 14:1-6. He read it aloud and said, "That's like Lord Krishna's teaching."

I said, "Compare this book with your Hindu scriptures and you'll notice major differences."

A female Indian accepted literature. I asked, "Explain the difference in our faiths?"

She answered, "We believe in 1000's of gods in one, but you only have three in one." I think she wanted to get rid of me.

Federation Square (Melbourne CBD)

Two Hindu students wearing spectacular sunglasses were sitting on a nearby parapet. Amit said, "We met not long ago. Remember? I still have your booklet." His shades (sun glasses) had masked his features.

His friend asked, "What happens when you die?" At that moment three gaudy show girls in brief skirts minced past and distracted the students big time. The students were dragged back to reality with Bill Newman 'Eternity' tracts and Gospels of John.

An Indian said, "Hinduism is like two men. The good man has a thorn in his shoe. The bad man has a gold coin. The good man suffered because of bad things in a past life. The bad man is being repaid for good things in his past life. It's up to me to balance my bad deeds with good deeds to get a better life next time." I explained God's grace in relation to the law. He said, "You mean the Ten Commandments are like a mirror. I look into them and see what I am like?" He accepted a Gospel.

Dev, a cocksure student, asserted, "I was born into a Hindu family. I don't follow any religion."

I firmly responded, "On the authority given me by God, I am putting the name of Jesus on you. May he bless and keep you; make his face to shine upon you, and be gracious unto you; the Lord lift up His countenance upon you and give you peace (Numbers 6:22-27)." He speechlessly accepted Gudgerati literature.

A South Indian was searching for work and accommodation in Melbourne. His wife would cease employment soon due to late-stage pregnancy. Recently his older brother tragically lost his life in England. This bitter blow caused him to lose his Hindu faith. He accepted a TPTL NT* and discussion on John 8:12.

Ghandi, (not his real name) said, "You gave me a booklet. Remember? I have troubles. Can we talk?" He accepted a TPTL NT*. His compatriot Gauren, (not his real name) accepted Tamil literature.

Looking at his booklet Gauren said, "I know this group. Their address is 67 Beracah Road, Kilpauk, Madras. I live at 129 Beracah."

I said to Gauren, "What is the pendant round your neck?"

He replied, "It says we believe in one god."

I said, "You worship cows in India."

He responded, "Yes."

I stated, "An Indian once told me that each cow contains 8,000 gods. Suppose you are killed in an accident in ten minutes, and the one true God asked, "Why should I let you into my kingdom? What would you say?"

He maintained, "If I do a hundred bad deeds and one good deed, I'll be OK." Both accepted literature.

An older Indian asked, "What is your date of birth?" I told him. He said, "You are Sagittarius - 1987 and 1988 were stressful years for you." Nothing startling here. Most blokes my age went through the stock market crash. I shared my testimony. He changed tack, "Now it's much clearer. Your forceful personality is a stress factor. Watch your heart!" With fierce frown, rising voice and jabbing fore-finger he continued, "Who made blood? God! Who made the heart that pumps it? God! Who made the world we live in? God! Who made the air we breathe? God! You don't own Australia! God does! I don't own India, God does!"

I interrupted, "I am a traveller on the way to the Celestial City. Thank you for visiting this country which I don't own. Please make a quick return to the country you don't own. Goodbye!"

An Indian explained, "The Immigration Department wants $100,000 to grant immediate residential status. Before I left India my mother gave me a calendar on which she wrote two Bible verses for each day of the year.

Today's verse is Psalm 23. Would you pray for me?" I prayed for him and his family. "He responded, "That was great."

Four Hindus from Mumbai were relaxing. The older one said, "What did you think of the test match (test cricket between India and England)?"

I replied, "Do you believe in the theory of evolution?"

He said, "Yes."

I replied, "Evolution allows people to call each other monkeys on the cricket ground."

After discussion about creation, he accepted literature and replied, "You are doing a good job. Nobody else is talking about these subjects."

Monica, a student from Delhi, was examining pictures of deities, including Jesus, on her cell phone. Her Hindu parents encouraged her to attend a Christian school for thirteen years to learn the basics of the Christian faith. She said, "I am ready to go to the mosque, the temple or the church." She accepted a Gospel of John and Hindi literature.

A Hindu student said, "I attended a Catholic School in India and know a bit about the Bible. I believe you must do good works and good things happen. If you pour drops of holy water from the Ganges into the mouth of a dead person, he is guaranteed entrance into paradise." He too accepted literature.

An Indian visitor from Perth was a Seventh Day Adventist. His wife converted from Buddhism but said, "All religions are the same and every good person gets to Heaven. God would not be so cruel as to turn a good person away. My parents were good people. Are you telling me they are in Hell because they didn't convert to Christianity?" She will believe what she wants, but the Bible says, "The Lord Jesus shall be revealed from Heaven with His mighty angels in flaming fire taking vengeance on those who do not obey the Gospel of our Lord Jesus Christ" (2 Thessalonians 1:7-8).

Another Indian said, "Religion is like a room full of incense sticks. Light them all and select the one with the best aroma."

I replied, "Religion is like pneumonia. Your doctor says, 'I have 1000's of medications on my shelf, choose which you like and it will cure you.' But select the wrong one, and you're dead'." He accepted Hindi literature.

A student from Bombay, who arrived in Australia fifteen days previously, worshipped Surya (sun) Bhagwan (god). The student rises early, takes a dish of water, washes, then offers the dirty water to the rising sun for cleansing, then eats his breakfast. In this way he feels physically and spiritually clean. He accepted a Gospel of John saying, "Thanks uncle. I'll get back to you." But he never did.

In Hungry Jacks

A student said, "I worship Shiridi Sai Baba, who died in his human form about eighty years ago. He is now alive in his godly form in the city of Shiridi in India. He heals the lame, gives sight to the blind, conducts miracles, and knows everything. Make a wish, he'll grant it. I did that for my visa to Australia. It was approved in record time. He is a realistic god."

Vihar accepted a Gospel presentation based on Genesis 1 to 3. He said, "There are 1,000's of gods in India but I've never seen one."

I replied, "Hinduism, Buddhism and Islam came into the world as a word and stayed a word. In Christianity, the Word of God became flesh and dwelt among us."

A Hindu was a 'Ror', a wealthy farming caste with membership in the Geeta Temple in KurukshelraI, Haryana. The Brahmin caste in India hold the power but few in number. The Dalits are the bottom caste - they have no power and millions of children. The 'Ror' are about halfway up. I said, "Is the caste system good?"

Vihar replied, "Not good. It causes problems. This is why I want permanent residency in Australia." He accepted literature.

In McDonalds

I put the BQ* to an extrovert Indian who replied, "Creating as much wealth as I can so I can look after my family."

I said, "I am over eighty years old, and you are only twenty-four. The most important question in all the world for me is what happens when I die and in time to come this will become your most important question too."

He accepted a Gospel of John saying, "I've never heard that before."

Sangeet, the twenty-eight-year-old waitress with whom I have had several conversations, has a boyfriend in India whom she loves dearly. However, her hopes and dreams were over-ridden by her parent's choice of a wealthier man. She said, "I would rather die single. If I can get PR my boyfriend and I will marry in Australia. If I can't marry him, I'll never marry."

The Indian, who failed to keep the appointment, phoned, and said, "Can we meet in McDonalds in fifteen minutes?" His good questions were based on the Christianity Explained question sheet he received a week previously. He had learned the Lord's Prayer at the Christian School he attended.

I drew the self-centred and Christ-centred circles and asked, "Which represents you?" Without hesitation he pointed to the Christ-centred circle. He took question sheet two.

Sometime later he said, "I haven't seen you for weeks."

I explained, "My wife and I went to Brisbane to meet our baby granddaughter. They live close to the Brisbane River with huge, beautiful trees along its banks. These trees remind me of Psalm 1:3. I want my life to be like a tree planted by the waters."

He said, "I have trouble with sinful thoughts."

I said, "Think of a wild rose growing in your garden. Into that rose you graft a beautiful choice rose. The wild rose is still a wild rose and if you aren't careful shoots growing from below that graft will suck away the life producing sap that feeds the new graft. Snip off the wild shoots and the beautiful new rose will grow and blossom. That beautiful rose pictures Christ being formed in you. We owe it to the Spirit (the new rose) to put to death and snip away the deeds of the body (the wild rose)."

> "But if the Spirit of Him who raised Jesus from the dead dwells in you,
> He who raised Christ from the dead will also
> give life to your mortal bodies
> through His Spirit who dwells in you."
> (Romans 8:11)

Swanston Street and Flinders Street Railway Station (FSRS) - Melbourne CBD

A lass from Himachal Pradesh (in the Himalayan foothills) asked, "Pray for me?"

"Which God do you want me to pray to?"

She said, in surprise, "Jesus Christ of course! He is the one true God" (now I'm surprised).

"What do you want me to pray for?"

She replied, "I lodged application this morning to join the Australian Navy."

A smiling Indian in the concourse has older siblings successful in medical and legal fields in India. But Praveen, unsuited for academia, was forced into a university course in Hyderabad by his overzealous father. He failed, thereby reflecting shame and disgrace upon his family. Deeply depressed, he turned to the Bhagavat Gita and the Koran but found no comfort in either. He read the Bible and found 'strength in every page'. He was contemplating a Bible College course.

A converted Indian said, "Returning to my Muslim family in Hyderabad could cost me my life. I have prepared myself for whatever happens, but I can't progress in my Christian life until my family are converted."

I said, "I run into this mindset many times. What should I do?"

He replied, "Befriend them. Get them reading the Bible. Lord Krishna asked the questions but only the Bible gives the answers and pray. It takes ages to change their mind set."

The male Indian nut seller, in referring to his booklet, received last week, said, "Hello Bruce. We have big problem" (referring to sin).

I asked him, "What's the answer?"

He said, "Jesus Christ."

"If your father offers a beautiful gift and you smash it on the floor. How would he feel?"

He replied, "Broken hearted."

I stated, "God's gift to you is Jesus Christ. Refuse Him and you break God's heart."

An Indian student said, "I am in trouble. I have no home."

I answered, "Have you told your parents?"

He replied, "I told them I live in a palatial residence. I cannot worry them with my troubles." He accepted testimony and a Gospel presentation but showed me a picture of Krishna in his cell phone and said, "My god will get me through."

The Hindu handing out fliers commented, "I remember what you said. People can spit on me, swear at me, do what they like. I don't care anymore. It's like that film, I have all those horrible things hanging out my brain but one little shoot in the centre is Jesus Christ. I no longer want to commit suicide, I am happy."

On the Train

Harshal said, "We met in the train remember?" He produced a tattered John's Gospel with my signature therein.

I asked, "Did you attend the Diwali Festival yesterday?"

He replied, "Yes. It is a Hindu festival of lights." I opened his Gospel to John 8:12. He read what Jesus said about being the Light of the world. He was impressed.

A Hindu salesman said, "We believe the same as Christians. Diwali (the evil god) did many bad things. Lord Krishna came down from Heaven and killed him. We celebrate that victory each year."

Suresh grew up steeped in Hinduism and now lives with his wife in Melbourne. He said, "I'm vegetarian. I don't like killing animals."

"But you are wearing leather shoes."

He replied, "It's hard to keep all the rules. I can only try."

I responded "It's impossible" and discussed the Law, Grace, and the Cross of Jesus. He accepted Gudgerati literature.

An Indian lady said to me, "I am reading an Indian Bible."

I asked her, "What version are you reading?"

She replied, "My name is Shefila. I am a Hindu. This is a book about Vishnu. Have you heard of him?"

I said, "Yes. You believe in 1,000's of gods?"

She replied, "Yes."

My response, "Do you believe in Jesus Christ?"

"Yes!" she enthused.

I asked, "Do you know anything about Him?"

She replied, "I read about Him years ago - somewhere."

I said, "If you believe in Him, you should learn about Him. This book is all about the Lord Jesus Christ. Please accept it as your own personal copy of the Christian Bible."

She accepted a TPTL NT* and said, "I really appreciate this. Thank you."

I told her, "Shefila is a beautiful name."

She smiled and said, "Thank you Bruce."

I received the following text: "Hi Bruce its Vahnya here 4pm fed square would just like to thank u for bringing the faith of god into my life as I have found a job. I would also like to thank u for ur prayers. Have an awesome day."

Puneet, from a clothing manufacturing family business in Rajasthan, is perplexed about his future - he accepted a Gospel presentation and a John's Gospel. Two days later the following text arrived: "Hi Bruce, this is Puneet. We met in the train. Thank you for your time and I really appreciate your views about life."

On the Bus

A young man offered me his seat on the bus. I didn't think I looked so old! In the train he said, "I am a professional musician. My guru is the current Jesus Christ. He owns two islands. The one near Fiji has 2,000 devotees. He teaches me to use music to unlock my spirit, to avoid drugs, alcohol, and materialism and to search for true happiness."

I asked, "What is true happiness?"

He replied, "A good question." He accepted a John's Gospel.

To an elderly Hindu couple, I said, "I am a Christian. Could you explain reincarnation?"

The man said, "Buy a copy of the Bhagavat Gita?"

I asked, "Do you have a Bible?"

He replied, "Of course. I attended a Christian School. All religions, Buddha, Islam, Judaism, and Christianity merge into one stream. There is absolutely nothing to argue about."

Raj said, "You spoke to me some time back. I cannot find work. My parents are supporting me, but I should be supporting them." Teary eyes betrayed his deep depression and despondency. I quoted the words of the famous old hymn 'What a friend we have in Jesus'. He soaked up these truths and gained strength before my eyes. He accepted a Gospel of John. I offered to get him a Bible.

He said "Yes. I want it." but never turned up.

A passenger I had previously met, extolled meditation. I explained, "My meditation is centred on the Cross. If you want to know the love of God, read about the crucifixion of Jesus. If you want to know the power of God read about the Resurrection. The Holy Spirit of God will help you understand."

A student said, "I am a vegetarian. I do not eat meat or eggs. The cow is holy. It is our religious mother." She accepted Gudgerati literature.

Vinod, a student from Himachel Pradesh said, "I am an ascetic."

I asked the BQ*. He replied, "Being happy."

I asked, "How do you get happiness? Does a doctor inject it into your brain?"

He stated, "Stop! You are asking questions I cannot answer." He accepted Hindi literature.

Our Doorbell Rang

At 3pm our doorbell rang. Jigar Parmar, an I.T. Masters' student was offering a special deal re the Internet. I said, "I have been to the city of Varanasi by the Ganges."

With eyes aglow and nodding approval as only Indians do, he said, "A very religious place."

I asked, "How does Hinduism help you?"

He said, "Hinduism has hundreds of gods. You can't go wrong."

I asked again, "But how does Hinduism help you personally?"

He said, "Hinduism is peaceful. Have you heard of Ghandi? He was a peaceful man?"

I said, "Yes, but Ghandi was assassinated by a Hindu. What hope does Hinduism offer for your future?"

He replied, "What can I say?" He accepted the booklet 'Who Else Could?' I quoted:

> "The powerful, incomparable all sufficiency of Christ
> alone is able to keep you from stumbling,
> and to present you faultless before the presence
> of His glory with exceeding joy.
> To God our Saviour, who alone is wise, be glory and
> majesty, dominion and power both now and forever.
> Amen" (Jude 24-25)

An Indian Telstra salesman at our front door defended Hinduism with spirit and good humor. Our front door key was still in the lock. A bad move on my part. He quickly locked the door, removed the key and with a mischievous grin said, "I won't let you out till you sign up." He accepted a Gospel of John.

Another Indian salesman at our door accepted Hindi tracts and said, "Mrs. Staines' forgiveness of her husband's murderers in India doesn't happen in Hinduism."

Light Community Baptist Church (LCBC)

An Indian lady, who had worshiped a short while at LCBC was encouraged by the fellowship she received. Having returned to Bangalore (India) she emailed with the following comments: "Though I am writing after many months, I want you to know what an encouragement it was to meet the two of you (Jan and me) while in Melbourne. I have to say being able to worship at the Light Community Baptist Church and meeting a few precious people, was the best part of my time there." She also mentioned her gratitude for counselling for some serious issues she was facing in her homeland.

We attended as guests at an enjoyable farewell dinner in the home of friends from LCBC. A young Indian couple, who worshipped with us were also invited. The Indians accepted Malayalam and Hindi literature and later a Hindi Bible. She quietly wept tears of joy when her husband prayed for the first time. She was pursuing studies in Adelaide. They organised a dinner at our church to celebrate his birthday. The meal was excellent. We arranged contact for them with a church in Adelaide.

East Ringwood Cafes

During discussion with an Indian waitress said, "Animals have hearts of gold."

I answered, "Animals respond with locked in instinctive thrusts. Humans made in the image of God respond with logic and sense. We respond either by instinct or God's way. How do you respond?"

She replied, "Thanks for telling me." On another occasion she asked, "How do you handle a broken heart?" She never specifically said what broke her heart and I never asked, but we discussed the issue in broad terms. She accepted relevant Christian literature and counsel with appreciation.

An Indian PhD career counsellor asked, "Can we sit with you?" She and her student son were returning to India because of his loneliness and homesickness. Using the story of the Sikh ten gurus, I shared the Gospel. She said, "I have read the Bible."

He said, "I am reading from Genesis. I am up to the story of Isaac, (Genesis 22) but I am puzzled by reference to the ram caught by its horns in the thicket" (v13).

I explained, "The ram was substituting for Isaac and foreshadowed the sacrifice of the perfect spotless Lamb of God in the New Testament (John 1:29*) who substituted for our sins."

The lady said, "My son's name means 'Light'." I quoted John 8:12 where Jesus said, "I am the light of the world. Whoever follows me will have the light of life and shall never walk in darkness."

A Malaysian Hindu businessman and his adult son queried me regarding aspects of Christian theology, Jehovah's Witnesses, Protestantism, Catholicism, and Creation. My response was centred round Philippians 2:11* with diagrams and references on a table napkin. He accepted literature. His son accepted a TPTL NT*. The parent said, "I am sorry to ask these hard questions, but you helped me a lot. Thanks!" Notwithstanding my protests, he purchased my lunch and coffee, grabbed the diagrams, and departed.

During our weekly prayer walk an Indian pedestrian was feeding ducks in a local lake. He unexpectedly extracted a photo of Vishnu his Hindu god and tapped it on my forehead. I said, "I refuse that!" He accepted a Gospel of John.

Conclusion:

Replacing the cultural Hindu mindset with the Biblical worldview is more a process than an event. Christ in partnership with believers, prepares sinners for salvation, however, He alone raises them to eternal life. Sharing Christ with eastern mystics (including the New Age movement) whose belief systems include direct contradiction to the first three chapters of Genesis, is an exciting, challenging, learning, and rewarding experience.

In my years of street evangelism, I have not seen or heard one bit of evidence that outweighs the Genesis account of God's fourfold harmony with Himself, others, nature, and me. If any part of the first three chapters of Genesis is incorrect why should anyone believe the Biblical message of salvation? The Bible is replete with examples of people who dropped everything to follow Jesus.

There is no need for hesitation in sharing the Gospel with your waitress, doctor, hairdresser, mechanic, neighbour or relative. That spiritually hungry person may be living just a few doors away. As you pray and that person responds to the claims of Christ, continue with them in ministry for some 'on the job training'. Do some search and rescue work wherever you go.

Taking it to heart –

1. Name some nearby localities in which your 'work of evangelism' may proceed.
2. What spiritual and physical resources might you need for such a ministry?
3. How/when will you begin this ministry?

References:-

Isaiah 40:29 – He gives power to the weak, and to those who have no might He increases strength.

Isaiah 49:15 – Can a woman forget her nursing child, and not have compassion on the son of her womb? Surely they may forget, yet I will not forget you.

Jeremiah 1:5 – Before I formed you in the womb I knew you; before you were born I sanctified you; I ordained you a prophet to the nations.

John 1:29 – The next day John saw Jesus coming toward him and said, 'Behold! The Lamb of God who takes away the sin of the world'.

Romans 8:13 – For if you live according to the flesh you will die; but if by the Spirit you put to death the deeds of the body, you will live.

Romans 13:13-14 – Let us walk properly, as in the day, not in revelry and drunkenness, not in lewdness and lust, not in strife and envy. But put on the Lord Jesus Christ, and make no provision for the flesh, to fulfil its lusts.

2 Corinthians 6:14 – Do not be unequally yoked together with unbelievers. For what fellowship has righteousness with lawlessness? And what communication has light with darkness?

Philippians 2:11 – That every tongue should confess that Jesus Christ is Lord, to the glory of God the Father.

2 Peter 1:5-7 – But also for this very reason, giving all diligence, add to your faith virtue, to virtue knowledge, to knowledge self-control, to self-control perseverance, to perseverance godliness, to godliness, and to brotherly kindness love.

BQ – Big Question – What is the most important question in all the world for you?

TPTL NT – The Pocket Testament League New Testament.

Samuel - Not his real name.

Chapter 15

Challenging Discussions with Israelis

No city on earth has captured the world's attention through the centuries like Jerusalem. In 2010 Jan and I visited this city with its ancient walls, Temple Mount, Wailing Wall, Dome of the Rock, Mount of Olives, the Church of the Holy Sepulchre, and walked the Via Dolorosa along which Jesus carried His Cross to Calvary. It is God's chosen city. Setting foot in Jerusalem was like living with one foot in a glorious past and the other in the tenuous present.

In a restaurant sitting next to us enjoying lunch, was a group of Israeli soldiers - males and females in full uniform, all armed with machine guns. The females' shoulder bags seemed incongruous along-side their weapons. Armed military personnel sitting close by while we had lunch was a confronting sight. But the Lord God said, "This is Jerusalem; I have set her in the midst of the nations and the countries all around her" (Ezekiel 5:5).

In Matthew 22:2-3 Jesus said, "A certain king arranged a marriage feast for his son. All things were ready. His servants went out into the highways and issued invitations to both good and bad!" Though many declined the invitation the wedding hall was filled. This parable encouraged me in issuing Kingdom invitations to Jews I encountered in street evangelism.

Two Jews in Swanston Street were close to being the most obnoxious people I ever met. One interjected. The other glared balefully. Both tried hard to redefine my testimony. They derided my New Testament theology with scornful laughter and refused Christian literature. Their deliberately imposed emotional pain triggered prayer for the peace of Israel on the spot. The Psalmist said, "Pray for the peace of Israel: may they prosper who love you. Peace be within your walls; prosperity be within your palaces" (Psalm 122:6-7).

To a young Israeli in Federation Square (FS) I said, "I met an American Jew reading his Torah at the Wailing Wall in Jerusalem. I asked what he was reading?"

The Israeli replied, "The story of Abraham sacrificing his son on Mt Moriah (Genesis 22)."

I asked, "Why did Abraham do that?"

He replied, "To test Abraham's obedience."

I said, "What is the significance of the ram caught by its horn in a thicket (Genesis 22:13*)?"

The Jew replied, "I don't know."

I stated, "The ram foreshadowed the sacrifice of Jesus Christ, the pure, spotless lamb of God on the Cross for the sins of mankind" (John 1:29*). My Israeli contact listened to my testimony and accepted a Gospel of John.

Two Israeli soldier tourists visiting after three years of military service in their homeland, had just returned from mustering cattle in the Kimberley district (WA).

I shared my story, "For twenty-five years I lived on a farm looking after sheep and cattle. For twenty-five years I worked in the Police Department caring for two-legged sheep. For fifteen years, I worked in churches looking after two-legged sheep. I am a shepherd, but I am not the Shepherd. The Lord is my Shepherd."

One responded, "I believe God." They accepted a Gospel of John each and gave me an excellent hearing. They departed our shores that night for their homeland.

A Russian Jewish refugee sitting in the sun at a local coffee shop, asked, "Do you mind if I smoke?" She gripped a cigarette in one shaking hand and a lighter in the other.

I explained, "I don't smoke but if you really must, don't let me stop you."

She replied, "Oh good!" She lit up and dragged hungrily. I reckoned if it's good enough for her to fill my space with smoke, I can fill hers with the Gospel.

I asked the BQ*. She replied, "Maintaining my independence," and listened to my testimony.

Over there was a Jew. Over here a Muslim. I tackled the Israeli. We discussed the theology of Judaism and Christianity but I got nowhere. A nearby street entertainer competed for the attention of my Jewish friend. I was losing the battle. I introduced my testimony. Then he was attending. I saw it in his eyes but at the first mention of the name of Christ, he said, "Sorry I have to go." He accepted a tract.

A young cosmetics sales person (looked like a twenty-year-old) in the main concourse at Shoppingtown turned out to be an Israeli army major on holidays. She was responsible for the supervision and recovery process of wounded Israeli soldiers in the Arab conflict. She accepted Christmas literature.

A secular Israeli couple with infant child, at the famous and beautiful Dorrigo National Park Sky and Bird Walk (NSW), were interested in the fact that Jan and I had visited the Wailing Wall at Jerusalem. They listened carefully to the story of Abraham and Isaac from Genesis 22. With reference to the ram caught by its horns in a thicket, I said, "It's a substitute sacrifice foreshadowing the coming of Christ the 'perfect, spotless Lamb of God who takes away the sin of the world'. It is by faith you are saved, not works, lest you should boast. God doesn't wait for guilty sinners to come to him for reconciliation. He comes to reconcile them. The Cross is the starting point. Now is the time."

She said, "We'll wait and see."

Several Jews in black suits and black broad brimmed hats were pounding city footpaths. Two stood on the Flinders Street railway station steps. I engaged one in conversation. They were seeking lapsed Jews to invite to a Jewish celebration. He was tentative and unsure. Maybe speaking with a Gentile was embarrassing. His colleague declined any involvement. I was given a card containing the seven universal laws (based on the Ten Commandments) of Judaism. I asked, "What happens if you obey these?" He pointed heavenward. I again asked, "What happens if you don't?"

He said, "We always obey."

I retorted, "Come on now, are you telling me you perfectly obey all these laws?" He declined to answer and reluctantly accepted literature.

Two large backpacks decorated the floor in McDonalds. Two muscular young men occupied nearby seats. One was dark, swarthy and intimidating. The other was blue-eyed and balding. I asked, "Where's your truck?" (pointing to their large backpacks). They smiled. I enquired, "May I sit with you?"

"By all means." They were Israeli soldiers. The topic of terrorism soon arose. Mr. Blue Eyes, the hardliner, said, "Kill them all."

Mr. Swarthy said, "Education is the answer."

I stated, "Education produces clever devils. Sin is the problem." The swarthy one, who sensed I was a Christian, addressed a genuine question at me, saying, "If a terrorist points his machine gun at your wife and kids would you turn the other cheek?"

I answered, "Let me think about that" and silently prayed for help. Other discussion points included euthanasia and Christian and Jewish heritage. I tried to work from the Ten Commandments to respond to their issues. Mr. Blue Eyes said, "In Israel, we lose five hundred Jews, including women and children, to terrorism each year. We envy the peace you have in Australia, and all you do is philosophise about abortion."

I stated, "Thousands of babies are murdered by abortion each year in Australia. Which is worse, abortion or terrorism?"

Suddenly, extracts from the book entitled the 'Heavenly Man' flashed up on my mental computer. To Mr. Swarthy I said, "Let me go back to your question. I have never experienced the pressures you face in Israel. I do not know if I would turn the other cheek. This is a hard question for me. But I do know there were more Christians martyred around the world for their faith in the previous hundred years than in all the other twenty centuries since Christ." Mr. Blue Eyes shook his head incredulously.

I continued, "In China, thousands are becoming Christians every day. They are thrown into jail, tortured, and killed for their faith. From this group is rising a missionary force trained in the school of hard knocks. They are not afraid to take the Gospel to the lands of Buddha, Hindu and Islam. They know they will be persecuted. They have no money, guns, or bombs. All they can do is pray and turn the other cheek. God will honour their faith and answer their prayers, and the world will be won for Christ."

The Jews gladly and respectfully accepted Gospels of John. I inserted their names in John 3:16* and read the verse aloud to them. Our spirited discussion concluded with genuine friendly smiles and hearty handshakes. It did my heart good to cross friendly swords with these hard bitten, toughened, battle scarred Israeli veterans. Pray that one day they too may know the peace of Jesus.

Taking it to heart:

1. Why did the Psalmist exhort us to pray for the 'Peace of Israel?' (Psalm 122:6-7)
2. How does this exhortation affect your attitude to the Great Commission?
3. How might you initiate ministry to your Jewish contacts?

References:

Genesis 22:13 – Then Abraham lifted his eyes and looked, and there behind was a ram caught in a thicket by its horns. So, Abraham went and took the ram, and offered it up for a burnt offering instead of his son.

John 1:29 – When John saw Jesus coming toward him, he said, 'Behold! The Lamb of God who takes away the sin of the world.

John 3:16 – For God so loved the world that He gave His only begotten Son, that whoever believes in Him should not perish but have everlasting life.

BQ – Big Question – What is the most important question in all the world for you?

Chapter 16

Italian Outreach

In my youth, the first of many Italian migrants arrived in our district. One family moved onto the farm next door to us and grew tomatoes commercially. There was much shaking of heads and many heavy speculations among us Aussies regarding how this influx might affect our nation. Upon joining the Police Service, I worked shoulder to shoulder with those of different heritage and cultures including Italians - most of whom were better looking and more intelligent than me. I now have a deeper appreciation of the significant contribution those early migrants and their descendants made to our national prosperity and a healthier response to the friendship our limited wave of Italian visitors offered.

Romano, a down and outer in Hungry Jacks, related his sorry saga of tragedy. He believed in 'a' Jesus but not 'the' Jesus and had constructed a list of good works with which he imagined would get him to Heaven. He accepted a Gospel of John with reference to John 8:12*.

In Federation Square

Mirca, a strongly built Italian tourist, was on a futile search for his pot of gold. He left school early to work in the family business, which went bust in North Italy. Approaching middle age with no job and low-level education, he was seeking opportunities for a position as a waiter. He said, "I do not know what my future holds." I asked him the BQ*. He replied, "To be happy I suppose."

I asked, "If you died tonight and God asked, why he should let you into my kingdom, what would you say?"

He replied, "I don't know." He accepted testimony and an 'Eternity' tract.

A Maltese retiree stated, "I have retired from everything. My brain has had it."

I replied, "You are ten years younger than me. Do you want to curl up in front of your TV and die? Pull your socks up!"

His Maltese wife added, "That's exactly what I tell him." They accepted literature.

Fabio accepted the BQ*, Italian literature, a TPTL NT* and listened to my testimony. Andrea accepted Italian literature. She appreciated the opportunity to practice English.

Some weeks ago, I was approached by Lory, a born-again Christian Italian, in Melbourne to learn English. She accepted Italian literature. Today she asked advice re street evangelism. She said, "I gave out lots of literature in Italy. I want to do the same here. Can you give me some booklets?" I was happy to oblige. She said, "Thank you for being my mentor. I love you in Jesus. May God bless your wife and family." She was involved with an Italian language Christian radio program in Melbourne.

In the distance on an upper step, sat a disconsolate young male with a large backpack. There being no future in his homeland, Mattia arrived with permanent residency in mind. After three months of fruitless searching, he landed a job as a waiter, only to be fired three days later. The boss refused to pay his wages leaving Mattia with ten dollars to spend and a concrete bed on the street. He accepted Italian literature and read aloud John 8:12*. I asked him, "What do you think?"

He replied, "Very good." Our Church Communications Director and I introduced Mattia to 'Urban Seed,' an outreach of the Collins Street Baptist Church, which provided free meals to the disadvantaged. They in turn, took Mattia to the Salvation Army for emergency accommodation.

An encouraging text arrived: "Hi Bruce, how are you? I'm Raimondo the Italian boy. I'm fine, every day. Follow the word of God, is easy live with faith in God, have good day. Pray and believe!!!!! Titus 3:5-7. Signed Raimondo.":

"Not by works of righteousness which we have done, but according to His mercy He saved us, through the washing of regeneration and renewing of the Holy Spirit, whom He poured out on us abundantly through Jesus Christ our Saviour; that having been justified by His grace we should become heirs according to the hope of eternal life."

Taking it to heart:

1. What, if any, prejudicial attitudes do you have to those of differing national or cultural heritage?
2. How frequently do you evaluate your attitudes?
3. How would you approach those with a different heritage and culture, including Italians, and share the love of Christ with them for example?

References:

John 8:12 – I am the light of the world. He who follows me shall not walk in darkness, but have the light of life.

BQ – Big Question – What is the most important question in all the world for you?

TPTL NT – The Pocket Testament League New Testament.

Chapter 17

Japanese Students and Travellers

In earlier years of my street ministry in Melbourne many Japanese students and tourists were evident, but in more recent years these contacts became less frequent. Of many good contacts among our Japanese visitors, two – Hitoshi and Kenitchi (Ken) stood out. You will enjoy reading something of their stories included below.

Whilst waiting at Circular Quay, Sydney NSW, for the Manly Ferry, Yuriko, with Emma her infant child born in New York, arrived two hours ago from Japan. With flawless English she would set up home for her daughter and Texan husband when he arrived in Sydney permanently. She accepted English literature and a TPTL NT* and said, "Bruce, this is my very first Bible."

Back in Melbourne, Yuki, a Japanese tourist with good English, thoughtfully struggled with the questions: 'Where do we come from?' Why are we here?' and, 'Where are we going?' We discussed at length Genesis 1, 2 and 3. He listened to my testimony, accepted my hand-written diagrams,

Japanese literature, and a TPTL NT* with reference to John 8:12*, which he read aloud.

Yamaguchi (Yama) Eiichi, a Buddhist Japanese tourist, who arrived in Australia twenty-four hours previously, sat with me over coffee in Degraves Street, Melbourne. Tax files, residency, accommodation, employment etc. were discussed with the aid of his Japanese/English electronic dictionary. He accepted Japanese literature and a bi-lingual Bible. Our one-and-a-half-hour discussion included reference to Creation and information on English language courses. Later that week he unexpectedly re-appeared. We discussed fruit picking opportunities in Beechworth, Shepparton, and Mildura. In so doing his English vocabulary and pronunciation improved a little. He had his bi-lingual Bible with him. I reminded him of John 8:12*. He repeated, "Thank you so much for talking with me." On Thursday he departed for who knows where. It was a pleasure to interact with him.

Two sad female students accepted Japanese literature. The tsunami and nuclear reactor meltdowns in their country deeply concerned them. One said, "All my family are Christians, but I don't go to church."

The coffee shop proprietor in Degraves Street drew my attention to an ESL college that recently ceased operating due to financial mismanagement. Many of his customers were Japanese students. Coincidentally, Shogo, with limited English, a mature aged Japanese man on a search for the meaning of life, showed me a report of this event in the Age newspaper. This closure left 1,000's of ESL students, including Shogo, in limbo. It may also adversely impact the coffee shop trade. Thereafter, followed a lengthy discussion on Creation with Shogo. We communicated with the aid of his Japanese/English electronic dictionary and diagrams. He would like to become a Christian but can't understand how. Later, Shogo accepted a Gideon Japanese/English NT, an English Bible, a booklet entitled 'Is there really a God?' and a covering letter. He spread his Bible and literature over the table and checked out English words on his electronic dictionary. Another subsequent loud and lengthy discussion over coffee surrounded by patrons within elbow distance, was conducted. His future in Australia considering his college closure, is unknown but what a wonderful window of opportunity for the Gospel.

Two young Japanese travellers sat beside my wife and me at an evening baptismal service in our church. During this service one gave me a hand-written note from which I quote: "Thank you for your kindness. I came here for the first time, and I enjoyed this time. So, I'll go back to Japan next week, cause my girlfriend lives in Japan has my baby. Anyway, nice to meet you. I hope I will get along with you."

A recently arrived traveller was reading a book in Japanese entitled 'Black Rain' which, he said, described the atomic destruction of Hiroshima in 1945. He said, "I am addicted to gambling. I came out $14,000 in front on the horse races in Japan but lost $30,000 at the Casino in Brisbane."

I said, "How will you stop your addiction?"

He answered, "I have learned my lesson." But that I doubt. Over coffee he listened to the plan of salvation and accepted a bi-lingual tract. The Christian Tongan waiter joined our discussion. The Mormon waiter materialised as if from nowhere and hovered within earshot, as usual. Our Japanese friend had no mobile phone and lived in city backpacker premises. My attempt to arrange a meeting for him with two Japanese speaking Australian Christians failed.

A tourist was reading a book in Japanese. I asked, "What are you reading?"

He answered, "It compares Islam, Christianity, Judaism, Buddhism, and Hinduism. All religions emanate from the same source, but religion causes war." His ignorance of Christianity knew no bounds. We discussed the Crucifixion and Resurrection. He accepted a bi-lingual tract and said,

"Thank you. I have learned much today." He declined to offer address or contact details.

In McDonalds, Takeshi, a Japanese tourist, said, "No one has ever seen God. I don't believe in religion." A fairly exhaustive discussion on Genesis 1-3 and God's remedy for sin followed. He accepted Japanese literature and departed for farm work near Sale, a small Victorian country town.

Sitting next to me in Hungry Jacks, was Kazuhiro Nazaki, a Japanese traveller, learning conversational English. He arrived from Perth two days previously. Kazu accepted an invitation to Matt Adams' home group at our church and Japanese literature. He had attended a church recently in Perth with a Christian friend, who gave him a Japanese/English Bible.

A Japanese student seated in the Mall spoke practically no English. He was applying to be a part time 'worrruntar'. I think he meant volunteer! Pronouncing L's and R's was almost impossible for him. My English-speaking lesson included extracts from the Gospel, but I doubt he understood. Sweat beads dotted his forehead as he wrestled with pronouncing the word 'volunteer'. God bless you Mr Japanese man.

In McDonalds, Kyohei Abe, a pleasant young Japanese tourist, enjoying an early lunch, was interested in spiritual topics. We walked together through a lengthy presentation from a Japanese/English version of the Four Spiritual Laws, but language, culture and religious background made communication slow and difficult. He eagerly prayed the prayer of commitment. As far as I can tell, he is now a baby Christian. He accepted Japanese literature to read on his journey that night to Adelaide. This was the first leg of his trip home (in more ways than one)? Japanese literature was mailed to his home address awaiting his return. He uttered an emotional farewell as we shook hands.

Hitoshi

Hitoshi attended the 10.30am service at Canterbury Presbyterian Church in Surrey Hills. The young, much loved, fluent Japanese speaking, Irish Presbyterian Pastor, preached on Romans 6:11: "Reckon yourselves dead to sin, but alive to God in Christ Jesus our Lord." Guitars and bongo drums accompanied the singing of 'Jesus Name above all Names' as four beautiful young Japanese people including Hitoshi testified with translation to their faith in Christ prior to their baptism by immersion at a Mentone Beach, attended by some forty-five people, later that afternoon.

The day was overcast. Sand was smooth and clean. Sea birds floated on ocean waters clear and pristine. Others effortlessly swooped, soared, and glided above. A large rock standing sentinel off-shore, reminded me of that famous old hymn: 'Rock of Ages, cleft for me, let me hide myself in thee; let the water and the blood, from thy riven side which flowed, be of sin the double cure, cleanse me from its guilt and power'. These baptisms were conducted with energetic enthusiasm, flair, and a sense of the presence of the Holy Spirit. The saturated ones received rounds of applause as they emerged shivering one by one from the icy waters. Each candidate registered in various and deeply emotional ways, their feelings as they waded toward us. The significance of their baptisms was uplifting for all concerned. It was a happy, joyous occasion.

Hitoshi and I lunched at McDonalds. To my surprise he quoted by heart Colossians 1:15-16* in English. He asked an explanation for 2 Corinthians 5:17* and mentioned the names of three Japanese non-Christian friends for whom he was praying. Several key young Christians from our church had significant spiritual input with him. A few short weeks ago he had zero knowledge of the Christian faith. He was racing against time to get the basics right before returning to Japan. After each agenda item was exhaustively discussed, and silently pondered, he nodded and said, "I understand."

Discussion took place as usual with the aid of his Japanese/English NT and electronic dictionary. Since his baptism he has received requests for advice from young local Christians and invitations to join or lead a small group. Those who know him agree that a huge lift in his understanding of the faith had occurred, incredibly so, as English is not his mother tongue. This impressive young man has potential for key church leadership in Japan in due course.

Hitoshi and a Korean, whose adopted Aussie name was Frank, turned up for our usual lunch hour Bible study in Hungry Jacks - an ideal location for this purpose. (Frank's inspiring story is more fully documented in the Korean section). Our study at their request, was based on the connection between the tongue, horses, ships, and fire from James 3:1-12. In conclusion, I prayed with Hitoshi and Frank, and later attended, as arranged, another weekly Bible study in Hungry Jacks. Frank went to soccer practice at our church the previous evening and was so tired he nodded off in the Bible study and excused himself from the proceedings. Hitoshi asked questions on how to share his faith. He is aware that testing times may arise and wanted to meet again next Monday.

I lunched with Hitoshi and Frank at Hungry Jacks. We were joined by two adults from the church group who cared for them. Referring to the testimonies of two of the Japanese girls recently baptised with him, Hitoshi said, "Each had experienced trauma and contemplated/attempted suicide. If I take leadership in the church back home and a suicidal person asks counsel, I won't know what to say." We discussed counseling and in conclusion prayed.

We met again in Hungry Jacks for our regular lunch hour Bible study. Frank, who was present at Hitoshi's recent baptism requested baptism.

Hitoshi and I checked out Frank's testimony and discovered, as suspected, that Frank is a not yet Christian. We revisited the steps of salvation with him. I was amazed by the grasp Hitoshi had developed of the doctrine of salvation in such a short time. I was impressed by his gentle, but firm way of dealing with Frank. Also, I did some teaching on the Lord's Prayer. This is excellent training for Hitoshi, who prayed in Japanese at the conclusion of our meeting.

I had lunch in Hungry Jacks with Hitoshi, Frank and Michelle, Frank's Korean girlfriend. I wondered what to say to Hitoshi before he was to depart for Japan. I referred him to Mark 5:2-6 - the man who was healed of massive health problems. He begged Jesus that he might stay with Him but was told, "Go home to your friends and tell them what great things the Lord has done for you" (Mark 5:19). I said to Hitoshi, in the presence of Frank and Michelle, "The Crucified and Resurrected Christ is the greatest thing in your life. When your friends and family ask what happened in Australia, tell them how Jesus changed you."

Hitoshi's spiritual growth during his last few months in Melbourne was incredible. His highlight in Melbourne, he said, "Was my baptism at Mentone Beach." We prayed. He had the Bill Newman 'Eternity' tract signed on 1st March 2004, the date he became a Christian, in his pocket. He had already said goodbye to his Japanese church group and farewelled me with a big hug. We may never meet again. I was sad to see him go. But surprise! Surprise! A knock on the door late one evening heralded the arrival of the church small group leader taking Hitoshi to the airport. They called in on their way for him to say one last goodbye on his departure from Australia. Also present were Frank and Michelle.

A female Japanese student and I chatted at the conclusion of our church's evening service. We walked through some Four Spiritual Laws material. She prayed the sinner's prayer and invited Jesus into her life. I prayed with her. She repeated to a leader accurately and clearly the details of her conversion. A leader from the youth department later said, "She is excited about her decision."

Among those present at an evening service were:

- Two Japanese students who were recently baptised.
- N who was Ken's Japanese friend and not yet a Christian, attended for the first time. N later said, "Hitoshi told me you helped him a lot."
- Ken, whose story appears below after becoming a Christian, later said, "Bruce, you got me into this."
- Frank the Korean student, who had recently become a Christian.
- Frank and Michelle - now married, live in South Korea, have two delightful children and attend church.
- Two Indian students from the Bourke Mall attended at their request for the first time and travelled by train from Footscray, a western suburb of Melbourne.

Another Japanese guy messaged me from Japan as follows: "Hi Bruce, Long time no see! How are you? I arrived in home yesterday! Home sweet home!! I remember we promised that when I arrive in Japan, I email you. Do you remember that? I remember it. Because I pray for you. Blessings."

And again: "Good morning. Thanks for your reply. I'm glad that you are still alive. Our group leader is ninety-two-years old and still talks a lot. He is my mentor and preacher. According to your journal, I invited you over for a noodles party in October, but if I'm not mistaken, we got to know each other before. We talked in church. I'm sending you some photos of our engagement ceremony. I hope we can meet again on earth. Blessings."

Much later: "Hey Bruce, Long time no see. Are you still alive? I hope so. I have major news. I am getting married to a Christian Japanese lady next year. I hope we can meet again here before we go to heaven. Blessings."

Kenitchi (Ken)

Many years ago, a baby boy was born to farming parents in Northern Victoria. Through a lengthy quest to discover the meaning of life he became a Christian as a teenager. Thirty-one years ago (at the time of writing), another baby boy was born and raised in Japan, a vastly different culture. A quest to discover the meaning of life launched Ken on a long journey to Australia. Amazingly, the lives of Ken and me intersected on a bench seat in the Bourke Mall, Melbourne. Ken listened carefully to my testimony and accepted a Gospel of John. He requested my phone number and church address. Soon after this 'chance' meeting, Ken, to my surprise, called requesting transport to our next evening church service. Jan and I collected Ken from his flat in nearby East Kew.

That particular Sunday morning I had preached (with interpreter) at the Vietnamese Service at North Blackburn Baptist Church (now NewHope). A young lady, not known to me at this service, was experienced with Japanese culture and language. She and her husband volunteered to attend the evening service specially to meet Ken and help with translation. I had also mentioned Ken to two young adult small group members from our church. The above-mentioned young lady and her husband welcomed us in the church foyer and sat with Ken during the service to translate. He enjoyed the service, although not fully understanding it. This was his first ever church service. Ken accepted an English Bible and was shown how to use it.

Ken, later that week, arrived at McDonalds in Swanston Street with a big smile. Together we went through the Bill Newman 'Eternity' tract with a fine-tooth comb. I asked him, "What stops you giving your life to Christ right now?"

He replied, "I prefer to do that in private."

The two young adults mentioned above, regularly transported Ken to and from railway stations, homes, outings, and included him in coffee, dinner, and home group meetings. It was an impressive new world for Ken. He was inspired and encouraged. A young man from our church had given Ken a Japanese/English New Testament. Soon after, Ken requested transport to another evening church service when Pastor Daniel Bullock gave a strong message. Afterwards, Ken said, "I have accepted the package. Now I am going through the contents."

Our church's young adults' group excelled at intentionally making our international visitor feel welcome. This is the body of Christ in action. Praise God for them. Their excellent, timely, high-quality support, encouragement and prayer was significant in Ken's adoption into the Kingdom of God.

Ken returned to Melbourne months later to renew acquaintances. He tracked me down in the Bourke Mall with a view to re-establishing his Christian faith. He still had his Bill Newman 'Eternity' tract from last year. I dined with him in a Japanese restaurant and discussed John 8:12*. Ken keenly pursued this verse as the basis for his study the following week. He also completed an overview of the Gospel of Mark with the above-mentioned two young men from our church. His understanding of the Gospel was increasing. Today, Ken invited me for a farewell lunch in a Japanese noodle bar in Bourke Street, Melbourne. He was disappointed by the poor quality of the 'Japanese' food prepared by Chinese chefs. This was my last opportunity to review his understanding of Christianity and to pray with him. His understanding of the basics was good and due in no small measure to the combined discipleship efforts of the above-mentioned firmly committed, dedicated young Christians. The Japanese Church in Canterbury connected Ken to a church in Japan. However, Ken found it difficult to attend this church because of his long hours at work and it was over an hour's drive to get there. Notwithstanding, he looked happier now and his grasp of the faith still seemed good. The linkage between the birth 2,000 years ago of a babe born in a manger, an old Aussie Christian from Northern Victoria, and a young Japanese tourist in the Bourke Mall was a miracle of grace that amazes me to this day.

Sometime later, Ken texted me as follows: "Dear Bruce, Hello! I am Ken from Japan. It has been a half year since the last time I met you. I enjoyed so much when I stayed with Matt. Australia is the best place to stay and relax. And it is very great to have friends like Matt and Kent. If I hadn't met you about five years ago, it would never have happened. I really appreciate that you gave me this opportunity. My new job is good so far, more challenging, and more spare time in my life. I would like you to keep healthy and I would like to see you next time I visit Melbourne. Take care."

I had tried to roll away a few stones of misunderstanding and unwind some bandages that blinded Ken to the truth but praise God, Jesus alone called Ken forth (John 11:41-44*). Thankfully, I was there when it happened.

(A treasured photo with Ken and three other young Asian visitors who became Christians at some stage during their Melbourne visit is included in the photo section).

Taking it to Heart:

1. How does the term 'accept the package and examine the contents' relate to the Great Commission?
2. How might you extend your influence locally and internationally?

3. In what ways will you encourage young Christians coming along behind you?

Bible References:

Mark 5:19 – Jesus said to him, 'Go home to your friends and tell them what great things the Lord has done for you, and how He has had compassion on you.'

John 8:12 – Then Jesus spoke to them again, saying, 'I am the light of the world. He who follows Me shall not walk in darkness, but have the light of life.'

John 11:41-44 – Then they took away the stone from the place where the dead man was lying. And Jesus lifted up His eyes and said, 'Father, I thank You that You have heard Me…' Now when He had said these things, He cried with a loud voice, 'Lazarus, come forth!' and he who had died came out bound hand and foot with graveclothes, and his face was wrapped with a cloth. Jesus said to them, 'Loose him, and let him go.'

2 Corinthians 5:17 – Therefore, if anyone *is* in Christ, *he is* a new creation; old things have passed away; behold, all things have become new.

Colossians 1:15-16 – He is the image of the invisible God, the firstborn over all creation. For by Him all things were created that are in heaven and that are on earth, visible and invisible, whether thrones or dominions or principalities or powers. All things were created through Him and for Him.

TPTL NT – The Pocket Testament League New Testament.

Chapter 18

Encounters with Koreans in Australia and South Korea

Interesting Korean Contacts in the Melbourne CBD

In Federation Square an elderly retired Pastor opened conversation by asking with obvious feeling, "Are you Australian? You sent your young men to fight for us (the Korean conflict). Many of them died to keep our country free. Thank you very much."

A brave but naive twenty-year-old lass arrived alone in Australia five days previously to make a new start. Our discussion included English word studies with the aid of her Korean/English electronic dictionary. She accepted Korean literature and surprisingly said, "I am a Christian." She was invited to visit our church.

White clad Asians singing Christian choruses, were handing out tracts in FS entitled: 'Steps to Peace With God' (STPWG) by Rev Billy Graham. These delightful young Presbyterian Koreans from Sydney, under the supervision of their Pastor, shared recently in an Aboriginal Church service in Shepparton (Vic). Following a few days seeking to 'save people for Jesus' in Melbourne, they returned to Sydney that evening. I issued several of their brochures to onlookers, including one to a man with whom I have shared many times.

Day Kim said, "My parents are Christian. I invited God into my life ten years ago but now I don't read the Bible or go to church."

I stated, "Read your Bible and pray fifteen minutes each morning. Attend a Korean Church every Sunday. Follow Jesus, shine for him and tell others. At the end of one month, tell me how you go."

He said, "I promise," and accepted Korean literature.

A male pedestrian and a female student appeared in FS. The man said, "What do you think about boys and girls living together?" I stated my position.

She replied, "I've been telling him this, but he won't listen. What do you think about church going?" Again, I stated my position. She replied, "That's what I tell him."

I said to him, "You better attend church with her, or I'll come looking for you." He sheepishly accepted Korean literature.

She excitedly informed me, "That's what we use. God has brought us together."

A young tourist declared, "I went to a Catholic University. My girlfriend is a Christian, but I don't believe in God. I believe in myself."

I explained, "Your girlfriend is walking the Christian road, but you are walking the road to nowhere." He accepted Korean literature with teary eyes. I prayed for him.

Seung Baek, a tourist, said, "I don't believe in religion."

I asked him, "Where does time, space and matter come from?"

He said, "Nature."

I asked, "Who created nature."

He replied, "Nothing. It is just there."

I stated, "It's impossible for nothing to create anything." He had no answer and listened to a Gospel presentation based on Genesis 1-3. I explained, "All men will die. All will be judged. Jesus will be that judge. All will be divided into two groups, the positive and the negative. That division will be permanent. What you do with Jesus in this life determines what he does with you in the next. Refuse Him now and He will put you in the negative side and that's a thought too terrible to think about. Give your life to Christ and He will put you into the positive side and you will live with Him in Paradise forever."

He answered, "Maybe later." This conversation was conducted with the aid of his electronic Korean/English dictionary. He accepted Korean literature and a Gospel of John and returned to Korea that evening.

I asked a Korean traveller the Big Question (BQ*). He had no answer. I said, "What brings you the most joy in life?"

He answered, "Travel."

I replied, "What brings me the most joy is giving you the answer to my first question?"

Moved by my testimony he stated, "I'll think about it." This gentle, polite soul accepted a Gospel of John. A student I previously met, smiled on the railway platform. A home Bible study near her address was recommended.

A polite young traveller raised his eyebrows when I shared my testimony. He said, "I am a science student. What you say is hard to accept."

I replied, "You accept the theory of evolution in the same way I accept creation - by faith." He accepted a Gospel of John.

Yet another young Korean listened to a Gospel presentation. We were surrounded by noisy secondary school students on an excursion. The kids took no notice. I pressed on. The Korean said, "I am not ready yet" but accepted a Gospel of John.

Two Koreans on holidays, accepted teaching from Psalm 23 and a related diagrammatic Gospel challenge. One said to me, "I went to church every Sunday when I was little. I cannot accept there is a God."

The other said, "I am the same."

I asked, "What will you say when you die and God says, 'Why should I let you into my Kingdom'?" They didn't know. They accepted bi-lingual Korean tracts with extra respect.

A recently arrived Korean girl, who enrolled in a local college to learn English announced, "I am a Christian. I pray with my friend every morning for one hour." She examined my bi-lingual tract and quizzed me at length regarding my understanding of the Bible, and the Cross. She continued, "I am looking for a church to attend." I gave her directions to Blackburn North Baptist Church (now NewHope).

A tourist told me, "I'm not happy. I broke it off with my girlfriend last night. It's weird because I have no family here to discuss with." He gladly participated in discussions, including reference to John 1:12* and the church family. Though reserved about Gospel doctrine, he accepted Korean Christian literature. Discussion seemed to lift his spirits.

Jim, a back-packing commerce student, tried to initiate conversation with an older Aussie lady seated adjacent. She repulsed his every overture with frosty glare. Feeling sorry for him, I struck up a conversation. He was seeking work, opportunities to improve his English and direction in life. Following a Gospel discussion centred on 'surrender' to the Lord, he accepted Korean literature.

Jiyeon, a lass on the bus, accepted Korean literature and joyfully asked, "You Christian? Me too. What do you do?"

I said, "Street evangelism."

She asked, "How do you do it?" During a half hour discussion, she learned the BQ*, tips on street evangelism and listened to my testimony.

A student on Platform 2 at Flinders Street railway station asked, "Is this the line to Box Hill?" He recently arrived to study English. He lived in Clayton and said, "I want a good church to attend." He accepted Korean literature and was put in contact with a good local church.

A pleasant tourist with Christian parents, said, "I don't like the way church denominations fight; Christians argue, and no one has ever seen God anyway."

I stated, "The issue is the eternal destiny of your soul. Give your life to Jesus now." He accepted Korean literature.

Two girls sat with me in Degraves Street. One was a Catholic. The other, a born-again believer, but I suspect a somewhat backslidden Christian. They are entranced by a comparison of the 38th Parallel at Panmunjom that divides North and South Korea and their own spiritual lives. The sign 'In Front of Them All' above the village entrance gate added weight to this illustration. The Christian testified to a miracle healing of a serious heart defect as a child when a Pastor prayed for her. The Catholic girl said, "I'll think about becoming a Christian when I return to Korea."

I replied, "Now is the hour." She smiled ruefully. They accepted literature.

A Korean girl I had previously met in Degraves Street, called and asked, "Can we come to your English speak night?" That evening, she with her Bulgarian girlfriend, arrived at Matt Adams' home group for dinner and Bible Study.

Three Koreans on work visas, accepted literature. Two said, "We are going to Echuca to work in an abattoir. We don't believe in God. But we'll go to church to improve our English." The third Korean listened closely as I exhorted them to give their lives to Christ.

A couple in Hungry Jacks were perusing their English as a second language homework sheets. I asked them, "How are you getting on with it?" Discussing rafts of issues inspired confidence in their limited English-speaking skills. I took them through Psalm 23 and shared the bi-lingual four Spiritual Laws tract. He said, "This is what I believe."

She uttered, "I believe that too." They departed for Mildura the next day for the grapevine pruning season. We arranged to meet at Hungry Jacks again. Will they turn up?

In McDonalds, a Korean student accepted a bi-lingual tract. He stated, "God is Buddha, Islam and Hindu all wrapped up in one." We began our discussion at Genesis 1 then skipped through to Acts 4:12: "Nor is there salvation in any other, for there is no other name under heaven given among men by which we must be saved."

Two Korean travellers struggled with a tourist map of Melbourne. Their English was not good. Another young Korean in FS was a Christian but communicating was difficult. A young man complained, "My family are all Christians. They kept preaching at me." He listened to my testimony and accepted Korean literature.

Lee, a middle-aged Korean journalist, in answer to the BQ* said, "I don't know."

I proclaimed, "For me it is what happens when I die?"

He asked, "Are you a Christian?"

I responded, "Yes," and shared my story.

He went on to say, "My mother is a Christian. She prays every day I will become a Christian. I attended church when I was young, but a corrupt Pastor turned me away. Many Korean Pastors are corrupt. I don't believe in religion." He accepted Korean literature and a TPTL NT*.

A traveller, who arrived in Melbourne one day ago, accepted a Korean/English Four Spiritual Laws tract, read partly through it but said, "I have a Christian background. I am not a Christian."

I took him through the tract again and asked, "Would you like to make Jesus the Lord of your life?"

He answered, "Yes" and prayed the prayer of commitment. Unsure of the depth of his commitment I referred him to the Korean Elder of the Canterbury Presbyterian Church.

An Asian in the bus offered me his seat. I must be getting old. He said, "I am a Christian." I offered him a Korean/English literature. He asked, "May I keep this? It will help me share with my friends. I attend a Korean Church in Box Hill every Sunday." He produced a Korean English New Testament from his shoulder bag and said, "I read and meditate on this book for one hour a day." I sensed spiritual strength in this young man.

A tourist in Hungry Jacks announced, "I am a Christian."

I replied, "How do you know?"

He answered, "My family are all Christians."

I diagrammed the self-controlled life and the Christ controlled life and asked, "Which one are you?"

He pointed to the self-controlled life and asked, "Can I be both?"

Following some discussion, I said, "Would you like to pray for Jesus to come into your life?"

He answered, "Yes." He prayed with apparent sincerity to receive Jesus into his life. His decision seemed genuine. He was heading home to Korea that evening.

Interesting Korean Contacts Interstate

On the ferry to Circular Quay (Sydney), I met Neenah, a Korean lass with good English. She was studying in London and holidaying in Australia. She listened to the BQ* and said, "My grandparents are Christian and want me to attend church, but I just want to enjoy life, so I don't go." She accepted testimony, a Gospel message, and a TPTL NT*.

Jayan, a banker and golfer of note, sat unhappily in the shade of a large tree on the bank of the Brisbane River in Orleigh Park, West End (Brisbane). Something within me said, "Speak to him!' Jayan welcomed me with a huge smile. Low grade English impeded his application for banking employment here. His wife, a health care worker with good English and living in Brisbane some years, does not want to return to South Korea. Jayan was reading his English as a second language workbook. With the aid of technology, we embarked upon a study of the words 'positivity', 'patience', 'persistence' and 'prayerlessness'. These English words were new to him. The 'prayer' word opened the way for spiritual discussion. He happily accepted prayer and the gift of Christmas literature.

Frank's Testimony

Frank (not his Korean name), a student came to Australia to improve his English language speaking skills. Somehow, he made contact with Matt Adams' home group at North Blackburn (now NewHope) Baptist Church. Soon after Frank and I rendezvoused with two members of Matt's group in McDonalds. Frank said, "I want to get baptised."

I explained, "Your first priority is giving your life to Christ then baptism follows." We discussed at length, with the aid of the Four Spiritual Laws booklet and his electronic dictionary.

Frank said, "I understand."

I continued to say, "Perhaps you should talk to a Korean Pastor because of language barriers?"

He replied, "No! I want to give my life to Christ now." He prayed the sinner's prayer and a flash of heavenly sunlight lit up his face.

The significance of Exodus 23:20* in Frank's conversion is inescapable, considering the spiritual warfare in which we are all involved. At a subsequent luncheon appointment in McDonald's, I led Michelle, Frank's recently arrived Korean girlfriend, through the Korean/English edition of the four spiritual laws. She, Frank, and I held hands as Michelle repented joyfully and prayerfully invited Jesus in Korean into her life as Lord and Saviour. She cried, smiled, cried, and smiled some more.

The roles and prayers of the Matt Adams' group regarding Frank and Michelle's conversions, must not be under-estimated. They played a significant role in the transition of this beautiful young couple from the kingdom of darkness to the Kingdom of God's dear Son. As we left, the Iraqi waitress appeared. I said to Michelle, "Tell her what happened."

The waitress agog with excitement, said, "What happened?" Michelle was still a little shell shocked and couldn't quite get it out. The waitress peered at Michelle. With louder intensity, she said, "Go on. Telllll meeee!" Michelle shyly said through smiles and tears, "I invited Jesus into my life." The waitress's eyes widened with astonishment. She looked quickly and fearfully over her shoulder and round the room and barked, "Where? How? Did you see Him?"

I said to the waitress, "The most important thing is not your job, money, house, or security. You will never be truly happy until you have Jesus in your life. I want to talk with you."

She said, "Tomorrow 4pm!" I had tried to nail the Iraqi for weeks, but Michelle's fifty second long, ten-minute old testimony grabbed her attention. At least I now have her focus, even if only for a moment. The impact of a personal testimony must never be underestimated. The Iraqi waitress never turned up.

At lunch with Frank in Hungry Jacks, we discussed the Sunday night sermon from Genesis 37 on Jacob's dream and linked it to 1 Corinthians

1:9-10 re Paul's suffering for the Gospel. The home group leader joined us. I said to Frank, "Tell him what we discussed." He responded with an accurate resume. Our satisfied leader departed.

Frank cooked dinner in our home one evening. To this auspicious event, he invited Hitoshi, a Japanese student, our son, and his home group leader. We enjoyed a Korean meal and good fellowship. Frank related some difficult aspects of his service as a soldier in the Korean army. He said with a shy smile, "But God is my general now and I am his soldier."

Later Frank explained, "My father prayed with me every morning by my bedside before I got up. We watched Paul Yongi Cho on TV together each week. He took our family to church every Sunday, but he stopped attending church a long time ago. How can I get him to church again?" After a lengthy discussion, a prayer strategy emerged. Frank is happy with it and later joyfully reported that his father has resumed church attendance.

Frank, Matt (home group leader) and I enjoy coffee in FS. This is my last meeting with Frank, who was returning to Korea soon. We prayed. He said, "With Jesus' help I'll never fall." As Michelle and Frank left our shores, it hit me for the first time, that I may never meet them again this side of Heaven. I was sorry to see them go. Frank and Michelle are now married with two beautiful children. They are involved in a Christian group in a good church in Korea. Frank later messaged me as follows:

"Hi! I am Frank. How are you? I hope everything is fine. I sorry that I couldn't contact long time. I am in Seoul nowadays cause I am preparing exam. I have been here around three months. I miss you and friends, especially Matt. I haven't studied English long time so I feel uncomfortable to write and Michelle is fine whenever I meet her, we are talking about Australia and you. You gave us new life. Thanks. God bless u. See u soon."

A Corporate Highflier

In McDonalds, a middle-aged Korean at the next table asked, "Can I sit with you?" He was a corporate highflier in a large international business firm in Melbourne. He had previously taken an early retirement lump sum payout, returned to Korea and lost his millions in a failed business venture, resulting in bankruptcy. Deeply depressed with a bleak future, his wife, who he still loves, divorced him taking custody of their only son. I phoned her at his request, but she declined to speak with him.

He listened to a Gospel presentation and said, "I have an appointment. Can we meet again at 4pm?" In the interval, he had tried to organise finance to tide him over his financial crisis. When he returned the bureaucratic reluctance of those to whom he turned for help, unleashed pent up fury and anger. Like a human volcano he exploded. With reddened face and pulsating neck arteries he thumped the table with a clenched fist, punctuated with vented shouts. Curious patrons watched. The tension was palpable. I called time out for five minutes and escaped upstairs to the street for a breath of fresh air. He was waiting for my return.

It was more of the same! I continued the Gospel presentation and said, "You don't take God like an aspirin and forget him when the crisis passes. He is your Creator, Saviour, Lord, and Master. You follow Him for all time. Do you understand?"

He said, "I have no job, no money, no family and no home. I am at the nadir (his word) of life. I have no one else to turn to."

I explained, "God loves you and loves to work with people in their nadir." He accepted a Bible and teaching from Hebrews 12:1* and Revelation 3:20*.

He prayed the sinner's prayer, asked Jesus into his life, and requested, "Can we meet at 7pm. I have more things to sort out."

At 7pm the Korean returned much happier, waving his new Korean Bible. Was his wide smile due to a mood swing or a genuine work of the Holy Spirit? Time will tell.

Homeward bound in the rear seat of the bus, an Iranian lady I had previously met had a loud conversation with me as I was sitting near the front. During that conversation I received a call from the above-mentioned Korean gentleman. Coincidentally, the lady realising she had overshot her stop, shouted, "Stop, stop!"

The bus driver jammed on the brakes, catapulting the lady down the aisle. Landing in my lap she yelled, "OOOH!"

The Korean gentleman who overheard her, exclamation via the phone, delicately suggested, "Would you like me to ring back?" Later a Korean elder of a Presbyterian Church to whom I had referred my contact, called saying, "His conversion is real and genuine. He is returning to Korea to get involved in church work."

Testimony – Ji (Jimmy) Sung Yu (2007)

We got to know Ji Sung Yu when Matt Adams asked if he could bring his Korean friend round to our home one evening to discuss salvation. This event marked the beginning of our acquaintance with this young Korean man nick-named 'Jimmy' who came to Melbourne on a journey of discovery. Matt and his group, who had done most of the hard yards discipling Jimmy, came to the conclusion that he needed to hear the Gospel message with a fresh voice.

Jimmy was attending church and reading his Bible. His sincere, thoughtful, and intelligent questions indicated that he had burrowed unsuccessfully into the deeper issues of life. Matt and I responded with the aid of a Korean English Four Spiritual Laws brochure and many diagrams. Jimmy found some answers. About two hours later he concluded our prayer time with a simple but moving prayer for salvation and commitment of his life to Jesus. He enthusiastically expressed his deep desire that we pray for him.

Later, Jimmy at his baptism powerfully testified to his salvation by God's grace. He also asked prayer for a good church to attend in Korea and for Christian friends. Jimmy returned to Korea. His testimony given on the occasion of his baptism at an evening service in the NewHope Baptist Church, is reproduced herewith for your encouragement.

> "Hi, my name is Ji Sung, some people also call me Jimmy. I am here to tell you my story about how I became a Christian. I grew up in Korea, and my family doesn't follow any religion so I have had a chance to visit many different types of religion. First, when I was about seventeen years old, I met a Buddhist monk because one of my high school teachers is Buddhist. One day he took me and a few friends to the temple to study when we had exams. While we were staying there, we bowed to the Buddha every morning and had training for our mind. At that time, I thought 'this is really good' and I wanted to believe in Buddhism, but I realised that when I had a difficult problem, even though I tried hard, I couldn't solve it because it was beyond my ability. At that time, I often prayed to an unknown man in the sky, "Please bless me".
>
> Second, I also had a chance to meet someone who believes in Animism, this is ancestor worship. When I was nineteen years old, I was working on the street and suddenly someone asked me about my family. The question was 'Is there someone who died recently in your family?' Actually, my grandmother had died about one year before. Somehow, he knew that I didn't go to the funeral. I was feeling very bad about this. Surprisingly

he knew about my feeling. I couldn't believe it! Then he asked me to come to a temple so I followed him and as soon as I got there, he asked me for some money to prepare food for my dead grandmother. He said my grandmother's spirit couldn't go to heaven until I paid the money. So, I paid it because I really wanted her to go to heaven. I trusted him when he wanted me to keep my eyes closed as I bowed to the food. After that I felt happy as I thought my grandmother could go to heaven. A few months later I saw the news about people who believe in animism. They were arrested for ripping people off so I realised that I was also ripped off. I prayed again to the unknown man in the sky, 'Please bless me.'

Lastly, when I was twenty years old, I wanted to study Christianity. When I was in the army I went to church and read the bible but I didn't understand it even though I studied it. I felt comfortable when I was in the church so I went there every Sunday with no real purpose. One day I got baptised at the church in the army because those who got baptised had a celebration meal and I wanted more food. This baptism had no meaning to me at that time. I was baptised again a few months later for similar reasons but after finishing in the army I never went to church again. So, I didn't find any religion in Korea that made me want to put my trust in something or someone. I thought that I could rely on just myself.

When I came to Australia one and half years ago, I had no religion. I came to NewHope Church on my second day and met Matt and Kent who I have lived with since. We spent good times together and we also have a small group bible study once a week, but I didn't want to hear what they said about Jesus. My only concern was about how I can prove the words of Jesus in the bible were wrong. If I wanted to prove this, I had to study what was in the bible so I went to church every Sunday and to the ESL bible study and small group. I have learned about Christianity bit by bit from this.

Whenever I spent time with friends from the church, I was very happy because they were kind to me. They didn't want anything from me; they just showed their kindness and honesty. So, I asked them "What makes you like this?" They answered, "I am Christian", which made me think about what it means to be a Christian. One day I visited Bruce Kelly's place with Matt, as I really wanted to know more about what being a Christian means. We talked about it for a long time. It was a really important time for me because I finally understood what being a Christian meant.

I believe that Jesus never lied and all he said is true. He said that he is the Son of God, he died so that I could live and know the true God. I decided to follow Jesus. Since I made that decision my outlook on life has changed. In the past I was very concerned about my future, making money, family happiness, and job. Now, I trust that Jesus will look after those things and I am learning more about him and how to live every day. Now I want you to ask yourself something: Did Jesus lie to us? My answer is no. Now I know who the unknown man in the sky is, he is the God of the bible and of my life.

> *I want to say thank you to everyone in the ESL bible study, my small group and NewHope Church. I am returning to Korea next week; please pray for me to find a church and Christian friends who can help me learn more. I have enjoyed my time in Australia very much and I hope God blesses you. Thank you."*

Matt, referred to elsewhere in this book, effectively led a home group consisting mainly of students from Korea, China, Japan, Taiwan, and his Australian team leaders. Some members of the group were earnestly evaluating a relationship with the Saviour. Matt assisted my street ministry in several ways over time.

Visiting South Korea

Jan and I attended the 100th anniversary of the Korean Evangelical Holiness Church (KEHC) in Seoul, South Korea, in 2007. We caught our first daylight glimpse of the Republic of Korea (ROK) through our hotel bedroom window. Sixteen tall industrial cranes facilitated construction of multi-storey accommodation units opposite. Expensive boutique shops, flash European cars, industry, pedestrians and thick burning, stinging, choking smog provide a foretaste of our remaining journey.

In 1907 One Mission Society (OMS) missionaries first stood 'in front of them all' with the Gospel in a mission hall in downtown Seoul. No one knew the actual address of that building. A modern shopping complex covered the area. A coffee shop aptly named 'Angel in Us' was situated on a nearby corner site.

We were guests at an excellent OMS Centennial Celebration Banquet at 6pm in the Palace Hotel. Following congratulatory speeches, reference to the 100-year mission history and future vision, several OMS missionaries who had each given over twenty years of distinguished service, were honoured. The Koreans kept a tight schedule. They served a four-course meal to 300 people in record time. The chamber music and soloist were first class.

The next day we travelled to the 1988 Seoul Olympic Stadium for the Centennial Celebration. Hundreds of buses and thousands of cars were parked nearby. Our touring party members were each served a McDonald's hamburger (shades of Swanston Street) and a can of coca cola as we entered the stadium.

An estimated 100,000 people joined in praise to God for His faithfulness and prayed for His guidance for the church as it began its second century of ministry. Brightly colored national dress, banners, and a conversation buzz added to the excitement. Two big screens replayed the on-stage action. Hymn singing was accompanied by a 7,000-voice choir. Distinguished church leaders were recognised. Nine individuals, each of whom had led over 100 people to Christ this year, were acknowledged. Incredible! Over 900 new Christians swept into the Kingdom in one year (do I have an award-winning faith like them)? A martyred Pastor's wife received her husband's posthumous award. A magnificently presented drama on the raising of Lazarus gripped our attention. The evening concluded with the release of thousands of multi-colored balloons over the floodlight stadium, combined with a breath-taking display of fireworks. The backdrop was a huge cross. Overhead the moon shone, and the sky was clear. Some celebration! It was all focused on the resurrected Jesus, the only one worthy of praise.

At the Sunday morning service at the First Korean Evangelical Holiness Church (OMS planted) a full choir sang beautifully with little instrumental accompaniment. A lady, converted last week, testified to applause. Dave Graffenberger, an OMS missionary, preached from 2 Corinthians 5:15-21* on the characteristics of an ambassador. He pointed out the importance of telling Bible stories about Jesus Christ. Everyone prayed in unison. After the service our party was treated to a free lunch (four course banquet) in a local hotel, and each was presented with a gift-wrapped embroidered towel.

My hair shampoo was missing. So, I raided Jan's cosmetic bag and selected a bottle labeled hair shampoo. But the contents weren't working. Maybe it was the hard water. Later Jan said, "Bruce!!" My heart sank. I knew by the tone of her voice I was in big trouble. "Bruce!" She asserted, "I'm very cross with you. Now I'll have to buy some more face cleanser and you won't even lift a finger to help. How could you?" The atmosphere was decidedly frosty. I later double checked the bottle. It really was labeled 'Healthy Hair Revitalising Shampoo'. Husbands just can't win!

A large stone cairn at the entrance of a folk museum at Suwon was festooned with handwritten messages to the deity dwelling therein seeking protection from misfortune. Friendly Korean school girls wanted to practice their English. I used a handwritten four Spiritual Laws presentation. The British OMS Board Chairman, Rev Jim Faulkner, who became a devoted prayer supporter of our street ministry, said, "You have planted a seed in their minds."

Warren Hardig, the International Director of Men for Missions, the Layman's arm of OMS, added, "It is who we are in Christ that matters." His comment reminded me of Colossians 2:6: "As you therefore have received Christ Jesus the Lord, so walk in Him." In the evening we were treated to a traditional Korean meal at Korea House followed by a spectacular and colourful nine drum cultural dance presentation.

We visited the Seoul Theological University - 2,400 under-graduate students, 900 graduates, 60 professors, 300 part time lecturers serve the Korean Evangelical Holiness Church (KEHC). Our touring party was provided with lunch at the seminary. We moved on to the headquarters of KEHC. The Aussie contingent dined in the evening with the General Superintendent, who was presented with a clock mounted in Australian Red Gum.

At 5.30am we attended with some hundreds, at a prayer meeting at KEHC. Afterwards, we visited the Yoido Full Gospel Church, the world's largest church. Senior Pastor Yonggi Cho was preaching. Some 26,000 were in attendance and this was Wednesday morning! Their total membership was 700,000. We were taken on a short tour of the very impressive National Assembly (parliament) building of the Republic of Korea (ROK).

Later, we visited the Far East Broadcasting Company (FEBC) headquarters. I was astonished as I viewed a promotional video to see a clip of myself in a crowd scene. We spent time walking around the Seoul Foreign cemetery. On a tomb of a UK missionary was inscribed: 'I would rather die in China than be buried in Westminster Abbey.'

The closer we got to North Korea the more razor wire, guard posts, mine fields and tank traps we saw. Superhighways were converted to airstrips in minutes. The signage **'In front of them all'** mounted above the entrance to the United Nations Command Security Battalion at Panmunjom, reflected high level military preparedness in South Korea. The UN Forces provided logistical and security support to all UN personnel in the joint security area known as the Demilitarised Zone (DMZ) at Panmunjom. They thoroughly briefed us regarding dress code and behaviour. The slightest misinterpreted gesture could trigger an international incident, even violence. Our parameters were strict. Soldiers who stood face to face with North Korean guards were our tour guides at the DMZ. Watching UNC soldiers in their immaculate uniforms and armed North Korean guards in their drab brown clothing facing off about twenty metres apart with only the armistice line between, was a sobering experience. Greetings between South and North are never exchanged. Hands are never shaken. The atmosphere is brittle, ever hostile. We are carefully watched at all times through binoculars by North Korean guards. The term **'In front of them all'** describes well the UNC Security Forces, who prevent the powers of evil overtaking the forces of good.

On October 17, 1978, an infiltration tunnel from North Korea was discovered near Panmunjom. This tunnel (one of several) could deliver 30,000 armed troops, with heavy armament per hour under the 38th Parallel to an exit point just forty-four kilometres from Seoul. From this point the enemy could pin down the UNC troops at the DMZ, operate behind the supply lines, and race to Seoul in one hour. Jan and I investigated this tunnel. After shopping at Etaewan we enjoyed a steak at the Outback Restaurant suitably decorated with Aussie artifacts.

The signage 'In Front of Them All' mounted above the entrance to the UN village on the South Korean side of the Parallel was adopted as my slogan for street evangelism ministry and the title of this book. In front of them all with the armour of God, the belt of truth, the shield of faith, the breast plate of righteousness, shod with the Gospel of peace, the helmet of salvation, the sword of the Spirit and prayer. Imagine nine evangelists standing in front of them all in Swanston Street each leading one hundred people to Jesus! Is this too much of a stretch for our imaginations? I don't think it hurts to dream big. Do you? Join me 'In front of them all'.

Taking it to heart –

1. Identify some examples of reluctance to respond to the Gospel revealed in this chapter.
2. You may have experienced variations of these responses. What were they?'
3. How did you respond? How might you respond?

Bible References:

Exodus 23:20 – Behold, I send an angel before you to keep you in the way and to bring you into the place which I have prepared.

John 1:12 – Then Jesus spoke to them again, saying, I am the light of the world. He who follows Me shall not walk in darkness, but have the light of life.

1Corinthians 1:9-10 – God is faithful by whom you were called into the fellowship of His Son Jesus Christ our Lord. Now I plead with you, brethren, by the name of our Lord Jesus Christ, that you all speak the same thing, and that there be no divisions among you, but that you may be perfectly joined together in the same mind and in the same judgement.

Hebrews 12:1 – Therefore we also, since we are surrounded by so great a cloud of witnesses, let us lay aside every weight, and the sin that so easily ensnares us, and let us run with endurance the race that is set before us.

Revelation 3:20 – Behold, I stand at the door and knock. If anyone hears my voice and opens the door, I will come into him and dine with him and he with me.

BQ – What is the most important question in all the world for you?

TPTL NT – The Pocket Testament League New Testament.

Chapter 19

Characters Encountered in McDonalds and Hungry Jacks

A significant slice of the evangelical pie existed in both McDonalds and Hungry Jacks, located side by side in Swanston Street in the Melbourne CBD. These venues contained a kaleidoscope of multi-cultural patronage on which many years of outreach activity was focused. With few exceptions the following contacts listened to my testimony/BQ* and accepted literature at first contact.

McDonalds Well

I departed Bourke Street Mall and head for Flinders Street railway station homeward bound. The Lord Jesus never seemed short of contacts (John 4:7*) but I have had none for over an hour. I must needs go via Swanston Street. McDonald's Well is there (John 4:6*). Being wearied and thirsty from much walking I entered and occupied one lone vacant seat. Customers are now in easy reach. Lord, help me share the water that springs into everlasting life (John 4:14*) with lost and desperately needy people.

Some McDonalds Encounters

An over-weight Asian student tucked into his Big Mac, chips, and Coke with obvious relish. To my surprise, he spoke flawless English with an Aussie accent.

A fifty-two-year-old Tasmanian derelict dressed in thongs, tattered blue jeans, and a flimsy coat looked seventy-two. He froze at night sleeping on concrete streets. His long straggly brown hair was unwashed. His unblinking watery blue eyes bored coldly into mine as I asked him, "What's the worst mistake you've ever made?" That was close to being the dumbest question, I ever asked. It triggered loud diatribe fixated on his catastrophic family background.

"Can I say something confidential, sir?" he began, "I should have killed my parents. I wish I'd never been born." He declined the offer of literature.

Whilst sharing with Shelly, a visitor from Sacramento USA, a nearby female said, "I've been listening to your conversation. I'm a Christian too. My life is simple, and I've never broken the law. I'm thirty-four years old, suffer from chronic fatigue and still looking for my true love."

A waitress contributed, "Our priest was a paedophile." Neither she or her family now attend any church.

An eighty-two-years old lady indignantly rejected my offer of literature saying, "Oh! You're not one of them, are you?"

I replied with affected indignation, "What do you mean 'one of them'?"

She replied, "They hand out religious papers and ram religion down your throat. I'm an atheist. I don't believe a good God would let little children suffer."

I broke in saying, "You can't blame God for that. Christ offers a better life."

She interrupted, "To tell you the truth, I am under stress. My husband had a bad stroke. We've just put him in a home. He asked me what future we have?"

I replied to her with the words of the old hymn, "What a friend we have in Jesus, all our sins and griefs to bear. What a privilege to carry everything to God in prayer."

She laughed and said, "You got that one in, but you still haven't converted me."

An eighty-five-year older person, with whom I have previously shared, ordered an ice-cream. My purchase of an apple pie for $1 entitled me to a free senior's coffee. The old man ate my pie. I drank my coffee. Everybody was happy. A joyful lady with five children sitting opposite said to the old man, "Excuse me, do you know God?"

He replied, "My conscience guides me."

She said to him, "My father was a sly grog merchant in Kensington. We were always in trouble with Police. I got into alcohol and drugs, but God saved me. Now I am happily married and paying off my mortgage. You have broken God's law, you'll be judged. Your only hope is Jesus Christ." She departed.

The old man commented, "She's wound up, isn't she?"

Krip, from Thailand, had some knowledge of Christianity and seemed fairly westernised but suspiciously said, "My English is no good."

I said, "Practice on me?"

He asked, "What do you do?"

I explained, "For twenty-five years I was a farmer, looking after sheep." We discussed sheep and shepherds. I said, "I am an under-shepherd and quoted the Good Shepherd Psalm 23. From this he saw himself as a sheep with only two roads to travel, two masters to serve, and two destinies to reach. He wavered on the brink of a decision, but finally asked, "Is there a middle road?"

A handsome and articulate American ex-marine veteran, who served in Iraq, related details of his Post Traumatic Distress Disorder (PTDD). His physical and emotional disillusionment manifested obviously. At the end of an hour-long conversation, he said, "Thanks for listening."

Joe, a year eleven student from Newcastle NSW on a school excursion, openly discussed his hopes and dreams. Three schoolgirls who replaced Joe, were intrigued by my testimony. A Yugoslavian Orthodox nurse with a child asked, "What do you do?"

I replied, "I am a retired Police Officer."

She said, "What do you know! My partner is a Police Officer." Regarding my testimony, she asked, "How does that translate to me?"

I explained to her, "If you were killed in a car accident today, and God said, 'Why should I let you into my Kingdom?' What would you say'?"

She said, "That's a hard question. I don't know. It's strange that we met today. It's a pity there aren't more like you. I am going to St Paul's Cathedral to pray."

A tall, slim, blonde, blue-eyed sixteen-year-old smiled and said, "Do you mind if I sit with you?" She had caught the early train in remote Victoria for an appointment in Melbourne with a view to launching into a modelling career. She stated, "I never expected to hear a testimony in Melbourne. Your conversation means a lot to me."

I replied, "It's a rough world out there."

She said, "Yes! It's frightening." She seemed too young and vulnerable to embark on such a life journey.

A blonde yelled expletives down her mobile phone. She sought approbation from nearby compatriots who walked on café seats and threw empty drink containers. Another sported a purple Mohawk. All wore black. They shouted, swore, and slapped each other. They declined literature with scornful laughter.

The Toe Rags gravitated to the Flinders Street railway station steps. Discarded newspapers waft back and forth in the breeze on the steps and adjacent footpath. I could clean this mess up in ten minutes, but the back doesn't bend as far now. The ground looks further away. Papers seem stuck to the footpath and a man in a wheelchair complained, "You are blocking my way."

A handsome young Asian, who observed these events said, "You ought to write a book. I go to Bible Study Fellowship (BSF)."

Another male gratefully said, "Thanks, but you don't need to do this! It's my responsibility." Peak hour pedestrians shuffled expressionless through the debris. The Toe Rags sat on the railway station steps like parrots on a branch still yelling, swearing, and laughing. Sternly glaring Police Officers prompted the Toe Rags to beat a hasty retreat. They will seek opportunities to create mayhem elsewhere, but the cultured young Asian BSF'er lifted my spirits.

A Vietnamese from Springvale, said, "I am not happy. I am forty years old. I have been in Australia twelve years. I am not married. I have no family and just been retrenched. Who will look after me when I get old?" I shared a Gospel presentation, and offered Vietnamese tracts, one of which contained a picture of a lion lying with a lamb. He said, "Lions eat lambs, how do you explain cruelty?" I used the diagram to explain the Cross. He said, "I have turned away from Buddhism. How do I become a Christian?"

I explained with the use of four spiritual laws diagrams i.e., the self-controlled life and Christ controlled life, and said, "What stops you from inviting Jesus to take control of your life right now?" But he declined a Vietnamese Bible or to provide contact details.

An older man had just arrived from Sydney. In response to my testimony, he replied, "My life has been a series of disasters, but I believe in a higher force." I explained the Crucifixion and Resurrection but he couldn't or wouldn't bow the knee to Jesus. I asked him, "How will you answer God when He says, 'Why should I let you into my Kingdom'?" He didn't know." A melee with accompanying foul language erupted with startling swiftness amongst pedestrians on the footpath outside McDonalds. Patrons evacuated the shop as if by magic. The grim-faced manager strode purposefully out to take control. An older lady invited me to sit with her. I suspected she was the one who knocked off my notebook recently. I walked upstairs, but she followed. I said, none too graciously, "Yeah, go on."

She said, "I'm upset. I've had a death in my family."

I asked, "Who?"

She said, "My mother died four years ago. My father died fifteen years ago. You wouldn't have some coins for a fag, would you?"

A rolled-up newspaper was unceremoniously thrust into my hand. I was somewhat taken aback. A male person parked himself on the seat opposite. This Filipino deaf mute pointed to articles, headlines, and photographs in the newspaper, then wrote upside-down adjacent to the article a related keyword for my benefit. By combining his key word with the article, I got the gist of his comment, then wrote my answer upside down for his benefit. This system avoided rotating the paper after each word. We progressed slowly through some articles. Three pages were covered with upside down squiggles. With his face wreathed in smiles we parted with a firm handshake. I am surprised (I shouldn't be) by the interesting people God brings across my path.

A young Chinese couple on annual holidays purchased food. It was no accident they travelled from Singapore and I from Doncaster, and our lives intersected at McDonalds. My heart warmed to them. They accepted testimony and literature. I silently prayed God would give them the Living Water, but the gentleman said, "I try to outweigh the bad with the good." I explained the role of faith and trust in the risen Christ alone and suggested they find a good church in Singapore. I thanked them for an hour of their time. What a joy to share Christ Jesus with such beautiful people. "I plant the seed, Apollos waters, but God makes it grow" (1 Corinthians 3:6*).

A young ballet dancer from Pittsburgh, Pennsylvania USA, listened to my testimony. He said, "I've given up church." He made a phone call and demanded, "Mother, have you been praying for me in the last twenty-four hours?" He handed the phone to me.

A tearful female American voice said, "Today, I prayed the Lord would lead my son into contact with a mature Christian. He is all mixed up. I do appreciate you talking with him. Thank you!"

He exclaimed, "I needed this talk."

A beauty school student from Narre Warren (Vic) sat with me. The tract unleashed a torrent of excited questions re church denominations and activities. She declined my offer to help find a church.

A Lebanese Sunni Muslim student of accounting said, "I have something to ask you." Then followed a long loud aggressive assault on my belief with the usual Islamic objections to the Christian faith. Among other things, he exclaimed, "Forget this Jesus bit. Just believe in God, you'd make an excellent Muslim. The Koran is a beautiful book. You should read it."

I replied, "If you want to know about Islam, don't ask Muslims, read the Koran. If you want to know about Christians, don't ask Christians, read the Bible." I read him several Biblical scriptures, but he recycled his arguments. I continued saying, "We've been through all this several times. We are getting nowhere." His fundamental, extremist Islamic tendencies were a tad frightening.

CHARACTERS ENCOUNTERED IN MCDONALDS AND HUNGRY JACKS

As I shared with an Asian male, an annoyed patron kicked the mop from a cleaner's hand and spat out, "@&%$!!!! Idiot" A derelict nearby sneezed volcanically twice. A pirouetting pink tutu, with pink stockings, matching butterfly wings appeared. A middle-aged derelict loudly said to another, "All I want is to marry and settle down."

A mother yelled, "If you kids don't behave, I'll take you down to the Police Station."

An aged lady with heavy accent called, "Free! Free!" as she handed out booklets written by Ellen G White.

"I've been off the drink for ages," said an Aboriginal.

An older female sitting opposite said, "You bailed them up well. It has been interesting. "Lord" I prayed, "I followed you into this darkness. Help me spread the light."

An Irishman cooling off in MacDonalds, had just finished cleaning outside windows on the 26th floor of a nearby city building. He said, "Where do you come from?"

I remarked, "Echuca."

He replied, "How interesting, That's on the Murray River. I want to swim in the Murray."

I said, "Watch out for toe cutters."

He asked, "What are toe cutters?"

I explained, "Giant freshwater crayfish that nip your toes off and eat them."

He said, "You are kidding."

I told him, "You have them in Ireland."

He asked, "We do? What are they called?"

I answered , "Leprechauns." He laughed.

An elderly aristocratic male from Townsville QLD, had watched Carlton Football Club trounce his beloved Collingwood. He asserted, "I'm $$##!! unhappy!"

To this feisty retired engineer, I said "I spent my first twenty-five years on a farm looking after sheep." He interjected with lurid details of his early experience on an Irish sheep farm. I continued to say, "I spent my second twenty-five years in the Police Department." He passed some unsavoury anti-police comments. I then told him, "I spent my third fifteen years in the church." He yelled "Woe! That's enough! I am OK with farms. I can cope with crooked cops but not the ???!!!*** church!"

I asked him, "What turned you against the church?" He muttered something about boys' homes and paedophile priests. I left him to it.

A lady in answer to the BQ* asked, "How can I get back to Mauritius?" But a protective wall of good works shielded her against Gospel truth. She said, "My father tells me I should go to church, but I tell him to back off. It's not right that people ram religion down my throat."

Sylvain, from Mauritius approached and asked, "Excuse me! Are you a Christian?"

I said, "Yes!"

He replied, "You spoke to me when I worked in MacDonalds three years ago and gave me a booklet (I don't recall)."

I asked him, "What did you think?"

He replied, "I've been to several churches, including the Jehovah's Witnesses, but I like the Seventh Day Adventists best."

An Indian student who was reading a 'New Believers' New Testament said, "Can I buy you a coffee?"

I asked him, "Are you a Christian?"

He said "Yes."

I uttered, "Tell me your story."

"I was a radical Hindu student in Calcutta," he recollected. "My father taught me to be that way. My girlfriend invited me to an Alpha Bible Study. I went along for her sake. After a couple of weeks, I got interested. I attended the Alpha camp and God touched me. I haven't told my parents yet."

A Kiwi National told me, "I'm a Christian feeling a bit down." I explained, "An older Christian told me, 'Great faith is the product of great fights. Great testimonies are the outcome of great tests; Great triumphs only come out of great trials'."

The Kiwi replied, "Thank you! I am glad I met you."

A depressed lady with a Catholic background had just arrived from Adelaide, having recently experienced a broken relationship, and the death of her beloved father, she was exploring the possibility of life anew in Melbourne. She returned to Adelaide to sort out her affairs. That evening, the following text message arrived 'Hello Bruce, S. here from today. It was very lovely to have that encounter with you. I've been having a very bad time recently and your note really touched me. Thankyou!'

A delightful young Ukrainian couple was catching the plane to their home in Kiev at 8pm that night. They had worked on a Warrnambool dairy farm for the previous twelve months. I declared, "Things are not good in your homeland."

He responded, "Our president is a lunatic. If they don't reach agreement this week." He fired an imaginary rifle, saying "Pop! Pop! Pop! There will be bloodshed." They were constrained to return to their families but reluctant to leave our shores. What a dilemma? We discussed their relationship with God and each other, their future hopes, and dreams. I encouraged them to seek a Christian fellowship on their return and promised to pray for them. I hope and pray they will be safe.

The following email from another Ukrainian contact regarding armed conflict in his country was received. He said, "War has begun. As protesters headed towards houses of parliament today, police started shooting, of course there were also people in the crowd stirring up trouble. The police/army have now also attacked the peaceful protesters on Independence Square behind the barricades. Police asked women and children to leave and will begin forcing the men into prison. Seven people died today and many, many, wounded. We are watching on our computers as chaos unfolds. Please! Please! Pray for Ukraine. They are fighting for freedom and losing their lives."

Encounters in Hungry Jacks

Chao, an attractive master's graduand in accountancy, was returning to China in five days. She said, "I am conflicted between returning to live in China with friends and family, or settling in Australia."

I told her, "Your greatest question is what will you do with Jesus Christ!" She said "Thanks! You have helped a lot."

Five young people – Jack, Jason, Anita, Doris, and Dominic were undergoing a training course for their employment at OK Tedi mines in PNG. All spoke good English. All had Christian backgrounds. Dominic said, "We are exposed to every aspect of life in Melbourne – good and bad. We must be careful. Our meeting with you today is a Godsend. Please pray for us now?" It was a delight to do so as we sat with heads bowed. Dominic continued and said, "There's another six of us. Could the ten of us meet sometime?" It never happened.

An extrovert Kenyan student of architecture was sketching St Paul's Cathedral. She said, "Why are you speaking to me?"

I answered, "I am a Christian. I share the good news of Jesus Christ."

She smiled. "I am a 'black' born-again Christian. What do you think of that?" I am gladdened and said so. "How old are you?" she queried. I told her. She said, "You don't look that old."

Jeff, from USA, sat next to me.

He asked, "How can you say Christianity is right and all others are wrong? How can you prove scriptures are not corrupted?"

A drama unfolded before my eyes. Two young people entered. He deposited his large corpulent frame on a seat and with head in hands sobbed at the table. His good looking but diminutive female companion appeared composed, and respectable. Intense conversation between them occurred. The irrational male produced a quantity of pills. His courageous, fearless companion tried to wrestle them off him, but he vigorously resisted and swallowed. A tall, older, unkempt male appeared and gruffly spoke to the young male. The female dumped her companion and walked. Her obese companion pathetically staggered after her like a wounded dog. I prayed, "Lord Jesus, send forth your angels, and gather out of his life all things that offend." The older derelict sidled up close and foghorn like, shouted, "Excuse me sir! I told that bum to take responsibility for his own problems." Like an exploding pressure cooker, Mr. Foghorn regurgitated the same dysfunctional family background stuff as when we met in McDonald's years before.

A twenty-one-year-old Aboriginal Torres Strait Islander lass now living in Ocean Grove said, "I made a mistake with my diary. I should have been here tomorrow. I thought I wasted my time but now I know we were meant to meet. I've been thinking lately I should go to church, but I don't know where to start. You are the second person who has spoken to me about the Bible recently, my grandfather was a Godly man in the Anglican Church.

Three noisy, hefty young Middle Eastern males approached. One sat directly opposite, one close alongside, the other hovered above me. They wore black uniforms, bullet proof vests, forage caps and silver badges. I felt cornered. In response perhaps to my expression of compressed stress one explained, "We are here to protect Australia from terrorists." He extracted a silver cross on a chain from his neck and said, "But we don't do it with bombs, guns and knives, we do it with prayer and the Word of God." Whew!! These muscular products of Syrian Christian refugees are on their muck-up graduation day from a Christian college in the suburbs.

Foko Tupou from the Cook Islands, now living in Broadmeadows, answered the BQ* and said, "I think God sent you to get me back on track." She appreciated my ministry and a referral to another church.

A waiter said to me, "You gave me a booklet twelve months ago (I had no recollection). I never had money problems, but the last two years have been the hardest of my life. I have no family here and now I have to earn my living. I've been reading your booklet, and God helped me. I turned away from religion but now I have come back."

I asked, "Are you sure who this God is?"

He said "No!" and read John 8:12 aloud and said, "That's good." I told him, "Read a section from this booklet each day and when you come to a part you understand 'follow'."

An Australianised Chinese businessman sat with me. After some conversation including reference to the fact that his mother attended church in China, I asked him, "If you died tonight, and God said why should I let you into my kingdom, what would you say?"

He replied, "I would tell Him I am a good man. I do good things. That's what I'd tell Him." We examined his life in the light of the Ten Commandments.

Whilst reading a newspaper with an open Bible on the table beside me, a man asked, "Is that a New Testament?"

I answered, "Yes" and read aloud the passage on suffering as a Christian from 1 Peter 4:1*.

He said, "I go along with that. I am a Jew. We all spring from the same stock. If we have good attitudes, do acts of kindness, and keep the Commandments God will accept us."

I explained, "The Commandments say, 'Do not commit murder', but Jesus said, 'If you are angry with someone you have murdered him in your heart.' Have you ever been angry?"

He said, "Yes."

I said, "By that criteria you have fallen short of God's glory and in danger of judgement."

He replied, "Jesus was a good man, closely connected to God, but the Saviour is still to come."

I continued, "I was at the Wailing Wall in Jerusalem a few years ago, and a devout Jew was reading the Torah and praying. I asked him, 'What are you reading?' He replied, 'The story of Abraham offering his son as a sacrifice (Genesis 22:13).' I said to him, 'Explain the significance of the ram caught by its horns in the thicket.' He looked it up but said, 'I don't know. I'll check it out.' I explained, 'That verse foreshadows the death of Jesus on the Cross as the spotless Lamb of God who takes away the sin of the world'." The explanation to my Hungry Jacks contact fell on deaf ears.

At another table a derelict complained of loneliness, injustice, and a raft of terrible experiences. I said, "What would it take to make you admit you have stuffed up; that you are a sinner and need to accept Christ as Saviour?"

He said to me, "I have never sinned. I have never looked lustfully at a girl, and I've never been angry at anyone."

I declared, "I've only ever known two people to make this claim. One is you. The other is Jesus Christ."

Irish Mick was in town for the Jim Stynes' (famous AFL footballer from Ireland) funeral service. Mick was visibly shaking from the effect of diabetes and had to eat urgently. Mick, who knew Jim personally, had lived in Australia for thirty years. He had replacement heart valves and suffered two strokes. He was pre-occupied with Catholic Church rituals and the higher power which delivered him from alcoholism, but did not know Jesus. He accepted a TPTL NT*. I drew his attention to the plan of salvation in the back thereof. He said, "You are the first person who ever told me these things. Thank you!"

Paddy tapped my shoulder. His Gospel of John was clearly visible in his pocket. He was up to John 9:5*. We adjourned for coffee. He said, "I'd sooner read this (the Gospel) than watch TV or talk rugby." He accepted a TPTL NT* and exclaimed, "That'll keep me going for a while."

Across the way sat a married couple from Uulam Bator in Mongolia. She was studying for a Master's in Education Administration. Theirs was a nomadic country background and understood as I shared Psalm 23. They accepted a gift voucher for Hungry Jacks.

An Asian male said, "I am in trouble. I got hurt in a church in Brisbane." He had donated big sums of cash to this church but was not born-again. He gambled away his remaining resources on the stock market. His Buddhist wife and mother-in-law turned against him. He walked away from his Brisbane home this morning with no intention of returning. This astonished man said, "I can't believe I walked into Hungry Jacks today and met another Christian." He listened to a Gospel presentation using the plan at the back of a John's Gospel. He prayed the sinner's prayer and acting on the combined counsel of the three Christians then present, returned to his family in Brisbane.

Jia, a Chinese businessman asked, "Where do I find happiness?" A Gospel presentation followed. He replied, "You have been very helpful, but where do I find a church in China to help me understand?"

A young Chinese student told me, "I'm a Christian. I often talk with friends about sharing Christ, but I'm no good at it. Do you have any advice?"

I asked, "Do you have a big vision for God's work in the world?"

He replied, "Yes."

I answered, "Select one tiny facet of that vision and pursue it with relentless intensity. God will develop it into a successful ministry." He accepted Christmas literature.

Two vibrant Asian Christian ladies, one, a Kachin refugee from Burma and the other, a Chinese from Hong Kong shared testimonies, discussions about Burma and Buddhism and we prayed together.

To my surprise, Big Foot, the Tasmanian derelict who I'd previously met, waved, and smiled. I quickly sat beside a South Korean tourist who accepted Korean literature, but Big Foot moved in anyway. He loudly interrupted. The Korean retreated. I asked Big Foot, "Feeling better today?"

He answered "Yes. What did you do for a crust?"

I said, "I was a Police Officer." Instead of scaring him off, it sent him into orbit.

He rasped, "Can I say something sir, no disrespect intended, police are the laziest, most bent, useless bunch of ???!!!****%%% I ever seen. By the way, you wouldn't have a few bob to spare, would you?"

I said "No!"

"Just thought I'd ask", he added.

The following edited extracts of an email received from a young friend, who said among other things, 'A man with a strong smell of alcohol on his breath in the Bourke Mall asked for money to buy food. He and his partner are street people. There was another friend on crutches with them. We bought them six whopper juniors at Hungry Jacks. They eagerly accepted three bibles. One flipped through the pages and did not look up until we said goodbye.' Well done guys!

The wheelchair evangelist said, "You challenged me twelve months ago to evangelise in Swanston Street, since then I've been coming here three or four times a week." The evangelist was placing a thoughtfully arranged Christian literature presentation in a phone box in Flinders Street. What a marvelous ministry for a physically limited man. God bless him! He is a Bible Study Fellowship attendee, the organisation in which Jan is currently involved.

Conclusion:

A blind man taps his way through pedestrian traffic in Swanston Street. His piercing tortured cries captured the attention of McDonald's staff who led him to a seat and provided him with free coffee. To blind Bartimaeus sitting by the wayside Jesus said in effect, "What is your most important question?" "Lord!" he pleads, "That I might receive my sight." His sight was immediately restored.

Our city is filled with spiritually blinded minds, souls, and spirits. Paul described their condition in 2 Corinthians 4:3-4 – "But if our Gospel be hid, it is hidden to them that are lost; whose eyes the god of this world has blinded, lest the light of the glorious Gospel of Jesus Christ, who is the image of God, should shine unto them." Acts 26:18 says, "Lord! Open their eyes, turn them from darkness to light and from the power of Satan to God."

"A woman of Samaria came to draw water......Jesus said (to her) 'Whoever drinks of this water will thirst again, but whoever drinks of the water that I shall give him will never thirst but will become in him a fountain of living water springing up into everlasting life'" (John 4:7). Jesus opened the woman's eyes to spiritual truth. Her Biblical illiteracy reflected a continuing matter for serious consideration by evangelical churches today. Luke, inspired by the Holy Spirit, recorded the fact that the Christian church, fresh from Pentecost, devoted itself to four things: 'Apostolic teaching, fellowship, breaking of bread and prayer' (Acts 2:42). Apostolic doctrine played a major role in the explosive growth of the New Testament Church following Pentecost. They are a continuing vital ingredient for the health and strength of the current community of faith.

The Psalmist said, "O Lord, our Lord, how excellent is your name in all the earth, who have set Your glory above the heavens! Out of the mouth of babes and nursing infants you have ordained strength, because of your enemies, that You may silence the enemy and the avenger" (Psalm 8:1-2).

Do not be afraid to get busy for the Lord. Multitudes are perishing all round us. If we don't reach them, anti-Christian sectarian groups and individuals are poised to pounce. Evangelism glorifies God. Worship occurs each time believers share their testimony. Testimonies are heartbeats of the Christian church.

The male toilet door in McDonalds, Swanston Street, carried a sign saying 'Unavailable, use Disabled Toilet'. A female voice from within the disabled toilet yelled, "Busy, won't be long." An impatient Asian male entered the adjacent female toilet. A startled female beat a hasty retreat. The disabled toilet door swung open. The female said, "Sorry I was doing a number two. It takes me twenty minutes. It's a bit dirty in there." This ignominious announcement signalled the conclusion to some twenty years of ministry in the CBD and pointed to a local outreach in the street where we live and in the vicinity of our church in East Ringwood.

Taking it to heart

1. Name some cultural and religious activities you might interact with in your locality.
2. How would you shape your testimony to gently counteract other belief systems?
3. Share your testimony with other Christians.

References:

John 4:6-7 – Now Jacob's well was there. Jesus therefore, being wearied from His journey, sat thus by the well. A woman of Samaria came to draw water. Jesus said to her, "Give me a drink."

John 4:14 – Whoever drinks of the water that I shall give him will never thirst. But the water that I shall give him will become in him a fountain of water springing up into everlasting life.

John 9:5 – As long as I am in the world, I am the light of the world.

1 Corinthians 3:6 – I planted. Apollos watered, but God gave the increase.

1 Peter 4:1 – Therefore since Christ suffered for us in the flesh, arm yourselves also with the same mind, for He who has suffered in the flesh has ceased from sin.

TPTL NT – The Pocket Testament League New Testament.

BQ – Big Question – What is the most important question in all the world for you?

Chapter 20

Interactions With Muslims

A recent TV documentary featured a refugee who became a champion rugby player. He openly and unashamedly attested to his Muslim beliefs on this program. So sincere was his presentation that for a moment, I thought I was watching a devout evangelical Christian speaker in action. Religionists, atheists, cultists, humanists, pantheists, spiritists stalk the streets of our country. Their representatives are gifted, zealous, earnest, and committed to deceiving even the elect.

In many countries, Christians are shunned, disowned, turned over to authorities, or killed, when testifying to family members and friends in the hope of leading them to Christ. However, we should not allow such challenges to impede our God-given ministry of sharing the Gospel. As a former Anglican Bishop put it: "Problems associated with ministry, are not barriers to ministry, they are the ministry."

Fear, prejudice, and suspicion are factors preventing Christians from evangelising Muslims, but as we genuinely seek to share Jesus, God creates within us a longing to impart to our contact, not only the Gospel but our own lives (1 Thessalonians 2:8*). God's love, grace, and mercy filtering through us differentiates the Gospel from all other religions. Contacts with hardened Muslims, angry sect members, and antagonistic critics weighed on my mind through the night. Jan reminded me of Psalm 43:5: "Why are you cast down O my soul and why are you disquieted within me? Hope in God!"

Dissimulation

To a Tanzanian I said, "What is the religion of your country?" He replied, "Islam and Christianity. Muslims and Christians are cooperating beautifully in my country."

A Quranic doctrine called 'dissimulation' allows Muslims to distort or conceal truth when dealing with non-Muslims.

Challenging Discussions

A Sudanese 'Sunni' Muslim threw some light on the well-known Islamic division between Sunni and Shiite Muslims. He said, "Ali, Muhammad's son-in-law, the fourth Caliph of Islam, was assassinated (as were others) in 661AD. His death established a great divide within Islam, which has never been reconciled. Sunnis are the major group within Islam. As the accusative question, 'Why so many different churches?' was fired at me by Muslims on several occasions, the above information was handy return fire.

The facial expressions and comments of a good-looking young male who invited me to sit with him, caused me to think he may be slightly retarded. Interspersed through his unrelated questions were comments like, "I am Turkish. I am Muslim. I was in jail for ten years. My girlfriend died of drugs. There is something about you. Are you a policeman?" The Lord kept me focused, but when I suggested he invite Jesus into his heart, he angrily shouted, "I would never do that!"

I said, "Would you like Christian literature?"

He angrily replied, "I would only throw it in the garbage." His agitated bodily jerkiness and wild look engendered insecurity. He said, "I've been to church and the mosque. They didn't help me." Surprisingly his imbecilic façade suddenly faded. Gone was the idiotic smile. The gaze was firm and steady. He chatted amicably and sensibly as we strolled towards Flinders Street railway station. He declared, "I don't know your name and you don't know mine."

I replied, "I think it best we keep it that way, don't you?" Mostly I can spot guys like this and avoid them, but this one bamboozled me.

Mansour, a Pakistani, kept his appointment. He produced his John's Gospel and the Urdu tract and said, "I will not change my religion, and do not expect to change yours, but I hope Christians and Muslims could hold forums to discuss the 'catastrophic' future our children face. I have made my points. Do you want to make yours?"

I said to him, "Can we meet next Monday?" On Monday he allowed me to put my case regarding the identity of Jesus, the Holy Spirit, eternal life, judgement etc. and requested another meeting on Thursday. On Thursday, Mansour appeared for our third meeting. As agreed, he spoke and I responded.

At our last meeting, Mansour asserted that the Quran is 100% accurate - thus inferring the Bible is corrupted. I had prayed in the small hours for a response especially for Mansour. When he raised his issue, I was ready. I suggested, "To claim the Bible is corrupt is like a drowning man in a stormy sea clutching at a straw." I read the story of Peter's rescue by Jesus from the stormy sea (Matthew 14:22-32). I further said "Jesus is no straw man. He is the great 'I AM' of the universe. He is the 'I AM' before Abraham was.

Jesus said, 'I AM' the door, 'I AM' the way, the truth, the life, the resurrection.' He is still the great 'I AM' of the universe who waits to pick you up in the storms of your life'." Mansour was impressed.

As usual, Mansour made notes of our conversation and showed me each entry to make sure he's got it right. He said, "Couldn't we just apologise to Allah and get on with life?"

I answered, "But that does not deal with your sin problem. God records every sin you commit and nothing you can do will erase them. Only faith in the power of the shed blood of Jesus will wipe them off your slate and save you from judgement."

He replied, "I think I understand now that the Jesus of the Quran and the Jesus of the Bible are different. I also understand you won't change to Islam, and I won't change to Christianity, but can we keep the phone lines open?"

I said, "It is not my business to make you a Christian or criticise the Quran but I am deeply concerned about the eternal destiny of your soul. I do not want you to spend eternity in everlasting torment."

An ageing, grey-headed Indian raised the usual Islamic objections to Christianity. I related one of Stuart Robinson's references to dreams and visions from his book 'Mosques and Miracles'. Most Muslims relate to dreams and visions. He seized my hand saying, "I'm a fortune teller. I will read your palm."

I exclaimed, "I'm a Christian, I cannot allow that."

Unfazed, he went on to say, "I also read faces. You have extra sensory perception and a sixth sense. You have great power to help the poor. You are a good man."

I explained, "My only power is from the Holy Spirit."

An elderly Sunnite Turk invited himself to my table and declared, "My father was a professor in an Islamic university. I learned the Quran (Koran) by heart. My parents taught me that anyone who is five years older deserves to be called Mister and their views must be respected." The context of his comments indicated an expectation of respect and deference to his senior position from me his junior. He thereupon launched into a loud one-eyed interpretation of Quranic principles from the Sunnite Muslim perspective. It quickly became apparent that he hated both Shiite Muslims and Christians. He responded with vehemence and vitriol to my testimony. When challenged he angrily growled, "You'll suffer in Hell."

An English-speaking Spanish 'Christian' convert to fundamentalistic Islam scornfully challenged the deity of Jesus, the Holy Spirit, salvation, and Biblical purity. I kept hitting the ball back in his court. He said with mock astonishment "You mean to say you believe a holy and pure God would come down to filth of this world to save me?"

I replied, "You mean to say you would turn your back on a just, holy, righteous, gracious, and loving God who came down to the mud, slime and filth of your world to rescue you from punishment for your sin, and promise you an eternity in Paradise in favor of someone who offers nothing. How stupid is that?"

He said, "You are mistaken, but you are too strong. I cannot argue with you." He accepted a John's Gospel.

An Eritrean Islamic intellect vigorously challenged my understanding of certain Bible doctrines. His carnal mind was not subject to the law of God neither could it be (Romans 8:7). Making Christ the hope of glory (Colossians 1:21*) known rather than challenging his intellect, might have pricked his conscience. I could have asked, "Do you consider yourself a good person? Have you been angry with someone? Have you lusted at a female? Have you coveted someone's property?" If he realised he offended God in these ways, and that eternal punishment awaited him, he may have asked forgiveness of God who is rich in mercy. It may take time, prayer, and patience for this simple Biblical model of evangelism to break through. I am learning valuable lessons on Islamic evangelism.

Another Muslim Pakistani I previously met, openly criticised Islam. I said to him, "Make a list of sayings of Muhammad and Jesus and compare them."

He maintained, "There again I am in trouble because Sunni Muslims and the Shiite Muslims use different books."

I explained to him, "Muslims have been murdering and torturing each other ever since Islam began."

He replied, "I know. I have this problem with Islam also. I can't answer it." He accepted literature.

A Pakistani said, "Muhammad had eleven wives. Why should he consummate marriage with a little girl?" Many Muslims are too frightened to ask these questions. He said, "Abu Bakr the first caliph after Muhammad, gave his six-year-old daughter Ayisha to Muhammad who consummated marriage with her when she was nine years old. Muhammad was fifty-three at the time. In addition to his eleven wives, he had access to twenty-three female slaves as listed by name in Islamic history. (Jesus and Muhammad - Pages 176 and 182 - by Mark A Gabriel, PhD, once a devout highly qualified Muslim scholar from Egypt but now a practicing Christian).

A Mauritian on crutches listened to my testimony. His estranged Muslim wife and two kids lived in London. He responded through the intellect saying, "Why Christianity? Why not Islam? What about 9/11, the Tsunami, the bombings? Basically, I'm a good bloke. I don't need religion!"

Getting nowhere with this approach, I switched to his conscience saying, "Have you ever told a lie?"

He answered, "Yes."

I asked, "Have you ever looked at a female with lust?"

"Yes."

"Have you ever been angry with anyone?"

"Yes."

I said to him, "You have just admitted being a lying, murdering adulterer. You are in danger of Hell." He was wounded. It showed in his eyes. He trembled visibly. I continued, "But God is rich in mercy and compassion and provides a way of escape through faith in Christ. He offers full pardon for your sin and the free gift of eternal life."

He stated, "I will give Jesus a go." But at that critical moment his girlfriend gave him a mobile phone blast due to him being overdue for their appointment. He quickly hobbled off in a state of acute anxiety waving goodbye with a Bill Newman tract and a Gospel of John firmly clutched in his hand.

A Captain in the Criminal Investigation Branch in the United Arab Emirates Police Service craftily initiated conversation by asking, "Explain the significance of ANZAC?" He moved on to an ardent exposition of all things Islam, with cunningly devised Islamic objections to Christianity. I responded with a Gospel message. His responsive assertation included this question. "You don't believe in Muhammad, do you?"

I was prompted to reply, "Why should I throw away the benefits of a relationship with God through faith in Christ? Give me a brief summary of what you have heard me saying."

He replied, "You are saying that Jesus Christ is God in human flesh, that He died on the Cross to pay the penalty of my sin and the Bible is an accurate document. How do you summarise my comments?"

I exclaimed, "You have been telling me that your Qur'an offers no guarantee of forgiveness of sin or eternal life."

He exchanged his business card for a John's Gospel saying, "Contact me any time."

A high-ranking official of a local Islamic organisation was fasting for Ramadan in an attitude of prayer. He accepted testimony, an Arabic Injil (NT) and a Gospel of John but said, "I read books by Christians from within the church who debunk the accuracy of the Bible." Before I can remind him, that ex-Muslims do the same with the Quran, he invited me to visit, or set up email or telephone dialogue saying, "We are all sons of Adam and Eve. You and I are brothers. We should discuss these issues. I must pray before I return to the office. Do come and see me."

I said to him, "Make a list of the attributes of Jesus from your Quran and the Injil, compare them and I will pray for you on the Night of Power." His words were soft like butter, but he had a knife in his hand.

Afghani Contacts

Intelligent brown eyes peering intently through a narrow slit between a large beanie and a voluminous scarf bored into mine with relentless intensity. He leaned closer as I testified. Was I under the microscope? Too right I was! Was he dissecting my faith and character? Very much so! If my witness to this Muslim was to be successful, my life and testimony must be transparently honest and openly Christian with no smudges. I offered a silent prayer. He said, "You spoke to me previously, remember?" I had not recognised him under his low-slung beanie. He continued saying, "Christianity is decadent but Islam will solve the world's problems."

I declared, "But I've had the experience of Christ."

He replied, "Yes. This is significant. Allah will bless you."

Murtaza, a persecuted Hazara tribesman from Afghanistan told me, "Each week my parents tell me a couple more friends or relatives were shot."

I said "But it's a Muslim country. Why shoot each other?" His downcast expression and sad reluctance to reply indicated these issues weighed heavily.

He declared, "I pray five times a day, fast, give to the poor and visit Mecca but I don't know what the future holds."

I asked him, "Would you accept a small book on the Christian religion?"

He said to me, "But the Christian and Muslim religions are similar."

I explained, "The Jesus of the Quran and the Jesus of the Bible vastly differ. The Jesus of the Bible says, 'Come to me all you who labor and are heavy laden and I will give you rest'" (Matthew 11:28). He listened to my testimony and accepted a TPTL NT*.

Imtiez and Sirfaraz sailed in a boat carrying 200 Afghani refugees to Christmas Island - their boat capsized in the Indian Ocean. Buoyed up by empty fuel cans they floated fourteen hours before rescue by Australians in international waters. Both were affected emotionally by their watery ordeal. They accepted Urdu literature.

An Afghani student accepted a Pushto New Testament and flipped expertly from page to page. Astounded he said, "Wow! That's Pushto! I am amazed you have this. I've always wanted one." On this our second contact, I showed him Hebrews 11:1,6* in his New Testament. He read these verses then said, "I don't believe faith is any different for a Buddhist, Hindu or a Muslim."

I explained to him, "Your faith is as valid as the object of your faith. Imagine standing on one side of a crevasse and you want to cross to the other. Across this crevasse is a wobbly rotten wooden plank. Though your faith in that weak plank is strong, it will drop you to the bottom of that crevasse, but a weak faith in a strong plank might get you safely across."

To Syed, an Afghani refugee, I asked, "What is the difference between Islam and Christianity?"

He answered, "All religions are basically the same." He listened to my testimony, accepted a Gospel of John, and said, "I am expecting to be sent back to Afghanistan soon. I do not want to go. I am worried, confused, and anxious."

I replied, "The booklet will encourage you."

A Muslim Afghani refugee family arrived in Australia three weeks previously with two infant children. The family had a Farsi Bible, which she had read. She accepted Farsi literature, and an English New Testament. She read John 8:12. I asked her, "What do you think?"

She said to me, "Beautiful!"

I sensed something special about this tall handsome young Afghani refugee as he walked toward me. I asked him, "Tell me your story."

He replied, "A man in Afghanistan gave me a Bible, and said, 'If you find it interesting talk with me.' I was fascinated by what I read, and became a Christian in my home'." This godly young man had experienced more tragedy in his short life than we could imagine but his faith gave him obvious peace.

Students from Bangladesh, Saudi Arabia, India, Indonesia, and Iran

A mature aged Saudi Arabian proclaimed, "Our government is subsidising 1000's of students to study in Australia. We want to learn your culture and leave something of our culture with you." He coughed delicately, smiled, drew breath, and launched into a carefully constructed process of dismantling my faith. He said, among other things, "Our Quran is accurate. Read it with an open mind."

I replied, "We have 1000's of historical documents that satisfy me that our Bible is accurate."

He said, "Where are they?"

I told him, "In libraries and museums round the world for all to see."

"Our religions have much in common," he stated.

I explained, "The Quran tells us Christ is a prophet. The Bible says Christ is God in human flesh. Our beliefs hugely differ."

He declared, "Afghan's Muslim cameleers opened up Australia. If the British government hadn't stepped in Australia would have been an Islamic country. Have you seen the camel driver's display at the Immigration Museum?"

I replied, "I have seen the old camel driver's cemetery at Wyndham, WA and the abandoned mosque at Maree in SA but Christianity was introduced into Australia by pioneer missionaries and early Australian settlers well prior to the arrival of the cameleers. Can I offer you an Injil (Arabic NT)?"

"I'd never read it," he responded.

I said, "Where's your open mind?" The unkempt cameleer's cemetery at Wyndham and the mud walled, brush roofed mosque now in disrepair at Maree, 685 kms north of Adelaide served Afghan families in the late 1800's. Now I can tell my Muslim contacts I have been in a mosque.

A Saudi Arabian student challenged Biblical accuracy, the identity of Christ, etc. I was running short of ideas and silently prayed. An Aussie sitting with us inadvertently threw me a lifeline. He said, "I once stood in the Arabian desert. All I saw was sand which is useless for concrete because of impurities – too much salt."

The Saudi indignantly replied, "But we separate the impurities with chemicals."

I said, "The human heart is like Arabian sand, full of impurities."

The Saudi stated, "We all have impurities."

I told him, "The only one who can remove our impurities is the Lord Jesus Christ." The Aussie somewhat taken aback, laughed, and left. I said to the Saudi, "Wouldn't it be good if you came to your own conclusions by reading the Injil (Arabic NT), rather than relying on advice from others?"

He replied, "Do you have a Quran?"

I said "Yes. I have read most of it."

He asked, "What did you think?"

I said, "I found nothing in it which promised me a clean heart and eternity in paradise." He accepted an Arabic Injil (NT).

Five Saudi students presented their Islamic viewpoint. Mr. Talkative said, "You should get a nice young wife."

I asked him, "How many wives do you want?"

He gloated, "I have one but I'll build up to four." He boldly asserted, "God has no sons. Muhammad is the last prophet. You should follow him." He insisted I listen to wailing prayers from a Muslim mosque on his iPod and carefully watched my reaction.

I said to him, "Before you criticise the Christian faith, draw up a list of the attributes of Jesus from your Qur'an and this Injil (NT) and compare them. You will be surprised." He walked with his Injil.

A student, who was returning to Indonesia the next day, said, "I'm glad Bin Laden has gone. He created a stigma with which the West paints all Muslims." He could not answer the BQ* but listened closely to my testimony. He said, "I'm not a good Muslim. I don't pray five times daily or read the Quran."

I answered, "There is a difference between religion and relationships. When you return home, your community will encourage you to be a good Muslim. This (a Gospel of John and Indonesian literature) explains how you can have a relationship with Jesus Christ."

A Persian student holidaying with relatives said, "There is no future in Iran. I don't want to go back. I don't trust the Government and I see nothing in Islam." He accepted a Farsi New Testament.

Another young male said, "I am Palestinian. I overheard your conversation. I am passionately interested in religion." Mr. Palestine hijacked the discussion in favour of Islam. I read to him from Philippians 2:9-11* etc. By God's grace his brash self-confidence deserted him. He accepted an Arabian New Testament. Mr. Persia, who was leaving for Iran the next day, listened intently.

As a male Bangladeshi student listened to a Gospel presentation, a female Aussie secondary school student broke into our conversation saying, "I am doing a survey. Do you mind if I take your photo and ask about religion?"

I said to her, "I'll do a deal. Take my photo in return for five minutes of your time." The Aussie sat hesitantly. My testimony was repeated in the presence and hearing of the Bangladeshi.

She asked, "Is this real?"

I said, "It surely is."

The Aussie took our photos and asked, "What difference has religion made in your life?"

I answered, "What do you think?"

She replied, "It must have been a huge change." She turned to the Bangladeshi and asked, "What difference has religion made in your life?"

He said, "It gives me peace." When the Aussie departed the Bangladeshi said "Actually, I don't have peace. I have some questions." Jesus and the Bible were discussed at length.

Ali, a young Indian, said, "My college won't release my marks for last semester until I pay my dues for the next." He was clearly depressed.

I asked him, "What language?"

He said, "Urdu."

I asked, "Which country?"

He said, "Guess."

I told him, "India."

He replied, "Yes."

I enquired, "Where?"

"Guess," he retorted.

"Hyderabad. You are Muslim?"

"Yes," he answered.

"And you name is Ali?" I exclaimed.

Somewhat puzzled, he replied, "How did you know?" I didn't tell him, but the information was all clearly written in large letters on a large key tag clipped to his belt. He accepted the tract entitled 'Life's Greatest Question' and said, "I am searching for answers to that question. Hindus, Buddhists, Christians all say they have truth."

My response included, "Jesus Christ is the only one who died on a Cross for my sin and rose the third day to give new life, that's why I am a Christian."

He said, "You have given me much to think about." He accepted a New Testament.

Refugee from Iraq

An Iraqi refugee said, "I am the son of Saddam Hussein. George Bush and Saddam were good friends at heart. Suffering is the will of God. Jesus is not the son of God."

I explained to him, "See that sparrow hopping round? It has no idea of the existence of God. The only way it will know God is for God to come down as a sparrow and speak in sparrow language. It is like that with us. God came down in the human form of Jesus Christ and spoke in human language so we could understand Him." I further said, "In appreciation of your listening ear, I offer you the very best possible gift I can give. It is the story of Jesus. Compare it with your Quran." He accepted.

Pakistani Student Contacts

My Pakistani mate with good natured sarcasm said, "How's the hunting going?"

I told him, "Some seeds fall on rocky ground, some on shallow ground and some on good soil. Some seeds die, some sprout and die, others take root and produce 30, 60, 100 times."

He said, "Why would God suffer on the Cross for me?"

I answered, "Nobody can ever say Jesus doesn't understand your sin. He was tempted in all points like you."

He questioned, "What is sin?"

I said to him, "It is falling short of the glory of God!"

He declared, "I will never change from Islam! If I die tonight, do I go to Hell?"

I said to him, "You will without Christ as your Saviour." He agreed to read Genesis 12:1-3 (blessed to be a blessing) and Galatians 3:2* (Law and grace) from the Bible, I recently gave him.

He exclaimed, "God contradicts himself in the Bible and the Quran."

I said, "Read the passages."

He uttered, "You are a hard nut to crack."

To a student I asked, "Is there a difference between our two religions?" Our discussion included reference to John 14:6* and Stuart Robinson's approach re dreams and vision in his book entitled 'Mosques and Miracles'.

The student replied, "I'll take your booklet (John's Gospel) and if I get one good thing out of it, you'll be rewarded."

I said, "My reward comes from me telling you the Good News."

He exclaimed, "You'll never make me a Christian."

I explained to him, "I cannot make anybody a Christian, but you are responsible before God to act on the information I give you."

Ardalon arrived in Melbourne four days previously. He said, "There is no guarantee in Pakistan that you will arrive home safely at night. I look for peace in a mosque, church - anywhere I can find it. Where do you find peace?" I read aloud from Acts 10:36*. He responded, "That's holy words!" and accepted the 'Jesus and the Qur'an' booklet, a Gospel of John and discussion on John 8:12*

Ahmad declared, "Islam and Christianity are like two streams. They gradually merge into one."

Another Pakistani student sobbed, "I am unhappy. I have health problems. My family don't understand. I am homesick. I want to die?" A third Muslim Pakistani student accepted a Gospel of John with reference to John 8:12* and the word 'Follow".

A student said, "Pakistani politicians are corrupt. Only 30% of the population follow the Quran."

I said to him, "Are you a 30%er?"

He said, "No, a 70%er!"

I told him, "I am a Jesus follower."

He replied, "Many Christians become Muslims but no Muslims become Christians."

I informed him, "More Muslims have become Christians this century than ever before." He accepted a Gospel of John.

Umar, the only son of a prestigious Muslim family, from Lahore, Pakistan, happily discussed his Islamic faith. I asked him, "Does your faith offer you a rock solid, watertight guarantee of paradise when you die?"

He said to me, "No! It all hinges on whether my good deeds outweigh my deficiencies. My religion tells me to pray five times daily. I don't. It tells me I must not drink alcohol. I do. That's my dilemma."

I asked, "Would you accept literature in Urdu about the Christian faith?"

He replied, "We are not Muslims unless we believe in Moses and Christ 'the prophet' as Christians do." He accepted literature.

A pleasant student said, "Islam is a religion of peace. The Taliban, government, corruption, and international interference cause the problems." He listened to my testimony and we discussed biblical peace from Galatians 5:22*, and replied, "What a beautiful story, but I 'insist' you read the Quran. It's the best place to find true peace. It proved Jesus is a prophet. Did you know Muhammad is referred to in the Bible?"

I said, "Can you read the Quran?"

"I do, but I can't understand it because it's Arabic, but I can give you Islamic websites of Muslims winning debates over Christian scholars."

I exclaimed, "And I can refer you to Christians winning debates against Muslims. Your only hope is for the Spirit of God to break into your conscience and reveal truth."

Various Conversations in Melbourne CBD

An elderly Pakistani male with a younger woman and child, sat beside me in McDonalds. She was an extrovert physiotherapist. She insisted I sample some of her curried mutton and rice lunch. The family, including me, took turns at eating her food with the same fork. He said, "By accepting our food you bring blessing of the god upon us." I introduced my testimony.

The young woman said, "We all worship the same God. If we do everything right, we'll all get to the same place eventually."

I explained, "Islam and Christianity have very different destinations." She accepted a Gospel of John marked at John 3:16* and John 14:6*.

To Saadia, a matronly lady, I asked, "Does Allah offer you a cast iron watertight guarantee of eternity in paradise?"

She said, "No! But I try to balance the bad with kindness. A long time ago, a prostitute offered a dying dog some water. God rewarded her kindness (I've heard this story before). Any little thing we do to help, God rewards. Soon after we married my husband fell ill. I cared for him twenty-four years before he died. I have done the Hadj, said my prayers, and fasted at Ramadhan. God will reward me."

A hotel manager and his wife, a practicing GP, strongly decried ISIS activities in the Middle East. He outlined the five pillars of his Islamic faith with which he proudly claimed to have complied. They listened to my testimony and seriously considered Ephesians 2:8-9 - "For by grace are you saved through faith; and that not of yourselves: it is the gift of God: not of works, lest any man should boast."

A Telegu speaking Muslim from Hyderabad, India, bemoaned the fact that he cannot live up to his ideals. I said, "What does the Quran say?"

He replied, "The Quran says God has the love of sixty mothers. He will forgive me. Jesus is a prophet, not the son of God."

I replied, "But Acts 4:12 says, "There is no salvation in any other name under heaven given among men by which we must be saved." He shrugged and accepted Hindi literature.

Ali, a Berber from Algeria, invited me for coffee. He was searching for an Aussie wife to facilitate his application for Australian permanent residency. I said, "The important thing is to have Jesus in your heart. Trust Him for all your needs. If he wants you in Melbourne, he'll make a way. If He wants you in Algeria you will know."

He replied, "There are many churches in my city. Stay with me. My house is empty. It has electricity and water and I'll give you a key."

I said, "I'll talk to God about that."

Ali declared, "You could conduct your mission and make many followers. When I get back to Algeria, I will get my house ready and call you for a date." Never did receive that call.

Kemal, and I lunched in Degraves Street as arranged. He reminded me, "I am a devout Muslim. I do not intend to change."

I said to him, "I cannot convert you. I can only give you an accurate understanding of the Christian belief." An explanation of the Cross astonished him.

He reverently accepted a Turkish NT (Injil) and said, "Where do you suggest I start reading?" I suggested John 1:1-5* because we share a similar belief in creation.

An Air Traffic Controller in the Malaysian Air Force, a Malaysian soldier and his wife were watching the world go by. The ATC claimed Islam is a religion of peace, that people can only become Muslims if it is their hearts desire, etc. To each statement, I said, "Is this what the Qur'an really says? Where does the Qur'an say that?" Trembling hands betrayed his emotions.

During this conversation he said, "I don't know how to put this." With delicate cough and genuine embarrassment, he continued, "If you don't become a Muslim, Allah will send you to Hell forever."

I replied, "Imagine walking down a road to a special destination. You come to a fork in the road but don't know which fork to take. Two men are there. One has never been to your destination and is dead. The other is alive and has been to your destination. Whose advice would you take?"

He said, "I don't understand."

I explained, "Muhammad is the dead man and Jesus is the living one. Jesus alone can get you to paradise." He accepted an Arabic Injil and a booklet for Muslims based on Hebrews. To the female I said, "Is it culturally offensive for a Muslim woman to shake hands with an infidel?"

She replied, "It's OK. I am wearing gloves, there is no skin contact."

To Francois, a French traveller and Saber, an Egyptian Muslim born in Luxor on the banks of the Nile River, I said, "I saw the ancient temples in Luxor. A Muslim guide explained the hieroglyphics.

"Death," he said, "equated to sunset on one side of the river. The soul flies across the river to the opposite bank where sunrise equated to life. Along that dark and dangerous flight between sunset and sunrise the soul was asked ten questions. Failure to answer each of these 100% correctly resulted in eternal punishment."

I asked, "Does your Islamic faith offer you a watertight, cast-iron guarantee of paradise in eternity?"

He replied, "No one can be sure of that." He accepted an Arabic Injil (NT). The Frenchman accepted French literature.

A Lebanese Sunni Muslim accounting student overheard my conversation with some Sikhs. When they left, he said, "I have something to ask you." Then followed a long loud aggressive assault on my belief with the usual Islamic objections to the Christian faith. He said, among other things, "Forget this Jesus bit. Just believe in God, you'd make an excellent Muslim. The Quran is beautiful. You should read it."

I replied, "If you want to know about Islam, don't ask Muslims, read the Quran. If you want to know about Christians, read the Bible." He accepted a John's Gospel.

Two Hazara males refused to believe the Christian viewpoint on the identity of Christ and authority of Scriptures. I drew attention to Surah Al-Imran 3:42-56 of the Quran, which says things about Isa (Jesus) which clearly lifts him above the status of a prophet and asked them as they read, to pray for God's guidance.

A man was reading the horoscope with two young sons beside him. I asked the BQ*. He replied, "I work for a supermarket but there must be more to life than that. I need a challenge." I shared my testimony. With chilling conviction, and piercing dark brown eyes, he replied, "We're just finishing the fast of Ramadan. During the fast everything became crystal clear. What God wants for you (an infidel) will never change. What he wants for me will never change but if an extremist burst through that door firing a machine gun, Islam would get a bad name and Christians would get good names." He accepted a Gospel of John and said, "Thanks for sharing your story. You are a good man. I will read this booklet."

Basil from Jordan openly discussed political issues in the Middle East in ways that would be dangerous for him to do so in his home country. He clearly articulated the Islamic interpretations of the identity of Jesus, Trinity, Bible, the Prophets, etc., then asked, "What does Christianity say about Islam?"

I explained, "Whether you are Muslim, Buddhist, Hindu or Australian is not the point. The point is all men will die. All will be raised. All will be judged. Jesus will be that judge. He will divide all men into two groups, the positive and the negative, and that division will be permanent. Say yes to Jesus now and He'll say yes to you then. Say no to Him now and your fate will be too terrible to think about." I offered him a TPTL NT*.

He responded, "I won't accept till I understand."

I said to him, "You have a high intellect. You just might understand, but what about the millions whose intellect does not allow for that? It would not be fair if God admitted people to Paradise on the basis of intellect. God accepts sinners based on faith in Christ alone." He accepted the New Testament.

Yasser, a Saudi Arabian student, had been twice on pilgrimages to Mecca. He firmly defended his Islamic faith. I asked him, "Does your religion offer you a watertight, cast-iron guarantee of eternal life in paradise when you die?"

He replied, "Definitely not. My only hope is to keep the five pillars of Islam, but I'll never know until I get to the judgement." He accepted literature.

An airline steward from Qatar, visiting Australia for the first time in the course of his duties, decried the lack of world peace and accepted an Arabic Injil. We read Galatians 5:22* together from a bilingual New Testament. He accepted testimony and Arabic literature and said, "Wow! I will contact you if I return to Melbourne."

Cross Cultural Experiences

Jan and I were invited to dine in the home of our Muslim Indian contacts from the Bourke Mall in the western suburbs of Melbourne. It was an intriguing cross-cultural experience with a difference. Some dishes were chilli hot. Others were toned down for our benefit. They hovered round our table as waiters in a restaurant. They will eat their meal after we leave.

Her family were wealthy. She was intelligent, confident, possesses university degrees and was experienced in hospital administration. His family were poor, but his two university degrees were reckoned as potential wealth.

Neither families had seen or conversed with each other prior to their wedding. Their respective families were unknown to each other. Matrimony was arranged by submitting CV's and photos to a marriage broker who negotiated their marriage on commission. The families were interviewed separately, photographs were exchanged, wealth distribution was considered, an agreement reached. Her photograph reminded him of a film star. He couldn't say, 'Yes' quick enough. Five thousand guests attended their wedding in India.

Queensland Visits

During a visit with my sister at the Gold Coast, an elderly Afghani and his wife in the nearby botanical gardens described the death of his brother and eight of his wife's close relatives in Afghanistan at the hand of extremists. They accepted English literature.

In Orleigh Park (Brisbane) Frank, a Muslim background Azerbaijan, believed in a creator god, but was thoroughly disillusioned by religion. At a nearby Ferry Terminal a Kurdish/Persian refugee said, "Issa (Jesus) and Muhammad are the same. It doesn't matter."

NSW Contacts

Jan and I meet with a faithful prayer supporter for coffee in the Corso, Manly NSW. This elderly Christian, together with her late husband, served ten years in Africa in literature distribution. Several churches now exist there because of this ministry. Our waitress was a Dari speaking Afghani whose family suffered at the hands of the Taliban. Our missionary friend, Jan and I discussed the Gospel with her and an Indian friend. Both accepted Gospels of John. The Indian reverently clasped his Gospel to his chest saying, "I'll read this tonight."

Box Hill Centro

At the Box Hill shops, I said, "I have never met many Moroccans, tell me about your country." He gave me a good run down. I told him, "I am a Christian. Explain the difference between Christianity and Islam."

He declared, "Christians say Jesus is God. Muslims say He is a prophet, but I am not a good Muslim. I do not pray. I drink and … '"

We discussed the Trinity. His Filipino partner arrived. She asked me, "Which church do you attend?'

I told her, "Baptist."

This clicked. She smiled and said, "My sisters are born again Baptists at Footscray." (a Western suburb of Melbourne). They insisted on buying me coffee. I shared my testimony.

His expressive brown eyes glowed with approval. "Beautiful!" he said.

She explained, "We have been having good times with spiritual issues lately. I'll tell my sisters about our meeting today." They accepted a Gospel of John.

A Moroccan previous contact was invited to attend our church Fun Day. With him was his Australian fiancée who I had never previously met. She was an Occupational Therapist specialising with brain damaged accident victims. The young couple were seriously considering attending an Alpha Course. He said, "I am grateful for the Arabic NT you gave me."

She said in an aside, "It all started when an old man like you talked to him about Jesus Christ on a Hawaiian beach a few years ago."

A Muslim student from Hyderabad accepted testimony and literature. I said, "A recent email told me of a Muslim who had visions of a man in white saying, 'Follow me.'"

The student replied, "When I saw the Jesus film, I was shocked to see several scenes in the film identical with my Ramadan dreams. Following this experience, I became a believer."

A Muslim industrial chemist from Bangladesh who arrived in Melbourne the previous week, was searching for work. He asked, "How long have you been married?"

When I told him he replied, "You are the Don Bradman of marriage.'

I replied, "I've faced a few bumpers in my day."

He countered, "Your wife is Brett Lee?"

I said, "I'm still batting because I have Christ in my life." He accepted a Gospel of John.

An Indian Muslim got the words 'agree' and 'ugly' mixed. In the context, each time I made a statement, he said, "I ugly" meaning, 'I agree.'

As he was learning English, I give him a soft landing by suggesting, "No, I ugly."

In a flash, he laughingly responded, "I agree."

Encouraging Moments

A weather beaten, cigarette smoking Palestinian gazed into space. Glittering brown eyes beneath dark bushy eyebrows probe mine. He was educated in Egypt and Germany, gained his PhD in English literature, taught English as a career in Dubai, loves Shakespeare, retired early, sat round for twelve months 'waiting to die', then found purpose through the purchase of a dry-cleaning business in Dubai. I asked the BQ*. He said, "Live for the day and enjoy it. What is yours?" He listened to my Psalm 23 testimony. The unexpected gift of an Arabic New Testament (Injil) was accepted without demur by this astonished senior Muslim who said, "I'll put it in my pocket next to my heart."

I explained, "When I die, I will live in paradise forever with God."

He replied, "I've learned something new!" He returned later that day to Dubai.

A young male said, "I left Morocco ten years ago. In America I watched Christian TV programs and became a Christian. I overstayed and was sent back to Morocco. I rang a church in America and asked them to pray for a Christian church for me in Australia." He accepted an Arabic New Testament and said, "Wow! This is a big day for me. This will help a lot." The name of a church was provided for him to attend.

A most confronting verse in the Bible is 2 Thessalonians 1:7-9*: "The Lord Jesus shall be revealed from Heaven with His mighty angels in flaming fire taking vengeance on them that know not God and obey not the Gospel, who shall be punished with everlasting destruction from the presence of the Lord." As their understanding allows, we gently, graciously, without prejudice, warn our Muslim friends to flee the wrath to come. They might then cry out, "What must I do to be saved?" and then you respond, "Believe on the Lord Jesus and be saved." God works in wondrous ways, his wonders to perform.

Praying for scriptural defenses against frequently voiced objections by representatives of other religions is a learning experience in terms of practical evangelism. Twenty years of street ministry has uncovered a variety of exciting ways of communicating the Gospel across religious and cultural barriers. Many lessons are yet to be learned.

Summary of Various Responses

- A Pakistani claimed the Bible is corrupted and challenged me to read the Quran.
- A Pakistani taxi driver disputed the Biblical view of Christ.
- A Turkish male said, "Islam is good. It's people that are bad."
- A Somalian Muslim openly condemned the Christian faith.
- A Serbian Muslim extolled the purity of the Quran.
- A Pakistani asserted, "In the Bible it is written there'll be another prophet after Jesus."
- A Pakistani Muslim said, "The Quran is the final authoritative word from God."
- An Afghani believed Osama Bin Ladin had nothing to do with 9/11.
- Two Kurdish refugees are disillusioned with Islam.
- Kalid, an aging Iraqi refugee said "I am alone. Can you find me a wife?"
- A Pakistani student said, "There are madmen in Pakistan."
- A Muslim said, "I cannot return to North Sudan; the Arab militia would kill me."
- A Palestinian male is disenchanted with Islam.
- A Saudi Arabian happily accepted Arabic literature and an Arabic NT (Injil).
- Muhammad, an Afghani refugee has lost contact with his family but accepted a Farsi NT.

- A refugee accepted an Arabic NT (Injil) and said, "My wife and four teenage kids refuse to leave Iraq."
- Maroof, a Farsi speaking Pakistani, said, "I have wanted an Injil (NT) for a long time."

Taking it to heart:

1. Islam and Christianity espouse widely divergent views about the identity of our Lord and Saviour Jesus Christ.
2. How would you respond to a Muslim contact who insists there is no God but Allah, and Muhammad is his messenger?
3. Discuss.

References:

John 1:1-5 -In the beginning was the Word, and the Word was with God, and the Word was God. He was in the beginning with God. All things were made through Him, and without Him nothing was made that was made. In Him was life, and the life was the light of men. And the light shines in the darkness, and the darkness did not comprehend it.

John 3:16 - For God so loved the world that He gave His only begotten Son, that whoever believes in Him should not perish but have everlasting life.

John 14:6 - Jesus said to him, "I am the way, the truth, and the life. No one comes to the Father except through Me."

Acts 10:36 – The word which God sent to the children of Israel, preaching peace through Jesus Christ – He is Lord of all.

Galatians 3:2 – This only I want to learn from you: Did you receive the Spirit by the works of the law, or by the hearing of faith?

Galatians 5:22 – But the fruit of the Spirit is love, joy, peace, longsuffering, kindness, goodness, faithfulness, gentleness, self-control. Against such there is no law.

Philippians 2:9-11 - Therefore God also has highly exalted Him and given Him the name which is above every name that at the name of Jesus every knee should bow, of those in heaven, and of those on earth, and of those under the earth, and that every tongue should confess that Jesus Christ is Lord, to the glory of God the Father.

Colossians 1:21 -And you, who once were alienated and enemies in your mind by wicked works, yet now He has reconciled.

1 Thessalonians 2:8 - So, affectionately longing for you, we were well pleased to impart to you not only the Gospel of God, but also our own lives, because you had become dear to us.

Hebrews 11:1,6 -Now faith is the substance of things hoped for, the evidence of things not seen. For by it the elders obtained a good testimony… But without faith it is impossible to please Him, for he who comes to God must believe that He is, and that He is a rewarder of those who diligently seek Him.

BQ - Big Question – What is the most important question in all the world for you?

TPTL NT – The Pocket Testament League New Testament.

Chapter 21

Nepalese Students and Tourists

The prophets of Baal are adjudged by Matthew Henry, a Bible commentator of yesteryear, as the most daring and threatening enemy ever faced by the God of the Old Testament church. Many, if not most current overseas students, are entrenched to some degree or other, in the carryover of these age old mystical religious belief systems. Such beliefs are becoming entrenched in Melbourne culture, more deeply than many Christians realise.

The Dashain Festival

While strolling through the Mary Cairncross scenic reserve adjacent to Melany, a township in Queensland, some years ago Jan and I met a highly qualified American Orthopaedic Missionary Surgeon. She had surgically treated during thirty years of overseas service, about 3,000 disabled Nepalese. Continuing conversation over coffee in the nearby kiosk, I asked, "What advice do you have for sharing the Gospel with Nepalese students in Melbourne?"

The surgeon related a redemptive analogy (refer to redemptive analogy in ch.23) based on a national religious ceremony known as 'Dashain' (it can be googled) which traps Nepalese in a hopeless reliance on animal sacrificial system to meet their deep spiritual needs. Many Nepalese students I have spoken with subscribe to belief in Dashain and similar philosophies.

'Dashain' as reported in the media, involves the annual sacrificial slaughter of thousands of goats, sheep, buffaloes, and poultry. This longest and most important Nepalese festival to commemorate the victory by the blood thirsty goddess Durga over evil spirits which binds adherents in a fruitless search of freedom from pain, sorrow and evil with no hope of an eternal destiny. When the ceremony ends, the temple courtyard runs ankle deep in blood. Such entrenched religious systems powerfully resist the spread of the Gospel around the world today. The surgeon suggested including reference in my testimony to John 1:29: "Behold the spotless Lamb of God who takes away the sin of the world" and Revelation 12:11: "They overcame him by the blood of the Lamb and by the word of their testimony and did not love their lives to the death" as keys to open understanding of Gospel presentations.

Nepalese Students in Federation Square (FS)

It occurred to me that different ethnic groups regularly frequented certain sections of FS. For example, Sikhs always frequented one corner. Nepalese students occupied another corner, and so on. The following Nepalese students with few exceptions, were contacted in their corner.

Two students happily discussed their homeland and families. Kanchan, whose grandmother is a Christian said, "She told me to pray each night before I go to bed and each morning when I wake." I replied, "And she'll be praying for you every morning and night." Sagar perceptively commented during our discussion.

The student to whom I recently gave a bi-lingual New Testament (NT), and another arrived. The recipient said, "I read it every day. I'll never forget what you did for me." We agreed to meet in the city in one month. I stated, "I'll be on the phone to remind you." They laughed and asked, "Keeping check on us?" and accepted more Nepalese literature, Gospels of John, and discussion on John 8:12*.

A student accepted Nepalese literature, and an explanation of John 14:6* and Rev 3:20*. He proclaimed, "There is something wrong with Hinduism. The gods are always fighting." I explained, "Recently an Indian student said Hinduism is like walking into a room full of incense sticks. Light them all and select the one that smells sweetest." The student liked that illustration. Then I said, "That's like suffering from pneumonia. Your doctor says, 'I have a thousand medications on my shelf, select whichever you want.' Do that and you increase your chances of dying."

A polite, intelligent young student, objected to Biblical conversion during a Gospel presentation based on Genesis 1-3 along the following lines: "How can I throw away the religion I grew up with? Conversion to Christianity would horrify my parents. What do you say happens to good people like my parents who have never heard of Jesus Christ?" He declined literature, but we parted friends.

Sudarshan, a Hindu student announced his arrival with effusive greeting, steady gaze, and a prolonged vigorous pumping handshake. He informed me, "I want to learn the Christian religion while I am in Australia. If I become Christian in Nepal the Hindu extremists will hurt me." His wife apparently attended church in Nepal. It so happened that 'New Life', Australia's Christian newspaper, carried an article outlining threats and violence faced by Christians in Nepal from Hindu extremists that week.

Sudarshan used my arranged meeting with Pratap as a platform to complain about lack of money and work, confidentially asserting with knowing wink, "If I marry Australian girl, I get plenty money." Not altogether impressed with his sense of humour I replied, "Stay married to your Nepali wife. It's cheaper." He asked, "Lend me $500." I replied, "My pockets have big holes." He asked again, "Find me work." I indicated the multi storey Rialto Towers building opposite and said, "Try window cleaning." He accepted Nepali literature and a Gospel of John and regularly attended a Nepali fellowship arranged through an Australian retired missionary to Nepal.

A bony talisman representing his god hung around the neck of Nirdosh, another student. "It's like Christians wearing Crosses," he explained. "When I have troubles, I go to the temple and pray. God always grants my wishes." He missed his family and recently deceased grandfather. He asked, "Do you have more booklets? I'd like some for my friends."

Bishowmainali, Bikram, Khgendra, Dinesh, Kamal and Nabin clustered round listening to a Gospel message based on Genesis 1-3. They accepted my remaining supply of Nepalese literature with amazement. Kamal commented, "It doesn't matter what we believe, we all get to the same place." Our lengthy discussion included an in-depth Gospel presentation. Kamal also accepted a John's Gospel and said, "I'll ring you. I need work."

Friendly Nepalese Students Readily Accept Literature

- A student accepted a Genesis 1–3 Gospel presentation and Nepalese literature.
- A student on his way to Rochester (Victoria) for farm work, said, "I am a Christian. Thanks for literature in my language."
- A trio of students and Praveen, another student, who overheard our conversation, all accepted Nepalese literature.

- Sunil was converted to Christ from Hinduism through a Christian correspondence course in Nepal. He was referred to a well-known retired Nepalese speaking Australian missionary.
- Bhoj Kumer Patil was a Nepali whose wife was a student here. He accepted Hindi and English literature and said, "I want to go to church." They were referred to a church in the western suburbs.
- Hemanta accepted a John's Gospel. He enthused, "I've searched for a Bible. I will read it from cover to cover and tell my friends about it." His friend also accepted a Nepalese booklet.
- Umi said, "I believed a mixture of Buddhism and Hinduism, but in the last five years my faith disappeared. I don't know what happened." Lengthy discussion followed during which he listened to my testimony, accepted the Gospel message, Nepalese literature, a TPTL NT* and the 'Way to God' tract.
- Rajah in discussing his Hindu/Buddhist faith, admitted to fear of illness, death and doubted the authenticity of his religion. He listened to my testimony, a Gospel message, and accepted a John's Gospel.
- To another I declared, "You look sad." He replied, "I am sad. I miss my family." He was joined by his Nepalese mate. They accepted a Gospel presentation and Gospels of John. Buddha's Day festivals were being advertised on the big screen in FS.
- Dibakar exclaimed, "I follow the best from all religions, but my life is totally futile." His is a wretched, pitiable, pathetically tragic story. Included in a lengthy discussion were two other Nepalese students. All present participated in good discussion on John 1:1-3* accepted literature, and Gospels of John.
- Suress explained, "We have political problems in Nepal. Our infrastructure is breaking down. We only have electricity two hours a day." He read John 1:5* aloud. A discussion on 'light' and 'life'

followed. He accepted literature, a John's Gospel, and testimony. He transferred to a Sydney (NSW) college the next day.

Mountainous Conversations

I would often open conversation with the Nepalese students in Federation Square by asking, "Have you climbed Mount Everest yet?" This question always generated puzzled interest with the usual serious reply. "No! It's too expensive." I would go on to say, "We have mountains in Australia higher than Mount Everest." Now they were really puzzled. Many protested "No!" there is only one mountain, Mt Everest."

I would then explain, "The mountains of unemployment, education, finance." They caught on quickly and laughed. Following on from this statement I said, "Trying to find true peace in employment, education, finance, or culture is like trying to climb Mt Everest!" and introduced my testimony and literature about the Lord Jesus who said, "My peace I give you." Mostly they listened and frequently accepted Nepalese literature with gratitude.

A diminutive ageing Nepalese 'claimed,' "I was a porter on Mt Everest. I have been to Base Camp many times, climbed Everest three times and met Edmund Hillary and Sherpa Tensing." He accepted testimony, and Nepalese literature, but added, "Can you find me work?"

More Encounters With Nepalese

An articulate, thoughtful ex-reporter of a national Nepalese newspaper said inter alia, "Maoist guerrillas in Nepal survive through blackmail, hostage taking and violence. My only hope is from within myself." I uttered, "I am a prisoner of hope (Zechariah 9:12)." He asked, "In jail?" I answered, "No! I am a prisoner of Jesus Christ," and shared my testimony. He accepted literature.

A couple suggested that Australia's history was replete with inhumane treatment of minority groups referring to our bad treatment of Aboriginals. However, she had seen Mel Gibson's film on the 'Passion of Christ' and understood why Christ suffered. I shared a Gospel message based on Genesis 1-3. Her Gautama Buddhism was a barrier. They accepted literature.

Tanka and Saru smiled a greeting. I had previously met Tanka and given him literature. This young couple attended a 'Protestant' church in Thomastown (Victoria). We discussed the meaning of the word 'Protestant'. In Saru's brief absence, Tanka confided, "She wants a divorce." As Saru returned Tanka said, "Tell her what God says about marriage." I mentioned that my wife and I have been happily married for many years and then discussed God's plan for marriage as referred to in Ephesians 5:23-31. I told him, "Tanka, love your wife as Christ loves the church. Saru, be subject to your husband's love as the church is subject to Christ. I think God has big plans for you both. I believe you could pastor a church in Nepal." Tanka replied, "That's strange. My Pastor said the same thing." Saru exclaimed, "Yes! I must love my husband." Tanka asked, "Can you find work for me?" They accepted literature.

Dipak the Nepalese chef accepted a John's Gospel. Gopul his friend said, "I like to empty my mind in a forest. God is in all the trees. It relaxes me." He listened to a Gospel presentation based on Genesis 1-3. I told him, "Fill your mind with the fruit of the Spirit – love, joy, peace, gentleness, goodness against which there is no law'" He accepted a Gospel of John.

Jan and I headed to Southbank for a birthday dinner celebration for two family members. On the train a young Nepalese student smiled. His father worked in Katmandu with chemicals to control insect pests. I said to him, "I am puzzled. Nepal is a Buddhist country. Your father is killing insects, which are reincarnated manifestations of human beings. Why is he killing people?" He smiled, read his tract and said, "May I keep this?"

On the train a student, who had resided in Australia for twelve months, was delighted to accept Nepalese literature which he had not read while residing here. This devout Hindu asked good questions about the church.

We attend the engagement party of a good friend. A guest at this party who worked with me in city evangelism for two years, said, "Remember meeting…… the Nepalese student? He called me recently and we had dinner in his house."

A young male and his compatriot accepted literature. Santeed related another religious practice in his homeland, which included shedding animal's blood in a ceremony believed to atone for pain and sorrow. He understood the 'Perfect Sacrifice' of the Lamb of God slain to take away the sin of the world (John 1:29). He accepted literature and a TPTL NT*.

Milan, a newly arrived student in Swanston Street, said, "The Mormons gave me this (literature). Is it the same as yours?" Then he asked, "Where do I find a Post Office to pay my bills?" We walked to the Emirates building PO and showed him how to pay electronically. He also obtained maps to help navigate the city. He said, "You helped me a lot. I am very happy I met you." Some six months later in Swanston Street Milan called, "Remember me?" His Nepalese friends, who had previously received TPTL NT's* and remembered John 8:12*, also appeared.

Sabin, who texted for an appointment, had previously accepted literature and recalled John 8:12. He recently married. His university fees were burdensome. His mother and brother in Nepal attended church, but he, his father and other siblings remained Hindus. We discussed Nepalese religious festivals and John 8:12. He accepted a TPTL NT* with the above verse underlined. I suggested he read a section of John each day and 'follow' the parts he understood.

Deepu, who spoke Suderpachim (I'd never heard of it!) from the far western Development Region of Nepal, accepted literature and his Indian friend accepted Punjabi literature. Sushil surprised me by accurately quoting the story of John the Baptist saying, "The bottom line is what we do with Jesus." He accepted a TPTL NT* and promised to meet soon.

Sus said, "I attend a Friday night cell group at an Anglican Church in the western suburbs. They told me to get a Bible." He gladly accepted a TPTL NT* with comment on John 8:12*. I stated, "Read a section of John each day for a month, and when you come to a part you understand 'follow'. Contact me and tell me how you are going."

The Soraj Saga

When I first met Saroj, a Nepalese student in FS, he said, "I am depressed. I spend my days locked in my room and attending classes. I miss my family." He listened to my testimony based on my Psalm 23 shepherd testimony and accepted a John's Gospel. I read the Psalm aloud. He said with delight, "My father is a farmer in Nepal." Soraj invited me to meet with him in McDonalds.

Later, Mr B. another Nepalese student, Soraj and I discussed the 'I AM' statements of Jesus in John's Gospel and linked them to Genesis 1, 2 and 3. Mr B. said, "They are celebrating the Dashain Festival in Nepal. It's big like Christmas for Christians, but I don't go for that now." "Neither do I" said Soraj. Mr B. who recently became a Christian in FS, had handed out four Nepalese booklets and shared his testimony. He repeated my prayer word for word.

Neither Soraj nor Rabin, another Nepalese student, could find work and were sad, and depressed. Nepalese believe in a god of light. I said to them, "It's my job to light a tiny Bible flame in your lives and to protect that light until it grows into a big flame." They read John 8:12* aloud. I explained, "Let the Lord Jesus be the light of your life and you will never walk in darkness." They were delighted to accept and read more literature in their own language.

In McDonalds, Saroj said, "I have been in Australia four months. I have no prospect of employment. My funds are running out. I'm unable to pay my rent. I've been disallowed the use of kitchen facilities, told to vacate my room, and haven't eaten for two days. My family can't afford to keep me here. I have nowhere to go. I am depressed."

The despairing Soraj didn't know how to use the food vouchers issued by NewHope Baptist Church and was facing deportation. He was in big trouble; however, he produced his John's Gospel saying, "Reading it frees my mind from problems."

Soraj and I trudged toward the Salvos HQ in Bourke Street searching for accommodation. Along the way in Swanston Street, the Bible reader (a Christian who regularly read aloud from the Bible at the curb side) offered Soraj a word of encouragement. Soraj later said, "That man's words good inside my head." Salvos couldn't assist with Soraj's accommodation. Well stocked Woolworth's shelves in a local supermarket were almost too much for him to comprehend. His purchase of pita bread, fruit, and vegies left him with enough credit on his church vouchers to buy food for another month. His diary contained four passages transcribed from the Gospels. He told me, "They help my depression." Saroj's brother, a Christian, attended a Baptist Church in USA. He mentored Saroj by phone and text. Saroj said, "I spoke with my brother about your booklets. He told me to become a Christian."

Saroj Nailed His Colours to the Wall

To gauge the depth of Saroj's spiritual understanding I asked, "What stops you becoming a Christian right now?" He opened his John's Gospel, grabbed my pen and without further ado, signed the decision section. He said, "Now I am a Christian!" His responsive smile and positive attitude indicated a heart change. I lead him in prayer. It was a joyful experience to share the Gospel with this tenderised heart. It was good to be with him in his special moment. He also accepted a study booklet on Genesis and a gift pack including a Dixon booklet. He requested information regarding baptism and permitted me to refer him to a church I previously pastored near his current address.

Saroj gave me an envelope saying, "Do not open till you get home." The following hand-written note described his short Christian pilgrimage. "Lord, I believe you not because you gave me something but I believe you because you know what I need. You are teaching me a lesson, yes, the lesson of hard work, patience and struggle. For every hard time, I need you Jesus one more time. In the name of the shepherd the only God – Jesus. Amen."

Later, while discussing Philippians 4:8-9*, more Nepalese students appeared. Soraj drew breath sharply, fear registered in his eyes. He quickly hid his Bible saying, "They are dangerous!" He would never tell me why. We retried the Salvos for accommodation to no avail. How could I cast hope into his life? We met again in McDonalds. We had lengthy deep level discussions regarding material and spiritual needs. He seemed to be developing well in his newfound Christian faith.

I later said to Saroj, "What happened during our conversation last week?" He replied, "I gave my life to Jesus. I still get homesick, but going home would disgrace my family." I said, "What happened when your parents found out your brother became a Christian?" He replied, "They were not happy." I asked him, "What will happen when they discover you became a Christian?" He replied, "I won't tell them until I get home, but they will not be happy." His questions indicated he had been reading his literature. We prayed together.

Not long after I received the following text: "Bruce am very sorry... am asking this sorry for my (Muslim) friend... if he's been rude to you sometimes. I don't want you to feel bad. Thank u Bruce keep in touch." Signed Soraj. I was delighted with my young friend's caring encouragement. That our mutual Muslim friend may feel unhappy for whatever reason increased my sensitivity to his feelings when, or if next, we meet (Romans 8:28*). It's all good.

I said to Soraj, "What do you like about the booklet (John's Gospel)?" He enthused, "The day I signed your booklet I was born again. I liked the prayer and the place where I signed my name to receive Jesus. No other gods for me." He explained, "I cannot describe the relief I feel. Tears fall from my eyes. Someone gave me work to carry furniture. I am not strong so I pray for strength. I work hard all day and feel good. They paid me $200. God helped me. I will never forget it. I am so excited I can't sleep. I nearly rang you at 2am to tell you."

His employment opportunity came out of left field and his financial reward was incredibly confirming to him. He said, "I'm amazed that Jesus forgive my sin. He cared for me this week. I am honoured you give me Bible. I was sad and heavy when you spoke to me. Now I have a friend and literature in my own language. This is a miracle. I'm telling a friend about Jesus." Soraj accepted a study booklet on Romans. We discussed study methods. He quickly caught on and said, "Good! I want to study the Bible. My brother in America wants me to find a Bible College in Australia."

Soraj said, "I told my mother I am now a Christian. She told me to believe what I want. I don't get depressed now and I sleep well. I get relief from writing poems. I get frustrated sometimes but I am happy. My brother and I will convert our family to Christ." He requested help to fill out an application form for a replacement Met railway ticket. We later met unscheduled in Hungry Jacks. His Bible study was progressing well. Some

NewHope Baptist Church folks had met and prayed with Saroj and assisted him with more food vouchers and short-term casual employment. A friend (from the church) also gave him money. His remarkable journey was reassuring and encouraging.

A text message was later received as follows: "People may be near or far but it's true that they can't 4get those who had played a vital role in their life. I too can't forget ur all help n support even though I am very far now thnx bruce you taught me bible n support me in various difficult situations. I will always remember. I miss ur teachings." – Saroj (Nepali boy u used to meet in city on tues n thursday). I assumed Saroj had returned to Nepal.

To Mr B who had proved to be a wonderful support to Soraj, I said, "I recently heard news reports of a large festival in Kathmandu?" He replied, "Yes, animal blood makes life smooth for the Nepalese." For the next half hour, we discussed Hebrews 9:13-14*. This intelligent, twenty-two-year-old articulated genuine doubts regarding the Hindu religion and raised my understanding of Hinduism with an outline of the role of religious ceremonies (pujas), chanting (mantras), and Hindu Holy persons (pundits). The families of Soraj and Mr B. were saturated with Nepalese religious customs which to the best of my understanding includes elements of Hinduism and Buddhism. Much prayer is required for the total destruction of these influences in their lives.

Conclusion

Winning the spiritual warfare in our current climate of anti-Christian sentiment is difficult. But the account of the battle referred to in 1 Kings 18:38-39* is instructive. Here, God's consummate victory over evil produced spiritual awakening in Israel. A single-minded accurate focus on the word of God was essential to win the battle. Sanitising or sugar coating the Gospel to accommodate other faiths opened the door for them to say,

"We have this in our religion. Why are we arguing?" God's Old Testament victories are still instructive for modern Christians as we spread the Gospel in the 10/40 window and elsewhere."

> "But we preach Christ crucified, unto the Jews a
> stumbling block and unto the Greeks foolishness,
> but unto them which are called, both Jews and Greeks,
> Christ the power of God and the wisdom of God.
> Because the foolishness of God is wiser than men, and
> the weakness of God is stronger than men."
> (1 Corinthians 1:23-25)

Surren said, "I lived in a Hindu culture in India but did not believe in any gods. You were the first one who ever spoke to me about God. Now I am a God follower. How long have you done street work? How many have become followers?" I explained, "For many years. I was a link in a chain of events which might result in some coming to Christ. Some say yes to Jesus, others might come to Jesus later. Some say no! But I thank God you said yes." He accepted a reading from Psalm 91:1-2*.

Taking it to Heart:

1. In what ways do some religious practices re shedding of blood compete for allegiance with Christianity?
2. What is meant by the term 'sugar coating' the Gospel?
3. How should Christians respond to the claims of other philosophies?

References:

1 Kings 18:38-39 – Then the fire of the Lord fell and consumed the burnt sacrifices and the wood and the stones and the dust, and it licked up the water that was in the trench. Now when all the people saw it, they fell on their faces; and they said, "The Lord, He is God! The Lord, He is God!"

Psalm 91:1-2 – He who dwells in the secret place of the Most High shall abide under the shadow of the Almighty. I will say of the Lord, "He is my refuge and my fortress; my God, in whom I will trust."

Zechariah 9:12 – Return to the stronghold, you prisoners of hope. Even today I declare that I will restore double to you.

John 1:1-3 – In the beginning was the Word, and the Word was with God, and the Word was God. He was in the beginning with God. All things were made through Him, and without Him nothing was made that was made. In Him was life, and the life was the light of men. And the light shines in the darkness, and the darkness did not comprehend it.

John 1:5 – And the light shines in the darkness, and the darkness did not comprehend it.

John 8:12 – Jesus said, "I am the light of the world. He who follows Me shall not walk in darkness, but have the light of life."

John 14:6 – Jesus said, "I am the way, the truth and the life. No one comes to the Father except through me."

Romans 8:28 – And we know that all things work together for good to those who love God, to those who are the called according to His purpose.

Philippians 4:8-9 – Finally, brethren, whatever things are true, whatever things are noble, whatever things are just, whatever things are pure, whatever things are lovely, whatever things are of good report, if there is any virtue and if there is anything praiseworthy – meditate on these things. The things which you have learned and received and heard and saw in me, these do, and the God of peace will be with you.

Hebrews 9:13-14 – For if the blood of bulls and goats and the ashes of a heifer, sprinkling the unclean, sanctifies for the purifying of the flesh, how much more shall the blood of Christ, who through the eternal Spirit offered Himself without spot to God, cleanse your conscience from dead works to serve the living God?

TPTL NT – The Pocket Testament League New Testament.

Chapter 22

Persian (Iranian) Visitors

Christianity is the most persecuted religion in the world. More men and women are being persecuted today for Jesus than at any other time in human history. Millions of Christians face intense persecution and risk their lives for the sake of the Gospel. The Iranian government is among the most oppressive regimes in the world. It is illegal to leave the Islamic religion. Conversion to Christianity is regarded as acting against national security. Even owning Bibles or talking about Christ can lead to harsh imprisonment, or death.

Some Iranians are left with no options but to flee the country (sourced from Voice of the Martyrs). A case in point: A young refugee on the bus, said, "I became a Christian eight years ago in Persia. My family and my government threatened to kill me if I didn't revert to Islam."

Throughout this chapter the word 'Farsi' frequently appears. Farsi is the main Iranian spoken language. 'Injil' is the title given to the Farsi Testament (NT). In 2012, a group of Persian refugees unexpectedly signed up for English as a Second Language classes on Sunday mornings at NewHope Baptist Church (NBC). They soon formed themselves into a Persian-speaking Baptist Fellowship with a Persian Pastor and continue worshipping in this church.

To some extent, by God's grace, I succeeded in facilitating an urgent need to encourage interaction between English and Persian speakers at the church. Some testified to dramatic conversion experiences in Persia - others became Christians during their tortuous journey across the oceans to Australia. Several expressed soon after arrival, a desire to become Jesus followers and witness to their faith through believer's baptism by immersion. The Persian Fellowship at NBC was a welcoming venue for newly arrived Persians contacted in my street ministry. The Persian Pastor issued me with a quantity of Injils for distribution in my city rounds.

The Iranian (Persian) influx taught me much about crossing religious and cultural barriers with an understandable Gospel ministry. A high percentage of these Iranians have proved themselves to be honourable friends and excellent citizens. Some of their stories are touched upon below.

These 'Injils' were accepted with astonishment and joy by both refugees and professional migrants who brought their work skills to Australia with them. Additionally, most of the following contacts accepted Persian literature and testimony. The daughter of longstanding members at NBC, lived in the western suburbs of Melbourne with a Farsi speaking Iranian (Persian) lass, who was asking about God. The daughter gladly accepted an Injil for her Farsi speaking friend.

On our flight home after holidays on the Gold Coast QLD, Roya, a Persian lady with good English sitting beside Jan, accepted a Gospel of John, read four chapters, asked good questions, then read more chapters. She was intending to set up business in Brisbane on return from holidays overseas.

Contacts at the Bus Stop and on the Bus

An elderly Persian gently tapped my shoulder and handed me a handwritten note endorsed with the words: 'Serpells Road Primary School'. He accepted Farsi literature with delight. The bus driver ensured his passenger would disembark at the appropriate stop.

They Would Kill Me

Two Middle Eastern males were waiting at the local bus stop. One said, "My friend arrived in Australia yesterday."

I said to his friend, "Welcome to Australia. Thank you for coming."

The other explained, "We are both doctors."

I asked, "Why leave Iran?"

One said guardedly, "I want to practice in another country."

The other openly stated, "There is something wrong with Islam, so I left it. If the authorities in Iran knew that - they would kill me." These comments, frequently corroborated by Persian friends were typical of those received over many years. They accepted Farsi literature.

- A young Persian couple unknown to me, accepted Farsi literature.
- Three young Persian males enthusiastically asked directions to our Persian church.
- A jeweller mentioned his love of Persian poetry. I quoted Psalm 23. He said, "Beautiful!".
- A young Persian woman testified to her recent exciting conversion to Christianity in another church.
- A male resident in Australia for three years said, "You gave me Farsi literature in Eastland shops."

One Sunday morning on the bus, a friendly Muslim couple were on their way to their first ESL class at NBC. They had seen it advertised on Face Book. After class, they enjoyed coffee in the church café and were introduced to Persians and English speakers. The woman remarked, "I love the atmosphere here. I don't want to leave."

A week later, we met again on the bus. This was their second church ESL class. They accepted another invitation for coffee in the church café. Impressed with the fellowship, she said, "We want to see a church service." They accompanied Jan and me to a service and later joined us at home for lunch and accepted an Injil. We prayed for her sister in Melbourne who was danger of a miscarriage. Her sister recovered miraculously, and baby was safely delivered. Later, we met this bubbly little girl in the church café happily bouncing on her aunt's knee.

The husband said, "Your church has very good people."

She exclaimed, "We cannot thank you enough. God answered your prayers for our baby niece. Her mother is coming to church." The couple regularly attended the Persian Fellowship.

How Did You Know?

A male accidentally bumped me in heavy pedestrian traffic. An excellent opportunity for evangelism. I quickly apologised. He said, "I am heading home tomorrow night."

I replied, "You speak Farsi?"

Surprised, he answered, "How did you know?"

I uttered, "Sit with me. I have a gift for you." He accepted an Injil but responded from his Islamic understanding of the 'prophet' Jesus. His attention was directed to Colossians.

I explained to him, "The Jesus of the Koran is different to the Jesus of the Bible."

He told me, "I have Christian friends who say that, but every religion has good. I was a devout Muslim, but I think wider now."

At various times my comment, "You are Persian?" proved an excellent conversation starter. They often responded, "How did you know?" Their question frequently led to remarks, which opened the door to testimony, gift of Farsi literature, and an invitation to attend our Persian church. Brief extracts of some of these comments are touched upon below:

- "When I first came to Australia, I was desperately lonely, but now I've settled in."
- "Come lunch with me in my city cafeteria."
- "I lost my job two months ago. I'm on my way for an interview."
- A young married couple said, "It's good to meet you. We are Christians too."
- "We met at Flinders Street railway station. You invited me to NewHope. I go to church there now."
- "I became a Christian through reading Luke in Tehran."
- A male skyping his brother in Persia, said, "Can I have that booklet?"
- An Iranian lady said, "Thank you for the Injil you gave me last week."
- A lonely refugee accepted details of our Persian Fellowship and became a valued member.
- A bio-medical student said, "I've never seen a Christian holy book. I'll read it. Thank you."
- Milad said, "I am a Christian" and accepted Farsi literature.
- An elderly refugee without English accepted Farsi literature.

Contacts in Melbourne CBD

In Federation Square a refugee decried political and religious persecution in his home country. He showed me his Farsi NT saying, "I read it every morning and evening and was praying for a Persian church when you came. You are God's blessing to me." He is now attending our NBC Persian Fellowship.

A student decried the lack of religious and political freedom in his homeland. Together we read and discussed various verses from a Farsi/English bilingual tract. It was an interesting exercise helping him locate Galatians 5:22-23* and Revelation 3:20* in his newly acquired Injil. His eyebrows rose when he discovered the Biblical Jesus, and the Koranic Jesus were vastly different.

A determined Eritrean Muslim refugee now resident in the western suburbs of Melbourne, tried every trick he knew to loosen my grip on faith in Christ, but eventually accepted Farsi literature.

A swarthy looking businessman with ill-disguised innocence, accepted Farsi literature, a Gospel of John and an Urdu tract. In response to the BQ*, he asked, "Who does the Bible say is the last prophet?" (I think he was setting a trap).

I said, "You will say Mohammed is."

He replied, "Yes, and that's what the Bible says too."

I said, "Show me?"

He answered, "I can't, but it's there. Anyway, the Bible is corrupted. The story of God having sex with Mary, the cross and the trinity is unbelievable."

A lady, who has just completed her PhD, said, "I am a Muslim but went to church once to pray for my father's heart problems."

I stated, "I am not here to compare Christianity and Islam. I don't want to enter a debate about Islam. I do want to find common ground from which to launch a discussion. She declined to comment.

Apostate Muslims

A refugee, who accepted a Farsi NT and literature, said, "Islam is my father's religion, but I have turned away from it. Islam is legalistic and unhappy."

Another male said, "I was born into a Muslim family, but I have turned my back on religion."

A refugee just returned from orange picking in Mildura stated, "I am finished with Islam." He accepted Farsi literature and contact details for our Persian Fellowship.

A non-English speaking mother was joined by her son with English only marginally better, and her pretty young daughter with excellent English. This Persian brother and sister team were here to study. Their mother would housekeep. The family became Christians in Melbourne. My testimony as translated by the young lady, intrigued them. They said, "It is dangerous for us to return to our homeland."

On my right sat an attractive female German backpacker - on my left was an elderly Persian tourist without English on holidays. An interested but unconnected Aussie male from New South Wales sat beside him. The Aussie typed in my question on his 'Translate' app and hey presto, we have communication in Farsi. The Persian, a retired General in an Iranian military government department, showed a photograph of himself in a uniform festooned with lanyards, medals and chevrons. He was unhappy with his government, but said, "It's safe if you keep your mouth shut."

A disillusioned Muslim couple beside me said, "We are non-practicing Muslims" and translated my Psalm 23 testimony for the benefit of his very pregnant wife. They gladly accepted Farsi literature.

To a couple studying for accreditation to practice dentistry in Australia I asked, "Does your religion offer you a cast iron, watertight guarantee of eternal security?"

They answered, "No one knows but we pray in St Paul's Cathedral sometimes and have discussed getting a Bible." They were astonished by the gift of an Injil. We read together from Galatians 5:22* using both Farsi and English translations.

Two young Persians were invited to share their stories. One said, "Yes, but tell us yours first." One was the son of skilled Persian migrants living in Perth. His university qualifications and sharp wit were impressive. His reticent friend arrived as a refugee in recent months. At first, the University graduate declined literature, but when the refugee accepted an Injil the bright one said, "I will take one, do you have an English version?" He returned to Perth. His reticent friend promised to attend our Persian Fellowship.

I said, "Who do you say that Jesus the Son of Man is?" They responded from an Islamic perspective. I pointed out that this belief will cause them to miss the benefits of the Cross. They gave me an excellent hearing and accepted Injils.

A female Malaysian student responded to the BQ* saying, "I don't know." She added, "The Bible and the Qur'an are similar."

I replied, "There may be some similarities but also huge differences." She read John 8:12* aloud. I said, "What do you like about that verse?"

She said "Beautiful." Her neighbours take her to church occasionally.

Miriam, (not her real name) a young lady who I'd never met, hurried toward me on Flinders Street railway station platform 2. I enquired, "Which country do you come from?"

She replied, "Iran (Persia)."

I questioned, "You are not wearing your burkha?"

She stated, "I only wear it in Iran."

I asked, "Does your religion offer you a cast iron watertight guarantee of eternal life in paradise?"

She replied, "No! Are you Christian?"

I said, "Yes. My faith guarantees me eternal life."

She tearfully said, "Two months ago in a dream I saw a man in white standing at my bedside. He said, 'I am Jesus. I love you.' Now Jesus lives in my heart. I can feel him. I am a Christian'." Her eyes glistened with tears of joy. The carriage was crowded. She explained, "I met a lady who takes me to her church. She gave me a Farsi Bible. Now you come along. I can't believe it. God did this." At Box Hill Plaza she asked, "Can you be a Christian without being baptised?"

I answered her, "Yes! But baptism is for believers."

She said, "I want to get baptised. Does your church baptise?"

I answered her, "Yes."

She added, saying, "I could not discuss this in Iran. They kill people for that." During her young life she experienced many episodes of God's grace but didn't know who was God? Where was He? or, how He looked? She accepted with astonishment, literature, including 'The Ultimate Questions' booklet in Farsi - her mother tongue, which she regarded as a miraculous gift from God.

Her baptismal testimony at the NBC included reference to two texts, which helped in her Christian walk - Matthew 7:26-27 (the house built upon a rock) and 1 Corinthians 10:4 (the supernatural rock, which followed). She was baptised with her brother and another Persian at a Sunday service. Approximately 120 Persians attended these baptisms. It was a privilege to be present at her dramatic life changing event.

Following a meal at our house, her text read: "Dear Jan and Bruce. Thanks again for having us today, was so lovely to spend our Sunday evening with you two. We feel we have found a good and lovely family in here. God bless you. With love." Signed...

A young man later messaged me requesting a meeting at NBC café to discuss a relationship with this young Persian lady. After some discussion alarm bells began ringing. She later showed me his text messages. His persistent, threatening texts were traumatic. She couldn't shake him off. She preferred to risk persecution in Persia than tolerate his unwelcome attention in Melbourne. In reply to a later text message from Persia, I suggested she return to Australia and seek a restraining order from police against this man. But she had deliberately melted into anonymity to preserve her safety. Contact was lost.

A Refugee's Journey to Christ

A retired Aussie chaplain to refugees on Christmas Island, emailed me regarding the location of M, a refugee with whom he had lost contact. M. had become a Christian on Christmas Island and had recently settled somewhere in Box Hill area. Unable to locate his contact I requested assistance from another Persian Christian at our NBC. He later texted me saying, "Hi Bruce, I talked with M. He will come (to church) this Sunday hopefully. God bless you." M. duly arrived at the next service. He has faithfully supported the Persian Fellowship since.

Subsequently M. said, "Thanks for helping me, Bruce." He asked if I would explain the Gospel to his Thai fiancée so they could set up a Christian home together. They arrived at our home with a pre-cooked, delicious Thai meal. It transpired that she wanted to become a Christian but didn't know how. During a six-week Christianity course in our home she became a Christian. Following that course, I had the privilege of baptising her at our church. At their marriage celebration the groom began his speech with prayer, and a powerful testimony to his many Sikh/Hindu/Buddhist guests from work.

In a later text message to M. I said, "Hello, how are you with the coronavirus lock-downs?"

He replied, "Hello Bruce, we passed oceans, passing Corona is easy!" M. is currently wrestling with his immigration status.

Unexpected Persian Hospitality

During a hot summer evening stroll, Jan and I were invited in for refreshments by a professional Persian couple sitting in the cool breeze on their front patio. They recently moved into the area from the Western Suburbs of Melbourne. We arranged to meet for dinner each Friday evening, taking turns to play the host. At these dinner engagements subjects such as the Holy Spirit, the identity of Jesus, and Koranic verses were openly and candidly discussed. On one occasion our meal together was cancelled due to illness. Our new friends delivered a bowl of hot soup for our dinner.

On another occasion, they had supper with us and left with a seven-week series of Bible studies to discuss. Additionally, he was reading the Bible chronologically, side by side with the Koran. I tried by the grace of God, to delicately fan their flickering Gospel interest into a flame. We visited our hospitable friends to celebrate their young son's birthday. Her beautifully prepared exotically flavored Iranian cooking was enjoyed by all. She insisted we eat far more than we needed. It's Persian hospitality at its best. When it came our turn to host, we invited an Australian friend and his Mexican wife. The conversation was scintillating, the company enjoyable and food excellent. This small dinner party in our home celebrated their first twelve months in Australia. A good time was had by all.

Though skilled with overseas managerial experience in high profile technical fields, he is ineligible for Australian government benefits, and recently received notice to quit their unit due to the owner selling. It was suggested that pre-occupation with current financial stress and difficult management at his workplace may dull his skills necessary for the submission of a successful curriculum vitae for a more enjoyable work environment. They were assisted by a church couple skilled in this field. The lady was invited to an ESL course at our church and returned a satisfactory report. Discussion on Christian faith, and prayer at the conclusion of each evening together, brought them some relief from homesickness.

When our own family came to live temporarily with us, the Persians brought food to help. Jan took our Persian friend's wife to our church cafe for a farewell coffee. The husband recently moved to country Victoria for new employment. His new CV may have helped here. She and their young son departed that weekend. Later, we dined with them in their new home in country Victoria. A local retired Pastor and his wife also attended. We were pleased to facilitate contact with these and other Christian friends in their new locality. These friends were working wonders in helping our Persian friends settle in. The husband and his son now attend a local Baptist Church. In our last visit, they appreciated a devotion based on John 1:12* and prayer in their new home.

Happy Refugees

A happy refugee at the Persian Fellowship reminded me of our first meeting in Federation Square (FS). At that meeting he sat with his head in his hands, a picture of dejection and hopelessness. He had said tearfully in broken English, "I've just arrived in Melbourne. I can't find a Persian church." Months later he said, "When you spoke to me in FS, I was praying for a Persian Church. Ten minutes after I pray you come, and gave me literature, and a church phone number. I still have that booklet! I'll never forget you." I had prayed with him and later attended his baptism at NBC.

Hamid, a refugee, said without preamble, "I have bad news from home. A close friend died two days ago in Tehran. I am so far away from my family. I can't contact anyone. It's hard." On the bus I showed him our church as we drove past and informed him of the Farsi speaking service on Sundays. He accepted with interest and gratitude, the Jesus and the Qur'an brochure, and a Farsi NT. He smiled and said, "Before I met you, I have no hope. Now I have hope." He now regularly attends the Persian Fellowship.

A refugee, who arrived in Melbourne, had spent twelve handcuffed months without the light of day in a small prison cell in Iran. He became a Christian and was baptised by Christians in a refugee camp in Indonesia. He accepted Farsi literature but had lost his Bible and couldn't find a church. Overcome with surprise and emotion he accepted an Injil and contact details for our Persian Fellowship, he whispered, "My God! Thank you! Thank you! Thank you!" I prayed with him. He gladly began attending the Fellowship.

Jan and I attended the South Yarra Presbyterian Church for the wedding of a friend, who attended the Persian Fellowship. We wished him and his new Aussie wife God's richest blessing. They now have four children and he is studying theology at a nearby Christian college.

A Persian lady at the church had received news that her brother-in-law's fiancée overseas was diagnosed with aggressive cancer. She stated, "I'd be happy for your church to pray for her, but I don't think it wise to tell them yet. I read in the book (Injil) you gave me and the story of Jesus sleeping peacefully in the storm in a boat. Jesus s given me that peace."

Surprising Answers to Prayer

Ali, an Iranian, (Persian) is waiting on the East Ringwood railway platform. He had arrived in Australia ten days prior to this contact I said, "I am a Christian."

He responded, "I'm not religious. But I have a high moral standard." This charming man with good English, listened to my testimony and accepted an Injil.

I told him, "This is your welcome gift to Australia."

With an incredulous smile he replied, "Is this for me? Oh my god!" He continued, "I am a nominal Muslim. My sister became a Christian in London fifteen years ago. She prays for me and sends Christian video clips and news."

I exclaimed, "Tell your sister about this funny old Aussie who gave you a Bible at the railway station. She will be encouraged."

That night his sister telephoned from London saying, "Hi. This is Sara from England. I want to thank you for giving a Bible to my brother. I have been praying for him such long time and especially during the time he was far from Iran and God gave me the answer. I really appreciate your Godly heart. It would be great if you could call me by WhatsApp or by IMO to share our testimony. God bless you and your beautiful family." In a later message, she said among other things, "It would be excellent if you kindly follow up with him because he is not emotionally in good condition, and I am sure God will soon survive him from evil." Ali attended a Saturday morning men's breakfast at our Light Community Baptist Church and soon after returned to Iran.

Taking it to Heart:

1. How might we minister to persecuted refugees who flee to Australia for safe haven?
2. How could we support our needy brethren who currently exist under harsh and difficult situations overseas?
3. In what areas do you see signs of religious or political discrimination developing in Australia?

References:

John 1:12 – But as many as received Him, to them He gave the right to become children of God, to those who believe in His name.

John 8:12 – Then Jesus spoke to them again, saying "I am the light of the world. He who follows Me shall not walk in darkness, but have the light of life.

Galatians 5:22-23 – But the fruit of the Spirit is love, joy, peace, long-suffering, kindness, goodness, faithfulness, gentleness, self-control against such there is no law.

Revelation 3:20 – Behold, I stand at the door and knock. If anyone hears My voice and opens the door, I will come into him and dine with him, and he with Me.

BQ – Big Question – What is the most important question in all the world for you?

Chapter 23

Seeking Sikhs

The Value of a Testimony

I hold a vision of Sikh contacts in Melbourne becoming Christians and returning to the Punjab to plant village churches. However, it became fairly obvious that a few contacts (of various religious backgrounds) reluctantly declined conversion for fear of estrangement, disinheritance, eviction, assault, abandonment or even death, from families or communities overseas. This knowledge sensitised my approach and expectations in street evangelism.

However, there are reports of remarkable revivals of the Christian faith from North India, the Middle East, and other locations. Church leaders in those cultures don't teach discipleship from textbooks involving six easy lessons; they base discipleship on lives lived under great pressure. Disenchanted with traditional belief systems, people yearn for change and are attracted to values they see in church leaders who victoriously survive severe testing and suffering, or even martyrdom. Many are prepared no matter what the cost, to follow the example of these leaders. As Paul said, "Imitate me, just as I imitate Christ" (1 Corinthians 11:1).

The religion of India is predominantly Hinduism. The national language of India is 'Hindi'. Sikhism is a distinct religious culture arising out of Hinduism. The Sikh language and literature entitled 'Punjabi' is centred mainly in the Punjab, a province of North India. Its users are mostly referred to as either Sikhs or Punjabis. Most inhabitants of the Punjab whatever their religious affiliation, are fluent in more than one language. Sikhs are identifiable by their highly visible colourful turbans frequently seen in our city streets.

Sahil and his young wife are devout Christians from the Punjab. Sahil said, "My father-in-law is a Pastor in the Punjab. Will you meet him?" I later introduced this Pastor to a tall turbaned Sikh and a Sikh student. The Pastor shared his testimony in Punjabi with both men. These Sikh contacts accepted Punjabi literature. The Pastor's church with 800 members, is located in the city of Amritsar (a major Punjabi city) in which is also located the famous Sikh Golden Temple.

Seeing tall, bearded, stern looking young men with dark complexions and colourful turbans in crowded Melbourne streets was intriguing. Curiosity launched me on a mission of discovery. Through frequent interactions with numerous Sikhs, I encountered friendship, intelligence, and an open willingness to share their historical and religious background with occasional minor variations.

An Explanation of the Basic Belief of Sikhism Gave Birth to a Redemptive Analogy

To an intelligent young Sikh (Punjabi) student in the Bourke Mall, Melbourne I said, "Could you please explain the basics of your Sikh faith?" His clearly articulated response provided a 'redemptive analogy', which providentially gained ready acceptance among many Sikh contacts over time.

He explained, "Sikhism has ten gurus. In about the year 1400AD the first guru initiated a breakaway from Hinduism, which eventually became known as Sikhism. He was followed by gurus numbered two to eight, all of whom added to his teaching but are now dead. When Guru nine lived around the year 1600AD a powerful Islamic force surrounded Delhi, intent upon wiping Sikhism and Hinduism off the face of the earth. Guru nine knew his little army was no match for the might of Islam so he offered himself as a sacrifice to the Islamic General if Sikhism and Hinduism could go free. The General accepted the offer. Guru nine died to save Sikhism and Hinduism from annihilation. Guru number ten is their holy book. There'll be no more Gurus."

I replied, "My Guru, Jesus Christ, offered Himself as a sacrifice to bring forgiveness for sin to the whole world, you and me included. He rose the third day and lives forever to give us victory over death and sin, and an eternal life in Paradise. No other god in all history did that. That's why I am a Christian. Do you have a god like that?" The young man accepted Hindi and Punjabi literature. The Guru nine story (actual history) is referred to by title or inference in much of this chapter.

The Uniqueness of Christ's Death and Resurrection is Centrally Important When Talking with Sikhs

A Sikh security guard said, "My guru teaches that if you choose any god, you're OK."

I replied, "Suppose your doctor said, 'I have 1000's of different medicines on my shelf. Anyone of which will cure your pneumonia. Chances are you'll choose the wrong medication and die. My guru, Jesus Christ, died to save the world from punishment for sin and rose the third day to conquer death and still lives. He's the only God who did this. That's why I am a Christian. To an articulate, handsome young Sikh enjoying the sun, I said, "I am a Christian. Could you explain Sikhism?" He explained that some pillars of his faith are hard work, sincerity, facing responsibilities, equality, and belief in one god.

He listened to my testimony but stated, "My experience is exactly the same." Kappow! We were on collision course! He reckoned his religion is as good as mine. His mirror-like reflection of my testimony from his non-Christian viewpoint was confronting. I wanted to freak out, disconnect in a huff, or bury him with a barrage of Bible texts? The Sikh had disorientated me, but the still small voice whispered, "Bruce, shut up and hang in a while." To my amazement, the Sikh volunteered his ninth Guru history. How could I forget!

I replied with a resume of the Crucifixion, Resurrection and ascension. I said, "No other religion offers this, only Christianity."

The Sikh bowed his head and declared, "You are right."

To another Sikh I stated, "I am a Christian. What is the difference between Sikhism and Christianity?"

He confidently asserted, "They are all the same."

"Explain the Sikh religion to me please."

He explained, "If we do enough good, we'll come back better in the next life. If not, we might come back as an insect, bird, or animal."

I said, "That's vastly different to the Christian story," and responded with the guru story and a Gospel presentation.

The British hired Sikhs as mercenary soldiers in bygone generations because of their physical strength and fierce fighting qualities. Sikhs are proud of their heritage. Two tall, dark, handsome, stern looking Sikhs approached. One was bearded and turbaned. I told him, "I am a Christian, could you explain the Sikh religion?"

He exclaimed, "We believe in one universal god, all men are equal, men wear beards as god created us. No alcohol or tobacco. Ten gurus contributed to our faith."

I replied, "How did the Sikh nation survive the advancing Muslim hoards?"

He confidently responded, "An excellent question Sir. Our ninth Guru offered himself as a sacrifice to save our nation from annihilation."

I said, "Isn't that interesting!" They responded to an explanation of the Cross with interest, smiles, and nodding approbation. To my astonishment, the bearded one with twinkling black eyes put his arm round my shoulder and gave me the biggest neck cracking bear hug I ever had. Never having been hugged by a large muscular turbaned and be-whiskered Sikh in full view of the public, I was absolutely disconcerted, but recovered quickly enough to return the hug.

Another Sikh student gave me the Aussie thumbs up salute. I said, "Let me get a coke, and I'll sit with you." Soon I was surrounded by four tall, powerful, rugged young Sikhs. I reminded myself that with God I am a majority and continued saying, "I am impressed with the high level of integrity of Sikhs I have met. Tell me about your religion." With excitement and rising voices, they vied with each other for the privilege of supplying the information. Deteriorating hearing is no barrier to communication in this case, believe me! Their mild religious contradictions and my puzzled expression caused one to say to his mate, "Be quiet!"

A second said, "We believe there are different ways to the same God." A third related the story of their ninth Guru (Teg Bahadurji). They asked about my faith. I quoted John 14:6* and discussed the uniqueness of Christ who died to save the world from judgement. I was given another pressing invitation to visit their local temple. They accepted Gospels of John. One kissed his copy and pressed it against his eyes as a mark of respect.

A Sikh student in Federation Square (FS) said, "I have seen the Jesus film several times. There is a Christian church near my house in Amritsar - each time I walked past I bowed my head in respect. There is only one God but many different ways to get there." He read aloud John 3:16* and John 14:6* with his name in the verse and exclaimed, "Tonight, I'll read the whole booklet but before I do, I'll ceremonially cleanse myself."

Most Sikhs Openly Discuss Their Religion. A Few are Opposed

A Punjabi Sikh and an Afghan Muslim were chatting. The Sikh said, "I have a drinking problem and many girlfriends. I never ask their religion when I take them to bed. Every religion is the same. When I do something wrong, I feed fish in the Yarra to balance things up a bit. That's what my religion teaches me. Do you drink the Sikh asked me?"

I said, "No!"

He shouted, "Whaaaat! Every Aussie drinks. I don't believe you." The Sikh responded to the Guru story and a Gospel message saying, "OK, I'll try to live a better life."

I said, "Wrong! You will fail every time. The first and only thing to do is trust the Lord Jesus Christ to wash away your sins and lead you in the way everlasting."

The Sikh repeated, "I can't believe this. You sure you don't drink? Do you smoke? Did you chase women?"

His Muslim friend said, "I am my own god. Every religion has good points."

I responded, "You will change your mind when you return to Afghanistan."

"Why?" He asked.

"The Taliban will execute you for views like that."

He said, "?!@# them. I'll tell them where to go." He read some Arabic literature but returned it. Discussion on the Christian moral code and judgement provoked snorts of derision and profane comments from both.

Four Indian students (three Sikhs and one Hindu) engaged in mildly boisterous behavior in Federation Square were irritated by 'Australian racial' discrimination, and high college fees. They transferred their irritation to me. One said, "We are going home." They were impacted by the Guru nine story.

Another added, "You must have dinner with us."

To the Hindu I explained, "I once floated down the Ganges in a boat with a man who worshipped the rising sun. Why did he do this?"

The Indian sternly answered, "We Indians are strong believers in our religion. We never change."

I replied to him, "You have a right to believe what you want. I defend that right. All I ask is an opportunity to explain my Christian faith, but you alone must make the decision to follow Christ."

Responses by Turbanless Sikhs

Two tall Sikhs sat beside me in Hungry Jacks. One was turbanless and beardless. Mr. Turban with piercing brown eyes, and beard proudly displayed his religious necklace, bangle, and ceremonial dagger. To Mr. Turbanless I asked, "Where is your turban?" He grinned sheepishly.

Mr. Turban broke in saying, "He is breaking god's law. We have a great religion. People like him are weakening our faith. He is doing wrong?" Whereupon he vigorously chided his wavering friend.

I answered, "But if he is doing wrong, why do you eat with him?"

He replied, "I am trying to get him back to god. All religions lead to the same god. What right do you have to change me to Christianity?"

I explained, "I cannot change you or anyone else to Christianity? It's up to you to decide which religion to follow, but surely you wouldn't deny me the privilege of explaining my faith." The temperature was rising.

Mr. Turbanless, who had carefully followed our discussion thoughtfully, bought ice-creams for each of us saying, "It's time we changed the subject." His intuitive response was appreciated but Turban's parting handshake was limp and expression stony.

Some Sikhs are Surprised by an Aussie Who Knows a Little of Their Religion

Two loutish Punjabi students sat with me as I wrote up my notes. With a frown and stern tone, I asked, "Where are your turbans?"

One said, "We don't wear them." The Guru nine analogy surprised them.

I stated, "Sikhism, Buddhism, Islam all have their little rules. This is religion. My God is a God of relationships. He won't exclude you from paradise for not wearing a turban."

The shell-shocked lads asked, "How do you know so much about our religion?"

Two young Sikhs responded to my question, "What will God do to you for not wearing turbans?"

They replied, "We don't know." A third turbaned Sikh approached. All three accepted Gospels of John.

The turbaned one indicated line drawings in his Gospel booklet saying, "This person is wearing a turban, why don't Christians wear turbans?"

I indicated the un-turbaned Sikhs beside us and said, "Why aren't they wearing turbans?"

He laughed in surprise and said, "The perfect answer."

Difference Between Religion and Relationship with God

An eighteen-year-old Optus salesman at our front door commented, "I am doing quite well in my sales." He proudly showed me his rookie of the week certificate, then added, "But how did you know I'm Sikh?"

I indicated his bangle and said, "But you are not wearing your turban. Are you a good Sikh?"

He said, "I do my work good. I never tell lies."

I commented, "Never tell lies???"

He replied, "Well sometimes."

I asked him, "How many lies does it take to make you a liar?"

He answered, "One I suppose."

I replied, "You have broken God's law, what will God say?"

He said, "My housemate gave me a Bible and takes me to church."

To a Sikh, I asked, "What will God say to you about not wearing your turban?"

He sheepishly replied, "He's already saying it. Inside I am suffering and miserable." We discussed the Guru nine analogy and written moral codes of our respective faiths and his failure to keep his laws. He agreed, "I am a sinner inside." I shared the Gospel message and invited him to follow Christ.

I asked him, "Will you make a decision to follow Christ now?"

He responded, "I will read the material first."

I said, "Let me know if I can assist."

Works/Rules-Based Understanding of Religion Displayed by Sikhs

To a Sikh Master's student, I said, "I am a Christian. Could you explain the Sikh faith?"

He asked, "What do you want to know?"

I replied, "Anything will do."

He said, "We have five Kakkars. (1) approved underclothes. 2) a silver bangle on the left wrist, 3) a replica dagger (Karan) suspended on a chain round the neck. 4) a beard, and uncut hair and 5) a turban. When I return to the Punjab, I'll grow my hair and beard and wear a turban again."

"Tell me about reincarnation?"

He replied, 'There are 840,000 different life species in the world. We could come back as any one of those."

I said, "I believe there are some parallels between your ninth Guru and our Christian faith." This grabbed his attention. I showed him the Ten Commandments and suggested, "We have all broken them. Somehow our sin must be dealt with." He agreed. The redemptive analogy based on the ninth Guru came in handy. I quoted John 14:6* which refutes reincarnation.

He said, "If you are really interested in our religion, come to the Golden Temple in Amritsar, or check it out on Google." He was pleasant, respectful, and attentive.

A Sikh student in Hungry Jacks had arrived in Australia four days ago. We discussed tensions he may face in Melbourne. I said, "You are not wearing your turban. What will God say?"

He replied, "It takes half an hour to put on."

I said, "What is your philosophy?"

He stated, "Don't hurt anyone, help others, and do my duty."

I asked, "What happens when we break the Moral Code of the universe?"

He explained, "There are 840,000 reincarnations. That's hell for Sikhs, but if we do enough good God will take us to Paradise when we die." But he admitted, "You were right. I have broken the Ten Commandments."

I said, "The perfect justice of the perfect God demands eternal punishment for your sin. But the perfect love of God through the perfect sacrifice of Christ on the Cross, paid the perfect penalty for all your sin."

Manjit, a Sikh student, said, "You shouldn't kill animals."

I replied to him, "You are wearing leather shoes and a leather belt that come from slaughtered animals. If it's OK for you to do that, it's OK for me to eat meat. Jesus, the spotless lamb of God, died on the Cross to pay the price of your sin. His body was broken, and blood spilt for you. If you drink His blood and eat His flesh by faith you shall never die."

Turbaned Sikhs

A Sikh on the train, was mildly startled when I sat in front of him and shook his hand. He and his wife had arrived in Australia three weeks previously. This was his first day on his first job. He takes his religion seriously and has visited the Golden Temple at Amritsar. I wondered how to share the Gospel without creating the perception of superiority. I prayed silently then followed up the Guru story with a Gospel message. He responded, "What do you do?"

I replied, "For twenty-five-years I was a farmer looking after sheep. For twenty-five years I was a Police Officer looking after sheep with two legs and for fifteen years I was a Pastor looking after people sheep." I then quoted Psalm 23.

He understood the analogy and accepted a Gospel of John and responded, "You take your religion seriously. Can I ring you?"

Picture this! My co-worker and I in Hungry Jacks were discussing and praying during coffee. Whilst surrounded by noisy, bustling, surging pre-Christmas patrons, loud wall mounted TV monitors advertising Christmas specials and busy staff, two Sikh students quickly responded to our overtures of friendship. Both had given names prefixed by the syllable

'DEEP'. One had arrived in Australia four days previously. The other had been here six months. Neither understood Christianity nor had heard of the Bible. Their ninth Guru story became the basis for a simple Gospel message. One sadly said, "Sikhism is brotherhood, but now Hindus and Sikhs don't like each other." My co-worker shared from his Bible the 'banquet' story with insights on 'the brotherhood factor' in Luke 14:13-14*. The Sikhs were intrigued.

I asked, "What does 'DEEP' mean?"

One explained, "It means light and guidance." At my request, he read aloud John 8:12 where Jesus said, "I am the light of the world. Whoever follows me will never walk in darkness." Then he translated into Punjabi for his friend. They insisted on my co-worker photographing me with one Sikh on either side, and the open Bible in front.

In Federation Square, Sumitpol, a Sikh student from Amritsar, exclaimed, "Life is hard in Melbourne. I ran away from my religion, culture, and family. The exchange rate on the Indian rupee is against me. I have no friends and no family to support me. No Indian or Australian has spoken to me except you. I am amazed. Your literature in my language has encouraged me. Thank you."

An Instructive and Timely Testimony

Aman, a sad looking Sikh in Flinders Street railway concourse, was waiting for his wife. Part way through a discussion on our respective faiths, Praveen, the Christian South Indian cook I had previously met, arrived. I suggested to Praveen, "Tell Aman your story." Praveen happily obliged.

He stated, "I failed university in Hyderabad, (a city in South India) bringing shame and disgrace on my family. I became depressed and tried to suicide twice. I read the Bhagavat Gita (Hindu Holy Book), and the Koran and found no God. But the Bible changed my life, and I became a Christian." Praveen's short, sharp, and shiny testimony highlighted the importance of including the Creation story from Genesis 1-3 in Gospel presentations to those of Eastern religious persuasions. Aman accepted literature but fired the parting shot. He said, "There are hundreds of millions of Christians in the world. They remind me of a great dull grey lump of iron ore. There are only ten million Sikhs, but we glitter like diamonds in the dullness."

A Sikh's Choice Between Two Roads

A Sikh listened to my testimony and asked, "Why so much drugs, alcohol, and immorality in Australia? Your girls are immodestly dressed. We never see this in our country."

I replied, "Are you telling me you have no moral problems in North India? Are you telling me you have no bad thoughts about the opposite sex? There are two kinds of people on earth – the lost and the saved - those who reject the Lord Jesus and those who accept Him. Which kind are you? There are two roads to travel – one down and the other up, one broad and one narrow, one crowded, the other sometimes deserted. Which road are you traveling? There are two masters to serve - one is Satan, the other is Jesus. One is the enemy of God. The other is the Son of God. Which Master are you serving? There are two destinies – one in hell and the other in heaven. Which destiny is yours?" A thoughtful Sikh departed with literature.

A Sikh indicated St Paul's Cathedral and asked, "Is that a church?"

I answered, "The true church is a brotherhood of people living in a relationship with God through faith in Christ." I drew the self-centred and Christ-centered circles and continued saying, "Which circle represents you?"

He indicated the Christ-centred circle and said, "That one."

I asked him, "When did you make that decision?"

He replied, "Now."

I explained, "You need Christians to help you grow in your faith." We discussed prayer, witnessing and other aspects of the Christian faith including John 14:6*. He declined follow up.

To a Sikh, who had visited the Golden Temple in Amritsar, I said, "How did your visit affect you?" He showed me a picture on his iPhone of a large pool inside the Golden Temple. In the centre of the pool was a smaller temple accessed via a causeway. I asked, "Have you ever visited this temple?"

"Yes! three or four times," he enthused. "I found peace there." I read him the story of 'the woman at the well' and emphasised Jesus' words to the woman in John 4:14* He replied with annoyance, "Why do Sikhs never try to convert people to Sikhism, but Christians try to convert Sikhs?"

I said to him, "Jesus tells me to go into all the world and make disciples of all nations, and you tell me I'm not allowed to. Whose advice do I follow?" He laughed.

A Sikh student discussed political corruption in his homeland. I suggested, "Everything begins in absolute truth, but corruption is inevitable. What is the answer?"

He exclaimed, "You overcome corruption little by little with religion. What do you think?"

I said, "There's a difference between religion and relationships in the spiritual sense. Religion is corruptible but a personal relationship with the Creator of the universe is your only hope."

A Punjabi Sikh pointed to a 'Herald Sun' photo of Harbhajan Singh; the English test cricketer embroiled in a recent racial controversy on a cricket ground in the UK. He asked, "What do you think of that?"

I said, "Do you believe in evolution?"

He retorted, "Yes."

I said to him, "Evolution allows us to call each other monkeys on the cricket ground, but my God created all nationalities equal."

Some Sikhs in Australia are Lonely, Cut off from Family and Home

To a Sikh student, I said, "You look sad."

He removed his glasses, wiped away tears and said, "I arrived in Australia two months ago. I cannot find work. I am short of money. I am too ashamed to tell my parents. I told them I am living in a good flat so as not to worry them," (many disadvantaged Indian students tell their parents in India this). This morning he had a cup of tea for breakfast, nothing for lunch and is recovering from chicken pox. He gulped down my gift of a vegetarian hamburger.

The Uniqueness of Christ's Death and Resurrection Central in Talking with Sikhs

A Punjabi (Sikh) student and his Sikh friend questioned the Christian faith. The Punjabi asked, "What happens when we die?"

I replied, "What you do with Jesus in this life determines what He does with you in the next. All people will be raised. All people will be judged. Jesus will be that judge. All people will be divided into two groups – the positive and the negative. This division is forever."

"But," this fine young man persisted, "what happens to the negative group?" To respond biblically to this genuinely, deeply religious young man's question could be regarded as hurtful arrogance.

I opted for a policy of utter honesty and explained, "Everlasting punishment in the eternal fire." If anything could sink our conversation this would, but they accepted Gospels of John with smiles and questions unabated.

A recently arrived Sikh student had seen the 'Passion of The Christ' film. As is often the case with Sikh's, he replicated biblical doctrines with reference to alleged events in his own faith. For example, when I mention the Crucifixion, he stated, "We have that too." When I read Matthew 16 with emphasis on the Resurrection he remained silent. Then, as I read 1 Corinthians 15:3-8 and had him keep count of the witnesses who saw Jesus alive after the crucifixion, he said, "I'll never forget you."

A Sikh student was softly singing. I said to him, "Tell me about your song."

He replied, "In the 1800's a terrorist fired shots in the Golden Temple in Amritsar. About fifteen hundred Sikhs died in the stampede to escape the Temple. The song commemorates the Sikh soldier who tracked this terrorist down and killed him."

I told him, "Each of us has anger, lust, and greed in our hearts. We all tell lies. Who will die to save us from God's judgement and the punishment we all deserve? Who will break the endless cycles of reincarnation that goes on for millions of years? Who will bring us into an eternal paradise? Islam cannot do that. They have no saviour. Buddhism is a philosophy. It can't save you. Only Jesus Christ, who suffered and died to pay the penalty for your sin and rose again the third day to give you eternal life, can do that."

A Sikh cookery student said, "I am required by Victorian law to shave off my beard when cooking." He considered himself a good Sikh. Beardlessness was against his religion. He went on to say, "We regard all animals as reincarnated human beings. When we cook meat, we are cooking human bodies. When I protested, my instructor said, 'If you don't like it, go back to the Punjab'!" His deep repugnance of this requirement was a huge weight on his shoulders. I spoke of the freedom by which Christ alone could set him free.

As a friendly Sikh sipped from his water bottle. I quoted John 7:37-38: "If any man thirst let him come to me and drink. He that believes on Me, as the scripture has said, out of his innermost being shall flow rivers of living water." His enthusiastic hamburger munching was contrasted by a noticeably unenthusiastic response to the gospel. I said, "If you surrender to Christ, you must turn away from your religious belief."

He exclaimed, "I could never do that." However, he accepted John 8:12 where Jesus said, "I am the Light of the world. Whoever follows me will never walk in darkness, but will have the light of life."

A bitterly anti-Indian Sikh recounted with expletives the history of his nation. He said, "Our nation recently petitioned the United Nations for Punjabi independence. We defended Hinduism against a superior Islamic military force generations ago, and in more recent times Hindus repaid our kindness with genocide." He showed me lurid photos of butchered Sikhs on his iPhone.

A Sikh student said, "I have told my family about you."

I responded, "Did you tell them I am a Christian?"

He said, "Yes. They are happy. I told them I want to make you my Australian mum and dad." This was getting a bit sticky! He went on to say, "I want to live with you. I want to meet mother (he meant Jan). I want to marry an Australian girl. I want to work hard but cannot get work and permanent residence, will you help me?" I alerted him to some pitfalls arising out of unrealistic expectations and helped him set some reasonable goals. I encouraged him to attend an ESL class at our church.

A Sikh student said with a touch of humour, "I want to be a gangster, so I am studying accountancy at university." The Punjabi waitress depressed by her parents overriding her choice of boyfriend with a wealthier match, listened to my testimony based round Romans 8:28*.

Mohit's Story

Some two years previously I made contact with Mohit, an enigmatic twenty-one-year-old Punjabi Sikh student with over-tones of Hinduism mixed into his belief system. It transpired that Mohit had come to Melbourne against his middle-class family's wishes. Their income couldn't support him. He couldn't pay his bills. His phone was disconnected. He accepted Punjabi literature.

Early in our relationship, this young Sikh invited me to accompany him into St Paul's Cathedral. As we walked through the front entrance, he suddenly grabbed his head and groaned, "I have a heavy headache. It happens each time I come here." Following further visits he suffered bouts of sleeplessness, made irrational decisions, broke promises, and fell out with friends. Mohit, while suffering yet another headache with head cradled in his hands, explained, "Ah! Home sweet home. Everything done for me at home. In Melbourne, nothing. No money! No cooking! No washing!"

I had offered Mohit a Hindi Bible. He repeated, "I don't have a bag to carry it."

I said, "Bring a bag next week."

He stated, "I will bring."

I continued saying, "And I'll bring a gun!"

He asked, "Why?"

I answered, "You'll find out if you don't bring that bag."

The next week he said, "You don't need a gun" and produced with dramatic flourish a bag from behind his back. He accepted the Hindi Bible.

Mohit phoned from the other side of Flinders Street railway station barriers and exclaimed, "I've lost my ticket. Can you come?"

I said, "Buy another ticket and they'll let you through."

Toasted cheese sandwiches are a free promotional attraction offered in Federation Square. I said, "You paid for your ticket but here's a free lunch."

Mohit continued saying, "I read your booklet (John's Gospel). I did what it said and gave my life to Christ. I felt high. I want to go back to that church" (St Paul's). I prayed with him. He further said, "I helped my relative get a job, but he emotionally tortured me because I was unemployed. I am angry. What should I do?" We discussed.

On return to the cathedral, I drew Mohit's attention to John 12:35b. The words: "He that walks in darkness knows not where he goes" prompted him to say, "That's me!" After praying with him, he wiped away tears. I asked, "Do you feel heavy now?"

He answered, "No!" That was good news. I bought him an apple pie and coffee. He repeated, "But what will I do with my flat mate who tortured me?" We discussed Matthew 18:21-22*. He asked, "Will you be my dad while I'm in Australia? I want to meet my new mumma too." Do I hear warning bells?

I said, "I will be your spiritual father, but I cannot offer employment, finance or accommodation."

With mounting excitement, Mohit said, "I will come to church with you this Sunday." But he never did.

Mohit arrived at McDonalds for coffee. He said, "My girlfriend in India wants to stay with you when she visits me."

I asked him, "Are you reading the Bible?" In the months that followed Mohit was repeatedly exhorted to read his Gospel of John.

He stated, "Last week I read."

I said, "Still getting heavy feeling?"

He replied, "Sometimes."

I said, "Pray and read your Bible. What should you do with the man who tortures you?"

He answered, "Love him."

I explained to him, "I pray for you every day. Do you still have Jesus in your heart?"

He replied, "Each time I think of Jesus I get headaches. It is like a ghost in me trying to get out. I have a big phone bill. I can't pay my rent. I told my girlfriend in India to forget me because I am surrounded by darkness." He accepted three food vouchers from our NewHope Baptist Church, Mohit confidentially asked, "I have applied for a security job. Could you arrange references from a teacher and a doctor for me? My immigration solicitor wants $500."

I said, "Mohit, that is dishonest. Give God your headaches and accept His happiness."

Mohit answered saying, "Can we meet again next Thursday? My cousin stole my passport, credit card and tax file number."

I said, "What would happen if your cousin did this in the Punjab?"

Mohit explained, "We would beat him. Break his leg. Break his arm." We discussed a Biblical response to his dilemma.

I purchased lunch for Mohit (no hamburgers for me). Mohit's decision of sorts some time ago was followed by frequent attacks of heaviness.

"Are you praying?"

He replied, "Yes."

I said, "Who to?" He mentioned his god of Eastern philosophy. I told him, "You are choosing to suffer under other gods who offer nothing, not the one true Christian God who heals." I suspect he was less than straight with me. I repeated, "Mohit, I've been through the Good News with you several times, but you are still following your god (Hanumanj). How many more times must I tell you to follow Jesus?"

He stated, "There is much to think about. Give me one week."

I replied, "What you do with Jesus in this life determines what He does with you in the next. Say yes to Him now and He'll say yes to you when you die. Say no to Him now and He'll say no to you then. If you refuse to follow Jesus there is nothing more, I can do for you."

Mohit and I discussed yet again, the basics of the Gospel. He would like to become a Christian but Sikhism and Hanumanj, his Hindu deity, are entrenched. He accepted a church gift pack with Dixon booklet and Punjabi literature and said, "I haven't had work for six months. I have to pay back an $800 loan. It's a big headache. I must be getting punished for something I did wrong. All I see is darkness. I cannot go back to the Punjab as a failure." We discussed Romans 3:23-24* and John 8:12. He said, "My worries make me forget the Bible." I bought him lunch. I drew his attention to Romans 5:1*.

Later, I offered Mohit a chicken wrap and coffee. He told me, "I am a vegetarian on Tuesdays. That's my religion." He recently transferred his met card at the railway barriers to his friend. They each received a $167 infringement notice. He asked, "Can you get me a Hindi Bible for my family in India?" Mohit's iPhone was disconnected until he paid his dues.

Mohit walked against the red pedestrian light. Police were ready to swoop. I called him back in the nick of time.

Later he called from the passenger side of the FSRS barriers. He called saying, "I'm in trouble again. I left my wallet at home. I have no money to buy a ticket. Will you come?"

I said, "I have things to do. Try your boss."

Later, Mohit stood on the passenger side of the railway barriers. I was on the exit side. Railway Police were in attendance. Mohit asked me to buy a ticket and pass it across the barrier. I said, "You are on the train illegally. Tell the inspectors the truth and ask for mercy." He talked his way through. I lent him money for a two-hour ticket which he never refunded. We adjourned for a chicken wrap and coffee.

Mohit's eyes were bloodshot. He had not eaten. His iPod contained pictures and images of his many gods. I said, "Surrender your life to God and delete those pictures."

He answered, "I have tried, but it's too hard and I'm scared of what mum will say if I become a Christian. I'll call her tonight and ring you." Mohit's spiritual oppression due to involvement with idol worship in the Punjab was real.

He promised to attend church the following Sunday. I drew up an agreement to attend church with Vishnu (a young Indian Christian) next Sunday, which Mohit signed. I said, "The desert palm does not find life in itself or in the burning blistering sand out of which it grows. Its life lies in the water far below, which keeps it fresh and green. The Christian life depends on being rooted and grounded in the water of life – Jesus Christ." But Mohit never attended church.

Mohit exclaimed, "I've paid my fine of $175." We adjourned for coffee. Mohit was introduced to Rhandir, another Indian Christian. Rhandir counselled Mohit against idol worship. We discussed again his spiritual oppression. Vishnu invited Mohit to his church again the following Sunday. Mohit, who lives close to Vishnu's church, responded with yet another broken promise.

Mohit said, "The Immigration Department advised me to change my college who refused to refund my $2000 fees. I have sent money to my father in India to buy a motorcycle for his birthday. I want to buy a good wristwatch - would you come with me?" I declined his invitation. He now had two jobs and had not slept for forty-eight hours. He told me, "I want to come to church with you on Sunday."

I fed Mohit a vegan hamburger for lunch and offered him scripture for life. He recently received from his parents in North India, details including photos of the girl they suggested he should marry. Mohit did not feel ready for marriage but said, "My parents have been so good to me. How can I refuse?"

I replied, "If you go to India for holidays, you are in danger of returning to Melbourne with a wife."

He said, "Will you and your wife come to my wedding?"

Mohit informed me he was returning to India for holidays, then would try his luck in New Zealand. I took the opportunity to reinforce the Gospel. Suddenly Mohit disappeared. Maybe the Immigration Department deported him, maybe he returned voluntarily for marriage in the Punjab, or was trying his luck in New Zealand? I can only pray for his salvation.

An Encouraging Conclusion

Rocky, a Sikh, phoned me for an appointment next day at 1pm. Rocky kept his appointment. He said, "We met about seven months ago on the train. You gave me a booklet." His concern was the 'religious media' of his Sikh teachers. He accepted a John's Gospel. I drew attention to John 1:13,* which he then and there read. He broke into a smile saying, "They are good words." In answer to further questions, he said, "I gave my hamburger to a hungry man. I hope this outweighs some bad things I did."

I explained, "When I started school, we used slates. If I made a mistake, I rubbed it out with a duster and started again. Later they gave me an exercise book and pen. But mistakes in exercise books written with ink cannot be erased with dusters. God has a book in which is written all your bad deeds, thoughts, and words but there is absolutely no way your sin can be erased from God's book with good works. The only way they will be erased is washing by faith in the blood of Jesus."

When Swapan, his girlfriend arrived, Rocky accurately recounted the nature of our conversation. She said, "I went to a Christian school in India. I know your moral code. When you spoke with Rocky on the phone, he was so happy. I also am happy to learn the meaning of this great teaching." I followed Sikh custom by placing my right hand on Swapan's head asking God's blessing on her.

Though unaware of any Sikh contacts returning to their homeland to plant village churches, the parable of the sower reminds me that some in whom Gospel seeds fell, will later bear fruit, much fruit and more fruit. That I had taken the trouble to learn a simple greeting in Punjabi often opened the door to interesting cross-cultural conversations in English. 'Sat Shavi Akaal' the friendly Punjabi greeting contains, it was suggested, connotations of future good wishes. Almost without exception my Punjabi contacts were respectful, honest, upstanding, and worthy people who readily forgave my atrocious Aussie accent. So, you might remember when next you meet to greet your Sikh contact with a good old-fashioned Aussie accented 'Sat Shavi Akaal.'

Taking it to Heart:

1. How might you develop a vision to reach the nations for Christ?
2. In broad terms how would you structure your vision?
3. Share some thoughts on how you might implement your vision.

References:

Matthew 18:21-22 – Then Peter came to Him and said, "Lord, how often shall my brother sin against me, and I forgive him? Up to seven times?" Jesus said to him, "I do not say to you, up to seven times, but up to seventy times seven.

Luke 14:13-14 – But when you give a feast, invite the poor, the maimed, the lame and the blind. And you will be blessed, because they cannot repay you: for you shall be repaid at the resurrection of the just.

John 1:13 – Who were born, not of blood, nor of the will of the flesh, nor of the will of man, but of God.

John 3:16 – God so loved the world that He gave His only begotten Son, that whoever believes in Him should not perish but have everlasting life.

John 4:14 – Whoever drinks of the water that I shall give him will never thirst. But the water that I shall give him will become in him a fountain of water springing up into everlasting life.

John 14:6 – Jesus said, I am the way, the truth, and the life. No-one comes to the Father except through Me.

Romans 3:23-24 – For all have sinned and fall short of the glory of God. Being justified freely by His grace through the redemption that is in Christ Jesus whom God set forth as a propitiation by His blood, through faith to demonstrate His righteousness, because in His forbearance God had passed over the sins that were previously committed.

Romans 5:1 – Therefore, having been justified by faith, we have peace with God through our Lord Jesus Christ.

Romans 8:28 – And we know that all things work together for good to those who love God, to those who are called according to His purpose.

Chapter 24

Sri Lankan Experiences

Melbourne CBD

In Federation Square a Sinhala speaking Buddhist and I had protracted discussions regarding the merits of Buddhism and Christianity. After he returned to Sri Lanka, we exchanged views through lengthy emails. He eventually texted saying, "You have studied your faith well. We'll leave it at that."

A Sri Lankan and his brothers attended a prestigious Buddhist school in Colombo, renowned for producing many of his country's elite soldiers and military leadership, but his beloved eldest brother an army brigadier, was killed in the civil war by a land mine. He thereupon lost interest in a military career and migrated to Australia. He said, "My brother's death is difficult. I miss him terribly." I quoted Psalm 23 and read to him John 8:12* with emphasis on the word 'follow'. He accepted the Gospel of John with thanks.

A Tamil refugee whose leg was blown off by a land mine in war torn Sri Lanka, was advertising in Swanston Street with a placard across his shoulders. He was seriously contemplating Christianity and regularly attended a good church in the outer eastern suburb. He was encouraged by the gift of Tamil literature.

In Federation Square a Sri Lankan extolled Buddhism and believed his good karma (he was not slow to tell me about it) will suffice to attain Nirvana. I said, "If you look at a female with lust you have committed adultery with her in your heart. If you are angry at someone you have murdered him in your heart - your Karma will not save you from judgement." He continued mud-slinging. I read to him aspects of Romans 5.

He exclaimed, "The Bible is wrong. Why should I believe it?" He angrily departed.

In Hungry Jacks, Dhrmaratne (his spelling), a retired high ranking Sri Lankan Police Officer, had just arrived to settle his son into university. Photos of his family, home and luxury car indicated wealth! He accepted Sinhala literature and returned to Sri Lanka the next day.

A Singhalese speaking Catholic lady, discussed Mariolatry, and Popeism. She read Hebrews 7:24* in its context and John 8:12* and said, "That's beautiful!" She accepted Sinhala literature.

A Tamil speaking Sri Lankan explained, "My Father is Catholic. My mother is a Hindu."

I replied, "Which do you follow?"

He said, "Both." We discussed Psalm 23, but his command of English was superficial. Finding our way round a Tamil Bible was difficult for him and impossible for me.

I asked him, "Can I put you in contact with a Tamil speaking Christian?'

He said, "Yes." I passed the information on to a Tamil speaking contact who will make contact with him.

Typical Responses from Sri Lankans to the Big Question – "What is the most important question in all the world for you?"

- A trainee nurse who felt worthless and undeserving accepted literature.
- S.D. Pathmanatian said, "I'm Catholic, we all worship the same God." He accepted Singhalese literature.
- A hospitality student replied, "That's a good question. I don't know."
- Umesha, with an engaging smile, admitted to occasional bouts of worry.
- Nalin said, "The fighting in Sri Lanka is nearly over." He accepted a Gospel of John.
- A friendly old man visiting family accepted Sinhala literature.
- A lady at Box Hill railway station said, "I've been to your church. I've heard about your work in the city."
- A student said, 'I've been reading the Bible. What's born-again mean?"
- An enthusiastic young student and cricket supporter accepted a tract.
- Pradeep, a Christian church youth leader, accepted testimony.
- A pleasant Buddhist university student accepted literature in English and Sinhala.
- A male who climbed mountains in Sri Lanka to worship his gods, accepted a Gospel of John.
- A student accepted a Gospel of John.

A family, including two young sons, watched me in McDonalds. The wife was reading a booklet in another language. I asked, "What are you are reading?"

She answered, "Extracts from the Bible."

I said, "I am a Christian."

She stated, "I know. I saw you praying."

I drew two circles, representing the self-centred life and the Christ-controlled life and said to her husband, "Which represents your life?"

Without hesitation he pointed to the Christ centred life and explained, "I recently converted from Buddhism." He went on to share his brief dramatic testimony, including reference to his victory over uncontrollable anger.

I said to his wife, "What's life like since your husband became a Christian?"

With a beautiful smile she softly said, "It's like being in heaven." I drew attention to Psalm 23, Galatians 5:22* and Ephesians 4:32*. She continued "God is speaking to me through these verses."

He said, "God brought you to us today. Thank you." Their boys hugged me as I departed. Their glowing, beaming faces bore eloquent and powerful testimony to a lively vibrant faith.

A Sri Lankan academic in our church car park surreptitiously puffed on his cancer stick. He asked, "What do you do?"

I replied, "For twenty-five years I worked on a farm, looking after sheep. For twenty-five years I worked in the Police Department looking after two-legged sheep. For fifteen years I worked in churches looking after people sheep. Now they reckon I look sheepish." He frowned. I continued to say, "When I say that to Aussies they laugh, but you frown. Why?"

He said, "In our culture, it is insulting to compare humans with animals."

I said, "Thank you for that insight, but did you know that our Christian Holy Book says, "All we like sheep have gone astray, and Jesus is the great Shepherd of the sheep?"

He replied, "No, I didn't."

I asked, "What does your religion say about reincarnation?"

He mischievously replied, "Depending on my Karma, I could reincarnate as a sheep." I quoted John 14:6*. He accepted a Gospel of John.

Sri Lankan Travel Experiences

I've met some memorable people in my ministry throughout Melbourne. One such attractive contact on the local bus described herself as a small 'L' Muslim. She had completed a degree in New Zealand, added a Masters in New York and was recently awarded a PhD in Melbourne, all on scholarships. She said, "I love the way you make friends."

I answered, "Everyone appreciates a listening ear."

She asked me, "Is that how you met your wife?"

I explained, "We met at a church function. Our faith held us together over many years." Later, she was introduced to Jan. They hit it off, so to speak!

During a subsequent conversation, she told me, "I came to your church and brought a friend, but you weren't there." Even though we had searched in the crowd, we missed her. They enjoyed the speaker. She warmly invited us to visit her and family in Sri Lanka should we ever go there.

We never gave her invitation another thought until March 2013 when Jan and I embarked with a group, led by John and Jenny Fearn-Wannan, on a journey to Sri Lanka. On arrival at the Galle Face Hotel, we made contact with our Sri Lankan friend. While awaiting their arrival, I shared with a high-ranking Government official in charge of re-settlement after the recent civil war. He accepted testimony and Sinhala literature.

True to her word our contact and her husband took us to their lovely home in a leafy Colombo suburb. Later, as we were departing, she said, "I have a reason for inviting you. I'll tell you about it later." They supplied us with a sumptuous, delicious, home cooked Sri Lankan lunch prepared by her mother. Our very personable hostess with humorous sparkle and spoken English far better than mine, had returned from Melbourne to her husband and three children on the Sunday prior to our arrival to live permanently in Sri Lanka and is pursuing a university lecturing career in languages.

Her father, a high-ranking military officer, was killed in the Sri Lankan conflict. Her mother, present with us at the luncheon, had survived unscathed the terrorist attack on the head office of her company in which 200 of her work colleagues were killed. Her family had also lost twenty-four relatives in the tsunami a few years ago.

During the meal our friend said, "My reason for inviting you is to say, how grateful I am to Australia for offering me a scholarship for my PhD. I want to give something back. I can't thank a government, but I can provide hospitality to as many Australians as possible."

Regarding the TPTL NT*, she said, "I'll accept, but don't know if I'll read it."

To her husband I asked, "What is the most important question in all the world for you?" He was not sure.

I exclaimed, "Surely it must be what happens to us when we die." Significant discussions followed. During my testimony, her mother's eyes were locked on mine, but she remained silent. Our friend's ex-landlady in Blackburn, had worked in our NewHope Baptist Church Cafe and was known to our tour group leader. It's a small world.

We endured a polluted seventy-five-minute ride back to our hotel in heavy traffic in an open sided noisy three wheeled 'tuk tuck' (three-wheel taxi). A sticker on the windshield said, 'Jesus is the way, the truth and the life,' but superstitious religious talismans swung to and fro from an interior rear vision mirror. This poverty stricken, non-English speaking driver happily received a higher-than-expected financial reward for his work and Sinhala literature.

A subsequent email received from our hostess: "It is still extremely hot and humid in Sri Lanka. We are told this weather pattern will continue until mid-May, alas. I wouldn't mind some of Melbourne's nippy weather here right now! Thanks for keeping in touch. I am very pleased you enjoyed your visit to Sri Lanka. I am also pleased to have met people like you during four of the most memorable years of my life. May God bless you." The attitude of our hostess and her family considering all their tragedy was amazing, admirable, and inspiring.

Next day we lunched at the Cinnamon Grand Hotel, Colombo. An attractive incredibly skilled Sri Lankan lady played golden oldies on the grand piano as patrons dined. Her repertoire was vast, all without sheet music. I loved the melody, and lyrics of music from the 1930's. At my request she played 'Blue Moon' beautifully:

> 'You saw me standing alone,
> Without a dream in my heart,
> Without a love of my own,
> Blue moon, you knew just what I was there for,
> You heard me saying a prayer for,
> Someone I really could care for'.

Months later, this grand hotel was destroyed by terrorist bombs; many were killed. Did this wonderful lady survive? I don't know. But the lyrics of the song make a point. Do I really care for that relative, neighbour, or work mate? Will they read enough of the Gospel in my life to want it themselves? They may never get another opportunity to accept the Gospel. You may never have another opportunity to share it. No one knows the future. Now is the hour. Tomorrow may be too late.

Some of us enjoyed an Allan 'Border Burger' at the world-famous Cricket Club Cafe with its wealth of cricket memorabilia. Sri Lankan/

Australian test cricket matches were played at the nearby Galle Cricket Ground. Walk the famous Galle Promenade where a Sri Lankan hailed a 'tuk' and insisted we attend the Buddhist elephant ceremony. He got angry when we declined his offer.

The Flower Seller

We journeyed on through the world-famous mountainous tea growing plantations of Sri Lanka down a steeply descending tightly winding, heavily trafficked road, bordered by verdant greenery, colourful flowers, streams, spectacular waterfalls, mountain peaks and forests – overwhelming, awesome, fantastic, and beautiful. It was close to being the most spectacular equatorial sub-tropical scenery we had seen on our journey thus far.

But a poorly clad little roadside flower vendor waving aloft a bouquet of dahlias, paled this magnificence into insignificance. He leapt into view as if from nowhere, running, broadly smiling alongside our slow-moving vehicle. We overtook this lightly built nearly middle-aged vendor of Nuwara Eliya with his surprising turn of speed and left him far behind, or so we thought. Around the next bend he sparked our interest by appearing again as if by magic, still running, waving his flowers imploring, pleading. We drove on. He surprised us all by unexpectedly re-appearing four or five more times by short cutting across the necks of tight road bends - each time lower down the mountainside. Thus, he marketed effectively and powerfully his wares along a kilometre or so of road. His initiative, determination, and herculean stamina lifted our surprise by degrees to something akin to astonishment.

Sensing that we felt his efforts should be acknowledged, and acting in accord with his own instincts perhaps, a group member called out with a trace of urgency, "Can we stop the bus and help this man?" The vendor appeared at the open bus door, breathless, sweaty, and utterly spent. The flower seller had seen his opportunity, pursued it relentlessly and conquered our hearts. His entrepreneurial skills and showmanship were generously rewarded. The exultation of his hard-won victory registered in a facial expression, which may best be described as a mixture of triumph and gratitude – a big step forward for him, and a random act of kindness for us. A fellow traveller accepted and treasured the flowers. Another of our party later succinctly and somewhat humorously put it this way:

> 'There was a man with lovely flowers,
> Who ran up and down for hours and hours,
> Our man had a thought,
> And these flowers he bought,
> And now these flowers are ours.'

Our local tour guide shrugged indifferently saying, "Many live this way." But the magnitude of the gift astonished the tour guide apprentice.

We booked in at Avani Beach Resort, Bentota, and shared a devotion based on Genesis 12:1-3 with the group, in lieu of church. Here I found a quote containing a phrase sometimes used by the retired engineer in our group. "We have genuflected before the god of science only to find that it has given us the atomic bomb producing fears and anxieties that science can never mitigate" (Martin Luther King).

We visited a Habitat for Humanity village and inspected several homes provided for those who lost family members and possessions during the infamous tsunami. One lady, who lost both her children was setting up a jewellery cutting business in her new home.

We then arrived at Chaaya Wild, Yala, Sri Lanka's most popular National Park. The jeep's square wheels and rough roads were not a good combination, but good views of wild elephants, water buffalo, spotted deer, pea fowl, the colourful jungle fowl and a profusion of bird life made it worthwhile. We discussed over an evening meal, our respective faiths with

Henry, our devoutly Buddhist tour guide. He politely accepted a Gospel presentation, Sinhala literature and a New Testament.

Lunch was provided at Ella Falls, Rawana, while a troop of monkeys played in the beautifully manicured garden, and we climbed to Nuwara Eliya. We stayed at the world-famous Grand Hotel and enjoyed the tea plantations on the hillsides. We attended an Easter morning service in a rotunda at the edge of a beautiful wetland at Cinnamon Lodge, Habarana, led by a group member. His text: 'He is risen' (John 20:19*). The O/C of security declined literature saying, "I am Buddhist," but requested my email address.

I said, "If you want my address, you must accept my literature."

He said, "OK."

Over breakfast on our final morning in Sri Lanka, whilst discussing religion with Henry our Buddhist tour guide, I offered Chandrani, a bright smiling forty-one-year-old waitress, Sinhala literature. Her eyes widened with glad surprise. "I am a Christian" she enthused and gratefully accepted a quantity of coloured pencils and related materials for her Sunday school class. This was another golden opportunity to get the message through to Henry.

I said to Chandrani in his presence, "How did you become a Christian?"

She replied, "I was a Buddhist, but my husband led me to Jesus."

Henry said, "My room is next to a church. Last night I heard Christians singing and praying, 'Lord, we are poor please help us,' but they are poor because of bad karma'." Chandrani the Christian hugged and kissed Jan and me as we departed.

Anuradhapura was generations ago the first capital of the island. We visited the city's famous sacred BO tree relic, said to have grown from a branch of the tree under which Buddha received enlightenment 2,250 years ago. A leaning trunk supported by gold-coloured props, is all that remains. It is supposedly the oldest documented living tree in the world.

The temple standing there contains statues of the Buddha. Buddhism in Sri Lanka is deeply entrenched.

Taking it to Heart:

1. Quantify the value of testimonies in evangelism.
2. What are some ways to prepare testimonies?
3. Share how you might present your story?

References:

John 8:12 – I am the light of the world. He who follows me shall not walk in darkness, but have the light of life.

John 14:6 – Jesus said to him, "I am the way, the truth, and the life. No one comes to the Father except through me.'

John 20:19 – Jesus came and stood in the midst and said to them, 'Peace be with you.'

Galatians 5:22-23 – But the fruit of the Spirit is love, joy, peace, long suffering, kindness, goodness, faithfulness, gentleness, self-control. Against such there is no law.

Ephesians 4:32 – Be kind to one another, tender hearted, forgiving one another, even as God in Christ forgave you.

Hebrews 7:24 – But He, because He continues forever, has an unchangeable priesthood.

TPTL NT – The Pocket Testament League New Testament.

Chapter 25

Three Sectarian Influences

Searching for God in Wrong Places

Blaise Pascal, an influential French philosopher (1623 – 1662) famously said 'There is a god-shaped vacuum in every man's heart which cannot be filled by any created thing, but only by God the Creator made known through Jesus Christ.'

Hare Krishnas, Jehovah's Witnesses and Mormons all downgrade the deity of Jesus and his atoning work on the cross. Without faith in the real Biblical Christ, they will spend an eternity in Hell like any non-Christian." Some lessons I have learned in dealing with sectarians are related as follows.

Some Lessons Learned in Street Evangelism

1. Hare Krishnas (HK)

The Christian life is a journey. Many Christians know about their conversion but understand little about living victoriously between conversion and eternity. I thank God for a challenging, satisfying, and exciting faith-based ministry that taught me much about the deeper issues of Christian doctrines. Curiosity led me to investigate the HK movement. Through this journey I learned a little of how to "defend my faith to everyone who asks a reason for the hope that is within me" (1 Peter 3:15).

Prayer, Christian scriptures, and trust in the Holy Spirit are vital keys in combating Hare Krishna's deceptive lies. According to Encyclopedia Britannica, the teachings of the HK movement are embedded in ancient Hindu scriptures, known as the Bhagavad Gita. Adherents believe that 'Krishna' is the Supreme Lord and that humans are eternal spiritual beings trapped in endless cycles of reincarnation.

The number and nature of cycles for individuals is determined by karma, the law of consequences of past actions which returns human beings to physical existence. According to the HK movement's doctrine, it is possible to change one's karma by practicing extreme forms of yoga; however, the Lord (Krishna) has provided an easier method. Believers spend several hours each day chanting the holy names, Krishna, and Rama - the HK mantra.

HK's are vegetarians. They have renounced the use of alcohol and drugs. Sex is allowed only within marriage for procreation purposes. Male devotees shave their heads, leaving only a small tuft of hair called a '*Sakha*', a sign of surrender to their teacher. Each morning male and female believers mark their foreheads with coloured clay as a reminder that their bodies are temples of Krishna. The following are selections of brief extracts from conversations over time with HK devotees propagating their religion in or near Swanston Street, Melbourne CBD. For privacy reasons, and because their names were seldom disclosed, and for convenience's sake, I have assigned English names in some cases.

A HK said, "I am a monk. Have you ever heard of a monk?" I think he wanted to impress me.

I replied, "No, but I have heard of monkeys."

He said, "I'm selling books about the Lord Krishna. He's a god of love." His religious book is covered with a picture of Krishna in a war chariot.

I replied, "Hang on! This is a contradiction of terms. He can't be a god of love and war."

I then quoted Psalm 23, but he stated, "I've got to get on with my book selling. Excuse me."

A further HK asked, "Have you read our holy book?"

I answered, "No! But have you read our Christian Holy Bible?" He admitted not. I countered with a defence from John 10:27-28. "My sheep hear my voice, and I know them, and they follow me. And I give them eternal life, and they shall never perish; neither shall anyone snatch them out of my hand." He reluctantly accepted a Gospel of John.

I prayed that another monk would see 'Jesus pierced for him, and that he would mourn for his sin as a father in bitterness for the loss of his first born and be washed from his idolatry by the blood of the Cross.' He shot me furtive glances and kept his distance. Using the same tactics, I silently prayed for a different monk who was aware of my presence. He droned an intermittent low chant. After some time, I was weary of praying. Somewhat burdened by my lack of spiritual energy, I said, "Lord, what do I pray now?" To my great relief, the Holy Spirit clearly reminded me, "Bruce you have prayed, now keep your eyes on Jesus."

A young lady from Botswana intercepted me. I got in first and asked, "What is the most important question for you?" She began to explain her relationship to the universe and offered me HK literature.

She firmly included in her comments, "I used to go to church. I know what goes on."

I responded, "Being an ex-church attender, you will know that all who rejected Moses' law died without mercy at the hand of two or three witnesses. What worse punishment do you suppose will happen to those who have trampled the Son of God underfoot, counted the blood of the covenant by which he was sanctified a common thing, and insulted the Spirit of grace?" (Hebrews 10:28-29). She rushed upstairs to the safety of their cafeteria.

Two males set up their book stall. To the one who approached me I asked, "Could you read to me from your book, and I'll read to you from mine?"

He answered, "I know you. I have spoken with you before. You are a Christian devotee, aren't you? I have no time for you. I have to sell books." He pronounced 'Hare Krishna' over me and turned away. I pronounced 'Jesus Christ' over him as he departed.

His co-worker intercepted an innocent female passerby. I peeked over their shoulders. He was showing his captive pictures of a large hideous serpent. He said to her, "You can show these to your kids."

I said to him, "Those pictures would give kids nightmares!"

He asked, "Are you interested?"

I said, "No! I'm a Christian." He ridiculed my faith by shouting, "Glory hallelujah! Praise God!"

An Albanian HK commented to me, "Your Ten Commandments say Christians should not kill animals." We discussed the topic.

He then contended, "I pay the council for the right to stand here."

I replied, "You are interfering with pedestrians. I have a right to stand here like you."

He chanted, "Hare Krishna. Hare Krishna."

I repeated, "Jesus Christ. Jesus Christ."

His Asian superior said, "My friend should not speak to you like that," and ordered him to apologise 'right away'! His colleague dutifully and meekly obeyed.

I explained, "That is a nonsense apology." Angrily, the superior demanded my name. I refused to give it. He refused to apologise.

An Aggressive HK Attempting to Indoctrinate Hapless Females

Outside a famous pub in Swanston Street, a towering, early thirties male HK intercepted a short and tiny teenager. She attempted to walk away. The overbearing man kept pace with her aggressively spouting his propaganda. He implemented the same aggressive tactics to another young female. I brushed elbows with him as we walked along crowded Swanston Street. So intent was he on conversation with the second young female that he failed to notice me. I overheard snippets of what he said, 'Auras,' 'Special diets,' and 'invitations.'

I interrupted this domineering man and said, "Excuse me! Please stop harassing young girls." Thus began a somewhat lengthy conversation which may best be summarised as follows.

He said, "I'm not harassing."

"You are! I've just seen you" I added.

He replied, "I'm humble enough to learn from what you say."

I responded, "Empty words! They mean nothing. Just stop harassing young females."

He defended himself saying, "If you don't like it write a letter."

I assertively stated, "I don't like what you are doing, and I will report you to the authorities for harassment."

He said, "Now you laugh at me!"

I responded, "And now you are angry."

He stalked off mumbling, "Stop shadowing me. Leave me alone." I continued to keep an eye on him. He later pestered yet another female.

I surprised him by speaking from behind, "You sure like the young females don't you."

He called out, "Not you again!"

A HK Throws Down the Gauntlet

Alec, with whom I had previously interacted, invited me to the HK cafeteria. I told him I didn't believe his religion. He countered, "All religions are the same." He threw down the gauntlet by confidently pronouncing the words, "Hare Krishna" upon me to invoke peace in my soul and an anticipated changed attitude.

I immediately responded, "Jesus Christ" to which he reciprocated, "Hare Krishna." I countered, "Jesus Christ." We continued our verbal exchange for what seemed an eternity. This exchange happened amidst a widening circle of onlookers. I began praying aloud along the lines of Acts 4:12: "Nor is there salvation in any other, for there is no other name under heaven given among men by which we must be saved."

He continued chanting unknown words with a sly grin but at the same time half turning from side to side handing out literature to passing pedestrians. I corresponded my movements by maintaining the position of my nose about two feet directly in front of his and continued praying aloud. A sense of calmness overtook me. He called for support from passing friends who didn't want a thing to do with the scene. His despairing appeal to a wider circle of watching, amused spectators also proved futile .

I prayed to God in Jesus' Name for help. Suddenly Revelation 12:11 popped into my head. "And they overcame him by the blood of the Lamb, and by the word of their testimony, and they did not love their lives unto death." I prayed aloud, "Lord, in the name of the blood of Jesus Christ, bind Satan and release this man into a personal relationship with you."

To his astonishment, and mine too, the man shouted, "Jesus Christ!" Non-plussed by the words of his own mouth, he stopped chanting, and with an expression akin to a mixture of fear and curiosity asked, "Why don't Christians chant the name of Jesus in the streets like we chant Hare Krishna?"

Ignoring his question, I stated, "My concern is the eternal destiny of your soul."

He hurried upstairs to his café yelling, "Hare Krishna, Hare Krishna." An old, grey-headed Aussie (me) verbally grappling with a shaven headed pigtailed young HK in all his flowing eastern finery, must have looked funny to the public, but I was fighting from the victory position for the Gospel's sake. The HK could never win. I left rejoicing in my Lord's victory.

- Annie, whilst handing out literature, smiled at me. Grateful for an implied invitation to talk I asked her, "What are you handing out?"
- She replied to me, "Spiritual books."
- I said, "You mean Hare Krishna?"
- She said, "Yes."
- I asked her, "Give me a run down on your holy book."
- She explained with the aid of pictures, the travel of the soul from here to eternity saying, "I recommend you read it. What books do you read?"
- I said, "The Bible."
- She stated, "My brother said he will send me a Bible."
- I inquired, "Do you have a Christian background?"
- To which she said, "Yes."
- I volunteered. "May I read you something from my Bible?" I opened my New Testament to Hebrews 10:31 so we could read the words

THREE SECTARIAN INFLUENCES

together: "It is a fearful thing to fall into the hands of the living God." She hurriedly disappeared.

A book selling HK monk told me, "I live a celibate life. Celibacy purifies the thoughts. These books answer life's greatest problems."

I asked him, "How many lives do you live before you get to God?"

He answered "If you live a good life, you go straight to God. If not, you could come back as another human or go down a level or two and become an animal, fish, or an insect."

I said, "It sounds like you have no confidence in your future."

He told me, "I've read the Bible. Christians change its meaning. It says you shall not murder, but Christians kill animals."

"Actually," I responded, "The biblical context of killing is referring to people killing people. But the Bible also talks about the blood sacrifice that matters most. Jesus Christ, the spotless Lamb of God was sacrificed for your sin and mine. He rose to life the third day to put an end to the untruth of endless cycles of reincarnation." Like so many Hare Krishnas he had enough and walked.

I followed him defending my handwritten scriptures, saying, "But we are Christians, and this is the Word of God."

He complained, "Stop hassling me!"

I didn't give up. "But I wrote it especially for you."

He stated, "You are too fundamental!" He turned away and harassed more pedestrians with increasing agitation and intensity.

Later that day I said, "You are still mad at me, aren't you?"

He quickly protested, "No!" And through gritted teeth he defended, "I was busy selling books, and I didn't have time to speak." Again, I offered him my handwritten script. This time he accepted.

To a monk aggressively selling books, I offered a handwritten script from 2 Peter 1:21: "For prophecy never came by the will of man, but holy men of God spoke as they were moved by the Holy Spirit," but he sharply replied, "No thanks!" and moved away.

Another monk offered me books, including one on Hare Krishna's food laws. I said, "I am over eighty years old and have used a non-vegetarian diet all my life. I still take no medication. Why would I change?"

He said, "Your Bible says you shall not kill. That includes animals."

I responded, "That prohibition applies to people killing people only."

He responded, "Your Bible is corrupted."

I counteracted, "Prove it!"

He said, "I'm sorry. I was arrogant. I shouldn't say that. I believe in Christ too."

I ventured to say, "The Christ you believe in and the Christ I believe in are totally different."

He quickly responded, "Now you are arrogant! Why so many divisions in the church?"

I bounced back saying, "Why did two of your leaders have a dispute over food laws in your restaurant (indicating the restaurant) with the result that one punched the other's nose and was convicted in court for assault?"

He said indignantly, "When?"

I reacted, "Last year. It was reported in the Age newspaper. I have the clipping."

He responded, "I haven't time to argue. You will never change me. I've got work to do."

A HK nun intercepted me with a wide smile and proffered hand. I declined her offer. She offered me books. I kindly declined to accept them. Thirty metres further up, another nun stepped in front of me and offered her hand. I declined her offer. She said, "These books are written about spirituality in India. Much blessing comes from India like yoga and meditation."

I told her, "I've been to India. It is full of problems, and it always has been."

She responded with a barrage of questions, "I was a Christian and attended church for years. Jesus is not God. What's God's name? Why aren't you selling Bibles? What miracles has your God done for you?" With a beautiful smile, she signaled the end of our interesting one-way discussion by pronouncing the words, "Hare Krishna" over me. I pronounced over her the blessing of "Jesus Christ." Her face flushed. Her smile disappeared. She intercepted yet another pedestrian.

At long last, a nun was on speaking terms. She asked me, "What has been happening in your life lately?"

I said, "The Lord has blessed me."

She enquired "How?"

I put the answer to her in plain words, "The blood of Jesus cleanses me from all my sin. The force of this verse came to me in a new way this week." I explained that the word 'cleanse' is not limited to remission of past sins, but it is also powerfully active in the present continuous sense. She seemed to be struggling with her emotions.

A monk countered with his own doctrinal spin. His boss appeared and interjected, "Did you get that Bible verse for me?" In a previous conversation he had asked me, 'Is there a verse in the Bible where Jesus says he is God?"

I said, "I typed up some verses, but I couldn't find you, so today, I didn't bring them."

He almost scolded, "Don't forget next time. I want to know." The next day, when I returned with the printed scriptures, he took the conversation a little deeper saying, "I've been in email contact with an American

Pastor who said Jesus is not God. Your verses (he had glanced at them) are inconclusive."

I asked him, "Provide me with the internet address of this American Pastor?"

He replied, "I'll get you the details next Thursday."

I said, "You realise there are criticisms of Hare Krishna on the internet, and we could go on swapping criticisms endlessly."

He demanded, "Are you saying you will not read the internet article?"

I replied, "Inspiration comes from the word of God not critics."

He stated, "That sounds like dogma."

I answered, "That's my experience. I enjoy telling people about Jesus. It doesn't get any better than that.'

He said, "Well keep up the good work."

I explained, "Jesus is the way the truth and the life, no man comes to the Father but by Jesus" (John 14:6). He never provided the information requested.

A young man in western apparel approached and said, "I am a HK monk. Could I interest you in some Himalayan philosophy?"

I immediately stated, "I saw nothing in India when I was there to interest me in Himalayan philosophy."

Unperturbed he said, "They elevate their minds above the material world."

I asked, "What about sex?"

He replied, "It is not right to join the two dirtiest parts of our bodies in sex, so we practice sex within marriage for procreation purposes only."

I countered, "That being the case, you were born in filth."

He nodded, "I was born in filth but left it behind."

I amended saying, "You were born with filth."

He bantered shouting, "This is developing into a clash of egos."

I responded, "Your ego is part of the filthiness of your flesh."

I observed another monk in western apparel accosting a young woman, offering her a similar small picture of a smiling face, saying, "I am giving away smiles." As was appropriate, I quickly interposed myself between him and the girl. He then had to address us both. He said, "What do you think of Hare Krishna?"

I said, "I attended your restaurant and have some of your reading matter. Your magazine states that Krishna is a god of war, violence, and polygamy. I would not want to follow a god like that." The young woman quickly departed. He angrily accused me of narrow mindedness and claimed that diet, sexual purity, and meditation are essential to achieve the higher state. I countered with, "It is by grace you are saved through faith, not works lest you should boast - all the fullness of the God head dwells bodily in Christ, and I am complete in Him." He stumbled at that and walked with a despondent expression.

A Snake Dancing Procession of HK's.

A gaggle of monks and nuns energetically snake danced their way through the busy throng in Swanston Street. Their leader was brandishing his weapon of musical destruction. A female taking up the rear guard focused her loud foghorn-like pronouncements heavenward. Her reverberating voice drowned out conversations and traffic noise. I was reminded of a different procession referred to by Paul when he wrote inspired by the Holy Spirit of God: "Thanks be to God who always leads us in triumph in Christ and through us diffuses the fragrance of His knowledge in every place" (2 Corinthians 2:14).

I observed another monk who said, "It is hypocritical for Christians to talk to me about religion with cigarettes dangling from their mouths."

I explained, "Recently, I saw one of your leading lights spit on the footpath three times. When I told him his behaviour was inappropriate, he denied spitting. And what about the 'punch up' your members had in your cafeteria kitchen over food rites, and the well-publicised court case which followed?"

He said, "I don't know anything about that." I shared some Christian doctrines to which he replied, "Yes, we have that too. I am reading the Bible. I'm up to John chapter five but can't understand it. Where does Jesus say anywhere in the Bible that he is God?" Without waiting for an answer, he declared, "Hare Krishna!"

I declared, "Jesus Christ."

He said, "Hari Krishna."

I replied, "I refuse that. May the blessing of Jesus Christ be upon you?"

He looked at me and repeated his curse, "Hare Krishna." He even called a couple of his mates for help. Thankfully they declined. The crest-fallen monk bolted upstairs to his vegetarian cafeteria.

Let the Bible loose and it will defend itself

I shared my testimony with a monk who unsuccessfully tried to convince me that we believe exactly the same thing.

He affirmed me by saying, "It's good to meet a holy man like you."

I quickly brought him to his senses saying, "I am a sinner saved by grace."

To which he commented, "It's good to meet a humble man."

I continued, "If I were humble, I'd become proud of my humility." He sighed in resignation. "I am tired of casting my pearls before the swine." He offered two books, which I may read to gain a perspective on their beliefs. He accepted literature on the guarantee he would read it.

The next day he called, "Hello Bruce, I thought I could feel you behind me. Did you read my books?"

I replied, "I read the first couple of pages, but nothing captured my interest, so I picked up my Bible and read words that were alive and powerful. These are some of the words I read: 'He who hears My word and believes Him who sent Me has everlasting life, and shall not come into judgement, but has passed from death into life'" (John 5:24). Engaging Hare Krishnas in philosophical debate is fruitless. I recalled the advice of a wise Christian who said, "You don't have to defend the Bible. It is like a lion. Let it loose and it will defend itself."

Yet another monk tried to entice me into the cult's cafeteria for a cheap vegetarian meal. He had asked me if I ate meat. I had told him I did, and I also stated I wear leather belts and leather shoes. He quickly brought to my attention that, "Your Bible says you shall not kill. That includes animals."

I corrected him saying, "That reference was to humans not animals."

He moved to his next tactic and said, "We believe in all gods."

I replied, "My Bible says Jesus is the way, the truth and the life, no man comes to God but by Him."

He said to me, "Come upstairs and read our Bhagavad-Gita scriptures. They give the complete picture."

I informed him that Jesus had said, "I am the bread of life. He who comes to me shall never hunger, and he who believes in me shall never thirst" (John 6:35). I have no need of your literature!"

One monk offered me a recipe book entitled: 'How to improve your karma'. He suggested, "If you eat vegetarian, and do not kill animals or eat meat, your karma improves and your chances of a better life next time round are improved."

I responded, "What stops you finishing up in the next life as a cockroach climbing trees in South America?"

He changed the subject saying, "Christianity is too narrow." He belligerently accused me of spiritual ignorance and reaffirmed his belief in the Biblical injunction not to kill - including animals.

Another monk told me, "If you eat animal flesh, you are eating humans from a past life. The Bible was written 2,000 years ago in the present tense which means it is no longer applicable."

I interjected, "The Bible was written in the present continuous tense, which makes it highly applicable."

He said, "Jesus was a vegetarian."

I corrected him saying, "Jesus ate fish." He smugly informed me that in the Greek, fish meant grass. Maybe he was quoting from an undiscovered Greek manuscript?

A seasoned monk in civilian clothes (a bit sneaky I reckon) was pressurising a pedestrian into accepting literature. He intercepted two more young males offering them books but my presence at his elbow upset him. Yesterday I had given him a New Testament and suggested he read Romans 8. Today, he said, "Good day Donald."

I asked, "Why do you call me Donald?"

He quipped, "You remind me of Donald Duck."

I declared, "There's no other name given among men by whom we must be saved except Jesus."

He demanded in rapid fire style, "Can you read Greek? How many versions of the Bible are there? What does God look like?" His tirade of questions made it clear that he really wasn't interested in hearing my answers.

I responded with his method, "Is your Bhagavata-Gita in English? Can you read Sanskrit?" How many translations are there? Have you read Romans 8 yet?"

He responded, "Yes, but I can't understand it." He protested loudly to young men lurking nearby saying "This man is going to ram his religion down my throat and tell me I am going to Hell." The startled pedestrians dispersed rapidly as did the Hare Krishna, not wanting to hear my explanation of Romans 8.

Arrested by an Angry HK and Escorted to a Police Station

- Another seasoned HK approached me and demanded, "Are you an agent of God?"
- I said, "I am a sinner saved by grace."
- He yelled with flushed face close to my nose, "Are you or are you not an agent of God?"
- I repeated, "I am a sinner saved by grace."
- He ranted. "Hare Krishna!"
- I declared, "Jesus Christ!"
- He repeated, "Hare Krishna."
- I responded, "Jesus Christ. Gnashing of teeth, wailing and the fires of hell await you, my friend. See if you can understand this. All men will die. All men will be judged. Jesus will be that judge. He'll divide all men into two groups, the positive and the negative. What you do with Jesus in this life determines what he does with you in the next life. Say yes to him now and live in paradise eternally or say no to Jesus and finish up in Hell forever. The choice is yours."
- He drew himself up to his full height and with an authoritative voice heavily threatened, "If you say that again, I'll take you to the Police Station."
- I wasn't about to let him get away with that, so I repeated, "Say yes to Jesus now or suffer in Hell forever."

- He yelled in my face, "That's it! I'm taking you to the Police Station. I've done this before. Come with me!" I figured he was bluffing, and I was supposed to be terrified.
- He seemed momentarily dumfounded when I began singing close to his ear, "Jesus loves me this I know for the Bible tells me so........." as we walked side by side to the Police Station.
- The Senior Policewoman said to the monk, "What can I do for you?"
- He bleated, "This Christian preacher keeps telling me I'm going to Hell."
- Quick as a flash she demanded, "And what religion are you peddling?"
- She then turned to me and said, "Leave the station!"
- I said, "But ... " I wanted to tell my side of the story.
- But she sternly emphasised "Now!!!!" So, I obediently left. She didn't even ask my name or address. I never saw that monk or any of his team on the street after that date.

Another bookselling HK told me, "All truth comes from Vedic scriptures in India."

I said, "Really! I understood that researchers have found, reproduced in ancient Chinese literature, the first three chapters of Genesis which predates the Sanskrit."

He redirected the conversation saying, "All gods are the same. There can only be one god." Then broke into some unfamiliar language which I presumed was Sanskrit.

I said, "Your language skills do not impress me. But I am impressed with Jesus Christ who said, "I am the Way, the Truth and the Life. No man comes to the Father but through faith in Him."

THREE SECTARIAN INFLUENCES

He countered saying, "The fact is that our eternal destiny depends on how good we are down here. We could come back to this life as a cat or a dog or a human."

I told him, "What you do with Jesus in this life determines what He does with you in the next."

He uttered, "I don't have to talk with you. I've got better things to do."

I warned him, "And I don't have to talk with you either - but remember this, if you deny Jesus in this life your future life will be too terrible to think about."

HK people use different methods by which to capture a potential victim's interest. Following, are two examples.

Equipped with a book in his hand, the Hare Krishna stares at an approaching prospect, then wordlessly points with his index finger to a spot on the pavement at his feet. The innocent pedestrian obligingly stands where X marks the spot. The HK immediately transfers the book to his victim's hand and begins talking hard and fast. Surprisingly the spellbound contact often buys the book. The HK focusses mainly, though not always, on young western adults, but seldom Asians or older folks. Pray that God spares our kids and grandkids from their blinding deceptions and lies.

Another trick is diverting their victims, especially Christians, with a simple threefold strategy. Firstly, offend with a mild or veiled insult against the Bible. Secondly, throw in some red herrings and thirdly turn their backs. One HK said, "I've forgotten your name already and you are going to say it doesn't matter. He curtly replied, "I follow Jesus Christ closer than anyone else I know, but what happens to those who don't even get to hear about Jesus Christ?" I suggested he read Romans chapters 1 and 2. He responded, "I thought you would tell me."

I replied, "But you won't listen! Go home and read the Bible!" I am learning to avoid foolish and ignorant disputes. I am resolved by God's grace, and as opportunity arises to cut through smug little red herrings and continue focusing attention on their responsibilities before God on Judgement Day.

2. Jehovah's Witnesses (JW)
J.C. Ryle, a famous highly respected evangelical scholar of yester-year, once said, "Since Satan cannot destroy the Gospel, he has too often neutralised its usefulness by addition, subtraction, or substitution." Such is the case with so called Biblical 'proof' texts supplied out of context by JW in support of their anti-Christian church stance.

Some brief extracts of a few of my interactions with Jehovah Witnesses are included herewith:

The Watchtower Movement
Assorted (JW) Contacts

Two bricklayers were relaxing in Hungry Jacks. In answer to the BQ*, the younger said, "I don't know."

The elder countered with, "How do we find peace in the world?"

I said, "You tell me."

He replied, "Peace will come when Jesus restores it. Have you seen our new Jehovah's Witness website? You should take a look."

I said, "My authority is the Bible."

"Good!" he said, and referring me to Hebrews 7 continued, "Jesus is our great high priest." It so happened I had read Hebrews 7 that morning. The Watchtower (JW) movement refers to the Trinity as consisting of the Father, the created 'man' Jesus, and a 'divine influence' called the spirit of God. I read Hebrews 7:3 regarding Melchizedek aloud to them: "Without father, without mother, without descent. Having neither beginning of days, nor end of life, but made like unto the Son of God; abides a priest continually." This mysterious Melchizedek referred to in the Hebrew context is quoted by Calvin, a highly respected evangelical scholar, who said, "In showing us Melchizedek as one who was never born and never died, scripture is setting forth in picture form, the truth that for Christ there is neither beginning nor end."

An elderly Greek complained bitterly with expletives about his treatment at Flinders Street railway station (FSRS) by a ticket inspector. He wept tears of frustration arising from ongoing health problems. But when I mentioned scriptures, he suddenly assumed a wise, pious, and holy expression, quoted numerous scriptures and asked crafty questions. I was wondering what was going on here? Suddenly it clicked. I said, "You are a Jehovah's Witness aren't you?"

He replied, "Yes." He accepted literature.

In the FSRS concourse sat a good looking well-dressed young man with a shoulder bag. He listened to my testimony and said, "'I'm a Jehovah's Witness. We believe exactly the same things."

I answered, "There are major differences in our belief."

He agreed, "Yes, there are."

I said, "Your people lose credibility when they walk up my driveway and tell me we believe the same bibles knowing full well there are major differences. That's annoying."

He replied, "It's a matter of interpretation."

I said, "And they even have the colossal effrontery of trying to redefine my testimony."

He said, "JW are no different to anyone else. We all make mistakes. It is good to meet a well-educated man like you, so well versed in the Bible." He gave me a leaflet and accepted a tract.

A black African American was busking in the Bourke Mall outside Myers. His loud voice, infectious laughter, red trousers, bib and braces, light mauve shirt and shiny black shoes fitted with steel heels and half soles, helped make his song and dance routine a class act. Pedestrians crowded round, laughed, cheered, applauded, and threw money. A man with a swarthy complexion and felt hat tipped over one eye, wearing a grey suit, white shirt, tie, and three-quarter length coat circulated amongst the pedestrians. He reminded me of Al Capone and the Mafia. A strongly built young man of pleasant appearance in 'cuckoo land' spoke behind me. I asked where he got his philosophy. He said, "Masonic ritual and Reiki." His voice was loud, his eyes intense. I became apprehensive of physical assault. I limited comment to reduce risk of aggravation. Unexpectedly, he placed his hand on my head and pronounced some dreadful curse, but I was protected by the blood of Jesus. I drew myself up to full height and stared him down. He walked. The tap dancer, a front man for the Jehovah's Witnesses, having finished his routine, was joined by Al Capone - so called.

Jehovah's Witnesses were trying to confuse the Christian black African security guard but he was savvy enough to understand their trickery. I said to the security guard, "The nation of Israel saw behind them Pharaoh and his army bent on their destruction. In front they saw the Red Sea waiting to drown them. They had nowhere to go and were as good as dead. Just so, the sinner sees God's justice pursuing him for sin. Ahead he sees Hell ready to swallow him. In this hopeless condition the sinner is unable to help himself. He will perish unless he is found in Christ.

An Experienced JW Contact in Swanston Street, Melbourne CBD

I had regular contact with an experienced JW offering literature in support of the Watchtower teaching on the Holy Spirit as a vague indefinable force. In so doing he removed the supernatural mysteries surrounding the birth, life, death and resurrection of Jesus and every hope the Bible offers

(Matthew 12:32*). As I recall, my initial contact occurred when I walked up behind him and quoted in his ear: "If anyone is in Christ, he is a new creation; old things have passed away; behold all things have become new" (2 Corinthians 5:17).

Startled, he sneered, "Oh yeah!"

Further, I said, "Jesus Christ is perfect God in perfect human flesh!"

He waved Watchtower literature under my nose. "Read this booklet," he spluttered.

Later, he claimed the King James Version and the New World Translation (NWT) were the same and tried to confuse me with textually misguiding Watchtower interpretations and supplied me with a handwritten list of texts framed in such a way as to destroy my evangelical faith by which he claimed the church had 'mislead' me.

Again, he cited a Romans text to support his Watchtower belief regarding death. I check his reference and said, "How does this substantiate your view?"

He got out his King James Version. "Oh!" he said, "I'm mistaken. Try this one."

I read the verse and stated, "But that's not it either."

He tried again. Finally, he pointed to Romans 6:7 and said, "Ah! This is it." and read aloud, "For he that has died is <u>freed</u> from sin." Puzzled, he exclaimed, "Freed! Freed! My version says dead. This says Freed! Freed!" He dropped his Bible on the footway in confusion. I offered to buy him a cup of coffee. He declined the offer.

He sarcastically demanded, "Who do you pray to? I pray to Jehovah read 1 Corinthians 15:24*. That will prove you wrong. Corinthians proves Jesus is not God. What do you think of that?" he crowed.

I read aloud from Matthew 1:23: "Behold the virgin shall be with child, and bear a Son, and they shall call His name Emmanuel which is translated

GOD WITH US." He got angry. I replied, "JW should be kind, tolerant, hospitable, and gentle. I'm the best friend you've got. It's time we talked through these issues over coffee." For a nano-second, a trace of a smile flitted across his craggy features. I remarked, "You nearly laughed then. For a split second your face looked almost human."

He replied through gritted teeth, "OK. You've badgered me into it but on one condition. You must listen to what I say."

On another occasion he yelled, "Your ideas on the Trinity are grossly insulting to God."

I quoted Isaiah 28:16* and added "Acts 4:12* They are Bible verses! Read them."

He replied, "You are an idiot!"

The man reneged on his coffee promise, and angrily said, "You are a dog. Get away from me!"

I re-iterated, "That's not nice. A good JW like you should never talk that way."

He altered his approach saying, "You know I really like you. You have a kind face and a nice smile."

I said to him, "But you broke your promise to have coffee with me and worse you called me a dog and an idiot. I am not impressed."

He replied, "I know. I meant you are dogged, persistent."

I greeted the old JW with, "I have a scripture for you." and quoted Hebrews 9:14*.

He didn't have a clue what it was but grated, "You've been hoodwinked. I have a list of verses from John 17 I want you to think about but remember there are mistakes in the King James Version."

I said, "I have read John 17 many times."

He demanded, "Who told Jesus to call God Jehovah?"

I responded by reading from Philippians 2:6*.

He replied, "You don't know what you are talking about." The man offered me yet another Bible verse and wheedled, "Just take a look. See what you think."

I said, "I think your ulterior motive is to destroy my faith in the credibility of scriptures and swing me to the Watchtower movement. I will not allow that."

He retorted, "I'll say this much. You're persistent!"

I asked, "Have you read the verses you promised to read recently?"

He said, "What were they?"

I replied, "Romans 9:5* and Philippians 2:6*."

He uttered, "Probably, but as they are of no consequence, I dismissed them from my mind."

Later, I invited myself into his conversation with a pedestrian. The JW was using Genesis 1 to convince his victim that Jesus is a created being. The pedestrian disappeared. At our next encounter, The JW with a saintly smile attempted to prove Jesus was a created human being. He frantically searched his notebook for more references.

I stated, "You will find no reference in the Bible to the creation of Jesus ANYWHERE! Your Watchtower doctrine is misleading."

He said, "I'll get one for you next week. Watchtower are the only ones. Christian churches are doing nothing."

I brought the Gideon NT distribution to his attention, he replied through gritted teeth, "The Bible is corrupt. You are misleading therm."

Gideons, an international Christian organisation, saturated Melbourne with 1000's of New Testaments (NTs) in a city-wide distribution during the week of 1-8 March with more than 70,000 being given directly into the hands of individuals! Two of their workers, a Queensland businessman and his wife standing a few meters away exhausted their stock of 600 Bibles in two hours. Praise God that His Word does not return void (Isaiah 55:11).

Hotels, motels, universities, colleges, schools, medical centres, hospitals, and individuals throughout the city now have access to a Bible. Over 4,000 locations were covered by the 300 Gideon volunteers and local church volunteers. The organisation is thankful for the partnership and prayers of many Christian supporters.

JW Influence Locally

Jan and I embarked on our Saturday morning walk to a local coffee lounge. A group of nine JW's were working their way along our street. I walked into their midst and shared my testimony. They were surprised to say the least. There is no better place to conduct personal devotions than on the street in the midst of a group of JW.

On another occasion ago a group of nine JW were door knocking in our street. Two visited our neighbours on one side, and two called on the neighbours on the other side, but they walked past our driveway. Was I blacklisted? Affronted by their deliberate neglect, I followed them up the street. They saw me coming and lined up for battle. Without further ado, I fired off my testimony. They were momentarily nonplussed. One lady said, "That's a nice story!"

I said to her, "I beg your pardon!"

She replied, "I didn't mean it like that."

The other female exclaimed, "We'll leave you to the men." They walked. The older male drew himself up to full height, adopting an imperialistic, authoritative, majestic, august, and magnificent posture. Flourishing his (NWT) with supercilious smile and in tones corresponding to pulsations of radiant light, he said, "Now let's have a look at John 17:3*." How smug, pompous, and self-righteous!

I pointed out, "I don't trust your translation."

He demanded, "What translation do you use?"

I said, "The New King James."

He said, "They are the same."

I asserted, "They are not, and you know it!"

In somewhat brittle tones, he replied, "You don't go door to door with the Gospel. You're no good."

I replied, "I have door knocked hundreds of times for the Gospel."

He grated, "No you haven't," and stormed off muttering something that sounded suspiciously like swear words.

To the younger guy, who had displayed interest in my testimony I said, "I believe we could discuss this issue. Come back one day. Let's make a date."

He said, "I might." They held a curb-side conference. I'd love to have been a fly on that wall.

Over the years JW's have called regularly at my address with their contorted views on Biblical theology. I was always uncertain how to respond. Their visits kick started research through which I discovered that side by side comparisons of their NWT, and the NKJV, NASB, and NIV reveal clear simple answers to their doctrinal errors. Literature from Christian bookshops assists in countering their favourite tactics and arguments with effective Biblical responses. I have developed sufficient understanding of the JW approach to knock some wind out of their sails when they come knocking on my door.

3. Mormons

- A lady from our church was buying Macadamia nuts in the Box Hill Plaza. She said, "These are a present for two lovely Mormon guys who have been visiting me. They are returning to the USA soon. Each time they put their Mormon doctrine to me, I respond with the Gospel message. Would you pray that God will speak to them

during our last meeting in the coffee shop at 3pm?" There and then, encompassed by the swirling throng, we prayed.
- Mormons offer an Asian in the Box Hill transit station another testament of Jesus Christ. I stepped silently between them and stayed there. The Mormons moved off. The Asian said, "I don't know why these blokes always pick on me. You're not religious, are you?"
- Nearby a well-dressed young man with a name badge 'troubles' an Asian student with another testament of Jesus Christ. I said to the victim in his presence, "You do not have to accept this literature." But she did.

Challenging Discussions!

Two American Mormons arrived at our door. Jan sent for me. They wanted to supply me with my genealogy. I told them who I was and suggested the book of Mormon was spurious and invited one of them inside to discuss the issue. To the other I said, "Go next door while we discuss." They wouldn't have a bar of that. I stated, "You are like the white-washed tombs of the Gospel - white, bright, and shiny on the outside but inside full of the rottenness, corruption and stench of the dead bones of Mormonism. Repent and turn to the Lord Jesus Christ for forgiveness of sin and salvation."

One called out, "Let's get out of here."

The other who must have thought I was deaf, yelled from the footpath, "You'll find out!"

Several attempts at conversation with the public by Mormons in Swanston Street aborted. One talked with a young lady named Adel. I prayed. That conversation ended abruptly. Another was seated with a young man. I asked the Mormon, "Excuse me! Can I sit with you?" He was telling the young man about Jesus Christ from the book of Mormon.

I interrupted saying, "I believe in Jesus. He saved from my sin. He acquitted my guilt. I have a right legal standing with God and an eternal destiny in Heaven."

He asked, "Have you read the book of Mormon?"

I replied, "Yes."

He said, "What did you think?"

I answered, "It has plagiarised slabs of the Bible and put them in a Mormon context." Then I shared my testimony. He excused himself. I continued to say, "Before you go, hear this. I do not need your book of Mormon." Before I could say more, he departed. He met with two other Mormons and doubtless earnestly discussed me. They quickly proceeded toward the railway station walking fast. I had the Mall to myself.

I approached another Mormon, saying, "Excuse me, why should I believe your Book of Mormon?"

Smiling confidently, he replied, "Yes, I can help you with that," and gave me the usual spiel. I responded with my full testimony including reference to John 3:16*and Colossians 2:9-10.*

I continued, "My sins are forgiven. My guilt is acquitted. I have a legal standing before God on the basis of what Jesus Christ did on the Cross and an eternal destiny in Heaven." The Mormon angrily turned away. I called, "Excuse me! Don't be so rude! I haven't finished yet."

He growled, "OK go ahead."

I said, "I have this one more thing to say to you. I do not need your book of Mormon." His face flushed. He walked away.

Mormons were rampant. One confronted Shalini an Indian lass, in Bourke Mall. She was uncomfortable. I tapped him on the shoulder and said, "Excuse me, are you a Mormon?"

He replied, "Yes, are you a religious man?"

I answered, "No! I am a Christian." His presentation was based on pictures in his 'Book of Mormon'. He offered me the book. I accepted, put it in my shoulder bag, then shared my testimony with unusual authority and power. He walked away. I turned to Shalini and asked, "Are you a Mormon?"

She replied, "No! I attend an AOG church, I had the feeling you were a Christian when you diverted him. I prayed all the time you spoke with him." Shalini and I prayed. Now I know where the power came from. Shalini originated from the city of Shimla in Himachel Pradesh, India and greatly encouraged me. I told her so. I searched for the Mormons, but they were gone.

A Mormon missionary was earnestly talking to a young lady. They were seated on a bench in the Bourke Street Mall. He was showing her pictures in his 'Book of Mormon' and saying, "Jesus went to America in the 18th century."

I said to him in her presence, "What right do you have to ram that garbage down her throat?" I think he was startled! Our heated discussion lasted some minutes. The girl departed. His Mormon supervisor appeared.

My Mormon contact said, "Talk to him."

I answered, "I don't want to talk to him. My purpose has been achieved. I have saved this innocent girl from your clutches."

As I walked, he shouted, "God will hold you accountable for this."

I replied, "God will hold you accountable for propagating lies about the Lord Jesus Christ."

Mormons with bags crammed full of Chinese literature, were focusing on Asians in the Box Hill shops. One, who claimed to speak Mandarin, could not understand why I didn't convert to Mormonism upon reading the 'Book of Mormon'. He therefore suggested, "As you did not convert when reading the book, you must be lying! You did not read this book, did you?"

I said, "I beg your pardon. I did read it. That's why I suggested you throw it in the trash. It is plagiarised from the 1611 King James Version of the Bible."

He said, "You are insulting me." I stuck to my guns. He backed off saying, "Why are we arguing? We believe the same things."

I replied to him, "The Jesus you believe in is totally different to the Jesus I believe in." He offered to shake hands, but I declined saying, "We are not in the fellowship of the Gospel" His not insignificant ego was dinted.

A huge Samoan with hands big like the end of five litre paint tins, listened to my testimony. He stated, "I am a Christian. We believe the same things." Instantly, the thought flashed through my mind, 'Be careful Bruce, this man is a Mormon.'

I said, "The Jesus that Mormons believe in is vastly different to the Jesus Christians believe." His brown eyes glinted with malevolence. He craftily and insidiously snipped away at my understanding of the Trinity with cunningly devised questions. He suggested among other things, that God and Jesus have bodies of flesh and bones as tangible as man's - thereby insinuating my theology is defective (but see John 4:24*, 1 Timothy 1:16-17*, 1 Timothy 6:15-16*). I sensed an evil spirit in him. I felt distinctly uneasy. Just then, his employer appeared and somewhat sharply redirected him. The Mormon glared, turned his back and walked. I waved and smiled. God saved me again.

I shadowed two Mormons walking along crowded Swanston Street. I was almost rubbing shoulders with them. They were unaware of my presence. Maybe God made me invisible. Now that would be a miracle! Some young Chinese folks were impressed with one of these Mormon's (a Caucasian) confident use of their language and accepted his literature.

I continued shadowing to Little Bourke Street. The Mormons split up. The Chinese speaker engaged with more Asians on the other side of the street. His mate trudged disconsolately toward Exhibition Street but made no contacts. He is in dreamland - it's my great opportunity. I materialised alongside him. He was mildly startled. I maneuvered him into a doorway. He thought he was on a good thing - I dropped my testimony into the middle of his presentation. It was a knockout. He was non-plussed. I challenged his thinking re Joseph Smith and the 'Book of Mormon'. He was wounded. It would be catastrophic for him to leave his organisation, but face the music he must, or live a lie the rest of his life.

Jan and I enjoyed a nice sunny walk in Ruffey Reserve, Doncaster. An overconfident well-dressed young American with a name badge and bicycle, was leaning on the bridge rail at Ruffey Lake watching the waterfowl. I thought - he was setting a trap. This spelt the end of my pleasant walk in the park with Jan. He smilingly asked, "Is that a Mallard?"

I said, "No. It's a Chestnut Teal."

He went on to ask, "Do you know about ducks?"

I answered, "Not much!"

He stated, "We are volunteers serving God. We come knocking on doors. Have you heard about us?"

I thoughtfully said, "I think so."

He asked, "Do you attend church?"

I said, "Yes."

He asked, "Which church?"

I replied, "I won't disclose that."

He asked again, "Do you believe in God?"

I said, "Yes."

He questioned me, "Do you believe in Jesus Christ and the Holy Spirit?"

I stated, "Yes."

THREE SECTARIAN INFLUENCES

He said, "Awesome!" in mock wonderment. "It sounds like we have lots in common. Awesome!" My testimony took some wind out of his sails. Undaunted, he continued, "There's another Gospel that tells us about Jesus."

I asked him, "Are you talking about the 'Book of Mormon?'"

He said, "Yes."

I explained, "I have read it from cover to cover." I attacked it from the standpoint of plagiarism of the King James Bible and lack of archeological support. I said, "All we need to know about Jesus Christ is in the Christian Holy Bible. We do not need your 'Book of Mormon'. Trash it! You guys are like the white-washed tombs Jesus spoke of. Outside you are white, shiny, and glistening, but inside full of the stench and rottenness of the dead bones of Mormonism. Take your Mormon glasses off. Read the Bible and you'll get a revelation of God that will transform your life."

He shouted, "You have insulted me."

I explained, "I am attacking your belief system."

He asked, "Where do you live?"

I also asked, "Why?"

He said, "If you want us to visit, we need your address."

I exclaimed, "I don't need you to visit."

He responded, "I'm not going to argue with you. I have done my job."

I said to him, "You are propagating mistruth!" He rode off fast and furious.

A Another Mormon propositioned a young male. I asked permission to sit with them. With barely a glance, the Mormon made room and I listened unobtrusively. Immediately he offered me the book of Mormon, but I injected my testimony into the conversation saying, "All we need know about Jesus is in the Bible. We don't need your Book of Mormon."

He was taken aback but lamely replied, "Are you a religious man?"

I said, "No, I'm a Christian, and I repeat, the' Book of Mormon' muddies the waters of Christian faith. We don't need it."

He asked, "What is your name?"

I said to him, "You don't need that."

He questioned, "What church do you attend?"

I said, "You don't need that either."

He retorted, "Please leave! You are interrupting!"

I said, "Excuse me! I will not let you get away with your Mormon propaganda." He turned his back. I shifted position, and eyeballed him again, like nose to nose. He could not possibly ignore me. I challenged each point as he raised it. He disappeared in a cloud of dust and smoke.

A young Mormon brother and sister in Federation Square listened to my testimony and accepted literature. She said, "What a lovely story."

He said, "We both worship the same God."

I explained, "There is a huge difference between the Jesus Christ of the Mormon church and the Jesus I know."

The diligent, conscientious, but ever hovering waiter, said, "What church are you from?"

I said, "Baptist."

He said, "I'm Mormon." I didn't realise my activities were being monitored.

Conclusion:

Sectarianists will try to unsettle our faith in the Apostolic teaching by making us feel misled and finally to reject it. They may not speak against the Bible initially but will tell you earnestly and convincingly of other prophets and revelations. If we fall for their diversionary tactics, we become lost like sheep without a shepherd. Holding firmly to Biblical truth gives us the victory.

Though some of my approaches may appear to emphasise the justice and vindication of God a little more than His love and compassion, I have found a more direct approach to gain the attention of my sectarian contacts who are gobbling up our evangelistic opportunities rapaciously with faulty interpretations of scripture.

I have taken on board the suggestion that more of the 'love' of Jesus in my approach to contacts, may have been helpful. However, I have rarely, if ever, encountered Christians addressing Sectarians with either God's justice and vindication or His love and compassion in the marketplace.

Taking it to Heart:

1. What importance do you attach to scriptures in life and ministry?
2. What will you do to increase your scriptural knowledge?
3. How will you apply it?

Bible references:

Isaiah 28:16 – Therefore thus says the Lord God: 'Behold I lay in Zion a stone for a foundation, a tried stone, a precious cornerstone, a sure foundation; whoever believes will not act hastily'.

Matthew 12:32 – Anyone who speaks a word against the Son of Man, it will be forgiven him; but whosoever speaks, against the Holy Spirit, it will not be forgiven him, either in this age or in the age to come.

John 3:16 – For God so loved the world that He gave His only begotten Son, that whoever believes in Him should not perish but have everlasting life.

John 4:24 – God is Spirit, and those who worship Him must worship in spirit and truth.

John 17:3 – And this is eternal life, that they may know You, the only true God, and Jesus Christ whom You have sent.

Acts 4:12 - Nor is there salvation in any other, for there is no other name under heaven given among men by which we must be saved.

Romans 9:5 – Of whom are the fathers and from whom, according to the flesh, Christ came, who is over all, the eternally blessed God.

1 Corinthians 15:24 – Then comes the end, when He delivers the Kingdom to God to the Father, when He puts an end to all rule and all authority and power.

Philippians 2:6 – Who being in the form of God, did not consider it robbery to be equal with God.

Colossians 2:9-10 - Whether thrones or dominions or principalities or powers. All things were created through Him and for Him.

1 Timothy 1:16-17 - For this reason I obtained mercy, that in me first, Jesus Christ might show all longsuffering as a pattern to those who are going to believe on Him for eternal life. Now to the King eternal, immortal, invisible, to God who alone is wise, be honour and glory for-ever and ever. Amen.

1 Timothy 6:15-16 – Which He will manifest in His own time. He who is the blessed and only Potentate, the King of kings and Lord of lords, who alone has immortality, dwelling in unapproachable light, whom no man has seen or can see, to whom be honour and everlasting power.

Hebrews 9:14 - How much more shall the blood of Christ, who through the eternal Spirit, offered Himself without spot to God, cleanse your conscience from dead works to serve the living God?

BQ – Big Question – What is the most important question in all the world for you?

Chapter 26

Endless Opportunities in Melbourne Business District (CBD)

Federation Square

Federation Square (FS) with its space, décor, coffee shops and galleries, attracts diverse crowds who ebb, flow, relax, and enjoy. A brief selection of some interesting experiences and encounters in the CBD follows:

The Victoria Police Band was entertaining. Their female vocalist, wearing police uniform was neat, sweet, and classy. The tattooed 'yobbo' was half drunk, sunburned (not tanned), obese, fair headed, crew cut, and shirtless. He danced in time to the music. His sweaty protruding stomach bounced like an overfull plateful of melting yellow jelly in the hot midday sun. The policewoman sang on. Tourists abounded. Waiters touted for business. Two elderly Chinese from Hong Kong accepted literature. Pepsi girls handed out free, cool, sugarless drinks. I demolished two cans in quick

ENDLESS OPPORTUNITIES IN MELBOURNE BUSINESS DISTRICT (CBD)

succession. A motor cyclist grabbed a drink can and sped off. A police band member and I enjoyed brief nostalgic discussion. A Muslim art gallery attendant patiently listened to my story and accepted a Gospel of John.

An ageing grandmother in Federation Square, who stood, not much higher than my waist, regularly evangelised among the mainly ethnic people in popular gathering places in Sydney. Her shoulder bag was filled with scriptures in different languages. She challenged all she could about their eternal destiny. This amazing octogenarian encouraged and inspired me.

The life journeys of a young Swedish tourist and a not so young Northern Victorian retiree intersected. The Swede responded to my greeting with spontaneous friendship saying, "I have travelled the world for five years."

I asked, "What are you looking for?"

The Swede replied, "That's a good question."

I said, "If you die tonight what would you say to God when he asks why He should let you into His Kingdom?"

He answered, "I don't know."

He listened with rapt attention to my story and said, "This morning I walked along St Kilda Beach. It was beautiful but uninteresting. I had a feeling I would meet someone special today. That someone is you." He accepted literature and a John's Gospel. The Swede put his literature in his backpack saying, "I'll read this on the bus for Sydney tonight."

A contact I first met in the street two years previously said, "You inspired me to talk to one person each day and hand out literature. I have done that and start Bible College soon."

An intelligent nineteen-year-old from a Baptist Church I was familiar with, is street preaching on the Ten Commandments during his lunch break from university. He's got potential. A security guard moved him on, unjustly so I thought. The preacher was causing no disturbance. Street entertainers are allowed to access this spot without objection. I suggested to the preacher, "Set up on the footpath. They can't touch you there."

He said, "You are the first Christian to encourage me in my ministry."

A young Aussie student asked, "What did you do for a living?"

I said, "For twenty-five years I worked on a farm caring for sheep. For twenty-five years I worked in the Police Department caring for two-legged sheep. For fifteen years I worked in churches caring for two-legged sheep."

He looked shocked and said, "What made you go into the church?"

I explained, "A spiritual experience when I was fifteen years old changed my life."

"Not many stick round church that long," he said.

"I've made many mistakes, but God uses even my foolish stupidity for good," I replied.

He shook my hand and said, "Good to meet you, Bruce."

I asked the Big Question (BQ*) to a local city council youth worker. He replied, "That's a hard one," paused, then replied, "I believe in fate. It always takes me to the right places." He listened to my testimony then said, "There are many ways to believe. I've always had help when I need it. There is someone out there, but I don't know who it is." He reluctantly accepted literature.

An older Aussie sitting pensively staring into space, was in the frame. He was recovering from yesterday's surgery. His respectfully framed questions were gentle, probing and stimulating. His philosophy of flexibility permitted him to accept Buddhist teachings. He cringed at John 3:16* which cut across his re-incarnational belief system. He insisted the Bible was the product of lively imaginations - he declined to acknowledge the saving power of Christ but acknowledged the existence of a powerful creative agency out there somewhere. He promised to read the Gospel of John but broke off the discussion saying, "I am tired."

I replied, "Anyone operated on yesterday would be. I appreciate you letting me share my story. Thank you." We shook hands, said friendly goodbyes, and parted with mutual respect.

A barefoot forty-year-old said, "I just got out of prison. I didn't kill anyone. I just happened to be in the wrong place at the wrong time (I've heard that story before). I just rang my '?!&#' father. He wants nothin' to do with me! My father transferred from Tasmania to Sydney when I was little. I couldn't cope and went off the rails. Do you mind if I turn on my radio?" Coincidentally, the song wafting out from his transistor at that very moment was 'Just a closer walk with thee, grant it Jesus is my plea.' He over-balanced as he reached for the literature. A loud rasping noise emanated from his lower portion. "OOOPS!" he exclaimed, then growled, "Music is music to me." and downed another swig from his flagon. He continued saying, "I'm an atheist. Where was God when all this B?!X S@#! started. I am a lover, not a fighter. (But his deviated septum suggested otherwise). I talk without guns." His left eye glared with baleful intensity. His right eye seemed permanently partly closed. Referring to my literature, he said, "I'll read this." He shook my hand and said, "Thanks for listening. You're a good man." He shook my hand again saying, "Look after yourself" and shook my hand a third time.

Christian, an electrical engineer from Chile, soaked up the sun on the steps. He was employed by an Australian company in Santiago and attended their recent company seminar here in Melbourne. This young gentleman listened closely and asked good questions. I walked him through a Bill Newman tract. The doctrine of grace as distinct from the doctrine of works was a revelation for him. He almost prayed the prayer of commitment but said, "You have explained many things, but I prefer to pray in my room tonight." He returned to Chile soon after. One morning as I was praying,

"Lord, teach me to number my days, that I may apply my heart unto wisdom" (Psalm 90:12) the following encouraging text message arrived:

"My apologies for the delay. I just got to Santiago last Saturday and I had to do many things this week. I hope you and your family are ok. I am working in Santiago again and as you see I still think in our conversation. For me always has been difficult to have the gift of faith. After our conversation everything was clearer, even though later I was not sure if I will go to the church. I have problems in believing in that institution, so I prefer to try to have my faith inside of me. I would like to have your opinion about that and also have some news about you. Regards, Cristian Salazar, Santiago, Chile." He did not respond to my return email.

Brando the super fit boxer from Acapulco, Mexico, had a flattened nose, which corroborated his claim of winning a bronze medal at the Seoul Olympics. Some three years ago in the Bourke Mall he accepted a Gospel of John. He had recently fought in Germany and will fight soon in Sweden but must be well past his prime by now. He said, "I want to be completely open with you. I cannot believe in God. If God is true, why does he allow suffering? What sex is God anyway? How do you know Islam, Hinduism, Buddhism is not the right religion? Who wrote the Bible, etc.?" He continued shaking his head. After a protracted discussion, he said, "Boxing is a hard life." He accepted the brochure 'Who Else Could?' and read it in my presence. He agreed, "Yes, this is true," and headed for the gymnasium.

An English tourist couple studying maps of the city, had been in Australia for two hours. I shared my testimony. He explained, "My girlfriend's mother in the UK is a Christian. When we were in New York, my girlfriend took me to church. Something happened in that church. After all the garbage of my life, I suddenly felt clean."

His girlfriend said, "I'd like to find a church for us to attend." They accepted a Gospel of John, which included the plan of salvation, details of our church services and a contact number.

A Basque nationalist from Spain had a good grip of English. He listened closely but gently said, "No thanks! Keep your literature for someone else. You look sad. Is this because I declined it?"

I said, "No! What I offered was a piece of paper which is nothing. What saddens me is that you turned your back on God."

A friendly honeymooning couple from Uruguay asked questions regarding tourism. To them I stated, "I have been married many years and I love my wife more now than ever." To him I said, "Love your wife and she'll stick with you through life. The best thing you can do for your children is to love their mother." With wide misty eyes, she handed their camera to her husband, snuggled up to me and said to him, "Take our photo."

He smiled and said, "In Uruguay, we husbands always have the last say – it is YES DEAR." They accepted a Gospel of John.

A stony-faced middle-aged man with piercing grey eyes was derelicted by bitterness. He was an elder in a Uniting Church. His wife eloped with their Pastor. He was stony broke, homeless and without family. His brother managed his business during his depression following the divorce, then fired him from his own business. He had MS. He listened to my testimony. I walked him through the salvation story with the use of a Bill Newman tract. He toned down his language, softened his attitude and said, "I board with a couple of Christian ladies. They witnessed to me, and I have started attending an Apostolic Church." He allowed me to pray and said, "I'm glad I met you." His nose began bleeding - profusely. He limped off. Life's bitter blows are hard to handle.

Despite an uncertain reception, I took the bit in my teeth and shared with a well-dressed young man in a grey suit, dark sunglasses, and shaven head. My discussion included reference to the druggy recently converted in the Bourke Mall. He said, "Your story about drugs resonates. I was on drugs and my parents institutionalised me in Queensland. It was terrible. This is why I am in Melbourne, but I am alone." He accepted a John's Gospel and read aloud John 3:16* with his name in it. His eyes glowed with pleasure.

I said, "These are not the words of some pastor or church leader. They are God's words, and I have the incredible privilege of speaking them straight into your heart."

He smiled and said, "That is inspirational. You've brought joy into my life."

Nils, on holidays from Switzerland, listened to my testimony and said with evident aggression, "My mother is a devout Christian, but my brother and six friends committed suicide. What God would let that happen? The church is full of hypocrites. One religion is as good as another. What's right for another person is OK by me." I put my face near the point of his nose and smiled. He asked good questions and gave me a fair hearing. He accepted a Gospel of John. Inside the fly leaf, I wrote, "'Dear Nils, thank you for allowing me into your life while I share my story. Bruce." He laughed in good-natured fashion and said, "Whoever discusses religion with me never forgets me."

I said, "That's for sure!" We shook hands and parted friends.

Milan from the Czech Republic was a champion national level soccer player in his homeland, but serious knee injuries cut short his career. He accepted testimony and literature. We adjourned for coffee. He later attended Dinner Tonight, an outreach ministry of our NewHope Church. Both he and a Chinese student attended our 9am service. Three years later I met Milan in Federation Square. He said, "I still keep God in my head."

Paulo, a crew cut young man is one of a few Portuguese speakers I recall meeting. Surprisingly, his eyes filled with tears and his muscular torso shook with uncontrolled sobs early in our conversation. Regaining his composure, he explained, "I split with my girlfriend this morning," and outlined his life-long struggle with deep depression. His heart was breaking because his Aussie girlfriend could see no future in their relationship upon which he had pinned many hopes and dreams for a brighter future.

I said, "Relationships on the human level are always prone to failure. Your first priority is a personal ongoing, dynamic relationship with the crucified, risen, Lord Jesus Christ who never disappoints." But the entrenched ritual, traditions, and religion of his Catholic Church, had soured him. Notwithstanding, he was interested in my testimony. He accepted teaching from John 3:16* and 8:12*. Later in McDonalds, during a lengthy discussion, Paulo understood his need for personal salvation but trusting in the Lord for him was difficult.

Minty, a young British backpacker on a pilgrimage to India, wore hippy clothes, ear, nose and lip studs and dreadlocked hair. She was searching for answers to life but was stumped by the BQ*. Obviously moved by my testimony she asked, "What do you think of Hinduism?"

After some discussion I said, "You won't find your pot of gold in India, Australia, the UK or elsewhere. You will only find it at the foot of the Cross." She accepted a Gospel of John and at my request read aloud from John 3:16* and John 8:12* with her name interposed in the texts. She smilingly accepted a salvation booklet and promised to text me with her progress. She looked so young and vulnerable. I feared for her future.

A young lady beside me was feeding pigeons. "It's therapeutic," she said and offered me breadcrumbs (for the pigeons).

I asked her, "Are you a Bible reader?"

She replied, "I like the KJV. I must get back into it. Can I change the question, are you a Bible reader?" Following discussion, she said, "I am not a Catholic and don't go with organised religion."

I replied, "Neither do I, but I believe in a personal relationship with the Creator."

She accepted a booklet entitled 'The Way to God' and laughing loudly said, "You got me, I didn't realise you were religious." She promised, "I'll read it tonight."

A Welsh Back Packer, (WBP) sitting on a parapet, was reading a book. Should I talk to him? A little voice on one shoulder said, "No! He won't be interested." A voice on the other shoulder said, "He might be one of my lost sheep." The WBP replied, "Science proves Creation is impossible!"

I said, "Creation is referred to in Genesis 1. Thousands of original biblical documents referring to creation are held in libraries and museums round the world for all to see. Genesis 1-3 points us forward to Christ. The central focus of the Christian faith is the crucifixion and resurrection. It has no parallel. This is why I am a Christian."

The man said, "What about sincere people who follow other religions, do they go to Hell?"

I replied, "There are only two classes of people in the world, Christians, and non-Christians. It doesn't matter what title they wear, if they don't follow Christ, they go to Hell."

The man said, "It's impossible to keep the Ten Commandments."

I stated, "I agree. Their purpose is to point us to the Cross for salvation." He accepted literature.

To a retired navy veteran from Albury (NSW) who was hobbling up some steps, I said, "Not easy getting old?" He replied, "I'm in Melbourne for back surgery." He thereupon explained his service details and how alcohol and navy life brought him undone. His speech was filled with more expletives than I've heard in a long time. In answer to my brief testimony, he said, "I grew up in the Catholic Church, but got a gut full of +!??*## religion and what I see in the world. I have a blue healer dog and a few Legacy widows to care for. That's my religion." I've served with several such ex-military personnel in the Police Department. My contact's attitudes reflect the culture of some of my old colleagues of long ago. There was a likeable streak beneath his rough gravelly voice and craggy exterior.

A male student offered a free 'purple heart' key ring to promote happiness and goodwill. I asked him, "What do you believe?" He said, "God."

I started my story. Seven of his group appeared as if from nowhere and surrounded me. I restarted my story. A senior lady watched carefully from a distance. She was the teacher in charge of this student group. Her attentive students exhausted my supply of English literature. One girl read aloud from John 8:12*. After discussion the students departed.

The teacher returned and confidentially said, "This is my psychology class. I have thirty-nine students. This morning my youth leader and I prayed that God would bless our excursion today. You have no idea what a blessing your testimony was to these needy kids. You spoke the right message to the right ones. The girl who read John 8:12* lost her mother recently and her father has another lady. Life is tough for her. I can't tell you about the others." She hugged me as we parted saying, "I'll be praying for you."

To my surprise, twenty-one-year-old Josh replied, "I have a testimony too. I left Tasmania at age twelve to live with my parents in Canada where I got involved with drugs, alcohol, tobacco and became suicidal." Upon returning to Tasmania, he miraculously became a Christian. While attending a large church in Melbourne in which he is now a member, he was delivered from the power of alcohol and drugs and is keen to serve the Lord in any capacity.

James, a twenty-five-year-old from California, arrived yesterday on a two-year work visa. In answer to the BQ* he said, "I'm not interested in the materialistic rat race." He listened to my testimony, including reference to Christian marriage, and said, "I needed to hear that. I am disillusioned with broken relationships and hatred." He accepted a Gideon New Testament with reference to John 8:12* and said, "Thank you! I have a Roman Catholic background but no Bible." In a follow-up text the drifter said, "Hi Bruce, this is James, we met at Fed Square not long ago. Just letting you know I am getting on okay, quit the job I started, wasn't for me, I'm now seeking new employment. Hope you and your wife are well. Take care. James fed sq."

A youngish Orthodox Lebanese male railed against 'heretical?' Christian denominationalism. He imperiously informed me that Orthodox churches are the only ones with the truth and that I should take very seriously what he said. After a lengthy rapid fire 'teaching' session he impaled me with a steely fanatical glare repeating in foreboding tones, "Take note of what I say," and departed with a superior satisfied smirk.

A retired couple arrived from the USA on a cruise ship recently. He seemed to know more about Australia than me. She is Methodist. He was an engineer with NASA. She exclaimed, "Don't start him on politics."

He said, "Obama can't solve our problems. We've even thrown out the 10 Commandments."

I asked, "Ever been angry at someone?" He replied in the affirmative.

"Ever committed adultery?" "No!"

"Ever looked at a woman with lust?" "Yes. All men do."

"Have you obeyed the Lord your God with all your heart, soul and mind?" "If I go to church the roof will cave in."

I explained, "You have broken the 10 commandments on three counts."

His wife commented, "It's time to go." He accepted literature.

A bearded bikie with a Harley Davidson parked adjacent the Tourist Information Centre, wore a studded tunic embossed with the God Squad emblem. His panniers were filled with flasks of hot coffee for street people living under bridges. I said, "What a wonderful ministry."

He answered, "Somebody gave me your newsletter. It's you! Yes, it is! I've always wanted to meet you."

An engineering student from Papua New Guinea, carefully listened. He accepted a Gospel of John and asked, "Are you a Christian? I was baptised in the Uniting Church but I've messed up."

We discussed the steps of salvation. I asked, "Have you done that?"

He replied, "No."

I questioned, "What stops you giving your life to Christ now?"

He said, "Nothing." He prayed for forgiveness and invited the Lord Jesus Christ into his life. I suggested a church to attend, offered counsel and prayed with him. He declined follow-up.

Swanston Street

Whilst conversing with Diego, the Colombian street side fruiterer, a male approached and said, "Do you know a gold buyer? I lost my money at the Casino last night and need cash to get home. He showed me some gold jewellery. You wouldn't like to buy it would you? It's not hot. I could give you a receipt."

I said, "No thanks!"

The fruiterer said, "I was thinking about you yesterday. I have a dilemma. My girlfriend is a Christian, but I am Catholic. We are conflicted over our differences." His fixation with Mariolatry also earned criticism from two Christian discipleship groups he had attended. Feeling judged he now declined to attend other such groups. He read aloud John 8:12*.

I said, "What do you like about this verse?"

He replied, "It's good. I believe it!"

I asked him, "What don't you like?"

He emphatically replied, "It's all good."

I said, "Read it again." He did so. I said, "What key word strikes you most?"

He replied to me, "Follow."

I said, "Take this booklet (John's Gospel) and read a section each night. When you come to a part you understand - follow."

An old-fashioned, fire-eating street corner evangelist handing out tracts as he preached, was new to me. His presentation seemed theologically sound and conveniently packaged for the benefit of waiting tram passengers. Surprisingly, many listened. A female derelict carefully and quietly read her tract entitled 'How near the end?' printed by Evangelical Tract Distributors, Canada. His style is such that he could touch people with the Gospel I could never reach. Some say street corner preaching is a thing of the past. I do not subscribe to this view.

A drunk sat on the footpath nearby with his cigarette lighter aflame beside him as he expertly rolled his own. He aimed an imitation pistol at the head of the preacher, pulled the imaginary trigger, and said "Pow!" and replaced the imaginary gun in his imaginary holster. His cigarette lighter was glowing hot. The preacher preached on.

I was occasionally reminded that God sometimes uses strange messengers to spread the Gospel. One such elderly man wearing tattered clothing, with scarred face and complexion like a walnut, edentate, coughing and expectorating but his arresting gaze and clear brown eyes reflected inner peace. He was surprisingly offering tracts that extol the virtues of Jesus to passing pedestrians.

A youthful-looking British backpacker sitting on a parapet said, "I am traveling alone and learning how to look after myself. I am also trying to find a higher power." A good opening for my testimony. He listened with rapt attention and exclaimed, "That's a good story but I have to think this through. My family are scientific evolutionists. If I became a Christian, there would be hell to pay."

I thought for a moment and said, "Science comes to its position of belief in Evolution in the same way Christians come to their position of belief in Jesus Christ – by faith." I produced my battered old Gideon's New Testament.

He exclaimed, "That's a well-worn Bible." I read Hebrews 11:1 and 6* to him. He accepted a Gospel with John 3:16* underlined.

Beto, an East Timorese student, said, "Your testimony is amazing! I've read the Bible but can't understand it. Last night I prayed for help. I was supposed to meet with friends but decided to come here instead. Now I meet you! Amazing! My friend will take me to church in the western suburbs." He permitted me to pray with him and accepted a Gospel of John.

To a lass handing out conservation literature, I said, "I'm an original greenie. The Lord God put man into the garden to dress, till and keep it. The more people who become Jesus followers the quicker the environment will be healed."

She explained, "I became a Christian a few weeks ago. I'd like to learn more about this. I've got a New King James Bible." She declined to offer contact details.

An Aboriginal man sucked from his can of beer. He was on a bender the night before and was worse for wear. I said, "I have seen you many times. My heart is heavy for you. You are killing yourself with alcohol."

He replied, "I have spent lots of time in detox but every now and again I break out." (I've never seen him sober). I quoted John 3:16* and gave him a Gospel tract. Though he had heard it all before, he said, "Thanks for talking with me."

A Jewish group commemorated the Exodus wanderings of their forefathers in the wilderness with a memorial palm roofed tent erected in Swanston Street. To a student rabbi from New York, who included reference to the Exodus event in his explanation, I explained, "Jesus talks about His own Exodus (Luke 9:31*) in the Christian Bible."

He replied, "There's an even more recent Exodus - when the Berlin Wall came down thousands of Jews came home."

I said, "When people become Christians they are transferred from the kingdom of darkness into the kingdom of light - thousands are becoming Christians every day. That is the most relevant and recent Exodus. Do you believe in the Ten Commandments?"

He said, "Beautiful. You shall not murder."

I replied, "Jesus said if you are angry with someone you have murdered him in your heart. Have you ever been angry?"

He said, "Yes."

I stated, "Do you love the Lord your God with all your heart and soul and might?" He replied, "Gotta go!" and walked.

Two male derelicts, leaning against a shop front, were involved in a heated discussion. Two Police Officers appeared - tensions were re-directed against the police. Meanwhile, one of these derelicts, a prickly older male engaged a nearby evangelist in heated discussions on church politics. The evangelist did his best to ignore the older man. Not to be deterred, Mr. Prickly got closer and shouted louder. During this discussion, the second derelict approached the evangelist and asked for literature. He said, "Just what I need. I am a bad Christian."

Mr. Prickly asserted, "You are either a Christian or not. Which is it?" Derelict number two angrily shouted his way back to the shop front. A third derelict directed filthy language at the undeserving evangelist, who with admirable restraint and patience, continued with his cause. Mr.

Prickly approached me and demanded, "Where do you go to church? I want to come to your church. Are you a Christian?"

I replied, "I am a member of a church that preaches the Crucifixion and Resurrection of Jesus. I attend a Bible-believing church with other Christians." He repeated his demand. I refused to elaborate. He stalked off with a withering glance in my direction. The derelicts settled down.

An Aussie university student listened to my testimony. His girlfriend and another male joined us. The female said, "I attended church for years. Church people are hypocrites."

I exclaimed, "Why am I not surprised? Tell me more." They tried hard to blow my faith off course. I said to the girl, "I take it you have never made a decision to follow Christ?"

"No!" she replied,

I explained, "Saying yes to Jesus is the first step. Until you do that the Bible is mumbo jumbo."

The Aussie male stated, "My good deeds will outweigh the bad." His male friend chipped in from time to time. I shared the story of the Cross.

Four young females and one male recruiting for the Wilderness Society, held a debriefing session. Kate said, "How did you go?"

Jane replied, "Not good."

John said, "I pick the roughest ugliest person first, and speak to him. After that it's a breeze."

I leapt to my feet and said, "Excuse me! I am the roughest, ugliest person in this city. You haven't spoken to me yet." John quickly recovered his composure. His comments provided a basis for a Gospel presentation using the four-fold disharmony resulting from the Fall (Genesis 2 & 3). I continued, "If enough people followed the Creator, our wilderness issues would get sorted." He accepted literature.

'L' sat on a seat against the Town Hall facade. His response to my story was, "Churches burn me. Now I worship alone." A pigeon on the third parapet took aim and fired. 'L' received a direct hit to his leg with a large missile. I thought, "Serves him right for turning his back on God's Institution."

But 'L' replied, "The drought is broken. Seven lean years are followed by seven years of plenty."

A man asked the newspaper vendor at the railway station for a magazine. The vendor replied, "Help yourself." The customer selected a magazine and walked without paying. The vendor yelled.

The customer replied, "You told me to help myself," and threw a $10 note on the footpath. The vendor put his foot on it. They wrestled for possession of the note.

The vendor won, held it aloft and shouted, "It's fake!" and shortchanged the customer. When the dust settled, the vendor asked me, "Like the hot weather?"

I replied, "Not too bad, but my wife doesn't."

He replied, "Put her in the fridge."

Three female Solomon Island Unification Church (Moonies) missionaries accepted Bibles from Private Frank the Bible Man. They said, "O yes, we believe that." But their founder, Rev. Sun Myung Moon, claimed among other things, to be the new Messiah and that Korea was God's chosen nation. Their cultic activity created within me evangelistic urgency. A squeamish presentation of Biblical truth is easily translatable into counterfeit philosophies.

A newspaper vendor with rotting teeth, (Fang) and his ancient mate with no teeth, (Toothless) stirred each other unmercifully. Toothless made unprintable accusations with religious overtones against Fang, who laughingly responded, "But I have repented," He then appealed for my support. His colorful pronunciations containing the letter 'P' were often associated with a saliva spray. Their banter was humorous, but I was learning to side-step at the appropriate time.

To Fang, I later said, "Some weeks ago you told me your old mate (Toothless) died. Last Thursday I saw him sitting in his news-stand. Did I see a ghost?"

Fang protested, "I didn't know he was on three weeks holidays. So, I sent him a wreath of flowers and a note saying, 'I thought you were dead'."

I said to him, "And you spread that story all over the city?"

Fang replied, "Yes, and he's mad at me. He won't talk anymore."

I answered, "No wonder."

Fang exclaimed, "He's got no sense of humour. He went white in the face and threatened to kill me." Further along Swanston Street Toothless, who was dead and now lives, was stirring with a different newspaper vendor.

Bourke Mall

Sidhu Shivray said, "When I see the light, I will be OK."

I questioned, "What do you mean?"

He explained, "When I get a secure job."

I told him, "I'm a Christian. Let me show you what God says about light." We read from 2 Corinthians 4:6*. He understood and accepted a Gospel presentation based on Psalm 23.

I asked him, "Would you like a Bible?"

He replied, "Yes, but who will help me understand it?"

I said, "I will. Meet me once a week." But always he had excuses.

It was a beautiful sunny day. A sleeveless, muscular Māori, with dread locks, tattoos, and missing teeth looked unsafe. I was constrained to talk with him but walked past a second and third time before I found courage to do so. This itinerant fruit picker turned out to be genial, friendly, and talkative. His parents took him to church as a child. He recited Psalm 23 from memory and said, "I sometimes think I should go back to church." He accepted a Gospel of John.

A black African retired professional basketball player said, "I am surprised by your friendship but are you peddling something?" I asked the BQ*. He replied, "What's it all about I suppose?" I shared my testimony. He informed me, "My mother in the States is a Christian. My name is up on her prayer board at home and in the church." He accepted a TPTL NT*.

I said, "I hope this book answers your mother's prayers." He and his partner were heading for Switzerland that week.

An eccentric, stringy-haired and shabbily dressed old Australian with eerie groans, weird songs, filthy clothes, and strange-sounding homemade electronically assisted instruments, was at it again. A small cardboard placard endorsed with the handwritten words ,'Yoyogi Yogis' was propped up by his side. The fact that gullible people donated money and purchased CDs from him astounded me. A Vietnamese Buddhist intently listened and said, "He is an honorable man." I gathered Yogi and his influence into a net of prayer and delivered it captive to Jesus for destruction. A thick-set man squatting nearby was physically and silently resisting Police. Yogi's ring of admirers disappeared. He stabbed me with a poisonous glare. With help from an electronic Vietnamese/English dictionary I shared my testimony with the Vietnamese. He accepted a Gospel of John.

I said to the Vietnamese, "Would you like me to put you in touch with a Vietnamese Pastor?"

He replied, "Yes." He shook my hand and said, "Thank you. You are a good man." I gave the information to a Vietnamese Pastor. God worked in mysterious ways His wonders to perform. It was awesome! Thank you, Lord.

ENDLESS OPPORTUNITIES IN MELBOURNE BUSINESS DISTRICT (CBD)

Strangers are Friends We Have Not Yet Met

A musing Afro-American was the producer, reporter, presenter, of a radio station on Wall Street, New York. He also wrote articles for well-known journals. This articulate, intelligent, engaging, conversationalist who had done his homework on Australia, was trying to stitch up a deal with SBS and the ABC. He concluded our wide-ranging conversation with the following comments, "The Holy Bible can be summed up in two words - Love others."

I said, "Thanks for allowing me to spend time with you."

He replied, "Not at all! I enjoy talking to strangers. You see," he continued, "Strangers are friends we've never yet met."

I said to him, "The Holy Bible also refers to the stranger many 'have never yet met'."

He said, "Exactly!" He gave me his card, shook my hand, and walked.

A retiree reminisced about his youth in Bega, New South Wales, and the nearby township of Delegate. His conversation peppered with foul expletives, is summarised as follows: "All I see when I look into my future is a big black hole. Maybe I should visit Bega. I might find some answers."

I explained, "You are seventy-two. You've had two strokes. If you don't visit Bega soon you might never do it at all. It was crunch-time for me but my decision to follow Christ as a teenager changed my life. It's crunch time for you. This booklet tells you how to make a decision to follow Christ now before it's too late."

He replied, "No one ever talked to me like that. Thank you." He accepted literature and shook my hand.

Scantily clad females modelling lingerie in Bourke Mall attracted the attention of a predominantly male audience. The surrounding crowd included burly Indian security guards, girls handing out balloons, loud music, kids, spruikers, humidity and trams. An Indonesian Catholic from

Bali accepted testimony and a Gospel tract. An Indian street salesman accepted the 'Four Things God Wants You to Know' tract in Tamil. He said in surprise, "Where did you get this?" We discussed the eternal destiny of his soul. He concluded, "My main concern is sorting out my vocation."

I stated, "What shall it profit a man if he gains the whole world but loses his own soul?"

Several male models conducting a fitness display in Myer's window, were dressed in revealing underwear. Their suggestive hip-swinging movements attracted admiring glances and waves of giggles from numerous young females crowding the display and blocking the footpath. The 'Seeing Eye Dog' display nearby was out-classed, out-maneuvered, and displaced.

A shaky old man who lived alone, arrived from Echuca (Vic) by bus for a medical appointment reckoned he may have Parkinson's Disease. I shared my story. He said, "Two good things happened today. I made a confession at St Francis Church, and I met you." His tremors seemed to intensify. I considered terminating our conversation for that reason, but he stalled me asking, "Could you tell me how I can get closer to Jesus?"

I said to him, "God took your debt of sin and nailed it to the most public place in the universe – the Cross. He has completely forgiven you. If you want to know how much God hates your sin and loves you look at the Cross of Jesus. Put your faith and trust in the risen Christ."

He said, "I asked a question and got a good answer. I am moved." He accepted the 'What a friend we have in Jesus' tract and a daily Bible reading programme. He is loosely connected to the Salvation Army in Echuca. I encouraged him to get more involved. Ministering to this frail, lovable, receptive old man touched me.

Leslie's Amazing Transformation!

A clean shaven, neatly attired, articulate, clear eyed, smiling, man caught my attention. He said, "103 days ago, the Lord saved me." He seemed vaguely familiar. He showed me enlarged photographs of himself curled up in a shop front doorway in the Bourke Mall in a drug induced stupor begging. (A freelance photographer had later handed him these photos). Like a bolt from the blue, it hit me. He was the drug addicted man I had frequently seen in years past curled up in that same doorway, unshaven, long bedraggled hair, clothing, and personage filthy, homeless - a picture of abject misery. I had always walked past believing Leslie was hopeless, I felt rebuked. I never envisaged God could make him the man he was meant to be.

This transformed man, at my request, showed an interstate visitor sitting nearby, his photos and shared his testimony. In essence, Leslie testified saying, "Look at these photos. That's who I was then…..Look at me now." The awe-struck Queenslander exclaimed in astonishment, "I never expected this!"

Leslie continued frequenting the proximity of that same doorway in the Bourke Mall in the hope of sharing his testimony with astonished pedestrians who 'saw him then and see him now'. On another occasion, Leslie was sharing his faith with an alcoholic beside that same doorway in the Bourke Mall. The drunk, who knows the basics of the Christian faith, was swilling alcohol as fast as he could. I said to the drunk, "Throw that down the gulley trap." Leslie shook his head saying, "He can't do it. Only God can reach down and lift him up like he did with me."

Later a tap on my shoulder in Swanston Street alerted me to Leslie's presence. He said, "I am going to the library for some Bible study. Happy Easter Bruce." Regular gymnasium activities are transforming his wasted muscular structure. His vice-like parting handshake was painful. "God is great!" he enthused.

Leslie's testimony reminds me of the story of the healing by Jesus of the man born blind (John 9:25) who said, "One thing I know: that though I was blind, now I see.' There is tremendous power in a testimony. It's an almost unanswerable way of dealing with objections. Leslie's testimony was powerful! He was transformed as an elderly lady stopped to pray over him.

The last time I saw Leslie, I asked him, "Do you remember the Queensland tourist who saw your photos and heard your testimony?" He replied, "Yes."

I told him, "That bloke was scratching his head when you shared your testimony."

Leslie laughingly replied, "Don't worry. I'm still scratching mine."

Too many opportunities are lost because the situation seems hopeless. Pray! Search for opportunities, share your testimony. God is more than capable of developing testimonies into Kingdom victories.

Taking it to Heart:

1. Do you find it difficult to initiate conversations with strangers?
2. What steps will you take to introduce strangers to the Gospel?
3. Are you aware that strangers are often friends you haven't yet met?

References:

Luke 9:31- And behold, two men talked with Him, who were Moses and Elijah, who appeared in glory and spoke of His decease (Exodus) which He was about to accomplish at Jerusalem.

John 3:16 – For God so loved the world that He gave His only begotten Son that whoever believes in Him should not perish but have eternal life.

John 8:12 – Then Jesus spoke to them again, saying, 'I am the light of the world. He who follows me shall not walk in darkness, but have the light of life.'

2 Corinthians 4:6 – For it is God who commanded light to shine out of darkness, who has shone in our hearts to give the light of the knowledge of the glory of God in the face of Jesus Christ.

Hebrews 11:1 – Now faith is the substance of things hoped for, the evidence of things unseen.

Hebrews 11:6 - But without faith it is impossible to please Him, for he who comes to God must believe that He is, and that He is a rewarder of those who diligently seek Him.

BQ – Big Question - What is the most important question in all the world for you?

TPTL NT – The Pocket Testament League New Testament.

Chapter 27

Melbourne's Maze of Laneways

Melbourne's maze of laneways began life as rear access to properties facing main thoroughfares. Some of these laneways were reborn in recent times and hummed to the rhythm of daily city life. One morning Jan and I commenced our odyssey in the Causeway (one such laneway) off Bourke Street Mall. Adjacent to the Causeway is Royal Arcade, allegedly the oldest shopping arcade in Australia. We crossed Little Collins Street and entered Block Place and Block Arcade enjoying its mosaic floors and fascinating old-world shops.

A Journey Back in Time

Visiting these alleyways was a nostalgia trip for me. As a probationary Constable my job description included patrolling these very same back alleys, sorting through piles of rotting garbage, kicking rats out of the way, uncovering sleeping derelicts from beneath piles of soiled newspaper and cardboard boxes, arranging transport in the Police divisional van to the

City Watch house, a shower, a bed for the night and a feed in the morning - courtesy of the taxpayer. Many drunks with little control over their bodily functions, reeked terribly and often, for some unknown reason, carried naked razor blades in their coat pockets. We carefully removed any instruments with which they could harm themselves or others in the cells, being doubly careful not to cut our fingers in the process. One of the more regular customers whose drunkenness made speech indecipherable, was dubbed, courtesy of an innovative sergeant, 'Sydney Harbour'. My attitude to fringe people considering the Jesus manifesto in Luke 4:18-19* still leaves much to be desired. Would my church (including me) make room for them in our fellowship?

Some young Constables I worked with have sadly passed on. One such colleague, younger than me, was tragically and deliberately killed while on duty by a deranged man on the steps of Flinders Street railway station. My capable and friendly young colleague had potential in his chosen field. Similar episodes have caused me to ponder more deeply on the meaning of life. It never occurred to me that I would return much wiser in a different capacity to these localities some forty years later with the Good News.

In the small hours one morning, whilst performing foot patrol on night shift, I was leaning against a parking metre in Collins Street sound asleep with bleary eyes wide open. Unbeknown to me, my supervisor had crept up behind and detonated a six-inch bunger between my feet. The resounding explosion launched me into orbit long before space shuttles were thought of. Years later I caught his wife speeding. By then he was a high-ranking officer. I deemed it unwise to book her.

Degraves Street

Degraves Street is an iconic Melbourne laneway that distils everything we love about our city into one pint-sized street. Sunlight filtered between tall buildings in Flinders Street and reflected as lights off wet footpaths at the end of long dark tunnels. The Flinders Lane end of Degraves Street was bedecked with outdoor umbrellas and gas heaters, tables, chairs, surging lunchtime crowds, young and old, poor, and wealthy, fat, skinny, homeless, waiters, etc. Buskers, drums, mandolins, coffee, cooking smells, barber shops, chemists and noise added to the ambience.

Unexpectedly, this heaving, convulsing mishmash of energy gave birth to Pedro, who appeared as if by magic, and occupied the seat beside me. He was joined by his French friend. They accepted literature. The Frenchman departed. To Pedro I asked the BQ*. Shocked by the harsh realities of a cold unwelcome world, he reacted with a cry of anguish, "I am trying to understand who I am, why I am here and where I am going." Testimony and a Gospel presentation followed.

I said to Pedro, "It is no accident that God arranged your path from Colombia and mine from Northern Victoria to intersect today in Degraves Street. You should give your life to Christ now." He attended carefully to my testimony and accepted Spanish literature, which could be life changing for him. For Pedro to understand and embrace God's plan, he must clearly distinguish between certainties and uncertainties – between multitudes of speculations and the fundamentals of our Christian faith. Christians need a soundproof understanding of the empowering historic Apostolic (Acts 2:42*) theology of the church's continuing struggle to maintain the truth, teachings, and explanations of the early church fathers to impart with clarity to the Pedros of our modern world.

I stopped for coffee as a middle-aged matron departed. The tail end of her conversation with a young man sitting slumped across the next table ran thus, "You'll have to help yourself before I can help you." With intense concentration, he slowly folded a napkin and laid it on his sweating forehead. With eyes dull and glazed, and speech slurred, he momentarily fell asleep with a fork full of food poised midway between plate and mouth. He roused and slurred, "Excuse me... " I broke in and said, "I can't help you."

He slurred, "I was only gunna ask the time." He staggered to his feet, knocking chairs and tables asunder in the process.

Four students sat with me – an Indonesian, a Thai, a Pakistani and an attractive female Mauritian. After some discussion I asked, "What is the most important question in all the world for you?"

The Mauritian burst out despairingly, "I don't know where I came from, why I am here or where I am going. I just don't know!" The perfect opportunity for a testimony. All the students listened carefully. Each accepted a tract entitled 'Life's greatest question' and sub-titled 'Where will I go when I leave this world?'

They said, "Thank you," shook hands and headed for the classroom.

The cafe waitress was going to visit her ailing father in Colombia. She hugged the Gospel of John saying, "I'm so excited. Thank you! Thank you!" She introduced me to her Colombian friend who also accepted a Gospel.

The lolly salesgirl from country South Australia, with whom I talked occasionally, said somewhat gloomily, "I'll wait and see what life throws at me I suppose."

I said to her, "Do you know about wedge tailed eagles?"

She replied, "Yes, I've seen plenty."

I stated, "I once watched a 'wedge tail' through my binoculars. He flew high above me as a small fast moving black dot among massive thunderheads. One minute he was in the north, seconds later he was miles away in the south without one flap. He simply used the gale force winds to his advantage. Be like the wedge tail (Isaiah 40:31*). Use the storms of life."

She said, "You always say good things. I'll remember that."

Some months ago, I met and shared with Allan from country Victoria. Later I received his phone call saying, "My wife and I will be baptised this Sunday in a Baptist Church." We had a good discussion regarding baptism.

I was intercepted by a female inviting me for breakfast and coffee in her recently opened cafe. An urgently required toilet stop and a cup of coffee was an excellent opportunity for evangelism. I was surprised by the ambience of what must be the closest to a five-star cafe I've ever seen. To this enterprising, energetic young Estonian lady with experience and management skills from Eastern Europe and Britain, I said, "I am a Christian. Let me tell you why I am here." Between mobile phone calls and staff questions, she accepted testimony and a TPTL* New Testament and supplied a gourmet biscuit to enjoy with my coffee.

A battered and bruised lady sat crying in a laneway off Collins Street. I asked her, "What's wrong?" She sobbed "My husband took all my money and kicked me out. I have nowhere to go. I am hungry, with a headache and no money to get to my mother's place in Mildura." I suggested the Salvos. She said "I have tried them, but they have no finance."

I offered to buy her a hamburger. "No!" she declared emphatically, declined literature and abruptly stated, "Leave me!"

A well-dressed female at a coffee shop asked, "What are you writing?"

I replied, "My journal." She included in our discussion reference to issues she was dealing with. Tears spilled from her eyes. Her equally well-dressed elderly mother sitting opposite, nodded sagely. The younger one apologised for her tears. I said, "Not at all. It is good to share your burdens. Strangers are sometimes the friends you've yet to meet."

She replied, "That's beautiful."

I said, "Here is a brochure about the stranger of strangers."

The sweet seller in the Royal Arcade said, "I am from interstate. I was a beauty therapist but there are only so many pubic hairs you can remove.

Now I'm a lolly girl. I don't know where my future lies." She listened to my testimony and accepted a Gospel of John.

A rowdy group of young people at the GPO corner attracted my attention. One of these, a shirtless youth with a disingenuous smile, offered me a tube of white cream saying, "Would you like to have it for fifty cents? It might help your relationship with your wife, or when you invite your girlfriend over." I gave him a tract and walked to the sound of ribald laughter and a thin reedy female voice derisively warbling 'Amazing Grace'.

To Juan Pablo Villota from Colombia, I asked the BQ*. With reflection and troubled expression, he replied, "How to cure the defects that spoil my relationship with God." He accepted a Gospel presentation, testimony, counsel, Spanish literature and said, "Many have spoken to me about God. You also have been a big help. I'll never forget our meeting. I will return to Colombia and fight violence and corruption."

I explained, "Three important things for you to consider. Ground yourself in God's Word, serve in the church, and tell others about Jesus." He made notes of our conversation.

Two Australians handing out copies of their Epoch Times, initially declined literature. I coaxed one saying, "Come on, you hand out your literature to me. It's only fair you accept mine." The other accepted literature but said, "I am reaching toward perfection. One day I'll make it. I commend the Falun Gong principles to you. Follow them and you'll never go wrong."

I asked two young male Aussie musicians the BQ*. Jessie was not sure. Chase, who had a church background, had visited Thailand, and dabbled in the drug scene said, "That is a hard question. Is there life after death?" They listened to my testimony and accepted a 'Life's Greatest Question' tract. Jessie left for class. Chase asked, "Do you believe in the devil? Should we kill animals? Is Christianity the only religion? Is life an illusion? Can we trust modern translations?" He accepted a good quality New Testament and a Gospel of John with the plan of salvation included.

It's a Different World in There

'The Pirate' appeared wearing a colourful bandana, platted beard, and exotic clothes. He came unstuck in the business world and now lives an alternate lifestyle. I don't dare even one quick glance at Jan's bemused expression for fear of cracking up. The Pirate was attending a drama course and recently 'imported' an abused female from Adelaide to be his travelling companion. Some of these alleys are a mecca for Melbourne's café society. Centre Place has cafes almost too small to swing a cat. We ordered a cappuccino at an espresso bar in Degraves Street. They charged $2.60 for any drink and two cinnamon donuts.

Later, Jan said, "Enjoyed your company Bruce, met lots of interesting people, and saw lots of interesting coffee shops. It's a different world in there."

Taking it to Heart –

1. Evaluate your attitudes to the socially disadvantaged/dysfunctional of our communities.
2. How might we address these issues personally?
3. How should the local church respond to the Jesus manifesto? (Luke 4:18-19*)

References:

Isaiah 40:31 – But those who wait on the Lord shall renew their strength; they shall mount up with wings like eagles, they shall run and not be weary, they shall walk and not faint.

Luke 4:18-19 – The Spirit of the Lord is upon Me, because He has anointed Me to preach the gospel to the poor; He has sent Me to heal the broken-hearted, to proclaim liberty to the captives and recovery of sight to the blind, to set at liberty those who are oppressed; to proclaim the acceptable year of the Lord.

Acts 2:42 – And they continued steadfastly in the Apostles doctrine and fellowship, in the breaking of bread and in prayers.

BQ – Big Question – What is the most important question in all the world for you?

TPTL – The Pocket Testament League.

Chapter 28

Public Transport Evangelism

Peter, a disciple of Jesus, lasted about five seconds on the stormy waves then began to sink. With an out-stretched hand Jesus caught Peter and lodged him safely in the boat. The wind ceased. The waves stilled. Jesus so glorified Himself in Peter's failure that those in the boat said, "Truly, you are the Son of God" (Matthew 14:26-27). As with Peter, Jesus rescued me from stormy times and glorified Himself, even in my many failures. Testimonies of Christ's protection, forgiveness and guidance often transcend cultural, racial, or linguistic barriers. "Hello! How are you today?" is an oft repeated simple introductory opening that facilitates relationship with strangers. A friendly smile with the greeting is often followed by the Big Question (BQ*), conversations and testimony.

Contacts at the Bus Stop and on the Bus

The local bus stop became a venue for regular friendly Sunday morning social events. For example, three Chinese seniors, who had previously accepted Chinese literature and testimonies, discussed with the aid of pencil sketches, last night's rain and its effect on their gardens. A Greek female, a Filipino hotel supervisor, Burmese, Aussie, Indian and Japanese students, a Sri Lankan Muslim lady, a Colombian fruitier on his way to the city, a Dutch waitress, a Peruvian and his Aussie girlfriend all accepted literature and testimony. Not all understood much of what the other said, but we enjoyed the chats. Suddenly we had cross culture communication. Frequently they waved goodbye as I disembarked at the church.

A young Asian guy looked unresponsive. Was I intruding on his privacy? He might be intellectually superior. Is it worth the effort? But folks are praying right now for this young man. By faith, I believe God preceded me into this young man's 'stormy' life. Faith took me one step beyond fear. By faith I made the approach. This Australian born Asian from Darwin was employed as a cook at Southgate. He listened carefully to my testimony, accepted literature and wistfully asked, "Do you really believe in Jesus Christ?"

A surprised Aussie lady accepted a 'What a Friend' brochure saying, "What a friend we have in Jesus!!!! Where did you get that? You must be a Baptist? I must get back to attending church."

An ancient wizened up Aussie said in a loud monotone voice, "Got an angina tablet under my tongue, had a stroke during a hernia operation, a double by-pass and can't see out of my right eye." He drew breath. I quickly dumped literature in his lap, but he continued, "We need good news what with China, Burma and America ... "

The sad looking man I had previously met said, "I met you in Federation Square twelve months ago. I was literally on my knees. You gave me a New Testament and an invitation to your church - but I returned to my old church. Everything is OK."

An ageing Chinese gentleman sat next to a quirky young Caucasian female wearing head scarf, ankle length coat, and reading what looked like a Bible in another language. To my surprise, her austere features split wide open with an ear-to-ear grin as she gifted the old Asian with a Chinese Christian calendar. Five minutes later she was giving, with equally bright smile, a calendar to another traveller.

A High School student, with whom I had shared previously, asked, "Do you go to NewHope Baptist Church? My boyfriend and I go there on Friday and Sunday nights. We like the singing. I was telling him about you. He wanted to know if you were that tall grey headed old guy called Bruce." She accepted a Gospel of John.

A middle-aged male and female who seemed half his age both smelling strongly of alcohol, boarded the bus at the Box Hill transport terminal.. I offered her the 'Finding Hope' booklet. She demanded, "Why give me this?"

I explained, "We're all on a journey. Everybody has issues. I hand out 100's."

An ancient female swiped her met card with no response. The driver said, "Put some money in your Myki account."

She shouted, "No!!" Taking a seat without payment she loudly accused the driver of various improprieties and me for stalking her and riding without a ticket.

The driver stage whispered, "I think she forgot her tablets."

A Saudi Arabian student, with one father and his two wives, and ten brothers and ten sisters asked, "What do you think of Islam?"

I replied, "I don't like terrorist killings."

He said, "It's media bias."

I answered, "Do you have a cast iron guarantee of paradise when you die?"

He said, "No," and accepted an Arabic NT (Injil).

An objectional young male theological student asserted the virtues of his 'beautiful' Catholic Church including teaching on holy communion (John 6) as necessary for salvation.

An elderly male shouted, "It's an illusion. The Bible is a myth."

He loudly ridiculed my faith, but an encouraging Christian Indian lady sitting nearby smiled and said, "Happy fishing."

A Few of the Many Train Contacts

A derelict female passenger who accepted a TPTL NT*, was invited to a café for coffee and a muffin, a luxury which I suspect she rarely enjoyed. Another lady reluctantly accepted a New Testament, read from it, and offered to return it. I said, "It's all about you and God. One day, you might cry, and this book will comfort you. Take it."

A twenty-three-year-old lost his mother and girlfriend tragically and broke his back in a motorcycle accident. He was unable to work, survived a recent attempted suicide, listened to my testimony, and accepted literature.

A shabbily dressed Irish born teenager asked, "What are you doing here?"

"I came specially to talk with you" I responded.

Surprised, he replied, "But we've never met."

I said to him, "You don't believe I came all the way from Northern Victoria and you came all the way from Northern Ireland to meet on this platform by accident, do you?"

He politely listened to my testimony, accepted literature, and said, "I hope we meet again."

At a sparsely populated local railway station, a middle-aged male hiding behind a platform pylon, leapt in front of me as I drew level and in the presence of a startled Asian lass, shouted, "Shoot me!"

I replied, "What will that prove?"

He exclaimed, "For God's sake find someone to shoot me!"

I said, "No one is going to do that."

He replied, "Don't worry," and subsided dejectedly onto a nearby bench seat. He accepted literature and said, "I'll read this!"

A skimpy-skirted female with wiry, green tinged hair, nose rings, heavily tattooed legs, arms, and shoulders boarded the train. I silently prayed for guidance on how to share with her who looked old beyond her years. A glimpse of the wide blue yonder through a cloud gap gave me a clue.

I said to her, "The only thing stopping me flying bullet-like through that cloud gap into outer space is gravity. I don't understand it but I believe it. It's the same with God. I don't fully understand God but I believe Him." In response to my testimony, she replied "My mother believes that, but I don't know if I can. I've had a hard year." She recounted details of the recent deaths of close family members and her beloved pet dog., Narrowing the Gospel to a definition of sin and forgiveness could have been counter-productive in her case. Acting under the authority that Jesus invests in all Christians, I pronounced upon her God's blessings that Jesus may fill her life with love, joy, and peace. She accepted a Blessing Card (BC*) and disembarked with tear-filled eyes.

Leon accepted the 'Where it all began' Christmas tract with a picture of an infant child on the front cover. He said, "Strange you should offer me that. My two-year old son died in my arms two years ago." He was invited to a complimentary 'Dinner Tonight' at our church.

A twenty-year-old overweight male with pimply face, untidy, shoulder length black hair, hoody, and holes in his trousers, was reading a book entitled: 'Treasury of Infamy'. His mum died last year, and he dropped out of college. His foster father remarried a woman with several kids who all moved into the family home. He said, "I was a Christian, but I respect what you're doing." He accepted testimony and literature.

A heavily tattooed young male wearing sunglasses, sat with me. After some discussion, he asked, "Is the air in Darwin clear? Do the moon and stars shine bright like they say?"

I responded, "They do. As a teenager I struggled with some issues. One night when the atmosphere was clear, stars twinkling in the night sky and the moon was shining bright. I said, 'God, I do not know who you are. I don't even know if you exist, but if you're there please help me.' Next evening, a Christian neighbour showed me how to connect with the Creator. That night I became a Jesus follower. I can trace a change in the direction of my life going back to that moment'." He was visibly impressed.

A respectable looking young man was heading to court on his fourth 'drive whilst disqualified' charge and would likely finish up in jail. His car was crushed and he wouldn't get his licence back for a long time. I quote John 5:24*. He replied, "I know, I'm Orthodox."

A poorly dressed lady with an obviously disadvantaged background, said, "One day in a tram, I felt sick and a man let me chunder in his shopping bag." She accepted a tract with a long drawn-out "Thaaaaanks." She was replaced by a Sikh student who insisted I listen to his Punjabi music. We transferred his ear plugs. I hoped his ears were clean. It occurred to me that the words of his eerie rhythm sounded rather like chunder, chucca, chunder, chunder.

An Indian student invited me to sit with him. I asked, "Do you read the Quran?" He believed merit was earned by reading the Arabic Quran even if not understood.

He reluctantly accepted an Injil (Arabic NT) saying, "Before we read holy books, we should first wash our hands."

I said, "Faith in Jesus Christ makes us clean on the inside. Take it. You might have an English-speaking Arabic speaking friend who can help you understand it."

He stated, "I was not a good Muslim. I don't know if God was judging me or giving me a second chance."

I explained, "I believe God is giving you another chance."

He said, "I have gone back to reading the Quran, praying and keeping the law."

I told him, "An encounter with the Lord Jesus Christ changed my life. Jesus paid the full price for all my sins. Have you had a personal encounter with your god?" I read John 12:46 where Jesus said, "I have come as a light into the world, that whosoever believes in me should not abide in darkness." I offered him a John's Gospel saying, "Take it. It will challenge your Islamic understanding of the identity of Jesus."

On another day, he asked, "Have you read the Quran yet?"

I answered, "Not completely, but I was reading it today." I showed him my copy.

He read it and declared, "This is not an accurate copy. I recommend you do not read it." But he indicated several passages within it that he hoped would convince me to renounce Christianity and become a Muslim.

A retired Indian Ophthalmologist offered me a seat beside him. He lived in Melbourne but found cultural transition difficult. I asked, "What is your main philosophy?"

He replied, "Giving light to the blind in their dark world." This opportune comment allowed me to introduce the words of Jesus who said, "I am the light of the world. Whoever follows me will never walk in darkness, but will have the light of life."

He said, "Those are powerful words." He accepted a Gospel of John.

Agilen, a student, accepted an invitation to help me with a crossword puzzle. He read my tract and said, "I thought you might be a Christian. I attend the ... Baptist Church."

I asked him, "How did you become a Christian?"

He explained, "Several years ago, I had a serious illness back home in Mauritius. My father was a witch doctor but could not heal me. He met a Baptist Pastor who prayed for me. I was healed. Our family became Christians. My father now preaches in local churches."

A filthy tongued derelict slurred, "I play the!?*# blues for a!@# donation." He let fly with loud discordant notes from his harmonica. Later in Degraves Street, the would-be musician with partly consumed plonk bottle, staggered past slurring, "Any change sir?"

A North Queensland teenager accepted literature and an outline of God's salvation plan. Later that day she sent the following text: "Hi Bruce, thank you for talking to me I feel great and I know I'm going to have a really good day because of you, I would love to have another talk like that again sometime – from ....."I replied, "Call me when you are ready." She never did.

A sad man was recently deserted by his wife and five kids. With no possibility of reconciliation and no job he was dejected and hopeless. He found his Bible hard to understand. Over coffee in Lilydale, I said, "What's your next move?"

He asked, "How do I get christened?"

I responded, "Firstly you must become a Christian." We read through the plan of salvation. He accepted Jesus as his Saviour. Months later, a Council team were beautifying a local bus stop. The sad man now a local counsel supervisor, advanced with hand outstretched. "Hello Bruce. I still want coffee with you. I'm reading my Bible."

A tattooed Darryl with Aboriginal heritage, was orphaned early in life and spiralled downwards to addictions, violence, criminality, jail, and serious ill health. I said to him, "May I pray for you?" He expressed gratitude with a vigorous handshake.

Recently, Jason, from another church, accompanied me to learn some finer points of street evangelism. On the train, he was introduced to three contacts – David, a lapsed Catholic Sudanese refugee who had previously accepted literature; long haired Eric, toothless and quirky heading for chemotherapy at Box Hill, and Briami, also toothless, an aboriginal lady from Redfern NSW swigging from a bottle in a brown paper bag. Jason invited Briami to sit in the only vacant seat, yes, you guessed it, next to me! Jason prayed for each contact.

Gilius, a Christian refugee from Wamena, Western Papua, greeted me. Jessie Williamson, a long-term retired missionary (now deceased) from P.N.G. and I had arranged to get him a Bible in his mother tongue a couple of years previously. He greeted me like a long-lost friend and was leading his Western Papua fellowship.

My co-worker and I talked with a Chilean student. This high grade, soccer player, just had his recently fractured leg set in plaster. My train arrived and I left them to it. My co-worker later texted: "Hey. Just thought I'd let you know I stayed with our Chilean friend; we even missed a train together. Shared the Gospel, got his number. Definitely catch up with him again. Praise God."

I had just finished reading Philippians 4:6-7* when a heavily tattooed male and a shoeless female boarded the carriage. I said to him, "How are you?" His immediate and unexpected response was explosive rage and loud expletives directed at me. I felt physically threatened. He stormed off, abusing his female partner as he went. His abusive response was a rare event in my street ministry experience.

A smoldering half smoked cigarette occupied space on a table in the Flinders Street railway concourse. A chair at this table was occupied by Milena, an attractive Yugoslav student. A derelict appropriated the cigarette, sat, and puffed. I shared my testimony with Milena. For reasons best known to himself, the derelict registered disapproval with head shaking and mono-syllabic grunts. Milena shook my hand. "A good story," she said. The grunts got louder. I quickly departed.

Mark complained, "Things aren't going well. I've been kicked out of home. My car has been repossessed. I have no money. What about you?"

I said, "I have a fulfilled life and an eternal destiny."

He asked me, "Are you a Christian? Did God tell you to speak to me?"

I replied, "Let me give you the question back. Do you think God sent me here?"

He replied. "I think so."

I said, "I'll buy you a coffee."

At the coffee shop he said, "I am born again, and Spirit filled, but Christians let me down. I have no purpose for life. I don't know why I am here. I even tried to commit suicide." He listened to my testimony and accepted literature and counsel. We enjoyed coffee together.

An older male said, "I lost my wife a couple of years ago. Life is lonely, I find things to do, but it's not the same."

I said to him, "If you could speak to the most important man in the universe. Who would he be, and what would you ask him?"

"Hmmm! No good speaking to politicians or scientists. I'd try Neil Armstrong and ask him what he thought when he looked down from the moon to earth. What about you?" I shared my testimony. My contact replied, "I'm atheist. As long as the sun stays up there everything else is irrelevant."

I answered, "An Indian business man once took me with him in his boat on the Ganges River. He was worshipping the rising sun. I commented to him, "I'm a Christian. I don't understand why you worship the rising sun?"

The Indian responded, "The sun gives warmth and light. Without them we could not survive."

I queried, "But the sun is a ball of molten metal and hot gas with no ears to hear, eyes to see, brains to think and no mouth to speak. Why not worship the Creator who made the sun?"

The older male responded, "It's all very complex." He accepted literature.

A lady with Vietnamese heritage had accepted a Gospel of John previously on the train. She said, "I was just starting out in the spiritual life. Reading that booklet helped me become a Christian. Our church is starting a study of John, reminding me to thank you for your gift of that Gospel."

Part way through a testimony a heavy hand laid on my shoulder. An accompanying voice excitedly affirmed, "It's true! It's true!" This was my introduction to a Baptist Pastor from Tasmania.

I replied, "Thanks for your encouragement." As I concluded my testimony, the overjoyed Pastor reiterated to my Asian contact, "It's all true!"

The Pastor said, "I am encouraged. If this man becomes a Christian, let me know. More people should share their faith like you." Soon after, a heartening letter arrived by mail from Tasmania. The Pastor wrote: "The Kingdom of God needs thousands of Bruce Kelly's riding on trains, in the workplaces, at the footy, desiring to catch an ear to tell their story."

Ministry Continues After Disembarkation

The Asian accepted a Gospel of John, shook hands, smiled, and said, "Very interesting!" and disembarked.

A druggy jailed many times, was on his way to court yet again. My interest in his welfare elevated his self-esteem. He said, "I'm OK on medication but can't kick the habit. I have no hope." He accepted literature and disembarked at the law courts saying "Thanks! You're a gentleman."

I was convicted to disembark at Flagstaff Station that services the Law Courts. Experience leads me to follow such promptings. Silks (legal professionals) were relaxing in the morning sunshine over coffee. Nearby a good-looking young man made notations on his writing pad. Enmeshed in a nasty custody battle in an adjacent court, he vented his bitterness at short notice. "My rights as a husband and father are taken from me!" I shared my testimony, then drew the self-centred and Christ centred circles.

I said to him, "Which of these circles represents your life?"

He said to me, "I've just started attending a church in Berwick. They are telling me the same thing."

I explained, "God can forgive your sins and give you strength and guidance. I will pray for you, your wife, and children." His case was due to commence. He accepted a Gospel of John, smiled, and hurried off.

A female was sprawled across three seats in a carriage. She loudly berated Connex Trains with filthy language directed into her mobile phone. An adjacent male was reading his large black gold embossed Bible. He remained silent and aloof. An Indian lady, preoccupied by her messy divorce, accepted a Gospel of John. Connex announced a change of trains. More invective from 'Loudmouth' who disembarked at Richmond.

A male Aussie passenger interjected with unhelpful comments into my conversation with two students from Hyderabad. A third curious Indian student broke into our conversation. All three Indians accepted Hindi tracts. After disembarkation at Flinders Street a female passenger on the platform said, "Good on you for sharing the word, but the man who sneered is trying to undo all your good work." This guy was walking through the exit deep in conversation with the Indians. The lady owned a dental practice and was under report to a government authority for sharing her faith in the surgery. She was interested in my range of tracts for her waiting room. She prayed for me.

Is God challenging you to be one of the thousands? Learning these lessons is a process, not an event requiring Bible knowledge, energy, and faithful prayer.

Taking it to Heart:

1. What does rightly dividing judgement and comfort mean?
2. Describe some helpful steps in maintaining true Gospel presentations?
3. How will you go about glorifying God this week?

References:

John 5:24 –Most assuredly, I say to you, he who hears My word and believes in Him who sent Me, has everlasting life, and shall not come into judgement, but has passed from death to life.

Philippians 4:6-7 - Be anxious for nothing, but in everything by prayer and supplication, with thanksgiving, let your requests be made known to God; and the peace of God, which surpasses all understanding, will guard your hearts and minds through Christ Jesus.

BQ – Big Question - What is the most important question in all the world for you?

TPTL NT – The Pocket Testament League New Testament.

BC – Blessing Card – Aaronic blessing.

Chapter 29

A New Direction - Local and East Ringwood Outreach

In the Street Where We Live

COVID 19 (see ch.36) created a new direction for outreach. Jan and I began prayer walking our street, park and local shops searching for opportunities to share the good news. A windstorm uprooted trees and played havoc with power supplies in our street. Prompted by a reading in our morning devotions, three widows and one elderly widower in our street were visited. These visits created goodwill and opened doors for continuing contacts with longstanding neighbours never previously met during many years of living there. Two friendly young female traffic wardens, performing traffic control duties supporting a power supply maintenance crew working on storm damage nearby, a curious pedestrian couple watching proceedings, and a nearby female all accepted 'Blessing cards' with gratitude. An Iranian couple strolling past our residence accepted a 'Blessing card' and a container of home-grown cherry tomatoes.

As Jan and I were departing for our regular Saturday morning walk, a happy young female with a bubbly personality, with her pet dog came running up to us breathlessly saying, "I've been wanting to speak to you. You gave me a card with a Bible verse at the local bus stop three years ago, but I was rebellious and didn't want to hear Christian stuff. However, following a near death experience, I began attending church, became a Christian and was recently baptised. I can't believe the difference in my life. I am sharing my new faith with friends."

Desolee, our neighbouring psychiatric friend, who often aimlessly shuffled past our home, phoned saying, "Jan, It is urgent that I take communion tonight." This sounded a bit ominous! Jan conveyed her to her Jewish case manager who asked, "What is communion?" Our friend overdosed soon after - Jan had frequently taken her to see her psychiatrist. Later, a card from her father in NSW acknowledged with gratitude our help to his daughter over several difficult years at different times as needed.

A single eighty-year-old Italian Catholic regularly wandered slowly down our street. I had sometimes taken him out for coffee. He had gone down physically in recent weeks. This self-funded retiree was obsessed with trivialities, money, his vegie garden, bad neighbours, and being fleeced by local businessmen. Though bitter about old age and frightened of death, he consistently refused testimony and declined literature.

During an evening stroll, Jan and I met an Asian lady, who expressed a desire to learn English. We transported her to the Sunday morning ESL class at NewHope Baptist Church, and afterwards she attended the worship service. In the evening, we visited at her nearby address. Her Asian ESL class teacher, who we'd never met, had later invited our contact to her home for a meal and informed her of a Bible study organisation with a branch in the large Chinese city where the contact lived. Our contact presented Jan with an expensive gift before returning to China the next day.

A Walk in the Park

Frogmouths are nocturnal birds roosting in trees during daylight hours. Gazing upward into trees through binoculars at nesting frogmouths attracted the attention of a retired nurse. She returned with her zoom lens camera, but the frogmouths were gone. Later, over coffee at a local café, she disclosed her previous connections with Wesleyans, Baptists, and Pentecostals, but no longer attended church. She declined to say why but happily accepted the 'Blessing card.' Several curious neighbours, overseas visitors and workers also accepted 'Blessing cards' while watching these frogmouths.

A holidaying middle-aged Persian couple, exercising in the park playground, were visiting with family nearby, but the covid virus lockdown trapped them in Melbourne. Their limited English-speaking skills made communication difficult. I said, "Wait! I have something for you." I hurried home and returned breathless with my gift (a Farsi language NT). She exclaimed in surprise, "Injil!" They accepted with interest, respect, and gratitude. Two weeks later in the park, she stated to me, "Injil very good!" He nodded and smiled. They accepted more Farsi literature.

Local Cafes and Nearby Streets

Andrew, sitting outside a local cafe, was a sixty-two-year-old postman with a cochlear implant. With a loud and gravelly voice, he responded to my greeting, "Eh! What was that. My hearing is … ed!" Our shouted conversation must surely have been audible court wide. He said, "I found peace in Thailand. They believe Buddha. I am divorced, but my new lady lives there. I want to return, but Covid-19 stopped me. I don't know what my future holds."

I explained, "If the object of your faith is valid, your faith is valid. If the object of your faith is invalid, then your faith is invalid. Christians validate their faith with actual history. Jesus said, "I am the light of the world. Whoever follows me, will never walk in darkness, but have the light of life." He accepted a Gospel of John with reference to John 8:12* saying, "Thanks! I'll have a read of that." Next morning Andrew shouted, "I read John 8:12" as he walked by.

A local resident, whose nearby English cottage garden we always admired, walked by my outdoor cafe table, and asked, "What are you reading?" I showed him the cover. He replied, "That means nothing to me." I answered, "It captures the essence of the book." He accepted a 'Blessing card' and volunteered, "My family grew up in India. My father was in the British army." I explained, "This booklet might interest you." He accepted a replica WW1 Gospel of John and stated, "How interesting! Is this for me?"

A Bangladeshi couple went to great lengths to explain their Islamic faith. I asked them, "Do you keep all the laws of Islam?" He said, "No." She exclaimed, "God is so merciful that one act of kindness, even to a dog, equals 1,000 sins." I replied, "But does the Qur'an offer you a rock-solid, watertight guarantee of forgiveness and eternity in paradise?" He said, "No. We'll find out when we die." They accepted Bengali literature.

Interesting Persian Contacts at a Local Persian Café

Most contacts listed below accepted 'Blessing cards', Farsi Injils (Persian NTs), the BQ* and testimony -

To the fifty-year-old proprietor of a local Persian café, whose ninety-three-year-old father in Persia recently died, I said, "We are praying for you and your family." To his wife I said, "Jesus Christ will take you to Paradise if you let Him."

A Christian Persian refugee showed me Farsi literature I had given him in Federation Square four years previously.

A NEW DIRECTION - LOCAL AND EAST RINGWOOD OUTREACH

Another Christian Persian related to the cafe management, in Farsi, my role in the unexpected Persian refugee influx at NewHope Baptist Church several years previously.

An attractive woman, a handsome man and a good-looking teenage student walked by. I guessed they were Persians. The woman, fluent with English, indicating the student by her side emphatically stated, "He is not my son. I am single." The student indicating the male adult by his side said, "He is my father." They disappeared inside the cafe. She returned with a tray of Persian delicacies and offered one each to Jan and me.

A landscape gardener declined a Farsi New Testament (NT) saying, "I've had my fill of religion!" and proceeded to test my faith. I stood my ground. Weeks later, I said, "I'm still waiting for the chat you promised." He replied, "Bruce, I really like you! When I said I don't want religion, I didn't mean we can't talk about it."

A friendly young lady nearby remarked, "I remember you from the cafe over there. I don't drink alcohol, but I'm trying to kick cigarettes. It's a filthy habit." With permission I prayed for her. She replied, "Thanks so much!"

A sprightly ninety-one-year-old Aussie lady used the word 'God' somewhat loosely in conversation. I said, "I have authority from God to pronounce His blessing on you." She accepted the 'Blessing card' and with sincerity, exclaiming, "God, how I needed that!" She, who recently lost her son with a brain tumour, was currently embroiled in a family dispute over his estate. She occasionally attended a local church with a friend.

A young Persian female in the street followed an ancient Middle Eastern religious sect. Her companion followed the majority religion. He said, "We had a car accident. I have permanent head injuries. In hospital I thought about God."

A couple, without English, outside the local pharmacy, were holidaying with their recently arrived son and wife, both skilled migrants applying for Permanent Residency (PR). The older couple extended with gestures and smiles, a pressing invitation for coffee at their son's home within walking distance. We were warmly greeted, introduced, and offered nuts and sweets for supper with fluent translation supplied by a pregnant daughter-in-law. In response to my brief testimony, the older man said in surprise, "Are you a priest?" The son asked, "Do you know where I can find work?"

A lady said to me, "I am a believer but I've never found a spiritual home." I asked her, "What's your favourite verse?" She replied, "Love your neighbours. What's yours?" I told her, "Jesus said, 'I am the light of the world. Whoever follows me shall never walk in darkness but have the light of life'." She stated, "That's beautiful!" I responded, "You will never find a perfect church. When I added my imperfection to an imperfect church, we worshipped a perfect Saviour."

Outside the cafe a domineering loud-voiced philosophical Mediterranean male introduced me sarcastically to the public as, "A fine Christian man from NewHope Baptist Church." How he obtained this information, I do not know. He then proceeded to rip the integrity of churches, denominations, and Christianity to pieces. I was more than happy to disengage with him.

On my way home, I tripped and fell in the middle of an intersection. Two Persian gentlemen, the above-mentioned café proprietor and another, stopped their cars and attended to my needs. Their concern and care were impressive. One directed traffic around me. The other drove me home in his two-door Mercedes coupe with accelerator flat on the floor and a throaty roar!

Mariam * - Divine Appointment

One pre-Covid-19 Saturday morning, Jan and I, with other Christians, met for our regular fellowship over coffee in a local cafe with Middle-Eastern paintings adorning its walls. The handsome, young male waiter clarified by saying, "It is Persian language." English sub-titles indicated these ancient poems were written about pretty flowers, and sweetly singing birds, etc. He had previously accepted the 'Life of Jesus' booklet.

An attractive young lady, with excellent English, who arrived in Australia fourteen months previously, sat reading a book. She thoughtfully offered to move to another table to create space for Jan and me. I said, "No! Please sit with us. Tell us about your book." During the lengthy conversation that followed she included information about Zoroastrianism, her family faith in Persia. Our friends joined with us in this conversation.

She listened to my testimony and said, "Fascinating, I have books on many religions. I respect them all. Do you think I am right?" I answered her, "There are books on thousands of philosophies and religions. They aren't all right. If the object of your faith is invalid, then your faith must also be invalid. The only trustworthy information we have about God is the Christian Bible. I have spoken with 100's about their belief. Not one offered a God who does more for me than Jesus Christ. This is why I am a Christian." She accepted a John's Gospel in which was written my name and phone number. She then read John 8:12* at my request. I asked, "What do you think?" She replied, "Wonderful. Thank you!"

Months later she messaged me saying, "My story and testimony are a miracle. Something marvellous happened. Can we talk?" The next day she powerfully testified in another local café to her recent conversion experience after a twenty-seven-year search. She declared, "I have known many Christians, but you were the first to share a John's Gospel with me. I am a baby in Christ. I have many years to make up." Her recently acquired Bible was heavily highlighted and her many philosophical books disposed of.

Later, she was intercepted in a car park by strange sect members and coerced into baptism in the name of god the father, god the mother and god the sect leader. A Christian friend advised her to read 1 Thessalonians 4:14-15*. She saw through their strange deception and studied a 'Navigators' study on 'Growing in Christ' in our home. I later had the privilege of baptising her at the Light Community Baptist Church (LCBC). Her testimony and baptism testified to the reality of her newfound faith. She treated us to a new cultural experience over dinner in a local Persian restaurant and took us to the Sunday market in Thomastown, an outer suburb of Melbourne, and introduced us to a disenchanted Orthodox contact with whom she was sharing her faith. The crowds were mainly Middle-Easterners and North Africans. It was a different world out there.

In time, she was subjected to demonic attacks in her apartment. Jan and I visited her and through prayer claimed God's victory and dedicated her and her apartment for the Lord's purposes and glory. Our friend has since moved to another suburb. Her faith is strong and alive by the grace of God. We are in continuing contact and encouraging her to become part of a Christian community.

Planting seeds takes time, but the harvest is assured. Jan and I were encouraged, despite the Covid-19 lockdowns and subsequent restrictions, God is at work.

> "And we know that for those who love God
> all things work together for good,
> for those who are called according to his purpose."
> (Romans 8:28)

A NEW DIRECTION - LOCAL AND EAST RINGWOOD OUTREACH

East Ringwood Outreach

We have also focussed on the East Ringwood locality situated some 25kms east of Melbourne's CBD. It's population of 10,265 with a median age of thirty-nine years, is located in the 'Green Belt' of Melbourne, with native vegetation and wildlife preserved in areas such as Wombelano Park and surrounding suburban streets. East Ringwood township is a small shopping centre with its own railway station on the Lilydale line. The shops are confined to and located along one side of the main street, parallel with the railway line. The railway station became a significant focal point for outreach.

On the occasion of my first stroll down the East Ringwood main street, the first person I met invited me to coffee at a local café. This worthy citizen with an Asian background turned out to be a regular attender at LCBC. I am grateful for her never-to-be-forgotten warm hospitality which set a good tone for our future at this church.

In the main street a friendly Asian, with an infant child, accepted testimony, and Chinese and English literature. She expressed interest in enrolling her child in a playgroup at our church and was provided with details. Another Asian lady also with an infant child asked, "Where's the playgroup?" We had previously door knocked at her address.

An African male with dread locks, rainbow coloured skull cap and baggy jeans shuffled by. I said, "Excuse me, do you know the area?" He said, "Yes, I live in Freeman Street" (I had visited his address on door knock previously). I asked, "Do you follow your God?" He answered, "No! I don't believe in any God." I replied, "Here's a booklet about the God you don't believe in." I read John 8:12* aloud and drew attention to the word 'follow'."

On arriving home from street ministry in East Ringwood one afternoon, I discovered with a nauseating feeling, that an unwelcome visitor had entered our home through a smashed our back window, rifled our bedrooms, and stole cash and jewellery. Police later attended.

East Ringwood Railway Platform (ERRP)

Gareth's tears rolled down his face as he accepted testimony, and the 'Picking Up the Pieces' booklet. Heavily medicated, he listlessly stated, "I must get a Bible." His energy level lifted a little when I handed him a New Testament. He asked incredulously, "Is this for me?" He added, "I've been to the LCBC a couple of times." I replied, "Only Jesus can unlock your potential. Follow Him."

Two youngish males were talking. I could only guess the nature of their transaction. One departed. The remaining one, tearfully said, "I've had a rotten week. My girlfriend kicked me out. We both hate drugs. I don't know why we do it. I've had my last chance." I replied, "I'll gladly help, even if only for a little while." He was catching the train, so I said, "I'll come too and shout you a coffee at Eastland."

Over coffee he described two relationship terminations, and his current girlfriend's recent miscarriage. He added, "I have no future. I'll never get a house. Nobody will employ me." He accepted the 'You matter' booklet (the Prodigal Son), a Gospel of John (John 8:12*), a Gideon's New Testament and an invitation to a church life group. He said, "Thank you. I appreciate what you've done. I've never told anyone except you about my problems." He departed with a lighter step and happier attitude, however, surrendering his ruined life to Jesus is his only hope.

A middle-aged, shaven headed, heavily tattooed male, wearing military apparel, colourfully described his chequered past. At first, he declined literature saying, "I lost faith in the church (Catholic) because of the way they treated my parents when they were dying. I'm a believer who has lost my way." Being assured that I was promoting a relationship with Jesus and not church membership, he accepted the 'Finding Hope' booklet.

A male known to me said, "Thanks for the literature you gave me and the invitation to your church." He accepted more literature and yet another invitation. This nice man, being treated for extreme anxiety said, "You'll see me soon." But severe panic attacks continued plaguing him.

On the platform, the oldest scooter rider I've ever met, was rummaging through his dilapidated untidy backpack. His long matted grey hair, beard, and clothing were filthy. His ramblings almost indecipherable. I offered him a 'Finding Hope' booklet. As he drank from a partly consumed coke bottle, he had extracted from the railway platform waste bin, another said, "I just gave him $10 to buy food." I stated, "When he put your money in his wallet, $25 was clearly visible." The donor shrugged and accepted literature. He informed me, "I have an illness. I'm on my way to get it fixed."

A mature young student nurse, in answer to the Big Question (BQ*) asked, "Don't know. What about you?" She accepted testimony and said, "I believe there's something out there, but I don't have your background," as she accepted a TPTL NT*. I answered, "Therein lies the answer to your BQ*."

Shabbily dressed Darryn, with a partly consumed bottle of wine asked, "Have you got some money. I am homeless and need food. It's cold at night." I told him, "I won't give you money, but I'll buy you a hamburger." He replied, "I have an appointment. I've got a train to catch." He was recently discharged from six weeks in a detox centre. I prayed over him for deliverance.

A tattooed, derelict, younger male wreck approached and said, "I'm homeless!" His eviction notice served earlier this day, ordered vacation by 5pm due to his drug addiction. He was on his way to the Salvation Army for help and accepted the 'Finding Hope' booklet.

A young mother commented, "I've heard of that church (LCBC}. You have a good playgroup." She further stated her mother was recently admitted to hospital. I said to her, "I could pray for your mother now if you wish." She replied, "Please do," and accepted church literature with thanks. She added, "I might come one day."

An elderly Christian lady and friend accepted a replica WW1 Gospel. These Gospels are a wonderful ministry opportunity to older Australians, of whom many are interested in Anzac Day. A key verse for soldiers in their great hour of need was - "But to as many as received Him, to them He gave the right to become children of God" (John 1:12).

A man, whose father suicided when he was nine-years-old, had lived in psychiatric institutions for many years. He said, "I pray every day, but it hasn't done me much good. I have thirty-five books on eastern religions and philosophy, but I can't be changed. I don't know what my future holds. I don't want your literature." These glimpses of life in the main street of East Ringwood raises a continuing issue. 'How will a small local church like ours reach out to these many disadvantaged locals?'

East Ringwood Shopping Centre

An American motor cyclist with Swedish Afro-American heritage, shared articulately and forcefully his belief in reincarnation, similarity of religions, and scriptural and religious corruption. The sceptical café proprietor, our local Pastor and his friend joined the fray. To a nearby Turkish male eating a hamburger I said, "I thought Muslims fasted during Ramadan." He replied, "I'm Christian!" and accepted Turkish literature.

An Aussie, devastated by the breakdown of his sixteen-year marriage, listened to my testimony and accepted a John's Gospel. A young British tourist replied, "What a fascinating story," and accepted Gospels for herself and her boyfriend.

G. was moving into a local community care accommodation unit. P. clutching his KJV Bible and suffering extreme anxiety, accepted literature. J. struggling with personal issues was known to me. Others from the same accommodation unit drifted slowly by. Two disadvantaged people, who occasionally attended our church, chatted nearby. A female shouted expletives in the distance.

George, an itinerant Queenslander, colourfully described his previous life as a tow truck driver, marriage breakdown, severe depression, attempted self-harm, and life travelling Australia in an ancient van. He accepted my story and a Gospel. He declared, "I'll read this tonight."

An elderly lady sniffed disdainfully as she looked at the church literature. She said, "There's lots of religious people round here. There were none in Balwyn (nearby Melbourne suburb) where I came from." An older Aussie male confidently elaborated on his views about Taoism, Yin and Yang, reincarnation, and idol worship.

Within the population of East Ringwood, a percentage of disadvantaged people could be seen slowly trudging the public places with eyes downcast. My earlier approach, though not always, was to evangelise along the 'Sinner believe or perish' line (Mark 1:15*). But most contacts didn't want to be reminded of what they already knew and found hard to forget. Jesus typically used a different approach. On one of those occasions, He said, "Follow me and I will make you fishers of men." He began with an invitation, "Follow me" (Matthew 4:19*). There was no mention of judgement or repentance at that point. It was about people coming as they were. Bringing the Good News is wider than focusing on sin. Our testimony should include an invitation to pave the way for the Holy Spirit, who awakens the need for salvation. This significant insight modified my approach to sharing.

Eastland Shopping Centre

Due to rain, I opted for ministry indoors at the Eastland shopping centre. A retired Pastor, known to me, said, "The amount of fish you catch is directly proportionate to the amount of times you go fishing."

To a female salesperson at an upmarket lady's shoe outlet, I said, "I'm not here to buy anything, but popped in to cheer you up." She replied, "I'm bored out of my brain. I've just ordered a coffee." In answer to the BQ* she said, "That's a good question." I replied, "Find the answer and you'll likely find your direction and purpose for life. I'm a Christian." She smiled and said, "So am I. I've just come from Sydney." She attended Hillsong Church there and now goes to an AOG Church in Richmond.

Two rough teenage 'rooftop boys' sought thrills late at night by climbing to the top of partially constructed city skyscrapers. They accepted Christian literature and shook hands. A puffing, sweaty one-legged wheelchair bound male, trying to propel himself backwards for better leverage up the steepish approach slope to Eastland shops, gratefully accepted a push. Now I'm puffing!

Selwyn Hughes, in an edition of his 'Every Day with Jesus' study notes in commenting on the parable of the Lost Coin, (Luke 15:8-10*) said, "God sweeps the universe with the broom of His redemptive grace until He finds the coin on which His image is stamped." Searching for 'God's Lost Coin' is an uplifting experience. The only Bible some people will read are the lives of Christians. We are a letter anyone can read just by looking at us. Christ Himself wrote it, not with ink but with His living Spirit, not chiselled into stone, but carved into our hearts and we publish it (2 Corinthians 3:2-3*).

An East Ringwood Café

While I was working on a crossword, the café proprietor asked, "Working out the puzzles?" I answered, "Life is a puzzle." He said, "Life is the solution." I declared, "God is the solution. I am a Christian." He told me, "People knock at my door and tell me their religion is right, and the Bible is contradictory." I replied, "Give me an example." He couldn't. I said, "I've read it for years but found no contradictions." He stated, "One of my staff is a Sikh. She would say her religion is right." I explained, "Christ died on the Cross for my sin. He rose the third day to give me victory over death, purpose in life and an eternal destiny. No other religion offers what Christ does. That's why I am a Christian." He said, "It's confusing." I exclaimed, "Don't be confused. The Bible is the only place you will find truth" and drew his attention to Proverbs 22:4* He later accepted an enlarged laminated copy of the 'Blessing card' superimposed over a photo of his business premises. He showed it to his staff, posted it in a visible position and excitedly said, "I must show it to my wife. She will like it."

Whilst enjoying sunshine at an outside table, an older female pedestrian with an ethnic background said, "Can I sit with you? I'm sick of being lonely and want someone to talk to." Her Greek husband abandoned her soon after the birth of their third child. One child was divorced, another has a retarded son. She said, "I've tried every church, but the only one that helped were the Mormons. I prayed and prayed but got no help. I don't want anything to do with church." She heard my story but declined literature saying, "You're a nice man." Later, she walked past with gaze averted.

A lass, who previously worked in the café, stated, "They were short staffed, so the boss asked me to lend a hand for the day. My boyfriend and I were talking about you the other day. He said you are the most interesting man he'd ever met." I asked, "How so?" She informed me, "Your story about the farm, the Police and the church is fascinating." I told her, "Invite him to see me some time."

An older male, with a friendly smile and handshake, said, "I'm not bad for a bloke who drinks, smokes, gambles, and chases women. Hedonism is a dying art. I want to revive it." I said to him, "Life is only as valid as your belief." He maintained, "If you go to a pond, you can drink all you want." I said, "Your pond is full of muck and filth." It might have been wiser to comment on the water from the well in John 4.

An ancient adage states, "Ask as many questions as you can; learn as much as you can and say as little as possible'. This adage served me well as I talked to an older male.

I asked, "How are you?" He replied, "S … H…!" His litany of woes included reference to his cancer, forthcoming surgery, weak heart, and medical expenses. This retired used car salesman colourfully confessed to questionable business practices, which admittedly created a lifetime of unhealthy pressure. In answer to the BQ*, he said, "That's hard! I don't know the future or what's round the corner." He accepted literature. I said, "When we meet again, tell me your answer."

An older man, with health issues, expounded philosophically his ideas about soul characteristics and geo-political solutions to world violence. Providentially, a Christian practicing barrister known to me walked by. With recent lecturing experience in an Asian Bible College, he was the ideal person to inject some Christian 'Philosophy' into this discourse. He has continuing contact with this man.

The proprietor said, "My friend (indicating a man at the counter) has cancer. He is not in a good place. Say a little prayer for him." This Christian cancer victim showed me graphic iPhone pictures detailing progress of his cancer. His attention was drawn to the Aaronic blessing in Numbers 6 mounted on the café wall. This is the first such request I had received from this manager after two years of patronage. I was honoured to pray for his friend.

An extroverted waitress had returned to Australia after attending her brother's wedding in India. She told me in good humoured conversation that she was glad to be 'home.' She intelligently asked, "What is the meaning of life?" I replied, "Love God with all your heart, soul, mind and strength and your neighbour as yourself." She said, "Thank you Bruce. Good answer. Write those words for me." Her handwritten response read: "Do kind deeds and they will come back to you." Shades of Karma? She had previously accepted a NT. She later sat with me for her lunch and stated, "I believe something good will happen to me." I explained, "Your belief will only be as valid as the object of your belief. Make sure you fixate on the right belief." She asked me, "How do you find the right belief?" I told her, "There's only one place - the Christian holy Bible.'

An elderly male customer had recently undergone a serious leg operation. After release from hospital his motorised wheelchair capsized necessitating further surgery. Having lost his daughter to cancer and with the death of his wife two years previously, he said, "Old age is not funny." He eagerly accepted a Scripture card, and a Gideon NT listing helps for life's problems. Tearfully he said, "I really appreciate this. Can I pay for it?"

A mother was a high-ranking technical officer in a large insurance company. Her infant child was well behaved. This impressive citizen attended a Christian home group and relied on their fellowship to keep her feet on solid ground. It was a privilege to encourage her.

The new Cambodian Buddhist manageress of the café I frequently patronise, asked, "What are you reading?"

I said to her, "Christian things."

She told me, "I go to church with friends sometimes. They gave me a Cambodian Bible." I suggested she read John 8:12* from her Bible. Next day she said, "I haven't checked out that verse yet. I don't want trouble with my Buddhist husband." At the next table two Christian ladies from another church were discussing preparation of testimonies.

The Buddhist said in their presence, "Life is meaningless!" Our ladies responded with well crafted, powerful, and impressive personal testimonies. We three prayed with the manageress present.

She responded, "I feel better already" and accepted literature. She smiled and said, "I have a Christian teenage son. He is always sharing his faith with me."

I asked, "Are you reading your New Testament (NT)?"

"Yes. Every night" She replied.

As I drank coffee, her Indian staff member, who I have gotten to know over time, asked, "What are you reading?"

I said, "The Christian Holy book called the Bible. Have you heard of it?"

She replied, "No!"

I said, "I can give you a copy if you like."

"I can't think of a reason why not." She accepted a NT and later said, "I am reading the Bible, you gave me."

I stated, "Good! If you have questions, feel free to ask."

The Cambodian proprietor had sold her business. The new proprietors are devout Korean Christians. Jan and I met with an elder of our church in this café for lunch. A wheelchair-bound, severely physically limited man, who I had previously met, and his carer entered. I bought him a small cake for Christmas. He instructed his carer to return with the gift of a lemon slice. The proprietor gave me some expensive chocolates and said, "This is for helping that man!" I divided the chocolates with the elder, the carer, the wheelchair patient, and an elderly customer at the next table. The elderly customer, who also accepted a replica WW1 Gospel of John asked, "Did you know …?"

"Yes, I know him."

He replied, "He makes toy cars with JN316 (John 3:16*) number plates for disadvantaged kids."

A middle-aged disabled female beside me said, "I'm not available."

I said to her, "What do you mean?"

She replied, "I thought you might be looking for a wife." Being assured that such was not the case she accepted literature and said, "I believe in God. I listen to readings every day." She continued, "I left my ticket at home. I was intending to jump the train. Now I've spoken to you I will catch a taxi!"

To an attractive young waitress in a different newly opened local cafe, I asked, "What do you think about the current crime wave?" I then drew attention to newspaper coverage of the recent Youth Forum called by the Chief Commissioner of Police. I suggested she consider pursuing a Police career.

She replied, "I'm concerned about crime and often thought about a Police career."

I said, "We must all take responsibility for law and order" and indicated the heading, 'It's reckless to ignore the cops on the front line' and said to her, "Read the article. I'll come back from time to time. Tell me what you think."

Conclusion

Jan and I were privileged to attend a memorial service for a devout Christian stalwart of the NewHope Baptist Church. She will be remembered as a faithful servant of Jesus Christ, devoted wife, loving mother, grandmother, great-grand mother with the epistle of Christ clearly written on her heart by the Spirit of the living God. Her life was a compassionate and beautiful invitation to come to Christ to all who came in contact with her. The

Pastor's concluding words at her service raised a question for me. How do I measure up as an epistle of Christ in my daily life? You are invited to consider her example as you witness to your faith.

It was also a privilege for Jan and me to visit, for the first time, an elderly lady in East Ringwood. She had received my newsletters from a friend and unknown to me had faithfully prayed for our street ministry for years. She also conducted two prayer meetings per month in her home. Jan and I were encouraged. There is no such person as an unnecessary Christian.

Taking it to heart:

1. Name some venues in your locality which may be suitable for outreach purposes.
2. Who should you approach in advance of your ministry?
3. How might you activate your approach?

References:

Proverbs 22:4 – By humility and the fear of the Lord are riches and honour and life.

Matthew 4:19 – Then Jesus said to them, 'Follow Me, and I will make you fishers of men.'

Mark 1:15 – Jesus said, 'The time is fulfilled, and the kingdom of God is at hand. Repent, and believe in the Gospel.'

Luke 15:8-10 – Or what woman, having ten silver coins, if she loses one coin, does not light a lamp, sweep the house, and search carefully until she finds it? And when she has found it, she calls her friends and neighbours together saying, 'Rejoice with me for I have found the piece which was lost.' Likewise, I say to you, there is joy in the presence of the angels over one sinner who repents.

John 3:16 – For God so loved the world that He gave His only begotten Son, that whoever believes in Him should not perish but have everlasting life.

John 8:12 – Then Jesus spoke to them again saying, 'I am the light of the world. He who follows me shall not walk in darkness but have the light of life.'

2 Corinthians 3:2-3 – Clearly you are an epistle of Christ, ministered by us, written not with ink but by the Spirit of the living God, not on tablets of stone but on tablets of flesh, that is, of the heart.

1 Thessalonians 4:14-15 – For if we believe that Jesus died and rose again, even so God will bring with Him those who sleep in Jesus. For this we say to you by the word of the Lord, that we who are alive and remain until the coming of the Lord will by no means precede who are asleep.

BQ – Big Question – What is the most important question in all the world for you?

TPTL NT – The Pocket Testament League New Testament.

Mariam – not real name.

Chapter 30

Church Planting and Interims

Handcuffs to Hymnbooks

My transition from handcuffs to hymnbooks began with an encounter with Rev John Simpson, then Mission at Home Superintendent, Baptist Union of Victoria (BUV). One Sunday morning in the North Blackburn Baptist Church car park, I remarked to John, "I'd like to learn how to preach. Do you know somewhere I could practice?"

He replied, "I'll come back to you."

Two weeks later John said to me, "The Wandin Baptist Fellowship want you to pastor them."

I accepted the invitation and was inducted as first Pastor on Sunday 1st February 1987. With John Simpson's encouragement I enrolled in a twelve month's part-time 'Front Line Training' Course conducted by the BUV. On 4th December 1987 I was appointed a Home Missionary at a meeting of the Assembly of the BUV and was presented with a certificate, having successfully completed the church planting course.

Hello Wandin Vic!

My induction into leadership at Wandin was a gigantic leap of faith for all concerned. The initial membership at that stage numbered as I recall about ten people. The following March sixty excited folks gathered in the sunshine, against a backdrop of shady trees, outside the tiny church building, to witness five baptisms.

In July 1988 almost 200 people crowded into the Senior Citizens Centre where the church now worshipped, for the celebration of the church being constituted as a member of the BUV with thirty-four members. Jim Plowman MP and Councillor Geoff Bailey representing the Local Shire and other dignitaries, were numbered among the guests. Just prior to my conclusion of ministry at Wandin in 1990, the average weekly attendance had reached around eighty.

During our ministry we lived at home and travelled on Sundays and one other weekday for the thirty kilometres journey to Wandin. Soon after my induction Jan and I commenced a programme of visitation. One afternoon we visited three elderly ladies at different addresses. One of these ladies informed her daughter of the visit of the new Pastor with the result that she and her daughter, along with the other two, became regular attenders and encouragers. In due course I had the honour and privilege of baptising several including the daughter in a portable tank. She has continued to support and encourage my ministry

The Lord knew my lack of expertise with music and provided a talented musician to organise the hymns each week to fit in with my sermons. Besides providing the music for the services, she set up a small choir who met together for weekly practice, which I was told, sometimes turned into fun times around the piano. Her supportive friendship continuing over many years was and still is a real blessing.

Think of it. A Police Sergeant with no pastoral or preaching experience with a vague sense of call to somewhere approached the Superintendent who had never heard me preach and did not know if pastoral gifts existed arranged for a small struggling fellowship to hire me as their first Pastor. This was a huge step of faith for all concerned.

On my last Sunday at this church, I spoke from Psalm 42 and 43 on the positive effect of good memories. I had glimpsed something of the art of preaching, marrying, baptising, and burying in this church.

Altona Meadows and Spanish Speaking Baptist Fellowships, Vic.

On Sunday, 11th February 1990, I was inducted to the pastoral leadership of a recently formed small group of Baptists wanting to establish a church in the western suburbs of Melbourne. Our first services consisted of a core group meeting in a school classroom used as a local community centre. As numbers increased, we relocated to the Altona Meadows Community Centre (AMCC) with the name change of Altona Meadows Baptist Church (AMBC) being adopted. Time passed. It further relocated and is currently called the Point Cook Baptist Community Church.

In December 1991, a young man in this congregation, announced that he had become a Christian in his home the previous week. Significant in his conversion was Romans 15:13: "May the God of hope fill you with all joy and peace as you trust in him, so that you may overflow with hope." His conversion triggered seven baptisms (including himself) in a portable tank at the AMCC. He, and others from this group, faithfully continued in leadership in this church which continues bearing a firm testimony of Christ.

The above-mentioned young man, who became a wonderfully supportive church secretary during and after our tenure, later sent this message,

"Hi Bruce, just thought of you. We are having some baptisms in the sea at Altona Beach at 12'ish this Sunday. You are invited." The candidates included a lovely couple, who became Christians during our pastorate, and some young adults. Years previously, I had baptised the parents of one of those young adults. Others I had baptised were also present. It was a wonderful time of celebration.

Soon after arrival in Altona Meadows Baptist Church (AMBC) I learned of some Spanish speaking families living in the area. At a Sunday evening service at the nearby Spanish speaking Newmarket Baptist Church, I stood at the conclusion of their service uninvited and informed them of these Latin Americans and asked what will they do about it? A Spanish speaking Fellowship soon joined with the AMBC. On Sunday 8th August 1993, we jointly celebrated our anniversaries - the fourth anniversary for the English-speaking church and the first for the Spanish speaking fellowship. Approximately 140 adults and fifty children were present. These fellowships worshipped at the same time in separate rooms in the community centre but shared the same Sunday School. John Simpson, our ever-supportive General Superintendent of the Baptist Union, wrote, "I can't recall this kind of approach having been adopted by any other Baptist Church."

Years later the AMBC invited me to preach at a morning service. Some street evangelism strategies to assist in their outreach programme, were transferred into this service. My text was:

> "I determined not to know anything among you
> except Jesus Christ and Him crucified"
> 1 Corinthians 2:2.

A recently widowed Indian lady later said, "I'll never forget your sermon. We regularly pray for the spread of the Gospel in the Point Cook area."

On Sunday, 13th November 2016, Jan, and I attended the induction service at the Point Cook Baptist Church (formerly AMBC) of their new Pastor. Later, we enjoyed afternoon tea and prayer with one of these leadership couples, who first believed during a Christianity Explained class conducted in their home all those years ago. We were also privileged to attend the 25th wedding anniversary celebrations of church attenders I had met on door-to-door visitation in Altona Meadows.

Kununurra WA

After six years of ministry at Altona Meadows an unexpected call from Rev Arthur Payne, Superintendent of the Northwest (NW) Association of Baptist Churches in WA, invited me to consider the position of worker/Pastor of the Kununurra Baptist Fellowship in the Kimberley region of NW Australia. Jan and I sought counsel and prayer from Christian friends and believing it to be God's will, accepted. I was inducted at the Kununurra Fellowship on 28th July 1996. The 'Kelly Kununurra Kick-off' was attended by about forty people, including visitors from Germany, Queensland, our home church at North Blackburn Baptist (now NewHope), Halls Creek, Fitzroy Crossing and Wyndham. Representatives from other local churches were also present. Arthur Payne preached and asked members of the Kununurra Fellowship to stand. All seven members present did so. A tiny but significant group in God's sight.

The fellowship was unable to support us financially. I signed up for three local national census collections that provided temporary financial relief and an interesting introduction into local culture. It was a nosey town. Chocolate skinned kids with runny noses everywhere. Cold wet noses sniffing my legs at front gates. Large varicose noses on red faces greeted me at doors. Red plastic noses on car bonnets. A nosy census collector bogged ankle deep in his 'foot falcon' in red, dusty unmade footpaths.

CHURCH PLANTING AND INTERIMS

Everybody 'nose' everybody else's business. Sticky, prickly grass seeds in my socks. Unrelenting 35deg temperatures - sweat, regular rehydration, shady Boab trees, Red Tailed Black Cockatoos, and fascinating characters. Over-shadowing everything was the ancient colourfully beautiful massive awe-inspiring Kelly's Knob and Cyril Mountain. A major redirection in life. I liked it.

Jan found part-time employment as a receptionist at the local hospital. A large Aboriginal population existed in Kununurra. Alcohol, gambling, promiscuity, and domestic violence were huge problems. Too many frequently ended up at the local hospital for treatment of wounds, alcohol poisoning or slept it off in the local lockup. I wondered how Jan would cope with drunken patients snoring on the hospital reception floor, employees rushing in with detached fingers wrapped in ice bags, stabbings, bleeding heads, and broken limbs. One patient had a live snake in his pocket. I needn't have worried; Jan never turned a hair.

During the tourist season (May to August) invitations were given at the morning church service to visitors/travellers to join us at the manse for a Sunday evening BBQ. Testimonies and occasional solos were much appreciated. Caravanners often formed friendships, which continued further along their journey. One letter I received told of the blessings the writer had experienced through meeting Christians they met either at other churches or caravan parks further along the way.

- Some church attenders became Christians during our pastorate.
- One Sunday, whilst preaching, a large goanna climbed the rafters above as. No one seemed worried.
- Due to accommodation shortages, we moved worship venues several times. One of these venues doubled as a venue for training of local volunteer ambulance crews. On one occasion a whiteboard listing

childbirth procedure was inadvertently left in the room during worship. One visitor wondered if they were my sermon points.
- Preached several times at evening services at the local Aboriginal Peoples Church.
- Featuring on local radio program was a new experience.

During a religious education at the local primary school, one young student sat in a far corner because his parents were anti-Christian. I spoke loud enough for him to hear. At the conclusion of the lesson, he threw his arm round my shoulder saying, "Thanks."

Paddy McGinty

One Christmas Eve Jan and I attended a BBQ in the manse at the local Aboriginal Church, at which a grey headed Aboriginal lady brought along thirteen grandkids. She gave up counting when the score reached twenty-eight. This ageing grandma enforced discipline with a smile on her face and a thong in her hand. Her beautiful, brown skinned, dark-eyed brood were happy, clean, neatly dressed and well behaved. Paddy, a stolen generation Aboriginal, reformed alcoholic and elder in this church, and I prognosticated about the future of these kids. Too many would become pregnant by age fifteen. I had taught Paddy a little ditty sent me by a Port Missionary to seafarers in County Cork in Ireland:

> "Yesterday God helped me,
> Today He did the same.
> How long will this continue?
> Forever praise His name."

We recited the ditty together, then Paddy said, "Goodnight Bruce, I'll see you in the morning." The words of this ditty, which I still find helpful, may have been the last he uttered this side of heaven. That night Paddy went to glory, dying peacefully in his sleep. His eleven-year-old granddaughter walked ten kilometres back to Kununurra in the searing heat of the tropical sun for help. Over one thousand mourners attended his funeral. His death shook me. I was honoured to have fellowshipped with him. I have fond memories of this Godly man.

Quarantine Check Point

Opportunity arose to sign on as a part-time Inspector at the Quarantine Check Point, located some forty kilometres from Kununurra on the main highway between Darwin and Perth. I didn't even have to submit a CV. Our job description required inspection of every vehicle crossing the border between the Northern Territory and West Australia to prevent the introduction of plant diseases, insect pests and harmful weeds riding piggyback on vehicles into the nearby Ord River Irrigation area. This area produced several million dollars' worth of fruit and vegetables annually. We intercepted and inspected road trains laden with cattle destined for consumption in Indonesia, trucks laden with tropical fruits for markets down south, cars, caravans, pedestrians, camel trains, cyclists were inspected, hessian bags, honey, foam boxes, etc. Anything that could hide insect pests, weed seeds and harmful plant diseases were quarantined, confiscated, or destroyed. During my final year, we successfully inspected 33,600 vehicles and confiscated forty tons of prohibited fruit and vegetables.

While on duty, I was usually the first-person travellers from Darwin met upon entering West Australia. The officialdom of quarantine tended to engender insecurity. Remoteness did too. International tourists and travellers were often astounded by our wide-open spaces and sometimes frustrated, angered, or even enraged by having their precious and expensive cargo of fruit and vegetables confiscated. Heat, loneliness, and the high cost of living compounded personal problems. Alcohol consumption made people feel ten feet tall and bullet proof for a while, but soon enough the mouth felt rough like day five on the pitch of a cricket test match between Australia and England.

The lonesome check point was a critical event for some, but it was also an opportunity for the Gospel. I tried hard to ease our clients gently into the state without compromising the integrity of the law. When we completed the official stuff, the way was sometimes clear to give a tract, or invitation to the church or its functions sensitively, and with due regard to circumstances.

Some interesting observations and comments from the check point:

- An American soldier in full battle dress, couldn't adjust his watch to the local time zone. He got upset when I suggested his watch was 'US'.
- The hostess of a bus laden with senior citizens suggested we use sniffer dogs and trained fruit bats. I suggested my boss was the fruit bat and I was the beagle.
- A quantity of live Victorian yabbies was confiscated. My department was in a quandary. Yabbies were not on our list of sizable items. The fisheries department were ecstatic. Victorian yabbies could infect WA waterways with serious parasitic diseases.
- 380 hatchling crocodiles from Darwin were inspected.
- A BMW came through. My female colleague and I concluded we would rather sleep with a tiger snake than trust that driver. Next day, he headlined the national news. Police had intercepted him near Halls Creek carrying thousands of ecstasy tablets hidden behind car door panels.

- To a man, with a guitar travelling to Kununurra to entertain at a local hotel, I said, "When God was handing out musical gifts, I was behind the door." He sneered, "What gifts has God given you?" I replied, "A fulfilled life and an eternal destiny. Jesus Christ made a huge difference to my life."

A customer in the briefest jocks, made a beeline for my female colleague. She escaped screaming through the back door. Station hands (ringers) hell bent on self-destruction, passed through, headed for the Bachelor and Spinsters Ball in Kununurra.

Our daily tasks included sending weather reports to Perth. The Weather Bureau designated the Quarantine Check Point as the 'Dingo Gap' Remote Weather Station. Their equipment was located on check point precincts. One Christmas, the check point being short staffed, appointed Jan to a three-day career as a quarantine inspector. Her sole responsibility was to phone Kununurra Police if I got in trouble with a client. On arrival, she kicked in the check point batwing doors, took control, and thereafter became famously known across NT and WA as the Deputy Sheriff of Dingo Gap.

On the occasion of our departure for Melbourne, one balmy evening under an enormous tropical moon bathing the rugged Kimberley landscape with a soft golden glow, the check point arranged a farewell BBQ. Some thirty staff said nice things about us and gave us lovely presents. The boss said, "I don't know what happened, but when you came, this place changed for the better." We had shared our faith with many staff and innumerable travellers. It was a magic moment, but it was time to hit the road again.

Thank You Faithful Prayerful Supporters

On our long journey home to Melbourne, we called on a ninety-year-old lady living alone in a one-bedroom unit in Perth. Her regular handwritten letters assured us of her prayers and the prayers of her Bible Study Group. She arose at 6am each day, prayed for two hours, and after breakfast prayed a further two hours. She maintained a folder of prayer/newsletters, conducted weekly missionary prayer meetings in her unit and sold beautiful treasures from her china cabinet, donating the proceeds to missionaries. We were privileged to have the support of this amazing old prayer warrior.

Upon return to our home church (NewHope Baptist) in Melbourne I was invited to lead devotions for the Indoor Carpet Bowls group. A dear old senior citizen from a local aged care facility said, "I have prayed for you each day since you first started church planting at Wandin." She also covered my street ministry in daily prayer over many years. She requested a TPTL NT* to hand out as opportunity arose. I did not recall meeting her prior to the above-mentioned bowls event. Years later, I attended this ninety-four-year-old prayer warrior's funeral. Her extensive family eulogised Edna Moran's life and Christian love in inspirational ways. She would be missed. I know for sure that my journey was birthed and bathed in the prayers of several such saints.

Jan and I are indebted to God for:

- The Pastor and members of our home church for their unwavering prayers and support during our ministry up north,
- Glen and Charlotte Crothers, our long-term small group leaders, who regularly circulated our newsletters in the church.
- NewHope Church groups provided an overhead projector, lawn mower etc. for the Kununurra church/manse.

- Untiring, unwavering support of the Chairman of the NewHope Church Missionary Committee.
- Friends (Men for Missions members in Vic) sorted out the extensive watering system at the manse.
- Letters and cards eagerly anticipated with daily visits to the local post office.
- Victoria Chemicals (VicChem) for generous support.
- Faithful members of the Waverley (Vic) and Naracoorte (SA) Baptist Churches for their many and varied encouragements.
- Friends/strangers from down south who arrived unexpectedly and treated us to dinner/morning tea.
- A Christian pilot of a Dauphin helicopter transporting employees, cargo and parts to offshore oil rigs, graciously invited us to a world class piano recital in Kununurra.

Marching to the Beat of a Different Drum

Evangelism as a concept had existed in embryonic form in my mind since the early days of my Christian experience. I had no idea how this dream would eventuate but firmly believed it's details would unfold as time passed. Our check point farewell was the beginning of a march to the beat of a different drum. In retrospect, I see my experiences of life including years of church planting and interim pastorates interstate as excellent preparation for twenty years of street evangelism ministries. Details of some of these exciting and hopefully fruitful journeys are referred to throughout the book.

Church Visits and Speaking Engagements

Over time I had preached at several country churches, some of which are referred to below. We stayed with Rev Dr Graeme and Mrs Maria Smith who, at that time, were interim Pastors at the Bermagui NSW Baptist Church. Bermagui is a world-famous big game fishing port. Graeme preached to an appreciative congregation from Galatians. His mentorship over many years had prepared me for an interim preaching ministry. We later heard Graeme preach at another NSW country Baptist Church where a lady who had previously accepted a quantity of John's Gospels for evangelism, forwarded the following slightly abridged email:

"Dear Bruce and Jan, it was just lovely to see you both today. You are such an encouragement to me. The Lord has been doing a great thing within my family. Two years ago, I was the only one coming to church, now my daughter and son have come back to their faith and since Father's Day my husband has been coming every Sunday. He is changing in so many ways and it is so exciting to watch the Holy Spirit in action without my interference for a change - just praying constantly which is all God has required of me!!! Our conversational English lessons we started this year (at the church) have been very exciting. During this time, we presented a bible to an Indian Sikh who was overwhelmed and said he had wanted a Bible in his language and didn't know how to get one! As well as our Japanese girl (Jan & I met her). I have never seen anyone so excited about being given a Bible it was a wonderful to see. She reads it every morning and brings it to church every Sunday. The Word of God is the most powerful tool. Lots of Christians take it for granted, it is very sad. I have been reading a lot about the persecuted church and to see how the New Testament (NT) is alive today and happening and know it's not a history book. To read how people are giving their lives to Christ after coming in contact with a Bible, reading it and without anyone else speaking a word to them, they discover our God. I believe in His word with all my heart and know the power it holds and will continue to pray for the work that you and Jan do. Bless you both, love and care …."

An outreach group meeting in our home was addressed by Stephen Downie, then Field Worker for The Pocket Testament League (TPTL). One young lady at this meeting said, "I can place 400 Gospels of John but can't afford them." Sufficient funds were raised at the meeting to cover this purchase on her behalf. She later informed us she texted over seventy people weekly with a scripture verse as a result of our previous phone conversation three years ago. At the Croydon (eastern Melbourne suburb) Baptist Church, Stephen preached on David and Goliath. He had recently returned from the Middle East where he was encouraged by the strength of the church. He also encouraged us with reports of literature distribution in difficult places overseas. I am honoured to serve with Stephen in a more localised role of street evangelism in God's huge plan of worldwide salvation. A quantity of English NT's and English/Arabic NTs for street distribution was purchased.

Following a speaking engagement regarding street evangelism at a men's breakfast at the Doncaster Holy Trinity Anglican Church, five TPTL NTs* were accepted. We visited Meeniyan Christian Fellowship (country Vic) and spoke at their request on evangelism. My text was 1 Corinthians 1:22-24*. The congregation members were each challenged to take one Gospel of John and hand it to a non-Christian the following week. They exhausted my supply of Gospels.

At the Melbourne School of Theology, a student group accepted discussion on street evangelism and then departed on the bus for action in Federation Square, laden with a supply of Christian literature.

Kathy, a Christian contact from earlier days at NewHope Church, said, "There is nothing more exhilarating than talking to a person, and asking if they want to know about Jesus. All of a sudden one morning, the word Dandenong came to me. I obeyed the Lord - I told Bruce Kelly. He was happy as it was he who gave me the idea to talk to people. I rarely go out without having opportunities to talk to someone about the Lord." She had letter boxed some 2,000 homes in recent times, shared her faith and distributed literature among different racial groups.

A lady in NSW, in whose church I had preached, sent the following email: "Hi Bruce, I wait each month with anticipation for your newsletter, they are so encouraging and inspiring. I use your answers myself when talking with people and pray that not a day goes by that I don't get an opportunity to tell someone about Jesus." I also received another email from a friend in South Africa requesting advice on suitable literature for his street ministry in Johannesburg.

Opportunities arose to share devotions on 'Sounding forth the Word' at NewHope Church with three groups containing significant numbers of 'not-yet Christians'. This devotional also formed the basis of a recent church website message. A lady in one of these groups said, "My husband kept the New Testament you gave him at his bedside. He read it each night before he died. It comforted him."

An elderly man at a Blackburn Square cafe said, "Since you talk to people every Friday, let me share something with you. I found out yesterday I have pancreatic and liver cancer. I have not told my family yet." He knew I attended church and was happy to receive literature.

One Cup Eve I conducted a wedding for friends at a chapel in Sherbrooke (Dandenong Ranges). At the reception afterwards, I was seated with a pleasant young man who was 'born again' some years ago. He was a state level basketball player until injury curtailed his career. Life after basketball proved difficult. His marriage broke down. His church attendance fell away. He accepted literature and was encouraged to continue reading his Bible, find a good church and a fatherly Christian mentor to stand alongside him. He promised he would.

A strongly built young male attended a conference in the western suburbs, at which we were present. His demeanor prompted me to ask, "Are you a Christian?"

He promptly replied, "No!" and disclosed his involvement in New Zealand gang warfare. Tired of the anger and violence, he escaped to Melbourne to find meaning to life. It was my privilege to roll away some misunderstandings and unwind some spiritual impediments. He was introduced to a leader of the church in which this conference was held, and surrendered his life to Christ. It was wonderful to see God in action in his life. He was being followed up by the church leader.

In 2009 Jan and I travelled to Yackandandah (small Victorian country town) to attend the wedding of two One Mission Society (OMS) supporters. I spoke by request, on Ecclesiastes 4:9-12: "A threefold cord is not easily broken." The delightfully historic Anglican Church, in which this wedding was solemnised, was located in a lovely bushland setting. We remained in regular contact with this couple.

Timboon (Vic) and Naracoorte (SA) Baptist Churches

At their invitation, I preached several times at the Timboon (a small country town in Vic) Church. Several missionary minded local farmers comprised the congregation; generous hospitality/accommodation was much appreciated.

I was invited by Bill Pomery, a friend and mentor, for a weekend of ministry at the Naracoorte Church, South Australia. Some twenty men responded well at a breakfast in a farmhouse, not far out of town. In the evening some forty people attended a bonfire organised by the church at another nearby farm. Testimonies of young people were encouraging. The congregation on Sunday was responsive to a sermon based on Isaiah 57:15*.

We enjoyed lunch with a church family before setting sail for home. These prayerful supporters always have our gratitude.

Temora NSW (Interim 2000)

Jan was born in Temora NSW. Several of her family connections still live there. A retired NSW Baptist Pastor we met in Kununurra suggested we consider an interim ministry in Temora Baptist Church during the absence of their Pastor who was following up orphan contacts after the East Timor war. Our Temora ministry took place March-June 2000. The weather was freezing – sleet, frost, and icy temperatures.

One of Jan's uncles, a Temora resident, was a WW2 veteran. He and his wife regularly took us for coffee and cakes at a local coffee shop. These were good sharing times. One of his family members later repeated aspects of my stories to Jan's uncle in his dying days. He died at peace. Another farmer with terminal cancer had doubled as a local shearing contractor. He said, "I'm glad to meet the man who will bury me."

His wife stated, "I'm so glad you called. He was happy to chat with a Pastor who understood the wool industry." We prayed together. Sadly, he passed away soon after we left Temora.

On the way home from Temora, and at the suggestion of the local Area Superintendent, we travelled to Lake Cargelligo where I preached a trial sermon. But we declined their invitation due to sub-standard accommodation. The highlight of our journey was a pine tree full of feeding Major Mitchells (pink Cockatoos) and Blue Bonnets (Parrots) along the roadside.

Newman WA

"Now to him who is able to do immeasurably more than all we ask or imagine, according to his power that is at work within us, to him be glory in the church and in Christ Jesus throughout all generations, for ever and ever! Amen" (Ephesians 3:20-21).

Craig Siggins, then ABMS missionary to the Martu Aboriginals in Newman, WA, invited Jan and me to Newman, an iron ore mining town in the Pilbara region of West Australia, to support his wife, Lyn, in their work among the local Aboriginal population. We were also invited to supply the pulpit of the Newman Baptist Church during his absence on deputation in Victoria.

Newman is an outback town, some 550kms inland from Port Hedland. We had known the Siggins family for many years. We arrived at Newman Wednesday evening, April 11 2001. The next morning, we walked to the local supermarket, purchased breakfast supplies, and spent the day clearing out a back room of the church for our bedroom. This would be home for six weeks.

Pilbara Aboriginal Easter Convention at Coobina River WA

Shortly after arriving in Newman, we were invited to attend the Pilbara Aboriginal Easter Convention at the Coobina River about 80 kilometres north of Newman. Having never heard of Coobina, we weren't sure what to expect. We were driven to Coobina on Good Friday afternoon and set up a tent in the dry Coobina riverbed under shady, bushy gum trees. The ankle deep, gravelly red sand in the riverbed had been churned up by numerous four-wheel drive vehicles, making it difficult to securely anchor tent pegs. I tried to keep the sand out of my shoes, but it was easier to empty my load every hour so. A few small water holes dotted the watercourse. Along the banks grow stately, white barked, green leafed ancient gum trees. The sky was cloudless. The evenings beautiful. Post card picture stuff!

We woke on Easter Saturday morning with aching bones. Hot sand made it feel like we had slept on an electric blanket turned high. We were not familiar with this camping caper. Shortly after sun-up I searched for bird life. Peregrine falcons were making life misery for budgies and zebra finches. Blue winged kookaburras, rufous whistlers, cockatoo parrots, grey crowned babblers abounded.

Camps were scattered along the riverbed for a couple of kilometres - 4WD's, swags, and people in small family groups dotted the landscape. An estimated 500 Aboriginals were present. As the sun rose about 6am, a group sang, "Jesus is Alive" from a distant hilltop. It was a wakeup chorus heralding Easter morning. People stirred. Campfire smoke curled lazily heavenwards from cooking fires. We searched for a wooden toilet (tree). One must carefully select a place to put one's foot but it's reasonably OK outside the camp vicinity. Some ladies disappeared into the distance in their 4WDs. Entrenched in the Aboriginal lifestyle are 1000's of years of traditional living. Aboriginals survived very well in the bush with blanket and billy.

We attended the morning prayer meeting. About sixty pray-ers sat in a sandy circle under a shady gum tree. Prayer intensity was high. Lots of praise, and a few announcements. Temperatures could reach 36deg that day. Jan and I found a cool spot - Craig's eskies kept food and drink cold. High spirited brown skinned kids with flashing white teeth played in sunshine, climbed trees, jumped into water holes, threw sticks and sand, pushed, yelled, laughed. Mischievous little creations they were, but with tremendous potential. A shade cloth protected the portable convention platform, speakers, singers and P/A gear from the burning sun. Groups from Roebourne, Kalgoorlie, Jigalong, Cotton Creek, Newman and others were in attendance. The Aboriginal name for Newman is Parnpajinya. Each group was allocated a meeting to conduct. Around 9.30am the first meeting began - the Newman mob conducted this meeting. Craig was up there with them, there were nine ladies and four guys. Clapping boomerangs and electric guitars provided rhythm for singing. A children's program was in progress. Lukas Butler and his wife from Christ for All Children, a Perth based children's ministry, was in charge. Some 100 kids enjoyed the games.

The mob sat in shaded groups listening intently. An Aboriginal layman from the Roebourne Church preached a fine sermon on maturing in Christ. The Roebourne Church had good musicians and there was lots of singing. Familiar choruses followed one upon another. Sometimes they sang in their local language, but we recognised the tunes. Communion consisted of damper (bread cooked in coals) and cold muddy tea complete with sediment. I raised the billy to my lips. Jan didn't even pretend.

A large tree stump adjacent to the convention platform, was smouldering. No one cared that smoke billowed across the speaker. No one cared about dogs fighting under the feet of singers. No one noticed the approaching whirligig raising dust and sand high into the atmosphere. People were focused. The Holy Spirit was working. Maybe fifty responded to the altar call - Craig and Lyn prayed with their folks who went forward. An AOG Pastor prayed for slaying of the spirit. A couple of his own group went down. Locals called them, 'the fall down mob'. Jonathan and Kathleen Bates, who we knew, well-respected Aboriginal missionaries to their own folks from Halls Creek were present. Three hours later the meeting concluded. We wandered back to our camp for lunch.

Around sunset Craig's portable generator died, so we completed our household duties in semi-darkness. The final meeting was scheduled for 7.30pm - it started about 8.30pm. This was known locally as normal rubber time. Each community mob brought their own items, many in their own language. Testimonies were shared.

At 9.30pm Peter Muramba, the featured guest speaker, and his wife Naomi, appeared on the platform. Peter, a Baptist Pastor from Kenya (Africa), ministered among the alcoholic, fringe dwelling, marginalised street dwellers of the Ngaanyatjarra people in Kalgoorlie. Exciting things were happening in that church. Naomi wore national dress and spoke for ten minutes. She was a gifted speaker. Peter, an accomplished guitarist, sang. His rich baritone voice in African rhythm and tempo was beautiful and unusual. He spoke to the Aboriginal culture out of his own experience as an oppressed African. His sermon presentation was biblical, balanced, and strong. His theme was, "1 am not ashamed of the Gospel of Christ. It is the power of God to salvation, for everyone who believes," from Romans 1:16.

We cleaned the generator spark plug, and the motor coughed and started. There was light! The Kalgoorlie mob departed for home round midnight – it was a 1000 kilometres trip. Coobina was not their country. They could get lost. Craig piloted them to Newman, found them some fuel, and returned about 3am.

I lit the fire and boiled the billy; It was 6am. I walked into open country; dry and stony. Red anthills dotted the landscape. Mulla Mulla bushes blossomed. Shrubbery was sparse. Grey crowned babblers flitted from tree to tree. A crested bellbird chimed in the distance, and a red capped robin flew by. Budgies and zebra finches were numerous - I was then far out in the bush. I could have got lost, but that faraway hill told me where to intersect with the Coobina. A high-powered rifle with telescope sight walked by. Goannas (large lizards), kangaroos or emus living near the Coobina would have rocks in their heads, and lead (bullets) if they were not quick. Bush turkey feathers fluttered in the breeze. Kangaroo bones strewed the sand. We preferred salmon and tomato sandwiches, while lazing away the afternoon under shady trees - a pleasant pastime while budgies chattered above. The billy boiled and we enjoyed one last cuppa.

I returned with Craig to Newman from Coobina and added Little Button Quails to my list of first sightings. Another bird resembled a rarely sighted Grey Honeyeater but Craig, an accomplished bird watcher, doubted this. Jan travelled with Lyn. We arrived brown and filthy at our little flat about 2.30pm. A most noteworthy event after Coobina was the shower at Newman. Four days of accumulated sweat and dirt disappeared down the drainpipe in seconds.

The next day Craig introduced me to some more Martu (local Aboriginals). They respected their dead by never using the deceased's name. There had been another Bruce Kelly in Newman years ago, so I was therefore introduced as BeeKay. They knew I was replacing Craig while he was absent on deputation. So many faces! Craig spoke in the Martuwangka language - Martu (man) Wangka (talk). Some Aboriginals told me that Craig's ability to speak their language was impressive. They heard better in their own tongue.

Ministry Amongst the Martu People

Craig and Lyn's home was the main Martu ministry centre. Used items, mainly clothes were sold here. Aboriginals called daily and sorted through boxes; a plastic bag of clothes sold for $5. The community room contained an urn, tea, mugs, sugar, powdered milk, biscuits, games, guitars, toy corner for the kids, Martu Bibles and related literature. The Martu came to read, sing, pray, participate in occasional Bible studies, greet, use the phone, eat, drink, seek advice, solve problems, leaf through photo albums of people they knew, things they had done, and where they went. Tattered, battered dog-eared albums were replaced.

Lynn also organised a special bargain sale day at the church, and opportunity for social interaction among the Martu people far and wide. Used clothing, household items and kid's toys were left in a shed at the church by public servants, mine workers etc. transferring down South on completion of their tour of duty. Jan and I sorted and priced these items and displayed them on tables under the church veranda, and on a large tarp on the ground at the rear of the church. Alistair's busloads of Martu ladies drifted in, sat on the tarp, and sipped tea from huge bucket size mugs (well almost), talked, rummaged, and purchased bargains. We netted $300, dumped the leftovers at the tip, hosed down the veranda, and cleaned the shed. Proceeds were used for Martu ministry expenses including fuel costs for evangelistic bus trips to distant communities. Lyn was happy - the Martu were happy and so were we.

Clarrie, Cliffie, and Shortie were talented guitarists. Clarrie, with his impish sense of humour, was a leader in the Martu Church. He was sharp, and not overawed by 'white fellas'. He asked permission to play me some 'Christian choruses' then sang 'Baa Baa Black Sheep' and 'Twinkle Little Star'. They taught me some Martu words. I repeated them. They looked puzzled and nervously giggled. Craig disappeared. The Martu language is different and difficult. Clarrie mischievously suggested we nick Craig's canoe and go paddling on Ophthalmia Dam. I suggested it was a good illustration of the church. He responded, "Yes, like a choir. Everyone pulls at the same time in the right direction. One cannot go faster than the other."

Craig received an SOS from a family lost in the bush - they were several days overdue. The Pilbara is an unforgiving place. There was cause for concern. Craig set out in his 4WD with other family members and a packed lunch. After nine hours of bush bashing Craig located the missing family. They were enjoying themselves under the shade of a tree in a dry creek bed.

Craig's communication gear interfered with his 4WD's electronics. They push started the 4WD. He arrived in time for the Martu service in the camping area (Parnpajinya). That meant loading and unloading a heavy P/A system, two large speakers, guitars, control box and connections. We assisted with setup. Craig was exhausted.

Community Care

The town rubbish tip was locally known as the Resource Centre. Good stuff could be obtained there for as little as a dollar per item. Lorna wanted carpet. Lizzie wanted a lounge. The lounge was dilapidated. The carpet wet and stinking. The load was delivered. Lorna's carpet was unrolled over kangaroo guts, rotting meat and bones on her front lawn to dry. She was happy. We tracked down Craig's trailer and shifted the dilapidated furniture infested with poisonous red back spiders. Lizzie was happy. The 4WD conked out. I cleaned the battery terminals – It then started, and Jan was impressed. About 10pm there was a knock on the church door. Someone was scared her drunken husband would bash her. Lyn took her to the shelter.

Lorna was writhing on her front lawn in agony. I offered to take her to hospital, but she declined. After lunch her daughter drove her round to Lyn's place. "Why don't you take her to hospital?" I thought. But the daughter's car was unregistered, and she was unlicensed. Fair enough! We transferred Lorna to the 4WD and took her to hospital. Lorna is a rough diamond. I enjoyed her company and did not like seeing her suffering.

I dropped the trailer at Sarah's place. This Martu lady loaded the trailer with rubbish. Jan and I dumped it at the tip. Lorna came with us. She must have been expecting guests. She purchased a single bed base and mattress, more carpet and a couple of filthy old lounge chairs ($20 total).

Back at Lorna's place, five burly, arguing, gesticulating, intoxicated young Aboriginal men unloaded for us. Maybe we distracted them from rioting. Lorna had eaten ginger and upset her stomach. She disappeared with a toilet roll and returned smiling. I took Lorna, her daughter and two snotty nosed grandkids into the bush to collect firewood (waru). Her electricity was cut off. She had forgotten to pay her bill. It was midwinter - 24 degrees was cold for them. She would light a fire to cook with in her backyard. One kid persistently rubbed her snot candles on the shoulder of my clean shirt. Lorna complained, "My head feels funny," and sat in the 4WD. So, I loaded alone.

We also collected a donated double bed for Eileen and Willy who were camping in the Capricorn rubbish dump. They were childless for years. The Martu Church prayed, then little Isaiah was born. He was their miracle child. It's ugly in the bush with a tiny baby and no roof when it rained. Lyn was battling the bureaucracy for a house for them. Eileen's husband was absent. Through not understanding our system, Eileen had accrued rental debts for years and the department held it against her. But with prayer and determination the department finally relented.

Eileen and Willy were granted a house on three months' probation. I set up the double bed and mattress. This bed was their first item of furniture. They and their two-year-old would now be sleeping high and dry, but nobody turned on the gas and electricity as promised. Then we drove out to Capricorn camp to collect her blankets and gear. To my surprise Eileen had a high-powered rifle stashed under the back seat of her broken down car - maybe she was hiding it from the drunks. I drove too close to those drunks. They besieged the 4WD. I omitted to lock the passenger side door, so one jumped in. I refused to take him to Newman and he aggressively refused to disembark. It was hard to get him out. Eileen fled to the roadhouse.

CHURCH PLANTING AND INTERIMS

The Martu were said to be the last tribal group to come out of the desert. Many hankered to return, but desert life as they knew it, had gone. Eileen was raised in the desert. Running houses, operating budgets, and paying bills was absolutely foreign to them. They didn't understand they could only spend what they earned. Lyn spent countless hours organising budgets, arranging debt repayments, making sure they were issued with receipts, getting power and gas switched on, etc. I talked with Eileen and her eighty-three-years old Dad. He saw his first white man when he was a teenager. "It was terrifying!" he said. We discussed tribal survival skills and social interactions. I hoped someone would get the story of that old man and his Nyupa (spouse) written before they died.

It rained all day, it was unseasonable, so I wore a pullover. Clarrie organised a Bible study on church leadership with Cliffie, Alistair, and himself. We never did nail that one down! Lyn ran a Bible study for two ladies in dispute about an old family tragedy. Lyn never missed an opportunity to challenge the Martu to live Godly lives. Another day Clarrie discussed church leadership with us. He was spiritually savvy for a four-year old Christian with no formal education.

Alistair's wife wanted me to collect her husband from the office. Then she asked me to go to Clarrie's place. The maggot infested kangaroo rump in her youngster's hand was turning black. It was on the nose. He dumped it on Alistair's lap. Alistair examined it for maggots and dropped it on the floor. That night they all enjoyed kangaroo stew. I was glad they didn't invite me!

At 1pm a large explosion rattled the crockery and released a cloud of red dust into the atmosphere. They always dynamite iron ore at the mine about the same time once a week.

An inebriated Aboriginal pedestrian near the church one evening mistook me for the local Police Sergeant. With slurry voice he said, "Don't worry Sergeant I'm goin' home."

Automatically and subconsciously, I slipped back into the old authoritarian mode, looked down my nose and sternly said, "That is the best place you can go. The quicker you get there the better." He stumbled happily and drunkenly homewards. It has been a long time since anyone called me Sergeant.

Lyn entered a Martu girls' netball team in the local competition. She thought it might raise their self-esteem but only one girl had played netball previously. The association's constitution required competitors to wear uniforms, unfortunately there was no uniform shop in Newman. Lyn nominated white polo shirts and black shorts, then raided the used clothing bins. She rounded up the girls for practice prior to the match and discovered they had no shoes. She did another run but still they were one pair short. She lent her shoes to the girl. The girls were badly beaten but happy. Lyn returned home minus her shoes and a pile of white shirts to wash and iron. Next week they trained and gave a better account.

Newman Baptist Church

It was 2.30pm and about 34deg outside the church, but the aircon was too cold. I preferred it warmer. Lyn and Jan had the order of service ready. In our first Sunday Service at Newman Jan would lead and I would preach - repentance was my theme. I never anticipated preaching at the Newman fellowship! They hadn't had a Pastor for nine months. Their leaders worked long hours - some were exhausted. Craig was an elder in this church but his prime focus was the Martu. About thirty attended including two guitarists, a keyboard player, and drummer. Craig's days were full.

Next Sunday the service was attended by thirty plus adults and a good roll up for Sunday School. The five-piece band provided bright music and helped with cheerful worship. Vic Heyward who was Chaplain at the local BHP Mine led the service and I preached. Vic's parents-in-law, Max and Verne Chapman were present. Max later became a seriously faithful prayer supporter of my street ministry.

We were invited to the Heyward family home for dinner. It was our wedding anniversary. The invitation was convenient indeed. I had intended taking Jan to a restaurant!

The Rabbit Proof Fence

Sam Dinah grew up at Roelands Mission (WA) where he knew Lloyd and Judy Masters, our good friends, and former caretakers at NewHope Church. Sam vaguely remembered seeing his mother when he was about three years old. That was the day he was taken from her. She died two years later. I asked, "Sam, you seem remarkably free of bitterness about all this."

He replied, "I struggled with it for years. Taking children from their parents was wrong, but the Old Testament story of Joseph helped me through. God used Joseph's suffering for good for the Jewish people in their time of need (Genesis 50:20*). Like Joseph I am helping my people through a period of transition."

At an Aboriginal service I preached on the Holy Spirit in the life of the church. Twelve adults attended. Sam's singing voice was a cut above the average. He was a great support for Craig and Lyn.

One day Sam took us along a gravel road to Jigalong, a remote Aboriginal Community about three hour's drive out from Newman. Sam represented the Aboriginal Legal Service in that area. Once through the Hammersley ranges, the country flattened out. The horizon was visible. There were no residences along this road. An occasional windmill dotted the landscape.

Windmills symbolised the outback. We crossed the Fortescue River causeway. Nankeen night herons roosted in trees along the stream bank. Small fish struggled upstream across the trickling causeway. Jigalong was alcohol free with a big general store. Ninety kids were enrolled in their school with an average attendance of forty-fifty. They had six white teachers and a few Aboriginal aides.

Sam got permission from the local community to take us to the last remnant of the Rabbit Proof Fence, constructed in the early 1930's. It traversed thousands of kilometres between Esperance and Wyndham in West Australia. The construction of the fence was a huge undertaking and a monumental failure. Not much of it remained except an old gateway, a few rotting posts and some rusty wire netting. Sam showed us a remaining strainer post at Jigalong. The 'Rabbit Proof Fence' is the title of an Australian made movie involving three stolen generation Aboriginal girls and is worth watching.

Sam copied us with a text he sent to the Masters. "Greetings Christian brethren in Victoria. Good morning, Lloyd, and Judy (Masters). The last time we met was at Don Cross' place in Bunbury, remember? Some years ago, now. You had lost a bit of weight and looked a bit older, but I recognised you. Praise the Lord, I ran into Bruce and Jan up here in Newman. I often pray for our old missionaries, so I say to you once more in Jesus' name, greetings to you. God bless." Sam's suggestions were helpful in preparing sermons for Martu services.

Outback Picnics With a Difference

The HACC (Home and Community Care) lady asked Lyn to take some elderly ladies out bush for a picnic. Lyn dropped this one on me! About 1pm we did the usual taxi run. Jan and I were embarking on a goanna hunting expedition out past Capricorn about 15kms beyond Newman.

Nine ancient Aboriginal ladies and three grandchildren guided us. A roadhouse straddled the Tropic of Capricorn. Alongside it lay an Aboriginal camp in a rubbish dump where we picked up a couple of older ladies. We turned off the main road, travelled a few more kilometres down a rough track, then turned right through an open gate. We continued a further eight or nine kilometres into the bush, lurching through churned up axle-deep sand. This was my first taste of four-wheel driving in low ratio. I seriously wondered if we would get through. We dropped the ladies off with their thin, light metal crowbars with which they excavated yams and executed goannas. In the old days they used wooden digging sticks. Clarrie turned up in his 4WD to make sure we were OK.

The ladies disgorged from the troopie (Toyota 4WD) and spread far and wide, keeping in contact with yodelling calls. They had already forgotten their domestic pressures. They scanned for vines with large purple flowers called bush potatoes. Jan carried a small child while its mother dug for her quota of yams. The child would not let the milk supply out of its sight.

One old lady with silvery hair, puffed out part through her excavation. She and I took turns with her digging stick (metal crowbar). She dug. I scraped. In that brief moment, we became immersed in a common goal and forgot the issues of colour, culture, and communication. I looked into her clear liquid brown eyes and saw intelligence, and appreciation. This episode illustrated a missionary principle that remains with me to this day.

Bush potatoes grew beside host trees. Tubers were located by following cracks in the earth from the base of the tree trunks made by vine roots. The ladies took soundings with their crowbars along these cracks. The resulting echo told them exactly where to dig. Some tubers measured a foot in length and two or three inches in diameter. They roast them in hot coals. Around 5pm we loaded up. One lady was missing so we honked the horn. They yodelled again. We heard the faint response. She slowly hobbled smiling from the bush toward us. It was a misunderstanding, they said. We delivered them home tired and happy. No goannas that day but we got some yams. Lyn provided them with warm meat pies donated by the local BP Service Station for their evening meal.

About 15kms out of Newman is a geographic feature called Round Hill which commanded a panoramic view of the surrounding countryside, including the roadhouse and adjacent Aboriginal camp located in a nearby rubbish tip. We drove some Aboriginal ladies to the camp specially to pray for an old couple who slept and ate on the ground. Their mattress was filthy and damp. Empty wine containers, kangaroo and bush turkey guts littered the surrounds. Their butcher shop consisted of a thorny tree suspended from which was a partially consumed rotting, maggoty kangaroo carcass. The indescribably squalid camp stank. Lyn and Craig ministered here, sometimes exhausted, sometimes frustrated but unfailingly cheerful. The people loved them.

On another occasion, we took some older ladies goanna hunting. It quickly became a saga. One passenger was a reformed drunk. She gave up the alcohol when she became a Christian. Her family were still drunks. Her daughter-in-law wanted to come with us but she was drunk. Our ladies shouted, "No! No! No!" and refused her entrance to the 'troopie'. The young woman dropped her jeans and urinated beside us. Not a pretty sight. Her inebriated husband sent her flying face first into the gravel with a well-directed right cross between her shoulders. He tried to drag her round by her hair. No wonder these old Christian ladies cleared out to the bush at every opportunity. Jan was distressed. Several ladies told Jan they appreciated our ministry at the church. We dropped them in the bush out through Capricorn and arranged to collect them at sundown. I placed a white plastic marker on a tree. The ladies disappeared. At 5pm we returned. They had captured five goannas. Their cooking method was simple:

- Dig a trench,
- Light a fire in it,
- Singe the goanna skin in the flames,
- When the flames subside, scrape the embers to one side,
- Place the goanna un-gutted in the trench,
- Cover the goanna with the embers,
- Roast to taste.

The women catch and cook 'em. The men cut 'em up and allocate pieces. That stops squabbling over choice cuts. They started another fire nearby to warm up as the goannas cooked.

In olden days, they scraped away the coals of a larger fire and slept in the trench on the hot sand on cold nights. Nomadic life style and hunting skills were deeply embedded in their life style. They were not comfortable with town life. They had amazing survival skills.

Thousands of hectares of pastel green spinifex grass hiding unsuccessfully beneath sheets of fading greyish seed heads, blanketed the flat and rocky countryside. Cloud cover dappled the spinifex with patches of light and shade. Snappy gums adorned the banks of the Fortescue River meandering lazily into the distance. The horizon stretched without a break, except for occasional low rocky hills. Welcoming gentle evening breezes gently caressed and cooled our sweaty faces after days reaching 34deg in the shade. We arrived home about 10pm.

One mid-afternoon we drove to Fortescue River with Lyn and some church folks for a BBQ. The river was flowing. The water was clear. In the wet season, we would be ten metres under. Colossal amounts of water dumped through this system were emptying into the ocean at Cambridge Gulf near Wyndham.

Martu Church

'Martu' is the name of the local Aboriginal group in Newman town and surrounds. They decide on the spot when and where they hold their next service. This night, it was at Alistair's place. My theme was the downfall of Samson. Jan reckoned thirty-five adults were present. Some kids curled up on blankets and slept. Others gathered inside the house. Three guitarists, with a small amplifier, accompanied the singing. Clarrie taught a couple of white kids, "Jesus loves me, this I know." Aboriginals preferred outdoor meetings.

Small groups clustered around fires in an open space at an evening service. The clustering might have something to do with regulating interaction between 'Skin Groups' under the old tribal system. Eileen explained the Martu's tribal Skin System (Tribal groupings) diagrammatically in my notebook. I think I understood broadly speaking. They gave Jan and me skin names. Jan was Milangka. I was Purungku. This naming system-imposed responsibilities on dealings with others of the same skin name and how to interact with tribal groupings of a different skin. One Aboriginal lady of my skin group made me responsible to find her a husband. I didn't do too well for her.

About 9pm the service started. Singing was interspersed with pauses, barking dogs, deafening squeals, and squelches from the P/A system. Part way through the service a dispute erupted. A microphone and a boomerang hurtled through the air. Dogs barked in a frenzy. People lost interest quickly. One party to the dispute disappeared in his motor car at high-speed, spraying gravel and clouds of dust as he went. Another vehicle followed. Craig gathered the remainder of the mob together to pray. Wearily we packed the gear into the 4WD and collapsed into bed at 12.30am. The devil was up to his old tricks again!

Next morning Lyn called with good news regarding last night's drama. Elders had met with the parties and resolved some issues. The boomerang thrower apologised. What relief! Craig would now travel to Melbourne on deputation released from that tension. Lyn could get on with the business. We praised God.

Lyn informed us that another Martu service would occur that night in the Newman church about 8.30pm. I would love to have been in bed by 9pm but preparing simple messages is not always simple. With Lyn's help, and some Martu guidance, I might get a point across. Twenty-five Martu adults and as many kids invaded our privacy. It was a full-scale assault. The kids' behaviour was raw and unbridled. They fought, argued, shouted, and squabbled. The P/A system squealed and squawked. Guitars were close to deafening. Singing good. The service finished round 11pm. This was church Martu style - somehow, the Spirit of God worked. The Martu people were encouraged. We put the P/A system away, vacuumed floors, cleaned hand basins, disinfected unflushed toilets, and mopped kitchen floors. About 9am next morning Jan was still in bed exhausted. They were considering another Martu service the next night. We wondered if we would cope. But that's the way it was in Martu land and if that's what they wanted we would do it.

About 8.30pm a Martu service was held on the veranda at Craig and Lyn's house. I gave a short presentation from Galatians Chapter 5 on spiritual warfare. They gave me hatred, fighting, alcohol, adultery, bad thoughts, bad language, as works of the devil. Then they reeled off the Fruits of the Spirit. I challenged them to opt for the fruit. They ran with it. Good discussion followed and we finished with prayer. Jan's freshly cooked pikelets disappeared in seconds. We delivered the old ladies home in the 4WD.

We arrived home to find a front church window smashed. Police night patrol also noticed the broken window. They thought they'd nabbed the two blurry crooks they'd seen through frosted glass windows in the act. I heard footsteps on the veranda and tyres in the gravel till about 1am. We were invited to dinner with Julie the local Policeman's wife. Her husband had recently transferred to Newman. They were Christians. Julie's husband replaced one of those four Newman Police personnel recently tragically killed in a plane crash.

At a Martu service at Lyn's, only Clarrie, his family, an Aboriginal guy from Perth and an old lady attended. Because of Aboriginal culture, certain men and women were not allowed contact. One old lady attended the service. A Perth visitor sat quietly in his ute parked in the shadows some distance away. Lyn got the service underway with the usual difficulties. Three people from various church families had 'gone off'. That meant 'berserk'. Too much grog (wama). I spoke on the 'Prodigal Son'. Preaching was hard that night. Spiritual oppression was heavy, like I'd never previously experienced. A huge centipede crawling across the floor, disrupted proceedings. Somehow Lyn kept the meeting together.

During a power blackout, a BHP technician pulled up at the front of the church. He said, "Is there any church today?"

"No! Why?" I asked.

He said to me, "I got a couple in the back of the ute who need it."

"What's happened to the power?" I asked.

He informed me, "The whole towns out."

I replied, "There you are. No church, no power!"

Newman is a BHP mining town. White mud stained, dusty Toyota utes with amber flashing lights, radio aerials and orange flags atop tall whippy masts are common. On my way to Capricorn, I went birdwatching and lost Lyn's BP key card. I backtracked and found it in the roadside scrub.

Amazing! I even surprised the Aboriginals with my tracking ability. Thank you, Lord. We arrived home and entertained a stolen generation Aboriginal from Perth for dinner. He worked for the Aboriginal Affairs Department and found bureaucracy difficult. He was a keen Christian and a great fellow.

Mother's Day was energetic, exhausting, enjoyable and satisfying. We set up the hall. Jan cooked scones and muffins. Angela and Ivan prepared white posies. Some twenty-five adults turned up. Jan kept the service moving with the aid of good musicians and old-fashioned hymns. After the service, men served the ladies Devonshire Teas and cakes, and washed up.

At 7pm Lyn informed us that a Martu service would be held in the church 'tonight'. Clarrie and his mob arrived. I needed time for preparation, but it was OK. Clarrie gave me clues about presentation. I chose the 'Rich Young Ruler' as my theme. Lyn couldn't get the bus started. Craig coincidentally rang from Melbourne and suggested changing batteries. It worked.

Cliffie, a Martu guy, collected the people and we started the service about 9pm. We endured the usual lengthy tuning process, crackling, squawking P/A systems and got under way with, "We are gathering together." The band consisted of three guitarists, clapsticks, and misbehaving kids kicking plastic toys across the floor. The Martu sat on the floor in family groups. God got me through! Clarrie summed up while picking nits out of his little son's hair. About 10.30pm they went home. We cleared the carnage, got to work with the mop and bucket and collapsed into bed about 11:30pm.

Northwest Pastors' Conference

We embarked on a 700kms drive to the Northwest Pastors' Conference in Karratha. Lengthy journeys are a walk in the park for people of the outback. Rev Norm Nix from Crossover Australia spoke on the 'Year of the Outback'. Windmills along the road would symbolise his challenge to southern and eastern Baptist churches to share their resources with the thirty-eight Baptist Churches above the 26th parallel. The Newman Church sat above this parallel. We attended morning service at Karratha Baptist, pastored by Rev Arthur Payne, Superintendent of the Northwest Association of Baptist Churches. After lunch with the church folks, we returned to Newman and arrived about 8.30pm.

Time to Leave

I walked over the brow of the hill into the valley beyond the church - the blossoms were gold and herbage was high. The Furtive Spinifex Birds were hard to spot. Distant hills were tinged blue and breezes gentle. Snowy barked Eucalyptus trees adorned with fresh green leaves lined the banks of distant dry watercourses. A kangaroo watched cautiously and safely from a distance. The sun sank slowly in the West.

Lyn reminded me of an umbrella. She cheerfully sheltered us from cultural bloopers. She sent us on tasks when the weather was clear metaphorically speaking, placed no unreal expectations on us, gave clear instructions and always debriefed us. She taught us heaps. We knew where we stood with her. She was an excellent supervisor. It was a privilege to work with her.

Jan and I have country heritages. We both love the open spaces. We were incredibly privileged to have this opportunity of appreciating once again, our beloved Australian outback and some of its wonderful citizens. This was an epic adventure we'll never forget. We have wonderful encouraging memories of the times we spent in Newman. We said farewell to Lyn and Craig, the Newman Church folks and our beloved Martu brothers and sisters, with lumpy throats and immense gratitude.

Light Community Baptist Church (LCBC), East Ringwood, Vic.

A devout Christian couple with Asian heritage from NewHope Church, became close friends. Jan and I were invited to become their small group mentors.

Once a week he and I worked shoulder to shoulder in regular evangelism excursion activities. The lady ventured once monthly for three years with other wonderful women into the CBD as our faithful, prayerful on-site support team.

Soon after transferring to LCBC our friend became an effective elder and regularly preached there. Jan and I had transferred to the LCBC with their encouragement. This predominantly young and multi-cultural church made us welcome.

A Burmese musician wondered how to minister to members of the local Burmese community who were doing it tough. A Farsi speaking Persian refugee said, "The booklet you gave me last week is true." He eagerly accepted more copies entitled 'The Bible or the Koran.' A Burmese mother requested copies of the 'Finding Hope' booklet for use in her outreach. The church is located in close proximity to the East Ringwood railway station and several local cafes where I have several good contacts.

Multiply Disciples Training Seminar in Darwin NT

In 2017 Jan and I together with our Pastor (the Multiply Disciples Coordinator) and another member of our East Ringwood Church, participated in a training seminar at the invitation of the Pastor of the Bagot Aboriginal Community Centre in Darwin. The two-day seminar was attended by twelve adults (mostly Aboriginals) and two children. The cool breeze wafting through the open-sided building provided welcome relief from the tropical Darwin heat. Three large dogs slept peacefully at our feet on the cool concrete floor. Meals were prepared by the Pastor and her helpers. The training seminar, led by our Pastor was appreciated by the attendees, who found it challenging, helpful and informative.

Upon marriage, a former respected member of LCBC and her devoutly Christian husband, moved, in the course of his employment, to Darwin where he was part of an organisation of significance. We were privileged to be their guests at a beautiful Darwin harbour-side restaurant where we enjoyed a delicious sunset meal and prayed together. While in Darwin we heard a wonderful sermon on 'Christian Unity in a Multi-Cultural Community' at the Casuarina Baptist Church. We caught up with a former denominational leader we had met in our Kununurra days.

The following email extract was received from an interstate lady I met whilst preaching at her church. It relates to the 'Push the Pedal' appeal for bicycles for Indian Pastors launched in one of my newsletters. Extracts from her email encouraged me. "Thank you for your literature that you sent me. I have shared it with a Bhutanese lady, and we are meeting regularly now. She took the tract, which explained the Gospel and we have talked about her wanting to become 'Christian'. We were meeting again that week. I haven't seen my Indian lady again but have the tract in my handbag for when I do! I would love to donate towards a push bike; I have some birthday money that I have been waiting on the Lord's direction for. Many blessings." Signed.......

I am forever thankful to God for letters and phone calls from supporters worldwide. Bill, a Naracoorte friend and mentor, in his nineties, regularly assured me that he and his church were praying. Prayer warriors from New Zealand, South Africa, America, United Kingdom and locally also prayed for our ministry.

Taking it to heart:

1. What are some ways you might respond to God's call to 'Do, Go and Give?'
2. In what ways might God glorify His name and extend His Kingdom through your obedience?
3. Who might you share your resolutions and actions with in this regard?

References:

Genesis 50:20 – But as for you, you meant evil against me, but God meant it for good, in order to bring it about as it is this day, to save many people alive.

Isaiah 57:15 – For thus says the High and Lofty One who inhabits eternity, whose name is Holy: I dwell in the high and holy place, with him who has a contrite and humble spirit, to revive the spirit of the humble, and to revive the heart of the contrite ones.

1 Corinthians 1:22-24 – For the Jews request a sign, and the Greeks seek after wisdom: but we preach Christ crucified, to the Jews a stumbling block and to the Greeks foolishness, but to those who are called, both Jews and Greeks, Christ the power of God and the wisdom of God.

TPTL NT – The Pocket Testament League New Testament.

Chapter 31

Overseas Adventures

Men for Missions (MFM) Trip to Indonesia

Indonesia figured prominently in our lives over many years. Jan and I were involved in three mission trips there. In August 1982 we travelled with a Men For Missions (MFM) tour group to the city of Malang, East Java. MFM is the layman's arm of One Mission Society (OMS). We were billeted with Don and Peggy Saum, a delightful American OMS missionary couple.

The Watchman's Gong

Don, then Dean of Students at the OMS Seminary in Malang, in his orientation, warned us of the activities of nightwatchmen hired by local residents to guard their neighbourhood streets and property. Residents suspended a large metal pipe from a tree in a local street. The pipe when struck by the watchman's gong, sent out a loud metallic clang. At 1am he struck the pipe once, at 2am, twice, at 3am thrice and so on. His twofold purpose was letting residents know their watchman was on the job and deterring criminal activity in that locality. Our nightwatchman struck his gong, right outside our bedroom window. Other watchmen quickly followed, some near and loud, others faintly in the distance.

Years ago, OMS missionaries 'sounded forth' the Gospel and the Malang seminary was established. From there students 'sounded forth' the Gospel far and wide planting churches across Java. I was privileged to preach (with translation) at one of these more recently planted churches. This worshipping band of mainly university students were continuing what Jesus began at Jerusalem. Paul picked up the theme in 1 Thessalonians 1:9 -

> "The Word of the Lord has 'sounded forth'
> not only in Macedonia and Achaia, but also in every place.
> Your faith toward God has gone out,
> so that we do not need to say anything."

Prayer Walking in Indonesia

Spurgeon said, "Illustrations are windows through which people see truth." Rev Dr Graham Smith alerted me to the use of 'Redemptive Analogies' through his frequent sermon illustrations - although the actual term was unknown to me then. Don Richardson's 'Peace Child' book further refined and refreshed my testimony with a deeper understanding of Redemptive Analogies. Glimpses of missionary strategies gleaned from our overseas adventures were developed into 'Redemptive Analogies'. The critical principle of my understanding of 'Redemptive Analogies' so called, are touched upon in other chapters in this book.

In a recent sermon our Pastor stressed the importance of engaging contacts with a question based on their cultural or religious background. If for example, your contact is Buddhist you might ask, "Do you have problems keeping the five laws of Buddhism?" Depending on his response you might reply, 'I have problems keeping the Ten Commandments of the Christian faith'." Now you have rapport which might pave the way for a redemptive analogy and testimony.

On another journey to Indonesia, we participated in a prayer walk under the auspices of OMS in and near the city of Medan, Sumatra, shortly after the tsunami in the next province Aceh. Our journey exposed us to a variety of different cultures and customs. One intriguing industry involved constructions of huge, grey colored concrete multi-storey bird houses (about the same floor area as a small supermarket). House swifts are attracted inside these buildings through port holes by the recorded amplified shrill rattling twitter of nesting swifts. Their nests, made of saliva, are harvested regularly, processed, and sold at profit for Bird's Nest soup. It is a lucrative industry. I never tried it!

One church of three floors was located near a bird house. Traffic noise and twittering swifts made the preaching difficult to hear. The bottom floor of the shop front was occupied by the Pastor. The next floor was used as the church. The third floor was occupied by the church team. The Pastor shared his testimony. His wife supplied lunch. She was a good cook. We prayed with the team. Rental for this building was A$700 per year. Money was not easy for them to come by. It would be an immensely encouraging project for an Australian Christian or church to underwrite a year's rental for a small Indonesian church (Donations can be channeled through OMS Australia.

A Tsunami Testimony

This Pastor's mother-in-law shared her testimony regarding her recent tsunami experience in nearby Aceh. She said, "At 8am on December 26 I was selling my wares in the market when the earthquake hit. I was very frightened. A second earthquake hit. People were saying a flood is coming but there was no rain, the coast is four kms away. I thought, so what. Then I heard this loud crashing noise. I looked up to see a black wave as high as a house coming toward us. Fast! I ran up to my house on the second floor of the building. I actually felt God's hand on my arm. A voice said, 'Go up to the roof.' Many people said let's go to the mosque. It is a very large mosque. Those who ran to the mosque were swept away before they got to safety. Only the ten people who were up on the roof with me were saved. I was too scared to come down. When the water receded after two days I came down. All my household things were washed away. The people on the second floor were washed away. Most of the houses in the area were washed away. Only the mosque is left standing. Men and boys put tables down across the rubbish for us to walk on. My son is a policeman. He was saved by getting up on the roof of the Police Station. We were both looking for each other. Miraculously we met up. My son was afraid I was dead."

When a Pastor in Medan told his wife about the tsunami, she was traumatised, frantic about her mother's safety. Reports were sketchy. Three days later they travelled with difficulty to Aceh by bus to find her mother. Merely getting out of Medan was a chaotic experience. They heard horror stories. It was a twelve-hour bus ride. They did not expect to see her mother again. Many survivors were trying to escape from Aceh. At the bus terminal the young couple miraculously met her brother. He told them their mother was alive. The mother lost many neighbours and friends in the tsunami, but she lost no family. The only thing she had left were the clothes she wore. She now lives in a refugee center. Tremors followed. People were fearful.

Later that day, conversation at the Tip Top restaurant in the city of Medan was difficult due to the noise of swifts returning to their roosts and traffic, but suddenly, as if by magic, the busy street outside converted into a shopping mall. Within the space of fifteen minutes vehicular traffic was replaced with hundreds of chairs, tables, food vendors and crowds of pedestrians.

To a local I said, "Apa Kaba?" It roughly means: "How are you?" He giggled, and said, "Say no more" and shot through. He may have been off colour, but more likely my atrocious accent embarrassed him. In a passageway a worker banged in a nail with a bottle. I said, "You need a hammer." He replied in broken English, "I am very well, thank you."

I met the Pastor and some of his leaders at another local church. This fellowship occupied a building owned by a local Christian businessman who hired it for nominal rent. A young worker was sleeping at our host's residence. Thieves sprayed her through the open bedroom window with a chemical substance that kept her asleep. They also cast a spell over her, then stole the dashboard from her car. She woke up in a heavy daze. Prayer was made on her behalf. Later, she led a group and felt God help her. I had not anticipated being asked to preach the sermon at her church on the next Sunday.

An Earthquake Experience

We visited Lake Toba, situated in the beautiful highlands about two and a half hours from Medan. A rotunda overlooked the lovely scenery of this lake and a nearby waterfall. Whilst enjoying the scenic views from this rotunda, colonnades suddenly swayed back and forth above me. I lost my balance and grabbed a colonnade for support. For a moment I thought I was going 'troppo' but quickly realised this was an earth tremor ('Gempa') of some significance! It was a new and eerie experience for me. Standing beneath the concrete slab roof of the rotunda during a 'Gempa' was not a good idea. The locals had rushed onto the street for safety, but I was in danger of finishing up flat like a pancake under a concrete slab. This 'Gempa' measuring 6.7 on the Richter scale was felt as far afield as Singapore.

Human technology and knowhow can do little to prevent earthquakes and tsunamis.

The Pastor and his wife from our next church were young. Their church membership was likewise youthful. The Pastor was praying for older couples to bolster the membership. A family of Christian weavers turned up. This was an answer to their prayers. The twenty young people in the church choir dressed uniformly, looked smart and sang beautifully. Their only instrument was a keyboard. It was a long time since I was so emotionally moved in worship - I preached with the aid of an interpreter. A low flying passenger jet roared overhead. Roosters crowed nearby. The acrid stench of a burning mattress near the church worried the congregation. They thought their PA system had caught alight. After the service, we rushed to our host's home for lunch, prayer time and an early departure for the airport. A captive monkey nearby distracted our prayer warriors.

China and Hong Kong Visit 2007

Our English-speaking Chinese guide took us on a tour of Guang Zhou, South China. We enjoyed the local beautifully manicured Yun Tai Gardens. On Sunday evening, we weaved our clandestine way through dingy back streets with its unfamiliar sights and smells to an unregistered house church in a poorer part of town.

An Unregistered House Church

Snails, water beetles, fish, crabs, oysters, freshly hatched chickens and dressed poultry were displayed in small glass containers lined up along the footpath for sale. There was no church signage to guide us - hand-written directions only. A non-English speaking local guessed our purpose and pointed us in the right direction, then we entered an unmarked single fronted rickety three-storey building divided into six chapels. Approximately 3,000 people worshipped in these premises during weekends. We were ushered into one of these chapels, sat on rough wooden seats and awaited the arrival of the Pastor. I had heard about him for years. Suddenly he breezed in, a little aged man with a cheerful grin and excellent English. He who fearlessly stood 'in front of them all' carried many battle scars. Imprisoned for his faith. He endured five years in a prison camp, and fifteen years hard labour in a coal mine and escaped death many times. He experienced extreme hardship, but shared a joyful victorious testimony. His request for prayer was a humbling experience. His business card bore the biblical text: 'Be thou faithful unto death'. I have his small, autographed book. He died in recent times as an effective triumphant Christian leader.

We embarked on an evening Pearl River cruise. The Chinese excelled with multi coloured lighting on buildings and riversides. Words like paradise, fairy world, and dreamland drifted through my mind.

A Registered Church Service

We attended the morning service of a registered church. The worship centre was colonial in style and under renovation. Members of the Chinese Republican Army stood rigidly to attention in nearby sentry boxes guarding the adjacent American and Polish embassies. The changing of the guard was not within cooee of the majestic changing of the guard at Buckingham Palace. Several services each weekend in this church were jam packed with 300 to 400 people. Worshippers also stood at the back and sat along the sides. The singing with little instrumentation and no backing choir was beautiful - no drums - no hand waving - no clapping. These parishioners were more than just an audience. They were joyful participators. We recognised the tunes of some old hymns, but English translation of the sermon left much to be desired. Our tight schedule required a hasty departure part way through the service.

Our next flight was to Guilin City, through which flowed the Lijiang River. Narrow bamboo rafts with battery powered floodlights captained by a fisherman and crewed by a row of hungry cormorants perched along the edge of the craft operated in this river. In mid-stream the captain swatted his cormorants with his paddle. They dived in, surfaced, and effortlessly kept abreast of their master's narrow raft. A ring fitted round the cormorant's neck allowed it to swallow small fish, but a large fish can only be swallowed as far as the ring permits. This enabled the fisherman to unceremoniously and not too gently, extract the fish from the unfortunate bird's gullet then fling the bird stream-ward for another try.

How many artistic works and paintings are inspired by the unusually green and magnificent mountain landscape through which the Lijiang River flows is any one's guess. It is a photographer's dream and painter's delight. We travelled eighty-three kilometres along this river in a convoy of some twenty tour boats - each carrying at least 100 passengers. The breathtakingly beautiful and unusual mountain scenery along each side of this wide stream was awesome. A Chinese lunch served aboard included several different courses and a serve of snake wine. Pickled snakes in large glass flagons held no appeal for me. One great Chinese poet from days of yore in writing of this place said, "The river winds like a blue silk ribbon, while the hills erect like green jade hairpins." The under-statement of the ages! At the end of our journey lay a quaint, bustling, picturesque little village with narrow winding paved streets where trinkets, crafts and coffee can be purchased. It is worth a visit. Whilst walking along this street, a tropical downpour encouraged us to purchase umbrellas from a street vendor for A$2 each.

I thought the Reed Flute Caves would be dark, dingy with narrow tunnels, where one banged an unprotected head against rocky ceiling protuberances and flying bats. Instead, we found ourselves gaping, open mouthed in absolute astonished admiration in a cavern some eighty metres wide and sixty metres high, chock full of various formations shaped over the millennia by underground rivers depositing calcium carbonate on rock. It is known locally as the 'Art Palace of the Great Nature'. Formations and reflections in glassy smooth pools were illuminated by continually changing, brilliant combinations of multi coloured lighting. Dreamland stuff.

The local zoo on the way to the airport, contained 1,000 tigers and 600 black bears used for conservation purposes. We fed some of the big cats strips of meat as they padded silently past with only a flimsy single barbed wire fence between us, and watched a black bear ride a small motor bike between two pylons along a tight high wire stretched about thirty metres up. These trained animals are used in circus presentations to raise funds. I was not impressed by their conditions.

The language barrier made life difficult during our hotel accommodation on our first night in Kunming. Changing hotel rooms due to faulty toilet and bathroom lights, was frustrating. The doorbell chimed mysteriously at odd hours. An incorrectly set wall clock caused us to miss breakfast. Giggling staff who refused to help, had lots to learn about customer service to foreigners!

Unusual rock formations an hour and a half from Kunming, were not petrified trees but rocks in what appeared to be a forest setting beautifully set out with green lawns. Even the local Chinese were disgusted at the persistently aggressive sales tactics of pesky local street traders who frequent this area to capitalise on 'wealthy' western tourists. The English-speaking guide took us to a restaurant in the hill tribe's area where we were treated to a typical Chinese style meal, accompanied by local folks dancing in colourful outfits. As was normal practice, the guide took us to the usual government owned shops on the way home – jade, tea, pearls and Chinese medicine.

We took a flight to the border city of Shen Zhen and crossed through Customs and Immigration to Hong Kong. Clearing government departments proved to be no problem but lugging heavy suitcases from the airport to the Kowloon Canton Railway (KCR) through elevators, car parks, freeways and heavy traffic was exhausting and stressful. The KCR was spotlessly clean, incredibly fast and very efficient. It was said to be one of the world's top railway systems. We made our way to the Baptist Seminary where we stayed for the next few days. We then proceeded by train to Kowloon Tong shopping centre and tucked into some beef and mashed potatoes (what joy) before picking up the mission vehicle.

Our tour leader navigated heavy traffic with consummate ease on a sightseeing tour of Hong Kong. After lunch we arrived at the well-known Stanley Markets where our ladies 'shopped till they dropped' while I enjoyed a coffee. Three Irish couples asked if they could sit at our table. They turned out to be Christians. Our leader may contact them when she visits the UK later this year. A long windy drive up to the Peak resulted in a meal without the view due to dense fog.

We attended the International Church and enjoyed a late buffet at the Marco Polo HK Hotel restaurant. We also enjoyed an evening ferry ride across the HK Harbour. Coloured harbour lights on luxury passenger liners and tall buildings were spectacular. On our return journey the cashier said, "You are senior citizens. No charge." Vessels disgorged cargo. Others loaded. They came and went. Helicopters flew overhead.

A friend recently said, "Ships line up outside the Hong Kong Port like cars on a busy freeway waiting to dock." A large diversity of men from many nationalities crew these ships.

The United Wesleyan Graduate Institute's fourth graduation ceremony was interesting. Eight new graduates were ready to serve the church. Whilst traveling home late in the OMS mission transit van, the engine coughed, spluttered and died. We were stranded on a new three lane bypass. Jan was concerned that fast flowing traffic might crash into us. How would we escape this predicament? I suggested, "There's one thing we haven't done yet. Pray."

Another member of our party indignantly emphasised, "I was praying for police to come and help us!!!" To my surprise my mobile phone worked in that country. Twenty minutes later a tow truck arrived. Two of our party caught a taxi. Another mission vehicle arrived and transported the rest of us to our nearby accommodation. We were thankful the breakdown occurred close to home and near the end of our time in Hong Kong.

The United Christian College in Hong Kong was highly regarded. Nine million dollars was granted by the Government (Communist) unconditionally to purchase land and buildings for this school. The government was so impressed by the quality of graduating students that they imposed no restrictions on the curriculum. Across the front of this building hung a large banner which read: *'The Lord God Is My Strength – Habakkuk 3:19'*. The principal also began a church in this school for students and their parents. They now have about 100 attenders.

We lunched with the OMS Executive Director for Hong Kong and visited the office headquarters. We shopped in downtown Hong Kong and dined at the YMCA before boarding the train to the airport to begin our journey home.

Into Africa

My grandfather, Alfred Ernest Kelly, at age twenty-six, enlisted in Pietermaritzburg, South Africa, on 21/11/1900 for service with the British army in the Boer War. He was promoted to Lance Corporal and awarded the Queen's SA medal with clasps of Orange Free State and Transvaal. He served as a member of the security team protecting the General. On return to Australia, he was allocated land at Wyuna in the Goulburn Valley of Victoria, under a Government closer settlement scheme where he and his wife Clara (nee Lobb) raised five children, including my father Keith Sydney Kelly.

In May 2006 Jan represented Australia at the One Mission Society (OMS) International Board meetings in the world-famous Kruger National Park, South Africa. Following a tour of Kruger, we journeyed across the border to the city of Maputo in Mozambique to attend the ten-year celebrations of the opening of the OMS Christian Academy at the conclusion of a seventeen-year civil war. Shops and homes pockmarked with bullet holes was a confronting sight. Cats and dogs were non-existent having been eaten by a starving population. The OMS goal of providing hope for young people exposed to killings, HIV Aids, drug and alcohol abuse, and extreme poverty soon created the need for a four-storey academy still under construction at the time of our visit. The structure when completed, will cater for 130 students. Its curriculum continuously evolved to meet the needs of its diverse community, while retaining its core values of quality Christian education. The humble, faithful, gracious missionaries and vibrant local Christians among whom they ministered, inspired us.

At the conclusion of our Mozambique adventure, Darwie Krouse, South African OMS Board Chairman, personally escorted a small group on a tour that included a journey through the Drakensburg Mountains in South Africa. 'Long Tom' a long-distance howitzer used by the Boers to harass the British in the Boer War, was resting silently by the roadside along the way. 'Long Tom' rekindled some barely remembered and fuzzy childhood stories of A.E. Kelly's military service with the British against the Boers in South Africa all those generations ago. Darwie also showed us several locations where skirmishes occurred between the Brits and Boers who invented the art of Guerilla warfare. What motivated grandfather, an Australian, to fight with the Brits in South Africa still puzzles me.

Middle East Trip - October 2010

An epic journey under the auspices of Middle East Christian Outreach (MECO), took us through Syria, Jordan, Israel and Egypt. Damascus was thought to be the oldest continuously inhabited city in the world. Abraham was reputed to have received his calling (Genesis 12:1-3) nearby. We walked the street called Straight (Acts 9:11) and visited the house of Ananias where Paul was baptised (Acts 9:18*). This home, converted in antiquity into the Chapel of Ananias, is now regarded as one of the earliest churches still standing where services continue to this day. We also saw the window, through which Paul was lowered in a basket, to avoid assassination (2 Corinthians 11:33*). We attended a lively vibrant, church service in Damascus. The responsive reading was Psalm 34. Our tour leader preached. The record of Paul's baptism in Acts 9 carries much greater significance now.

Caravanserais and Dragomen!

Our journey through Damascus took us past a Caravanserai. Our guide informed us that Caravanserais in olden days provided shelter, rest and refreshment for travellers and their animals after each stage of their journey, but now motor cars, aeroplanes and rail transport have largely replaced caravanserais. The usual practice of travellers then was to send a 'dragoman' ahead to prepare the next resting place that travellers may find food, comfort, and shelter ready and waiting on their arrival. This was life in Jesus' day. The dragoman caravanserai story clarified in a flash my own journey onward and upward to the eternal destiny awaiting all Christian pilgrims.

Where it all Began – Israel

The following verses are streetlights that have illuminated my way:

- Hebrews 12:2 – Jesus is the Captain and Perfector of my faith.
- Philippians 3:14 – I press toward the goal for the prize of the '*upward call*' of God.
- John 14:2 – In My Father's house are many mansions.
- John 14:3 – Jesus comes again to receive me to Himself.
- 2 Corinthians 3:18 – With unveiled face beholding as in a mirror the glory of the Lord, I am being transformed into the same image from glory to glory.
- Hebrews 12:1 - Laying aside every weight and sin which easily ensnares, I run with endurance.
- 1 John 1:3 - What we see and hear we declare to you; that you may have fellowship with us; and truly our fellowship is with the Father and His Son Jesus Christ.
- Philippians 1:20 - My earnest expectation and hope is that I will not be put to shame in anything, but that with all boldness, Christ will even now, as always, be exalted in my body, whether by life or by death.
- Philippians 1:21 - When death takes all I have, but gives me more of Christ, I count it gain. For me to live is Christ and to die is gain.
- Psalm 119:105 – Your word is a lamp to my feet and a light to my path.

Without prayer, Bible study, fellowship, testimonies, and worship we forfeit the companionship of our Lord, but upon repentance, He is beside us again. Jesus is my 'Resting Place'.

No city on earth has captured the world's attention through the centuries like Jerusalem. Jan and I felt incredibly safe in Israel. We sailed on the Sea of Galilee, trod the footsteps of Jesus along the Via Delarosa (The way of pain), Christ's traditional journey to the Cross (Mark 15:20-24) and gained a deeper perspective on our relationship with Christ. A friendly retired German couple in a coffee shop on the Via Delarosa accepted testimony and a Gospel of John.

The Empty Tomb

At the request of our tour leader, I was privileged to conduct a communion service for some forty co-travellers in the Garden surrounding the empty tomb where Christ was buried - a beautiful peaceful spot in which to commemorate His Resurrection.

The Wailing Wall

To a devout Jew at the Wailing Wall in Jerusalem I said, "Excuse me Sir, what are you reading?" He replied, "The story of Abraham taking Isaac up the mountain to be sacrificed." I asked him, "Can you explain the significance of the ram caught by its horns in the nearby thicket?" (Genesis 22:13). He thoughtfully replied, "A good question."

The Jordan River

Under the watchful eyes of an armed Israeli soldier standing guard on the Israeli side of the Jordan river and an equally watchful armed Jordanian guard on the opposite bank, four of our party were baptised where Jesus was baptised.

Tel Aviv

At an adjacent table in a Tel Aviv hotel a group of young male and female Israeli soldiers in full battle dress, armed with light machine guns were enjoying their lunch break. During our journey we saw female soldiers shopping with light machine guns slung across a shoulders and a handbag swinging from their free hand. These confronting sights introduced a whiff of tension into our atmosphere. In a sense we had one foot in Jerusalem's glorious past, but today our other foot was firmly planted in the present.

The Dead Sea

On one memorable occasion we travelled to the west bank of the Dead Sea. I have seen nothing in Australia which parallels the dry, unforgiving nature of this Middle Eastern desert region through which we travelled. Arriving at a trickle of pure clear water gurgling gently across a rock studded stream bed flanked by shady palms and greenery, with wild mountain sheep grazing among the craggy rocks above, and cavorting conies beside the stream edges abounding, was refreshing, a haven of rest in a sea of burning sand.

This was the desert through which David and his men travelled as they escaped from the wrath of King Saul. Imagine travelling with blistered feet, flies, exhaustion, thirst and sheer relief and joy on arrival at this spring called 'Engedi' in the Bible. Locals call this desert 'the torment', and its nearby oasis the 'Smile of God'. Learning about Genesis 12:1-3 in the Bethel Course gave me a glimpse of the torment and smiles revealed in the broad sweep of Biblical history stretching from before the beginning of time and pointing to the eternal future. There is Blessing and Torment in the Genesis 12 passage. "I will curse those who curse you" (torment), and "I will bless those who bless you" (smiles). God's smile in the Old Testament points forward to the 'Old Rugged Cross'. Church history points us back to that same 'Old Rugged Cross'. Billy Graham's crusade song book No. 69 puts it this way:

> 'On a hill far away stood an old rugged cross, the
> emblem of suffering and shame, (Torment)
> And I love that old cross, where the dearest and best died,
> for a world of lost sinners was slain.' (Smiles)

The Flight of the Soul

In Egypt we glimpsed 'Redemptive Analogies' unwittingly provided by sincere, proud Muslim tourist guides at ruined temples in Luxor, the Valley of Kings and archaeological sites in Alexandria. To the Big Question (BQ*) another sharp point for my testimony was added in the city of Luxor. I entitled this sharp point the 'Flight of the Soul.' One eloquent Muslim guide explained the ancient's belief in afterlife with the aid of beautifully preserved 4,000-year-old hieroglyphics on temple walls. He said, "Death is symbolised by the sun setting on the west side of the Nile. Souls leave the body and fly eastward across the river toward the rising sun, symbolising resurrection. But each hour as the soul flies through the long, dark, and dangerous night, it is asked a question by a god – a total of ten questions all told. To gain paradise 100% of these questions must be answered 100% accurately 100% of the time. Failure at any one point meant hell for eternity."

I asked our guide, "What are the questions?" He began, "Did the soul kill someone...?" The Ten Commandments immediately sprang to mind. I was reminded of my own ineptitude at law keeping for salvation. I am saved by faith alone, in Christ alone, by grace alone. With increasing confidence, I said to the guide, "I am aware that you do not believe in mythology, but this story does make a point. What is the greatest question in all the world for you?" He replied, "Have I kept all the law? Do I pray five times a day? Am I a good Muslim?' I asked him, "Have you succeeded?" He replied, "I think so." I declared, "By definition God is perfect and you are not. A perfect God cannot allow imperfection into his presence. Does Islam offer you a rock solid, watertight guarantee of eternal life?" He said, "No one can say that for sure." Herein lays one huge difference between Christian and Muslim belief. Christians are guaranteed forgiveness and eternal life through faith in the risen Christ. Muslims can only rely on a programme destined for failure.

I related this story to another Muslim guide in Cairo and asked the same question. She said, "Am I a good Muslim? Do I keep the law?" I asked her, "Does your religion offer you a rock-solid watertight guarantee of eternity in paradise with God?" She answered, "No one can be sure" and listened graciously to my response.

Sarah, our charming Muslim guide in Alexandria, listened to the story of the 'Flight of the Soul'. I said, "What is your greatest question?" She replied, "Making sure I obey all god's law." I informed her, "As I understand it, you are guaranteed entry into paradise only if you 100% obey 100% of God's law 100% of the time." She said, "God will overlook my failures." I maintained, "That's my problem. I am not perfect, where does God draw the line? You don't know where your line is. You have no guarantee you'll make it. But Jesus came to earth 2000 years ago as a perfect God in perfect human flesh and paid the perfect penalty for all my sin. By God's grace I am guaranteed salvation." She smiled and continued her commentary.

We embarked on the long flight home from the Middle East. My cramped seat was located directly behind a young mother with three infants, one of whom screamed continually. A hostess kindly offered me a roomier seat by an exit door. For this I was deeply grateful. Ammar, the gentle, tragic Iraqi refugee in the newly allocated seat beside me, had travelled at risk to visit his family in Baghdad. He had fled Saddam Hussein's regime and spent eight years as a refugee in Indonesia. He arrived in Australia on a boat and now lives in Footscray. I related the 'Flight of the soul', story, showed him Colossians 2:13* on my iPod and asked him the BQ*. He replied, "I'm not perfect. I'll have to wait for God to judge me. I do not know if I'll get to paradise or go to Hell." He didn't realise he was reading the Bible and said sharply, "Who wrote that?" I said, "It's from the Christian Holy Book." He accepted a Bible website, a Gospel of John, and an invitation to meet for coffee in the CBD in due course.

To a phone card salesgirl in Hungry Jacks, I said, "I was in Damascus last month and walked along the street called Straight" (Acts 9:11). She read the details of Saul's conversion on my iPod. This Syrian Orthodox Church member knew the story.

To Vanuatu with Christian Fellowship Group May 2018

Knowing practically nothing of Vanuatuan (formerly New Hebrides) history, Jan and I embarked on a Christian Fellowship Tour of that nation - a collection of small islands in the Pacific Ocean. We visited a 'Person of Peace' as part of One Mission's strategy of establishing a Christian witness amongst the unreached Chinese shopkeepers in Luganville, capital city on Santo Island. During dinner at a beach front resort, we met with the Principal of the Talua Theological Institute and his wife and children. He outlined some concerns about local ministry.

Not many had heard of the famous European explorer Pedro Fernandez de Queiroz. It was he who proclaimed the Southern region of the Pacific including Australia, as the 'Great South Land of the Holy Spirit'. Col Stringer in his stirring book entitled 'Discovering Australia's Christian Heritage' reminded us of the 'de Queiroz' proclamation and its significance to Australian churches. When de Queiroz landed at Big Bay near the island of Santos, he planted a large Cross and read the following proclamation:

"Let the heavens, the earth and the waters of the earth with all their creatures and all this here present witness that I, Captain Pedro Fernandez de Queiros ....in the name of Jesus Christ hoist this emblem of the Holy Cross on which His person was crucified; and whereas He gave His life for the ransom and remedy of the human race.... on this Day of Pentecost (14/05/1606). I take possession of all this part of the South as far as the Pole in the name of Jesus Christ... which, from now on, shall be called 'The great South Land of the Holy Ghost to the end that all natives, in all the said lands, the Holy, Sacred Evangel may be preached zealously and openly."

Our group visited an evangelical Christian village at Big Bay, near where the di Queiroz proclamation is now etched in a granite memorial. The Headman of this village traced his family history back to the di Queiroz's visit. This village was wonderfully welcoming and provided a delicious lunch at short notice. They accepted material and cash for use in their Sunday School. Many Vanuatans claim Jesus Christ as Saviour.

Geoff Bullock may have gained inspiration from the de Queiroz declaration to compose his famous song entitled: 'The Great Southland'. At the suggestion of some Koori brothers and sisters Bullock's song was later revised to include more acceptable lyrics for our 'First Nation' people, who are hereby acknowledged as equally beneficent in the de Queiroz proclamation.

One afternoon Jan and I visited Mount Yasur, an active volcano on the island of Tanna. We arrived after traversing in a 4WD along rough roads including a wide plain of hardened, barren volcanic ash surrounding the foot of this mountain. In the distance two teenage village kids trudged barefoot along a volcanic ash track homeward bound for the evening. They walked 10 kilometres to school and the same distance home daily.

Local guides carefully and gently led us oldies on foot up the remaining challenging, exhausting, and short steep rocky incline to the crater rim. Frighteningly massive explosions from deep within the crater shook the earth. Each vibration was accompanied by large glowing red fireballs of molten lava launched high in the evening sky. Clouds of steam, sulphur fumes and ash billowed through the atmosphere into the rays of the setting sun – a never to be forgotten experience.

Beneath the protection of the crater lip, and between explosions, I put the name of Jesus in front of our tour guide, a deserted wife with three unemployed adult sons with no money or food in the larder. She was encouraged as I shared God's message and furnished her with a small amount of financial assistance. It was only a few dollars loose change I happened to have, but she accepted it and Christian literature, with joy.

A book published in 1903 by Rev. Paton B.D., for six years resident Presbyterian missionary on the west coast of the island of Tanna, described how he got 'in front of them all' with the Gospel and how it changed the warring savagery of heathenism into an island of Christianity. He said, "I believe that nowhere else in the world, can there be found a more direct and irresistible demonstration, of the supernatural origin of the Word of God, and the miraculous effects of the Gospel of Jesus Christ."

After our return home, we were loaned another book entitled 'Lomai of Lenakel, sub-titled 'A Hero of the New Hebrides' (Vanuatu). Lomai became a Christian under Paton's ministry. This book detailed a significant chapter in the progress of the Gospel in Vanuatu. Lomai figured prominently in that progress.

Rushing winds, tongues of fire, and needy people were reminiscent of our Biblical Pentecost, but its power was not to be compared with Holy

Spirit power that launched the Christian Church from Pentecost as reported in Acts 2. Something big happened there. The Holy Spirit changed persecuted, discriminated, weak-kneed disciples into fearless proclaimers of the Gospel. Some 3000 souls repented and were baptised following the first sermon. That was God's volcanic launch of the church. Nothing changes! The Holy Spirit still 'fills us' in a world torn asunder! The promise is still for us, our children, to all far off, 'even as many as the Lord our God will call' (Acts 2:39). The church still grows!

Pedro Fernandes di Quiros, a man of faith, and missionary zeal, believed in the Resurrection (Luke 24:51*) and the descent of the Holy Spirit at Pentecost (Acts 2:41*), which launched and currently maintained the Christian Church across the world and through the ages.

On Pentecost Sunday 20th May, we attended a worship service in a local Presbyterian Church with approximately 175 attendees. No band, no choir, no song leader just magnificent singing of old-time hymns translated into the Bislama language (a variant of Pidgin English). Singing by the beneficiaries of those early missionary endeavours was inspirational and magnificent. The preacher's texts Ezekiel 37:1-15 and Acts 2:1-17 were combined for a Pentecost Day memorial sermon based on 'dry bones made alive by the Holy Spirit.' Inspirational! At the conclusion of the service, I was asked to bring greetings from Australian churches. My brief response included an invitation to send choirs to our Australian churches!

This tribute by a converted heathen (Lomai) was recorded in page 164 of Paton's book. "It is wonderful to meet in God's House with God's children. It is good to praise our Father in Heaven. There is for us only one Heaven, the Heaven that Jesus leads to. There is no other road for us but the road which Jesus made. We may think of earthly things, but they will not lead us to Heaven. Only Jesus can take away our sins and lead us to Heaven. Long ago the Light came into Dr Paton's heart. He said, 'I must not hide this light. I must let it shine.' And so, the Gospel was brought to the islands of Vanuatu. Do not hide your light, let it shine. Take the light of Jesus to your neighbours and those far away. Take the light of Jesus there. Let it shine. This is what Jesus told us to do."

Our early Australian explorers, pioneers and politicians did their best to put Christian principles 'in front of them all' through legislation, leadership, correspondence, and speeches. They emphasised Biblical principles as indispensable foundations for life and government. But humanists are dismantling our Christian heritage, stripping our great 'Southland of the Holy Spirit', selling it for a mess of pottage – materialism, eastern philosophy, transcendental meditation, martial arts and strange religions. Aussies follow these in droves, but God still pours out His Spirit on sons, daughters, old men, young men, servants and handmaids to spread the Gospel against all odds in this Pentecostal church age. Getting in front of them all with the Gospel is the answer. One Sunday in July 2018, I preached a sermon based on Acts 2:2-13 at Light Community Baptist Church using Mount Yasur to illustrate Pentecost.

New Zealand

An attractive Czech Republic waitress in a coffee shop in Hanmer Springs (South Island NZ), an indescribably beautiful resort town with thermal springs ringed by snow-capped mountains accepted the BQ* and a Gospel of John. At my request she read aloud from John 8:12 where Jesus said, "I am the light of the world. He that follows me shall not walk in darkness, but shall have the light of life."

Later, in the TV lounge, a youthful Chinese couple (cyclists with tent) and Graham, a lone middle-aged British diesel engineer (motor cyclist with tent) accepted the BQ* and listened to my story. The Chinese lad said, "My grandmother is a Christian. She gave me a Bible, but I left it at home." The Brit said, "What a wonderful story." Both accepted literature. An Irish lass raising funds for the heart foundation said, "My boyfriend and I read the Bible every weekend but don't attend church." She declined literature.

Sounding Forth the Gospel

The never to be forgotten watchman's gong illustration and the wonderful fellowship of churches we visited in the course of our adventures, sharpened an understanding of my role in the worldwide Great Commission. A pointed three-fold mantra developed by the MFM founder is based on three questions. 'Will you do anything God asks? Go anywhere God sends? And give anything God wants?' He'll never ask us to do, go or give without providing resources to do so. Will you play your part in 'Sounding Forth' the Gospel to the uttermost parts.

References:

Luke 24:51 – Now it came to pass, while He blessed them, that He was parted from them and carried up into Heaven.

Acts 2:41 – Then those who gladly received his word were baptised; and that day about 3000 souls were added to them.

2 Corinthians 11:33 – But I was let down in a basket through a window in the wall, and escaped from his hands.

Colossians 2:13 – And you, being dead in your trespasses and the uncircumcision of your flesh, He has made alive together with Him, having forgiven you all trespasses.

BQ – Big Question – What is the most important question in all the world for you?

TPTL NT – The Pocket Testament League New Testament.

Chapter 32

Interstate Journeys

South Australia (SA)

At Port Augusta we paid a surprise visit to Willy and Vera Austin, Aboriginal friends of long standing. We last saw them many years before. Willy, surprisingly recognised me at their front door. Willy was a champion bronc buster in his early years. He was miraculously saved from the grip of alcohol. Vera was converted as a teenager. She never touched alcohol. They pastored Aboriginal Fellowships around Copley, Leigh Creek, and Coober Pedy etc. for many years. Getting old they maybe but with hearts filled with love they continued ministering the Gospel to their people.

While Willy was attending an all-day church meeting in Port Augusta, we took Vera for a picnic lunch to the small satellite township of Wilmington. Later, we shouted her a slice of Quandong cheesecake with cappuccino in Quorn, another nearby country township north of Port Augusta. Quandongs are tasty little red native fruit growing in that region. Vera thoroughly enjoyed her day. We thoroughly enjoyed our time with her.

We headed for Wilpena Pound via Quorn where we attended a shop front Pentecostal church service. A lady preached on praise and worship to ten people in the congregation. A cafe on the adjacent corner tempted us. We enjoyed more Quandong pie and cappuccino. The Wilpena Pound road snaked through undulations toward a long jagged purple blue tinged range of hills far ahead. Beyond this first starkly beautiful delineation of heaven and earth lay another range of different hue and beyond that another. Roadside paddocks were patchworked with gold and purple spring flowers. A bright blue sky was flecked with the occasional fleecy white cloud. A wedge tailed eagle soared effortlessly high above. The remains of occasional sandstone ruins of homes built long ago dotted the landscape. Who knows how many broken hopes and faded dreams lay buried beneath those piles of rubble? Dead trees lined a dry creek bed meandering into the distance. A lazy blue tongue lizard dawdled across the road in front of our vehicle. This was my kind of country!

We pitched our tent on an unpowered site at Rawnsley Park Station Caravan Park close to Rawnsley Bluff (near Wilpena Pound SA), which turned pink or red according to the dictates of the setting sun. We stayed five nights. The ground was hard to sleep on. Enjoyable bush walks eased resulting hip stiffness.

'Chook', a local tour guide, took us for an all-day tour through the Flinders Ranges. Our first stop was Uloudna Lookout. It was a steep climb even for his 4WD. At the top a tiny flicker of movement in the scrub caught my eye. It was a family of Red Throats. The sole claim to fame of these elusive little brown birds of the rugged inland is a small orange patch at the throat of the male. They are secretive, uncommon, and difficult to locate. I was thrilled by this first sighting. Some whining anti-Victorian Eagles (WA) football supporters travelled with us. They harped on saying, "The venue for the Australian Football League (AFL) Grand Final should be Sydney or Perth, not the Melbourne Cricket Ground (MCG) and Barry Hall should be rubbed out," referring to one of Barry's many recent on-field football indiscretions. The Sydney Swans had just begun their return journey with a bucketful of West Australian Eagles' heads (AFL premiership). We drove onwards through scenery comparable in majesty to the rugged Kimberleys in far NW Australia. It is difficult to find superlatives sufficient to describe the beauty of this rugged inland locality.

We broke camp and headed for Copley, a small country township. Willy and Vera who made the three-and-a-half-hour journey from Port Augusta, met with us. They drove us to see the Leigh Creek Coal Mine. I had camped many years previously with them in the old United Aboriginal Mission Church in Copley. Vera then cooked for us. Willy shared, as always, from his wealth of cultural background knowledge flavoured with generous lashings of outback humour.

Hawker, the hub of the Flinders Ranges, is famous for its Wilpena Panorama superbly portrayed by artist Jeff Morgan, who also served as a local Baptist Pastor. This circular painting in his gallery, which took months of painting time, can be viewed from the ground floor or from the staircase landing. It was as good as it gets – a 360deg. view of the most beautiful country in South Australia as seen from the highest point of the Pound, St Mary's Peak. Jeff used his gallery for Christian outreach. He offered Bibles, tracts, and Christian books. Brass plates with Scripture verses were affixed to stair rails (Matthew 11:28-30, Romans 1:20, Psalm 46:10, Psalm 19:1 are examples). Four-wheel drives, cars and large passenger buses were parked outside. Tourists crowded the gallery. The skeptical bus driver said, "Be careful or they'll start preaching at you. That is their pulpit (indicating the stair-case landing). I had a bus load of Christians once. All they did was sing choruses." I asked, "Were they good?" He said, "Just ask them." I replied, "I'm asking you," but he refused to be drawn.

An old Aboriginal busker with his guitar, was seated beside the entrance door to this gallery. He shared with pedestrians and bus passengers through song and testimony of his salvation from debauchery and drunkenness. His singing voice was not the best I've heard by a long shot, but his sincerity was unquestioned and message clear. I asked him, "Do you know an Aboriginal lady named Vera?" He answered, "Vera Austin? Yes. She's my cousin." We travelled on. At every motel in which we stayed we found a Gideon Bible. I always left it open on the table at a selected passage for the benefit of cleaning staff as we departed. So, we said farewell to this lovely land as flocks of Galahs, clown princes of the bird world, screeched, circled and swooped acrobatically through tree tops and rays of the setting sun.

Victorian Touring Holidays

I said, 'Where do you want the esky Jan?' She replied, 'Ntheboodledoo.' One last quick flick of the powder puff and we were off like a larrikin's hat in the breeze. We booked in for two nights in a caravan park in Moama NSW, a twin town to Echuca (Vic) on the opposite bank of the mighty Murray River, habitat of the famous giant toe cutting Murray Crayfish (referred to elsewhere in this book). A nostalgia trip took us to the historic inland port city of Echuca, where I attended Technical College and graduated in unspectacular fashion. We students sometimes ate lunch under the famous wharves on the banks of the mighty Murray and occasionally enjoyed a quick dip on a hot day, until the headmaster got wind of our lunchtime activities and that was that!

In Portland, a coastal town in country Victoria, we attended the Baptist Church and lunched with former acquaintances from NewHope Baptist Church. At nearby Nelson we enjoyed afternoon tea overlooking the Southern Ocean with more friends from NewHope. The sky was clear, the ocean ruffled by gentle breezes was blue, and the beach golden. A Rufous

Bristle Bird, an almost Australia Treasure, flitted across our path. Back to Portland we went and signed in our car to a personal contact for minor body repairs, then visited the only mainland Australian Gannet (sea birds) breeding colony.

At Fawthrop's Lagoon, near Portland, we hoped to see a Lewin's Rail (bird) but found instead Kathleen sitting lonely and dejected on the bird hide steps. This fifteen-year-old tragic looked old beyond her years. She lived with her stepmother and had a history of drug addiction and heavy drinking. Our hearts went out to her. I asked the BQ*. She said, "I'd really like people to look past the studs in my nose and see me as I really am. My brother is injecting hard drugs, but there's no future in that for me. I would like to start my own restaurant. My friend invited me to church a couple of times." She listened to my testimony and accepted a Gospel of John. Her attitude throughout demonstrated a discernible softness to the Gospel.

At a cafe in Heathcote, a small country Victorian town, a wheelchair bound gentleman with heavily a plastered left leg said, "You won't believe this but I fell in the doctor's waiting room and broke my leg!" He appreciated genuine friendship and a Gospel of John.

I prayed for a needy person to cross our path. Jan and I just happened to spend an hour or two on the banks of the mighty Murray River at Thompsons Beach, Cobram Vic, under a cloudless blue sky with a gentle breeze caressing our faces beneath magnificent shady old river gums. Whilst sitting on a nearby riverside seat a family of four walked past. Without a word of greeting or invitation an agitated older male broke away from this group, hurried over and sat with us. This interstate truckie said, "I have cancer in both lungs and face more surgery. I think about it all the time. I've given up smoking but it's closing the stable door after the horse bolted." He gladly accepted the Dixon booklet 'How to Handle a Crisis' and rejoined his family. The Holy Spirit brought us all the way from

Melbourne to intersect with a needy man, not far from where I spent the first twenty-five years of my life.

New South Wales

From Moama Vic, we drove on to Mathoura NSW in the Millewa State Forest, which I last visited as a young teenager fishing the clear flowing nearby Gulpa Creek with my father and our neighbour, Gordon Allen. Jan and I walked hand in hand along the banks of this beautiful little stream flowing through the world's largest Red Gum Forest. I had caught bagfuls of Red Finn, Yellow Belly and Murray Cod at this location. The weather was mild. The sun was shining. The stately red gums were beautiful and welcome first rains had transformed the forest floor with a refreshing green tinge.

A bed and breakfast homestead on the banks of the Darling River out from Wentworth NSW, seemed a good place to stay. The owner, a famous Australian Football League (AFL) footballer and interstate cricketer of yesteryear, reckoned all stories including mine were interesting. Vehicle wheels drummed loudly across cattle grids on the nearby highway. Bitumen was edged with purple blossoming Salvation Jane noxious weeds. A line of trees merged with the horizon in the shimmering distance. The clear blue sky hosted a brightly shining sun. The country was fresh and green. High-powered electricity pylons reared their ugly heads into the atmosphere. Emus with chicks, graze by the roadside. Pine lined creeks came and went. Cruise control and audio tapes quickly ate up the outback mileage and hey presto, we are setting up tent in Broken Hill, a mining town in far west NSW.

Broken Hill NSW

An elderly man from Young NSW, in a Broken Hill caravan park, said, "My wife is a devout Christian. I am coming back to the faith. I am encouraged to hear your story. Thank you!" The wife of an employee recently walked out of their thirty-year marriage for a younger man. The employee was heartbroken. I offered a listening ear and literature. A farmer from Lake Grace in Western Australia accepted my testimony. He and his wife invited us to their cabin for coffee. A French geologist accepted testimony and a Gospel of John.

The temperature was down to six degrees. Pelting rain against the tent wall a hands breadth from my head interrupted sleep. Sloshing through twenty meters of mud in heavy rain and biting cold wind at 3am on the toilet run was no fun. The mobile phone was out of range. Emails wouldn't work. The Alfresco Coffee shop was a shocker. The coffee was cold and the fruit loaf burnt and stale. Jan walked out. I shared my faith with the proprietor of a near-by art gallery. The local State Emergency Services (SES) and Flying Doctor put out gale warnings and hailstorm alerts. We dismantled our tent. The only cabin available had two large holes punched through the roof by a low flying branch. We took it!

The Psalmist said, "God inhabits our praises." Selwyn Hughes said, "Praise awakens our conscience to the holiness of God. It feeds our minds with the truth of God. It purges imaginations by the beauty of God. It opens our hearts to the love of God. It helps devote our wills to the purpose of God." Proclaiming God's praises everywhere, any time in every circumstance is vital for spiritual health in Christians. Storms passed. Rains stopped. The sun shone. Emails and mobile phones worked. Lunch was enjoyed at the Musicians Club. We slept well. Praise God!

Sydney NSW

At the Manly Ferry Terminal, Joe, a Polish refugee, surprisingly said, "I've been in Australia two years. I want somewhere for my kids to get a start. The world is in a mess. The Bible says this will happen." In answer to the BQ* he said, "I don't know." He accepted literature and discussion on John

8:12 and the word 'follow'. At an adjacent table Jason, a lonely Tanzanian, sat drinking from a tankard of beer. He was seeking Permanent Residency and worked as a builder's labourer. He read John 8:12, listened to my story, accepted a John's Gospel, and words of caution regarding alcohol consumption. We later spied him drinking from a fresh tankard.

On Melbourne Cup Day (celebrated Australia wide), a world-famous horse racing carnival, Jan and I enjoyed some seaside scenery along the Manly Esplanade, a suburb of Sydney. Ladies promenading in Cup Day finery strutted their stuff. Females in the street loudly and proudly announced that, "A lady jockey won the Cup!" I said, "You're kidding." But it was true! Overseas interests with their million-dollar-mounts in a premier event on the world racing calendar were beaten by a local broken-down hack ridden by a young woman jockey must have been scratching their heads!!

In the Three Beans coffee shop, Nathan, a British tourist who now lives in Auckland, New Zealand stated, "My relationship broke down recently. It has taken some adjusting to." A lone Japanese tourist who arrived yesterday, accepted literature. He was replaced by two Swedish travellers who had never heard of the Melbourne Cup. In answer to the BQ*, Emily replied, "How to be happy." Johanna answered, "What is the meaning of life?" All contacts carefully listened to my testimony and eagerly accepted my last supply of New Testaments and Gospels of John.

Maitland NSW

We attended the 90th birthday celebrations at the Maitland NSW Uniting Church for Jan's only surviving aunt on her mother's side. The aunt was much encouraged by attending our 50th wedding anniversary in Coolamon previously. The birthday event was catch up time for Jan with relatives from Wagga, Sydney, Bowral, Coffs Harbour, and Gosford attending. Jan's sister-in-law later expressed gratitude for Jan's Testimony Card (JTC) with the following message: "To my very special sister-in-law. I found some quiet time to read the lovely card you gave me on the weekend. Thank you, it made me cry it was so beautiful. We were privileged to experience God in our lives, especially through the actions of loved ones." A Christian cousin was also grateful for a JTC.

The following contacts on our journey north accepted copies of JTC – two cleaning ladies at a Maitland (NSW) motel. A friendly Aboriginal grandmother of eight in McDonalds (Maitland). My sister and her husband on the Gold Coast. He was facing urgent 'Thoracic Aortic Dissection' surgery. Without the operation his condition was terminal.

Lightning Ridge NSW

Lightning Ridge is an opal mining town located in outback NSW. We attend the local Community Church morning service – the music was provided by the Curate's wife on the organ accompanied by a blind bongo drummer. The 7:30pm Bible study led by the Curate in the manse was attended by a coke sipping male who burped loudly and frequently; a shoeless male with remarkably large, battered, misshapen horny toes, and a gracious Kenyan Christian lady relief nurse from the local hospital. All made insightful, articulate, contributions.

Moree, Forster and Weethalle NSW

At the Gwydir caravan park, Moree NSW, a male accepted testimony, and a Gospel of John. At our motel in Forster, a heavily tattooed middle-aged male in decrepit clothes, used rough language when accepting literature and said, "I can't tell you how !!!??? much this means to me." A beach bike with wide tyres was his pride and joy. A replica skull and cross bones adorned the handlebars and a miniature human skeleton swung from the parcel rack at the back. The motel manager also accepted literature.

An impressive soldier, on leave with his wife and infant child, joined us at the only wayside picnic table in the main street of Weethalle, an outback township in NSW (Yvonne Goolagong who won a Wimbledon singles tennis title was born and raised there). The soldier on home leave served three tours of duty in Iraq and Afghanistan. They accepted literature with thanks.

Queensland (Qld)

In the small township of Montville Qld, Dr Tas Walker on the editorial staff of the well-known 'Creation' magazine, was seated sleepily reading under a shop veranda the book entitled 'What Jesus Started' by Steve Addison. To my surprise he gave me the book, which offered helpful Biblically based insights for outreach ministry.

We spent three days at Caloundra (Sunshine Coast) with Michelle Taylor, an OMS missionary on leave with acute medical issues. Whilst there we enjoyed, with Michelle, the inspiring Christian movie 'I Can Only Imagine' at Maroochydore. Michelle appreciated a JTC. Brent Weaver, a NZ OMS missionary who served as a church multiplication facilitator for Eastern Europe, arrived to catch up with Michelle. They had worked together overseas years before. Brent offered much needed advice about evangelism multiplication. Whilst Jan, Brent and I strolled along the foreshore, we met and discussed with a pleasantly extroverted Chilean family patriarch who asked the usual questions like, "Why does God allow suffering?"

We journeyed with our son and family on the ferry to North Stradbroke Island, Qld. The sun was shining brilliantly. The sky was cloudless and intensely blue. Breezes caressed our faces sub-tropically and gently. Clear blue/green oceanic waters washing onto golden sands, supported a pod of playful porpoises surfing and leaping in rollers offshore. Ospreys and

Brahminy Kites patrolled the beaches. Double Bar Finches, Tawny Grass birds and a variety of Honeyeaters populated the surrounding scrubland.

On our way back to the Gold Coast to visit my sister, we dropped in at the Brewers Pantry next to South Brisbane railway station for coffee. I hand wrote a thank you note for the South Sudanese waitress as follows: "Thank you for your friendly, cheerful, and efficient service. Jesus said, 'I am the light of the world. Whoever follows me shall never walk in darkness, but will have the light of life' (John 8:12). Read the Bible and when you come to a part you understand 'follow' with all your heart and soul and mind'." She read and responded with warm smile and a sincere, "Thank you!"

Waiting in the lounge of the Gold Coast Airport, Qld. were two sisters with Italian heritage. One was married to an Italian citizen. They now lived overseas. The other couple lived in Melbourne. I invited them to read a New Year's Eve Facebook entry entitled: 'God's miraculous intervention', reporting an atheist's change of heart during the bushfires in Mallacoota, SE Victoria, where he prayed for deliverance and God intervened with an unexpected, miraculous wind change - 4000 marooned people on the beach were kept safe! A wonderful platform for discussion! They listened to my story and accepted two Gospels of John with reference to John 8:12 'follow.' One sister read the verse aloud from her Gospel and said, "I remember that verse from school." The other sister asked, "What advice do you have for young married couples?" I replied: "Be kind to one another, tender hearted, forgiving one another, even as God for Christ's sake has forgiven you." Ephesians 4:32. I also added, "Find a group of like-minded people to share, study and pray with." One sister replied, "I am already on that journey." I told her, "Keep your eyes on Jesus and your chin out of the dust." The other sister said, "Good advice." We parted with handshakes. Meeting with this delightful foursome was a God-incident.

Orleigh Park, Brisbane Riverside Qld

Leroy, a Kiwi, sitting on a park bench in Orleigh Park said, "It's not often strangers are willing to talk." He had travelled to many countries, dabbling in Buddhism, Hinduism, Islam and various other philosophies. He questioned me respectfully on my views on each, then raised issues re Christianity, the Bible, the church and accepted a TPTL NT*. He said, "I've enjoyed our conversation and will be sure to read this. Thankyou."

In this park an Aussie dad, his wife and infant daughter had arrived two days ago from Brazil. In answer to the BQ*, he said, "Australia is a safe country, but the cost of living is high." He then joined nearby friends. His Portuguese speaking wife smirked in accented English. "If God is a God of love, why did He allow so much suffering? I travelled forty countries and saw so much. I lost faith years ago."

A tall, straggly haired, bony, middle-aged, glittering green eyed derelict reacted without preamble to my overture of friendship by yelling, "Why should I talk to you? Goodbye!!!" I replied, "No reason." He assertively responded, "Absolutely right!" This was not the first time he had treated me this way. I said, "One day you'll be nice to me and we'll both be surprised."

A Uruguayan tourist sucked Yerba Mate (South American green tea) through a metal straw from a hollowed calabash gourd - a national pastime in his homeland. The tea was prepared by pouring hot water from a flask over powdery leaves resembling dried marihuana. I asked him the BQ*. He replied, "I've travelled the world but can't find the answer." He accepted my story and literature.

A strongly built aspiring professional weightlifter sat with me. Her father, a retired Air Force Officer, served in Butterworth, Malaysia, married her mother, a local Malaysian Muslim, divorced, remarried, and died last year. My contact did not enjoy a good relationship with her foster mother. In answer to the BQ*, she said, "I don't know, but I am a Christian." I asked her, "When did you become a Christian?" She answered, "I've always been a Christian. I sometimes attend an Anglican Church." She listened to my story and accepted the booklet 'Picking up the Pieces.'

I said to an older man, "May I sit here?" He replied, "By all means, but I have friends coming in ten minutes." After some minutes of silence, he opened the conversation saying, "By the way have you heard of …?" He gave me his take on political leadership, then said, "When I was fourteen, I realised that animals, birds and humans are all gods. Everything that happened to me since has confirmed that belief. Nothing has changed my mind." I said to him, "I speak with young people from India who say the same thing. What is your vocation? He replied, "I have two PhD's, lectured at university and then became CEO of a large land development corporation." I asked him, "What would you say to a soldier on the beach at Gallipoli or in the trenches at the Western Front in WW1 who was fatally wounded but still alive with only ten minutes to live?" He replied, "In ten minutes I'd have plenty to say." But he quickly switched to more philosophy. I told him, "I became a Christian when I was fifteen. That decision changed my life. A man with an experience, need never be at the mercy of a man with an argument." Half an hour later he still sat alone. No sign of his friends.

To a one-armed indigenous pedestrian on the river walk I asked, "How did it happen?" He said, "I fell through a window I was cleaning." I said to him, "How do you cope?" He replied, "For a while I was suicidal but survived with positive thinking. I'm now doing a management course." He listened to my testimony and said, "I am a Christian. I read my Bible every night." He accepted a Gospel of John with reference to John 8:12 'follow.'

Pedjo, an ex-Yugoslav national, converted to Christ in NZ, married a Māori lady and now practices dentistry in Brisbane, approached me. We shared stories. Pedjo said to me, "You shouldn't be sitting alone. I'll talk with you." Pedjo was the son-in-law of a disorientated elderly male slowly shuffling past. The elderly man accepted Christmas literature and asked, "How old are you? Are you vegetarian?" With surprise he added, "And you still have your own teeth!"

An African trudged disconsolately along Montague Street, West End Brisbane, with steps slower and slower. Following discreetly, I watched him slump onto a seat in nearby Orleigh Park, as he gazed sadly across the beautiful Brisbane River into the distance. Dossei from the African Republic of Togo in answer to the BQ* said, "I miss my family and there is no peace in the world." I replied, "A world without peace is a world in darkness." He possessed some Bible knowledge and accepted a TPTL NT*. I directed his attention to Matthew 5:13-16 (salt and light) and asked him to read it aloud with his name in verse 14 then said, "God sees you as a very important person." A smile lightened his tired and sad features. I went on to say, "I spoke to you two years ago." I recalled his Scottish family name and his relationship with the Togoland royal family.

An Asian Monk in saffron robes at the West End ferry terminal was meditating with the aid of his electronic device. This non-English speaking Tibetan showed me an APP in English of his guru, the Dalai Lama, then reverted to his incantations.

In Brisbane, our burly, muscular, tattooed taxi driver became suicidal during his fifteen-year prison sentence, but through Bible reading was miraculously saved and now shares his faith at every opportunity. He related this story of a farmer who rescued a fluttering eaglet and kept it with his chooks, ducks, and turkeys. A friend offered to release it, but the eaglet refused to fly. It was returned to the chooks, ducks, and turkeys. Another friend offered to teach it to fly but the same happened. A third friend took it early one morning to the brow of a hill. When the eaglet saw the sun rise, it spread it wings and soared into the atmosphere as all eagles should.

I was reminded of Isaiah 40:31 - "Those who wait on the Lord (the Son of Righteousness) shall renew their strength; they shall mount up with wings like eagles, they shall run and not be weary, they shall walk and not faint"

On the plane, Teague, a young male, immediately engaged me in conversation - the tenor of which made me wonder what I would endure for the next two hours. This product of a broken marriage was about to visit his separated father now living in Bali. His grandparents and cousins were church attenders. The BQ* alerted him to the fact that he may be speaking with a Christian. He immediately moderated his views and respectfully asserted among other things that, "I am not concerned about my future. When I die my spirit is put in a bottle and flies into the unknown, after that I don't know, but what do you think?" Jan was praying. During the rest of the journey, he listened to a Gospel presentation, my testimony and accepted a Gospel of John. As we prepared to disembark at Melbourne, he shook my hand, waved his Gospel and declared, "I will read this!"

Back to the Kimberleys WA 2019

In preparation for a nostalgic three weeks return visit to the Kimberleys WA, we took delivery of a motorhome in Darwin NT. The French national employee who serviced our needs, accepted a Gospel of John. He said, "I am a Catholic Christian, but I'm not sure about the 'follow' bit" (John 8:12).

On our first stop in a Katherine NT caravan park a German backpacking couple and American waitress at the local Pop-Up-Cafe accepted Gospels of John. To an older tourist couple with British accents, I asked, "Are you interested in British military history?" "Oh yes," they replied. "Would you be interested in a WW1 replica John's Gospel?" Following a short resume of the background history of this Gospel, they accepted. Two

French backpackers travelling the world in search of reality, listened to my testimony and accepted the 'Finding Hope' booklet.

In a Kununurra WA supermarket, Lucas, an Aboriginal shelf stacker, accepted a Gospel of John, looked at it and said, "I am rebuking Jezebel." I asked "Have you been up to no good?" He replied, "You could say that." I said to him, "Confess and repent!"

Three English tourists at a caravan park, listened to my story, accepted literature and Gospels of John. Donna and Trevor at the Nitmiluk NT National Park kiosk were Māori's residing in Queensland who were impacted by a JTC.

Petra, a good-looking German tourist in Litchfield Tourist Park NT, was born in East Germany. When the Berlin Wall crashed, she relocated to West Germany and became a wealthy businesswoman. She said, "I was born where God was not accepted. As a teen I searched for spiritual reality and concluded that all religions are the same." She accepted a JTC and a John's Gospel. Her attention was drawn to John 8:12. She posed for a photo and hugged us on departure.

Wagga, Young, Rannock and Coolamon NSW

During one of our many journeys to visit relatives and friends in Jan's home country (NSW), we attended a Wagga Baptist Church service. A friendly voice said, "Hello. Do I know you?" Her husband pastored the Baptist Fellowship in Mt Tom Price WA when we pastored in Kununurra. He was now an army chaplain at nearby Kapooka Army Base, where some 800 recruits regularly attend Sunday services. What an amazing evangelistic opportunity. In the afternoon we attended the 50th wedding anniversary celebrations of Jan's friend from Coolamon school days. Her husband worked with Gideons, a Christian outreach group.

Also, we visited friends in a remote farming district near Young NSW. The district was lush after recent rains. Wide horizons, and brilliant sunsets were sights to see. We enjoyed sightings of the magnificent Major Mitchell (pink) Cockatoos and endangered Superb Parrots.

We called in to encourage a wonderful single Christian farmer who was recovering from a major health set back, in the Wagga Hospital. His family and Jan's had been next door neighbours (in Rannock NSW) for over 100 years. Sharing a devotion based on Galatians 2:20* and praying with him was a privilege. Our sister-in-law, with whom we stayed that night, accepted Jan's Testimony Card (JTC).

Rannock, near Coolamon in the northern Riverina district of NSW, was the peaceful Christian farming community in which Jan spent her childhood days and where she learned many of her Christian values. Jan's mother (at ninety-four-years old) was buried in the Rannock cemetery in 2009, alongside Jan's father.

Marrying Jan was the wisest decision I ever made. She is the glittering diamond in the dull greyness of my life, a wonderful life partner during fifty-eight years (at the time of writing) of marriage. She has, among other things, played the larger role in successfully raising our three children. She accompanied me in many exciting missionary adventures, and provided technological know-how and invaluable editorial skills in writing this book.

Taking it to Heart:

1. Why should we understand the cultural and religious background of our multi-cultural neighbours?
2. What are ways by which we might familiarise ourselves with their religious or cultural backgrounds?
3. Discuss how we might personally utilise these principles in daily missionary activities.

References:

Galatians 2:20 – I have been crucified with Christ; it is no longer I who live, but Christ lives in me; and the life which I now live in the flesh I live by faith in the Son of God, who loved me and gave Himself for me.

BQ – Big Question – What is the most important question in all the world for you?

TPTL NT – The Pocket Testament League New Testament.

Chapter 33

Medical Procedures and Birthday Celebrations

New Experiences - Facing Surgery

I commenced fasting at 7.30 am in preparation for surgery scheduled for 1.30 pm at Cotham Private Hospital. At 7.30 pm the anesthetist searched for a vein. He said, "You're being hard to get on with." He finally sent his needle home. The anesthetic burnt its way up my arm.

I said to him, "See you in an hour." I awoke at 9.15 pm with an IV drip in my left arm. A catheter tube emptied into a large drainage bag and also irrigated the site of the surgery with a salt solution. Medical staff calmly chatted as they attended to post operative routines. I was wheeled back to the ward ravenously hungry, however, soggy sandwiches induced nausea and an abrupt loss of appetite. The charge nurse cheerfully removed two blood clots. Instant relief! It was great to be in the care of experienced and capable staff.

MEDICAL PROCEDURES AND BIRTHDAY CELEBRATIONS

Another charge nurse barged in. "I want the colour in your urine clear. You must walk to prevent formation of clots and drink liquid. Take a shower now!" she asserted. Never one to buck authority, I meekly submitted but transferring a weakened wobbly body still affected with anesthetic, fasting and connection to a catheter, from the bed into a small shower cubicle was a major undertaking.

Nurses undressed me. I turned on the tap. Steamy hot water accentuated a prickly hot flush. Dizziness intensified. A strange grayness replaced reality. I hit the red panic button on the way down and sink into oblivion thinking, "Lord is this it?"

Five nurses had somehow man handled my dripping figure complete with attachments onto the bed. My naked glory was now concealed with a blood speckled hospital gown. The charge nurse previously referred to, silently and sheepishly, I think, listened as another nurse with a different focus, steady gaze and confident voice, kindly and firmly explained, "You have been fasting twelve hours, you are losing blood, your IVP drip was removed. Your blood pressure is still down. Take it easy for a while." This made sense.

A tender-hearted Chinese nurse in her first year, was my Carer. She and I discussed life in China. She listened with interest to my testimony. The bed linen, still damp from yesterday's episode, clung to my body. It was changed at my request. Later, they shifted me to another ward. To a Catholic nurse I said, "What is the hardest thing about your job?"

She replied, "Telling relatives their loved one is dead."

I asked her, "But what happens to me when I die?"

She said, "You go to Heaven."

I questioned, "What's your criteria for getting into Heaven?"

She answered, "I am a nurse. I do good things. I've raised kids."

I declared, "I'd like to continue this conversation when convenient." She raced off to her next chore. Despite Herculean efforts not to, I fell asleep during Jan's afternoon visit.

At 6 am the next day, a nurse arrived saying, "I am going to remove your catheter. Hang on to the bed rails. Take some deep breaths. This might tickle a bit." She reefed up my gown. No place for modesty in hospitals! The unceremonious sudden withdrawal of the catheter was accompanied by a shriek from yours truly - loud enough to wake the dead. It felt like my heart and lungs were coming out with the catheter. The nurse apologised with barely concealed laughter. With mock contrition, she cheekily smiled and said, "Would you like some Panadeine?" The pain was already subsiding. The trick now was to get my system working again.

Later, the Catholic nurse, previously referred to, accepted a Gospel of John. I explained, "It might throw more light on yesterdays' question."

- She said, "Thanks, I will read it. My mother is always sending me religious stuff."
- Jan arrived with cheerful news: My first ever speeding infringement notice was withdrawn because of a plea. I also received a generous gift to support my city ministry.
- My Moroccan contact and his fiancée attended the first Alpha class at our church.
- The hospital chaplain visited and asked perceptive questions.
- The pathology report confirmed no malignancy.

An early set back - waterworks were not functioning! The specialist sent a message that he would call on me at 5 pm. He didn't turn up. Nurses conducted regular ultrasounds, prescribed two pain-killers and a sachet of Citralite to relieve razor blade sensations. The problem resolved. I tracked down the Chinese nurse and gave her Chinese literature and thanked her for her tender care. Jan brought me home at midday.

Fainting was a new experience for me. My shrunken, shriveled, dehydrated, blue veined hands made me realise I was not getting any younger. This sight shocked me somewhat. No post-operative pain was experienced. I was unaware of whether or not I received a spinal anesthetic to relieve pain but may have. The surgeon prescribed no medication. I expected large doses of antibiotics. Jan and I enjoyed incredible peace of mind during that week. God did it in answer to prayer.

I had been on my feet too long. I purchased a cappuccino in Box Hill Centro. Two uniformed Salvation Army Officers were sitting nearby. It occurred to me that I should speak to them. But how? Maybe I should draw their attention to an Easter theme? I leafed through my New Testament. I know – post resurrection! I wrote on a notebook page the following text: "And they went out and preached everywhere, the Lord working with them and confirming the word through the accompanying signs" (Mark 16:20). Beneath this verse I wrote, "Lay not down your swords" then dropped the note on their table. One said, "Bless you brother." Maybe they reckoned I was a fruit cake. I hope they were challenged.

My physique following post operative surgery withstood the rigors of street ministry well. It seemed, 'I will lay not down my sword' for a while yet –

> "Onward Christian soldiers marching as to war,
> With the Cross of Jesus going on before,
> Christ the royal Master leads against the foe.
> Forward into battle see His banner go!
> Marching as to war with the Cross of Jesus going on before.
> My battle cry. Hallelujah!"

Old Men Should Never Run in Rainstorms!

However, some ominous black clouds were looming up in the western sky. Soon after disembarking from the bus, the heavens opened. Threatened with thunder, soaked in seconds, and harassed with hail, I ran huffing and puffing, up a nearby friend's driveway towards shelter in their carport, but my legs gave out. Down I went, base over apex and hit the concrete with a resounding thud. The immediately following chest pain seemed 10/10 in severity. I was struggling to regain my feet and breath. Rain, hail, and wind with runnels of water on either side was daunting.

Thinking I'd had a severe heart attack, I wondered if I would make it. Jan arrived home in the nick of time and drove me to the Emergency Department at Box Hill Hospital. They checked for heart function, but swinging bricks don't respond to medical technology. They searched for my brain to check for strokes but couldn't find it. Every movement was difficult and painful due to several fractured ribs. Getting wet was better than broken ribs - all of which proved a point. I was getting older and sillier every day, but praise God, I'm still here. The doctor reckoned I would be out of action for a few weeks. The lesson learned – old men should never run in rainstorms.

Medical Procedures

I attended the Box Hill Gardens Day surgery for a medical procedure. Colonoscopies are no big deal these days, however, the lead up preparation is harsh, the thought of needles appalled me and the surgeon warned it could go wrong. I read my copy of the tract 'When I am afraid', which included these words: "The Lord will watch over your coming and going both now and forever more" (Psalm 121:8). I surrendered my anxiety to the Lord, believed His promises and received His peace. They wheeled me off. The needle sting was faint. I said to the surgical team, "Did you hear about the drunk who staggered out of Young and Jacksons? Two approaching nuns dressed in identical habits split and passed by - one on either side of him. The old drunk said, 'How did she do that?'" The surgeon smiled. The anesthetist couldn't get the needle in quick enough. Drowsiness overwhelmed me. I said, "See you shortly" and hey presto!

The nurse called, "Wake up Mr. Kelly you are in the recovery room." It was a beautiful sleep but the lady in the next bed was hallucinating. Soon after I was diagnosed at Box Hill hospital with pneumonia and was promptly shunted off to Bellbird Hospital and treated with intravenous antibiotics. Four days later discharged with a further prescription of oral antibiotics. During hospitalisation a Vietnamese nurse, a Mauritian male nurse, a Filipino nurse, and an Indian nurse accepted TPTL NTs*.

One night, I experienced excruciating pain. I attended Cotham Road Clinic for keyhole surgery for removal of my gall bladder. I was introduced to the anesthetist. In an effort to delay loss of control of life for as long as possible I said to the surgical team "Do you realise seven-fifths of all people do not understand fractions?"

The attending nurse, with impish grin said, "You've got time left for half a joke." The needle was home. I was gone for an hour and twenty minutes. Ghastly apparitions with bulging bloodshot eyes surrounded me as I woke up. They gaped with mouths as raging roaring lions with teeth sharp like spears and arrows. Their tongues were sharp swords. My breathing was partially obstructed. Couldn't yell! Couldn't move! I was momentarily terrified! The surgeon had removed a large gall stone and gave it to me as a memento. I still have it at the time of writing. Nurse number one listened to my testimony but thought I was still hallucinating. My sheets were blood stained. Nurse number two thoughtfully cleaned my bloody incisions. Number three applied waterproof dressings. By 3pm I felt better and showered, forgetting to remove my glasses. The patient next door persistently and powerfully dry reached.

Everyone, including the dedicated, hardworking nurses, were exhausted. The dry-reacher and a nice old gentleman with a bypass from Barham NSW, accepted literature. I arrived home about 1pm. I went to the bathroom and put Jan's glasses on over mine. I must've been off the planet! I needed reassuring. Our church prayed for me at both Sunday morning services. Several good folks assured me by telephone of their prayers. Two contacts from Blackburn Square also telephoned. Seven visitors arrived at various stages during the afternoon. Several cards were received in the mail. I was assured, encouraged, and honoured beyond measure.

An Unexpected Broken Ankle

An unexpected life changing event for Jan and me occurred as we headed for our regular fortnightly Friday Church Coffee morning. On the way, an appointment took Jan to the local hairdressing salon. She said, "I'll get my hair fixed and come back for you."

I suggested, "No! I'll come with you, and we'll go directly to the function." Bad move! I'd forgotten the descending step immediately inside the salon rear car park entrance.

Down I went, with agonising lower left leg pain. (refer to 'Foreword') I waited over one hour for ambulance transport to Box Hill Hospital where my dislocated ankle was reset. On Sunday afternoon I was transferred to an Epworth Eastern Hospital Orthopaedic ward where the next day, two screws were surgically implanted in the broken right side of the ankle and a metal plate on the left side fracture. My leg was encased in plaster.

To a night duty nurse, I said, "My wife and I have been married fifty-five years."

She asked, "What is your secret for marriage?"

I explained, "We follow Christian guidelines." She accepted the 'Blessings' card, but at 2am, realising I hadn't related even one of these guidelines to her, I hand wrote Ephesians 4:31* on note paper and called her back.

She said, "I'll treasure this for the rest of my life." A beautiful floral arrangement arrived from our daughter-in-law in Brisbane. A kindly Mauritian born cleaner, who accepted the 'Blessings' card, returned at the completion of her shift and watered the flowers.

A Respite Patient!

Because my accident occurred just prior to Christmas, no 'Rehab' facility was available. Impossible independent mobility meant I could not negotiate the front or rear steps of our home in a wheelchair. An Occupational Therapist and Physiotherapist explored all avenues with the only option being the Blue Willows Aged Care Facility in Ringwood, as a respite patient. A friendly competent Asian male nurse, who prepared me for discharge from Epworth, accepted a 'Blessings' card saying, "My mother is Christian, but father is communist."

On arrival at Blue Willows, the supervising admissions nurse began weeping during the admission procedure. She apologetically told me, "I've just received news that my dear friend since school days was killed in a motor car accident in Canberra this morning." Heart-broken, she accepted a 'Blessings' card, and prayer. With relief she exclaimed, "I needed that!"

My accident triggered an array of financially disadvantaging, administrative, and physical difficulties for the year ending 2020 and a game changer for 2021. Rick Warren, an American Pastor, authored a best seller entitled 'The Purpose Driven Church', which sold millions. Warren channelled the huge profits from the sales of this book into church ministries. During the fame, accolades and plaudits which followed, his wife suffered with cancer. Warren's example of care in the midst of difficulties helped guide me through my bruises of life.

One evening, while talking to Jan on my iPhone, a nurse's inadvertent comment triggered a fusillade of loud frustrated complaints. Jan, still connected, overheard our conversation. The nurse departed. Jan said over the phone, "Bruce, you unloaded all your frustrations on that poor nurse who was doing her best to help you. You should apologise!" So, I apologised unreservedly and was forgiven. Paul said in Philippians 4:11, "I have learned in whatever state I am to be content." This 'contentment' lesson further eased the recovery process for both Jan, me, and the nursing staff.

The Apostles Creed says the chief end of man is to glorify God and enjoy Him forever. This maybe truer in suffering than elsewhere. What happens when health and life are in jeopardy? If we would glorify Christ in our dying, we must experience death as gain, Christ must be our prize, treasure, and joy. God must be so deeply satisfying that when death takes all we love but gives us more of Christ we count it gain. When we are satisfied with Christ in dying He is glorified in our death. Christian joy whatever the pain, powerfully testifies to Christ's supreme and all satisfying worth. Though our worldly foundations may crumble:

a) God provides every need for our ransomed souls forever.
b) Christ died for us.
c) and sits at God's right hand making intercession for us.
d) Scriptures never fail us.
e) The Holy Spirit interprets Scriptures to guide and comfort.
f) Prayer and faith make bitter waters sweet.

A Christian song puts it this way:

> "As I travel through the bad and good,
> Keep me travelling the way I should,
> Where I see no way to go,
> You'll be telling me the way I know.
> And so, from the old I travel to the new.
> Keep me travelling along with you."

Later, another nurse confided that she lost her mother with cancer when she was seven. She herself was diagnosed with MS as a teenager. Rick Warren's experience of blessings and bruises and my testimony gripped her. Acting under God's authority I pronounced His blessing upon her (Numbers 6:27*). She said, "That's lovely!" and accepted the 'Blessings' card'. Removal of the plaster cast by a locum doctor and fitting the moon-boot three weeks after surgery in the dining room of the respite home, stimulated the interest of several curious residents.

A second locum, a devout Christian, later removed some stitches. His gentle disposition and tender care were reassuring. The Filipino waitress asked, "Are you Christian?"

I responded, "Yes."

She stated, "I am too." She accepted a 'Blessings' card and said, "This is so lovely.'"

An elderly resident conducted a small service each Sunday in this facility with tapes of sermons by her deceased relative with three elderly and infirm residents. The oldies listened to my testimony and received 'Blessings' cards. A gentle, tender, and intelligent young Muslim nurse accepted a TPTL* New Testament with reverence and thanks. During my convalescence more than twenty 'Blessings' cards were accepted.

Upon discharge from Blue Willows on January 13, I was conveyed home by Patient Transport. A welcoming committee of family and friends assisted me up the back steps. The ankle bones had healed well. Two follow-up surgeries were required to remove the plate, clean up infection, and re-suture. The healing process continued for eight months.

Regular follow-up treatment by excellent home care nurses, and muscle strengthening exercises supervised by a visiting vibrant young physio, enabled me to progress not fast enough from the wheelchair, to crutches and a walker. Thankfully, I began to walk unassisted to and from the local shopping centre.

My ankle may never fully recover but with some adjustments I have mobility and can get back to normal life. In all this I have developed a better understanding and huge admiration for our health care professionals at every level. Our family blessed us with transport to and from hospital on several occasions, lawn mowing, and loving care. Friends turned up with encouragement, equipment, and meals. Neighbours also offered helping hands. Our wonderful church provided pastoral care, prayers, and moral support. Jan and I are eternally grateful to one and all. Thank you!

Birthday Celebrations
70th Birthday

To help celebrate my 70th birthday at the NewHope Baptist Church, my beautiful, capable, lovely wife induced 100 guests to attend this function in my honour. How she achieved this miracle beats me. Maybe she called 'Renta-Crowd?'

To my surprise (I actually wasn't sure what to expect) our son-in-law, Peter, unfolded a 'This is your life' presentation in dramatic fashion. One after another of the guests related briefly certain aspects of my life as they saw it. One guest told the story of a magnificent (????) winning partnership in which we shared on a local country cricket ground.

Included in the guest list were former members of the Wandin Baptist Church, and the Spanish and English-speaking folks from Altona Meadows Church. Some became Christians and were baptised during our ministry in both these churches. Craig and Lyn Siggins, Baptist missionaries to the Aboriginal folks in Newman WA where Jan and I ministered in interim roles on two occasions, happened to be in Melbourne on holidays from Perth. Their appearance pleasantly astonished me.

Six Indian students from the street ministry in Bourke Mall attended. At least one of whom had taken a significant step to be a follower of Jesus. They had visited our home and cooked an Indian meal for us and our family. Their hot curry made our Aussie foreheads sweat, noses run and tears flow. "But we made it mild specially for you," they laughed. A student from my Bethel Bible teaching class and friends from China, Taiwan, and African countries also attended. Two of the world's most beautiful grand-kids read short tributes they had composed. We have hand-written transcripts for posterity. Jonathan (our youngest son) made an encouraging and moving speech.

Soon it was time to respond, but Peter had pinched most of my material in his 'This is your life' segment. Jan had hidden my notes and my daughter with heavy emphasis and stern looks, stressed, "Dad, don't speak too long!" I opted instead therefore to introduce the Men For Missions 'Hope For Haiti' video with an invitation to finance the purchase of solar-powered, fix-tuned radios with Gospel ministry for Haitians living in the world's second most poverty-stricken nation. This gift helped facilitate good quality Gospel broadcasts from radio 4VEH to disadvantaged locals. Praise God, some $1,600 was donated for this project in lieu of birthday gifts.

80th Birthday

My 80th birthday was celebrated in the Light Community Baptist Church (LCBC) community hall with some sixty people of multi-cultural backgrounds and members of our own family present. The church ladies produced a huge array of delicious desserts, with Matt as MC, several speeches, Zac on violin and two singers leading guests in singing 'Amazing Grace', Pastor Dean's prayer and the cutting of the large birthday cake, concluded the celebrations. The following borrowed comments (I'm not sure who from) were in essence the basis of my speech:

> "God works in mysterious ways His wonders to perform!
> There comes a time when we must realise life is short
> And in the end the only thing that really counts
> Is not how others see us, but how God sees us.
> For the believer there is hope beyond the grave,
> because Jesus Christ has opened the door
> to Heaven for us by His death and Resurrection."
> My key verse was -
> "Now that I am old and grey, O God, let me proclaim your power
> to all who come after me." (Psalm 71:18)

We thanked God for the gracious provision, loving care of His people and the Pastor and members of the LCBC - a church that follows Jesus - a place of hope where people encounter His love, power, and truth.

I resisted retreating into a holier than thou Christian ghetto called Christian fellowship. I have also resisted (not always successfully) surrendering to the values of a secular, materialistic, post Christian society - not the easiest confluence in which to practice faith. But there's no turning back, for in this maelstrom of struggle I have encountered God and met many beautiful people. I wouldn't trade places with Shane Warne, posthumously awarded an OA medal for his services to Australian test cricket, for millions of dollars. My birthday bashes were memorable. I thank God for Jan and family and the many friends who helped make each celebration a memorable event.

A favourite chorus sang each Tuesday evening at our two-year Bethel Bible study course says it all:

> "Something beautiful, something good.
> All my confusion He understood,
> All I had to offer Him was brokenness and strife,
> But He makes something beautiful of my life."

References:

Numbers 6:27 – So they shall put my name on the Children of Israel, and I will bless them.

Ephesians 4:31 - Let all bitterness, wrath, anger, clamor, and evil speaking be put away from you, with all malice.

TPTL NT – The Pocket Testament League New Testament.

Chapter 34

Legendary Mentors

Rev Dr Graeme Smith, Frank Jenner, Arthur Stace, Rev Charles Spurgeon, Frank Sladek, Rev Jim Faulkner, Rev Dr Wesley Duewel, and Bill Pomery.

Rev Dr Graeme Smith

Graeme mentored me significantly during his tenure on the pastoral team at the North Blackburn Baptist Church over several years. Without his consistent Biblically based preaching and in-depth training in a two-year Bethel Bible study series, I may never have embarked on a twenty plus year street ministry. I thank God for Graeme's mentorship, which is referred to in greater depth elsewhere in this book.

Jenner of George Street

In May 2003, while I was undertaking cleaning duties at the North Blackburn Baptist Church, a lady walked back and forth along the Springfield Road footpath outside the front entrance of the church. I felt constrained to talk with her. She began attending church. Later, she gave me a book, for which she paid $1 at a local Op Shop and said, "I thought you might like it." This book entitled 'Jenner of George Street' still challenges, encourages, and inspires my adventures in grassroots outreach ministry.

Frank Jenner arrived in Australia from the UK in 1928 as a troubled young sailor. Twice he had jumped ship. He was hopelessly addicted to gambling. He had limited education and was plagued with life-long health problems. Though gloriously converted he was never invited to take leadership in any church, however, many of his converts became well-known Christian leaders.

The central business district of Sydney (NSW) has always been big and full on. I was on a pilgrimage to nearby Hyde Park and George Street, where Jenner prowled in the late forties and early fifties. I wanted to capture some inspiration from his extraordinary ministry. His modus operandi was simple. He would materialise unexpectedly from behind a tree or building and place his hand on the shoulder of some startled pedestrian. With vocal intensity unmatched and piercing gaze, he bluntly confronted his victims with direct reference to their eternal destiny. "Excuse me!" he would say. 'If you die tonight and God said, 'Why should I let you into my Kingdom?' What would you say?'" He aimed to speak to ten people daily. He did so for twenty-eight years. It was estimated he challenged 100,000 people with this same simple, brief, and powerful one sentence sermon.

Later, one Sunday evening, the Rev Francis Dixon, a famous British Baptist preacher, opened an evening service at Bournemouth Baptist Church, England for testimonies. A Christian in Dixon's congregation stood to his feet and said, "I was walking down George Street, Sydney at the end of WW2. Suddenly this strange man appeared from nowhere and asked, 'If God said, why should I let you into My Kingdom?' What would you say?'" Unable to dispel these words from his mind and under increasingly intense conviction, this ex-sailor gave his life to Christ.

A second man in the congregation that night likewise stood and said, "I'm another."

On a world-wide preaching crusade, Rev Dixon visited Australia and told this story wherever he preached. In Adelaide, an individual said, "I'm another!"

In Perth an ex RAN sailor proclaimed, "I'm another!"

In England a young woman also shouted, "I'm another!" A British missionary in the Mediterranean, a female missionary in India, an Australian in the West Indies, and American servicemen, all told the same remarkable story.

Rev Dixon located Jenner in Sydney. When told the news, Jenner cried for joy. He never knew if any of his contacts went on with the Lord but kept faithfully 'sounding out the Word' and trusting God for the harvest. One lone man standing in 'front of them all' with a one sentence sermon challenging thousands, inspires me to this day.

The gift of a secondhand book from a woman with two attention deficient little boys, running uncontrolled through the congregation during services, encouraged me. I still wonder if that lonely, disadvantaged soldier's wife, last heard of in Darwin, realised how much her gift inspired me? I am forever grateful to God for her ministry.

Marius, a smiling tourist next to me in Hungry Jacks, George Street, Sydney, was killing time reading a book while waiting to board his plane for Germany that evening. He listened to my testimony, including Jenner's question and accepted a Gospel of John. He said, "I hope there is someone up there, but so far, I have managed to achieve all my goals in my own strength."

A spruiker in Swanston Street Melbourne, challenged the accuracy of scriptures. She believed about but not in God. I asked her the Frank Jenner question. "If you died today, why would God let you into His kingdom?" She accepted Dixon's booklet based on John 3:16*. I have used the Jenner question in my testimony countless times since.

Arthur Stace and the Millennium Bug

It occurred to me that our 2000 New Year celebration activities should be recorded. Millenniums don't come around very often. It was a milestone in history, but like most milestones, details fade from memory unless documented. I had never given thought to millenniums. However, as 1999, with its speculation about the millennium bug molehill developing into a mountain approached, I wondered how to record this special event for my own posterity. Some friends came to our rescue. They invited Jan and me with others to their home to celebrate New Year's Eve millennium celebrations together.

We watched some interesting video footage of early Australian history and at midnight, on wide screen the fireworks with the word 'Eternity' emblazoned across Sydney Harbour Bridge. The 'Eternity' word went global on TV networks.

Arthur Stace, a simple Christian, through this single word 'Eternity' handwritten in chalk on thousands of footpaths so long ago, became a world-famous graffiti artist. His 'Eternity' testimony lives on.

Under the ministry of an Anglican Priest in Sydney, Arthur Stace, an unlikely hero with a horrid background, at his lowest ebb attended a service at which a well-known Baptist evangelist, John Ridley, preached. A record survives of Ridley's sermon notes. He began by quoting Isaiah 57:15:

> "For thus says the High and lofty one who inhabits
> ETERNITY whose name is Holy.
> I dwell in the high and holy place,

> with him who has a humble and contrite spirit
> to revive the spirit of the humble,
> and to revive the heart of the contrite ones."

Then, in his strong, earnest voice, Ridley let rip. In his final plea, Ridley raised his voice even louder and shouted, "Eternity! Eternity! I wish I could shout that word to everyone in the streets of Sydney. Eternity, friends you have got to meet it. Where will you spend eternity?" Mr. Stace left the Tabernacle with that word 'Eternity' ringing through his brain. 'Stace was converted.'

Suddenly he felt a powerful call from the Lord to write 'Eternity' on the footpath. He had chalk in his pocket, and outside the church, bent down and right there, wrote it. From that moment on, he wrote 'Eternity' on thousands of footpaths all over Sydney and beyond. That one-word sermon by one lone Baptist layman, standing in front of them all, was shared with millions. We will never know how many lives he influenced. Stace's life story is recorded in the book entitled 'Mr. Eternity' by Roy Williams with Elizabeth Meyers. It is inspiring reading. May all who come behind find us faithful. May the fires of our devotion light the way. May our footprints lead lost souls to believe.

During the early hours of New Year's Day, the millennium bug died in its sleep, but the world's problems continued. Populations have increased from millions to billions. Each person with Eternity written on their souls needs the Saviour. This monumental evangelistic task was too big for one person to grasp, but not too big for God. Though God may ask us to share in this massive task, He will always lead us on in triumph (2 Corinthians 2:14*).

Stace was a special kind of man specially used for God's special purpose at a unique time in history. Immortalised by that word 'Eternity' blazing forth from Sydney Harbour Bridge on the Millennium, Stace is a classic illustration of the 'one man standing principle.' You're unlikely to read stories like this in today's news media. Some of us have remarkable stories to tell in this regard.

In the Block Arcade, Melbourne, a young blue-eyed blonde, who recently arrived from Sydney, handed out free samples. I told her, "I made a pilgrimage to George Street and Hyde Park in Sydney."

She asked "Why?"

I said, "To soak up the atmosphere created by Mr. Eternity. Have you heard of him?"

She replied, "I think so." I asked the BQ*. "She replied with furrowed brow, "I'd love to know why I am here." She accepted the tract entitled 'Life's Greatest Question' and listened as I shared my testimony.

Rev Charles Haddon Spurgeon

On a bitterly cold Sunday morning in January 1850 a young man set off on foot through a snowstorm in appalling weather to find a place of worship. He came across a small chapel with about fifteen people in attendance. The young man sat alone. The preacher, uneducated, uncouth, and unknown couldn't even pronounce his words properly but what happened there changed this young man forever. The preacher's text was Isaiah 45:22:

> "Look to Me and be saved,
> All you ends of the earth!
> For I am God, and there is no other."

The congregation was urged to 'Look to Christ'. God used this simple direct challenge from an ordinary speaker to open the eyes of that young visitor. The identity of the preacher may never be known but God used his stammering faltering message to convert a young man who became the best known, popular preacher in Victorian Britain - Charles Haddon Spurgeon.

We may feel we are not specially gifted and don't have great opportunities to serve Christ. We may never be another Charles Spurgeon or Billy Graham; however, God uses ordinary Christians who stay faithful to Him. Who knows who God will bring across your path, and how He will use you to bring glory to Him? ('The People's Preacher C.H. Spurgeon' by Peter Morden).

Private Frank Sladek

Pte Sladek, a most remarkable evangelist, handed out thousands of New Testaments (NTs) over years of ministry in various Australian cities. The following comments are compiled from information supplied by Pte Frank in our frequent conversations outside Young and Jacksons' famous pub in Swanston Street, Melbourne. Also, from a copy of Frank's circular letter which I still possess; his autobiography, and an article in the Brisbane Courier Mail. Frank, in his military uniform purchased at a disposal store, looked every inch a front-line commando in God's army, under the command of Jesus Christ.

Frank was born in Czechoslovakia in 1928 where he lived until he was recruited into the communist army. He escaped but languished in a German refugee camp for two years. He then fled those over-crowded often inhumane conditions by jumping on board a passing circus train. After working as a labourer with them, he reached a British occupied part of Germany, applied for a visa to Australia and arrived in Adelaide as a displaced person in 1950, where he spent time in another camp, which he found luxurious by comparison. Frank was employed by the South Australian railways as a greaser for many years, but an upheaval, he was reluctant to discuss, changed his life. Reading a Good News NT in 1990 launched him on his lone crusade to save troubled souls.

Pte Frank was hired for two weeks by the owner of a mansion to build a retaining wall on Mount Lofty, Adelaide SA. He was accommodated on the property for the duration of his employment but finished up staying fourteen years in the same tiny shed with a bed, a sooty old fireplace, no power or running water, a few personal belongings, and possums cavorting on the roof top at night to keep him company. Frank called it his divisional HQ. Various jobs, including gardening, supplemented his pension, which enabled him to purchase and distribute 165,000 NTs free of charge to strangers in the streets of Brisbane, Sydney, Melbourne, and Adelaide since 1990.

In Swanston Street I watched surprised as pedestrians, often student groups, lined up to receive their copy of the NT. Frank offered me one to give away. Twenty meters up the street, a homeless West Australian selling magazines for profit, accepted Private Frank's NT. I invited the vendor to tell me his story. People are often more willing to share their stories than some Christians are to listen. By mid-afternoon that day Frank had given away his 320th copy. Each NT hand-over was accompanied with a snappy salute. He kept plenty of ammunition (NTs) ready to ensure he never ran short of bullets. Frank invested all his savings and much of his pension money in the purchase of NTs from the Bible Society Bookshop, 133 Rundle Mall, Adelaide SA 5000.

Occasionally, Frank, then seventy-five years old, found it necessary to defend his innocence in law courts for breaching council by-laws by handing out literature without a permit. Once he paid $500 for a plane flight from Adelaide to Brisbane to fight charges. He pushed his trolley bearing an Australian flag and a box full of Bibles into the court as an exhibit. The charges against him were proven but the Magistrate recorded no convictions and awarded no costs. She suggested Private Frank not return to the City Mall to hand out Bibles until he had liaised with the local council.

After the court, Frank was filmed on the streets for half an hour, appeared on Channel 9, plus radio reports and was written up in the Brisbane Courier mail. Following this publicity, people accepted Bibles with the comment "I saw you on TV." The things which happened to Frank actually turned out for the furtherance of the Gospel (Philippians 1:12*). He signaled his intention of applying to Brisbane City Council for a permit.

A feature article appeared in the Adelaide Sunday Mail on 8/11/2002 entitled 'Bible Man Frank's Life of Poverty'. He also appeared on Channel 9 TV evening news. He was a classic example of 'one man in front of them all' with the good news of the Gospel.

Pte Frank conducted many missions interstate during which he was evicted seven times, arrested, and issued with infringement notices. His crime? He was not licensed to give away Holy Bibles. In the Queen Street Mall, Brisbane a licence cost $425, which he refused to pay, so he was a lawbreaker. He was summoned as follows: 'You are hereby commanded in Her Majesty's name to appear in courthouse No. 15, 5th floor, 179 North Quay, Brisbane, at 10am on 16/4/2003. Failure to do so will cause the court to proceed accordingly.' "This is it my Lord! I will defend you my Lord before my Gallio" (Acts 18:12*).

Frank's Letter 18/4/2003

I arrived at Anzac Square Arcade in Adelaide Street, Brisbane at 2pm giving out Bibles. The harvest was big, fish were biting, a passing Anglican Clergy told me, "My friend you are doing a good job for the Lord."

Pte Frank replied, "Not much longer Reverend, tomorrow I go to Court here in Brisbane and hopefully I go behind bars to serve for my crime."

The clergyman replied, "What? I cannot believe they can do this to you." He got angry. "I will see to it that everybody in Brisbane knows about it." Half an hour later I had TV cameras, filming my activities from every angle - the camera had the Channel 9 insignia.

The cameraman said, "Tomorrow, they will interview you for our programme."

When I appeared at the courthouse the next day to my shock three TV cameras were pointing at me. I thought they were filming passers-by. I was wrong. As I was climbing up the long steps with my carton of Bibles on my trolley for the Magistrate's exhibit, the filmmakers focused their cameras on me. From the waiting room I could see her Honour, the Magistrate. She was about fifty and looked like she had a face of steel. I was her last client. As she called my name, I rolled with my carton of Bibles on my trolley plus a display poster which said, 'It is not too late Adelaide, Sydney, Melbourne, Brisbane' with the Aussie flag flying over, plus the sign Private Frank on the board. As I bowed before her Honour, she asked me, "Mr Sladek you have been distributing Bibles in Queen Street Mall without a permit, do you feel guilty?"

Frank replied, "Yes, your honour, I feel guilty because I could not afford to come here all the way from Adelaide and pay $425 for a permit plus $500 for the airfare."

She said to me, "It is your duty to obtain a permit." The clerk of the court read the charges against me. Nine missions without a licence plus three infringement notices. I noticed her Honour's face looked more friendly toward me. To my shock, her Honour stopped the court clerk reading further charges against me, then she stated, "Mr Sladek tell me more about yourself."

"Yes, your Honour. I was a refugee in Germany after WW2. I was in a refugee camp, hungry – no future for employment and alien in that land.

Your government paid my fare to come here and gave me new hope in my life. When I discovered that our young people become refugees in their own land, I started to give out those Good News Bibles in capital cities in Australia. If I only saved one criminal from gaol to society, I saved the Queensland government over $100,000 a year. If I save only one teenager from drugs - to mum and dad, I have paid my debt to this great country. I became a beggar for the sake of my belief."

Her Honour said, "I am discharging all the case against you and all the costs. Also, I am taking into account you came all the way from Adelaide to come before me and you have paid more than $500 for the airfare. This case is closed." She took her bundle of papers with her and left with a smile for me.

The cameramen had been waiting two hours and the man from Channel 9 asked me many questions - so did a lady. They told me the programme would be on that night after the news. I went back to Anzac Square Arcade and gave away my last two cartons of Bibles.

Signed Pte Frank Sladek."

Written at Mt Lofty Shed, Adelaide SA on 18/4/2003

"The next morning, I stood in a long queue at the airport when a pretty airport hostess said, "Sir I saw you on TV last night, it lasted half an hour. It was good."

I replied, "Young lady would you like my last Bible?"

She said to me, "I would be honoured."

On the plane the lady sitting next to me told me, "I saw you on TV last night, I liked it." When I got to Adelaide I did two hours of gardening, then went to the Bible shop to pick up Bibles for the Mall.

The manager told me, "You have been on TV in Brisbane, in newspapers, plus radio - the newspaper headline said, 'Brisbane City Council Took God to Court'." I was 100% sure I would be fined for my nine offences and three infringements and was willing to serve it in Her Majesty's prison, but my Gallio did not see it that way, nor did my Commander and my Lord Jesus Christ. "My Lord, I served you for Your glory as far as I could, have mercy on me."

Frank's strenuous pick and shovel gardening work paid for the bulk of his Bibles, but his ageing body was cracking up. He was getting beyond hard work. How many more Bibles could he give away? He would love to retire and give out Bibles full time, but funding concerns drove him on. "If I close my mission, thousands of empty souls will miss out on reading the Good News of Jesus," he lamented. The Bible Society sold Frank's biography. The profits went a small way toward paying for his Bible distribution programme.

Bill Pomery

Our dear beloved prayer warrior, Melva Pomery, passed away peacefully, surrounded by her loving family. I pray for her husband Bill, ninety-eight years old (when writing this book), as he adjusts to life without his wife of sixty-nine years and soldiers on for His Lord and Saviour in Naracoorte, SA.

We first met Bill, on a One Mission Society (OMS) Indonesia Missions trip in 1984. Bill, a former Mayor of Naracoorte, Stawell Gift finalist and prominent local cricketer, has won many to the Lord, supports missionaries world-wide through extensive prayer, letter writing and literature distribution, and remains remarkably influential in the Naracoorte Baptist Church. He has sacrificially prayed and supported Jan and me over many years. He carefully insists that all is by the grace of God.

Rev Jim Faulkner

In August 2006 Jan and I attended a One Mission Society (OMS) International Board Meeting in the Kruger National Park, South Africa. We have a long involvement with the Australian OMS ministry going back many years. Upon arrival in Johannesburg, South Africa, on our way to the board meeting we met Jim Faulkner, Chairman of the British OMS Board.

Upon learning of my street ministry in Melbourne, he replied, "How interesting! Last week I watched a Christian TV documentary in the UK. A man who shared his testimony on that program said, 'A grey headed old Aussie talked about Jesus and gave me a Gospel of John as I walked along Swanston Street, Melbourne." Through that conversation and the Gospel gift, he became a Christian and now leads a British Christian mission organisation. Jim reckoned that old Aussie was me. I have no recollection of that event. It could have been me, but the point is someone gave out a Gospel and God grew that gift into a Kingdom victory. Jim signed up to receive my monthly newsletters, and faithfully prayed for us and communicated regularly. His wonderfully encouraging messages contained assurances of prayers for protection and ministry opportunities. One scripture he forwarded:

> "Do you not know that those who run in a race
> all run, but one receives the prize?
> Run in such a way that you may obtain it.
> And everyone who competes for the prize is temperate in all things.
> Now they do it to obtain a perishable crown,
> but we for an imperishable crown.
> Therefore, I run thus: not with uncertainty. Thus,
> I fight: not as one who beats the air.

> But I discipline my body and bring it into subjection,
> lest when I have preached to others,
> I myself should become disqualified." (1 Corinthians 9:24-27)

In another reply, Jim said, "I see a light beginning to break through the dark clouds. You are an encouragement. Thanks too for your article on Wesley Duewel. I'm so pleased to have had fellowship from time to time with him." Wesley was an OMS missionary leader of long standing, missionary statesman and author of repute.

Jim posted several entries, one of which is attributed to A.W. Tozer, renowned evangelical author, pastor, and theologian. "God never negotiates with men. Jesus Christ's death on the cross put an end to any negotiations. It is now Christ or nothing. It is now God's Word in its entirety or nothing."

In one of his regular emails, Jim wrote, "I meet with JW's every Monday morn as they have a display outside a shopping centre in our town. Also, at the invitation of Weatherspoon's (owner an Australian!), I and a fellow minister spend two hours with an invitation to folk who wish for prayer or a talk. We are kept quite busy each Thursday am. The battle is the Lord's. Keep going (regards to Jan)."

When news was received that Rev Jim Faulkner died in the UK in November 2018 after a protracted illness, I felt I had lost a wonderful prayer partner and a good friend. Vale Jim. We miss you. An English male asked, "What do you do?" His question led to an opportunity to incorporate the Faulkner story in my testimony.

Dr Wesley Duewel

Reading interesting missionary strategies always grabs my attention. A book entitled 'Touch the World Through Prayer' authored by Dr Wesley

Duewel, a world renowned One Mission Society (OMS) prayer warrior was one such book. Though Wesley went to glory at an advanced age not long ago, he continues mentoring me through his many books. Some of what follows is inspired by the afore-mentioned book.

His book triggered a search of Jan's carefully recorded but somewhat dusty photo albums for further insights. Jan, and I had travelled with Wesley as back seat passengers in a car driven by Rev Mr Cole from Calgary to Camp Caroline, a retreat centre nestled in the foothills of the Rocky Mountains in Canada. We were headed to a Men For Missions (MFM) convention at which Wesley was listed as guest speaker. During this trip, Coles and Wesley, being old hands in the Mission, shared a wealth of mostly humorous and encouraging insights into their missionary adventures. Prayer seemed natural to Wesley.

As I recall, Wesley prayed for most of that journey. Winter had set in. The road surface was icy and slippery. His reminiscences were punctuated with prayers for safety whilst negotiating dangerous conditions along the highway. Unsurprisingly, we arrived safely, allowing Jan and me, a perhaps never to be repeated, short lived, and novel opportunity of cavorting in real Canadian snow.

If you're like me, you may not consider yourself a great Prayer Warrior. Through reading Wesley's book my desire to 'Touch the World Through Prayer' was fortified. Dr Duewel proved from scripture and personal experience that we can not only touch the world through our prayers but help change it. The great lack today is not people or funds, but prayer. God needs us to touch the world through prayer. Fast forward a few years and we find OMS building on the prayer legacy of Wesley and those of his ilk. The Mission was asking God, by His power and grace, and for His glory alone, to enable OMS and partners to give one billion people, the opportunity to hear, understand and believe the Good News of Jesus Christ over the next ten years. Spend a few minutes each day in prayer for the lost and desperately needy. Begin praying for that special person nearest to you.

The early years saw much fasting, prayer, and hard work on the Indian mission field, with little to show for it. For the first twenty-five years, the OMS established Evangelical Mission, planted only one church per year. On a return flight from India to the USA, God challenged Wesley to raise a team of 1,000 homeland prayer supporters to pray each day for the growth of the Indian church. On the night before the Duewels sailed for India in 1940, Mrs Charles Cowman, cofounder with her husband of OMS, reminded the Duewels of a promise God had given her for the opening of OMS work in India: "I will do better unto you than at your beginnings" (Ezekiel 36:11*). Church plants soon dramatically increased to four or five weekly. God rapidly multiplied the work in India in answer to ceaseless prayer (1 Timothy 1:3*).

Now as never before, church doctrines are being weakened by the introduction of fables, legends, old wives' tales, slander, and false doctrine (1 Timothy 1:3*). A case in point: A Sikh taxi driver, on the way to the Melbourne airport, believed the physical world was illusionary, and reality was mystical, thus denying the transcendence of God and the immanent loving Redeemer. Islam, Hinduism, and Buddhism are said to be the fastest growing religions in Australia. Eastern philosophies and the New Age movement values are creeping into our Christian values unawares. The challenge for Christianity is to stand in front of them all with the Crucified, Resurrected living Lord Jesus Christ (1 Corinthians 2:1-2*) in Holy Spirit power.

Prayer, in the power of Jesus' name, more than counteracts the influence of Satan. Make a prayer list. Organise a prayer group. Hold a prayer retreat among your friends who have a burden for evangelism. And pray:

- That churches will remain steadfastly focussed on evangelism, and discipleship by multiplication.

- That churches will faithfully minister the Gospel especially to the underprivileged and marginalised.
- That I will die multiplying and discipling.

Paul wrote, "This is a faithful saying and worthy of all acceptance, that Christ Jesus came into the world to save sinners of whom I am chief. However, for this reason I obtained mercy, that in me first, Jesus Christ might show all longsuffering as a pattern to those who are going to believe on Him for eternal life. Now to the King eternal, immortal, invisible, to God who alone is wise be honour and glory forever and ever. Amen" (1 Timothy 1:16).

Taking it to Heart:

1. Why is it so easy to trust human philosophies rather than the Gospel of Jesus?
2. How can Christians defend the true Gospel?
3. Discuss some ways of extending the Gospel into a pagan society?

References:

Ezekiel 36:11 - I will multiply upon you man and beast; and they shall increase and bear young; I will make you inhabited as in former times, and do better for you than at your beginnings. Then you shall know that I am the Lord.

John 3:16 - For God so loved the world that He gave His only begotten Son that whoever believes in Him should not perish but have everlasting life.

Acts 18:12 - When Gallio was proconsul of Achaia, the Jews with one accord rose up against Paul and brought him to the judgment seat.

1 Corinthians 2:1-2 - And I, brethren, when I came to you, did not come to you with excellence of speech or of wisdom declaring to you the testimony of God. For I determined not to know anything among you except Jesus Christ and Him crucified.

2 Corinthians 2:14 - Now thanks be to God who always leads us in triumph in Christ, and through us diffuses the fragrance of His Knowledge in every place.

Philippians 1:12 - But I want you to know, brethren, that the things *which happened* to me have actually turned out for the furtherance of the gospel.

1 Timothy 1:3 – As I urged you when I went into Macedonia – remain in Ephesus that you may charge some that they teach no other doctrine.

BQ – Big Question – What is the most important question in all the world for you?

Chapter 35

Sacrificial Service – 'Wars, Wounds & Wisdom'

> "But as many as received Him,
> to them He gave the right to become children of God,
> to those who believe in His name."
> (John 1:12)

The story and publication of the Replica World War One John's Gospels designated hereunder as War Gospels (WGs) became a centrepiece of my ministry during ANZAC Day and Remembrance Day celebrations. War Gospels facilitated numerous opportunities for Gospel presentations locally and interstate, including our 50th wedding anniversary celebrations.

Sacrificial Events to Remember

Four serving Victoria Police Officers were killed on Wednesday 22nd April 2020 in the line of duty. Their death, a tragedy unequalled in Victorian policing history, overshadowed the Police service and all Victorians. Although I did not know these officers, their deaths impacted me as a retired Police Officer. This episode highlighted the danger our serving officers face every day while on duty. They are heroes – never to be forgotten!

The coronavirus has impacted our planet in unprecedented ways. Hours, days and weeks of sacrificial duty by medical and support staff in combatting this disease have resulted in many contracting the virus and even loss of life. Their selfless service should be recorded as heroic in the annals of Australian medical history.

ANZAC Day – 'Lest We Forget'

I do not espouse warfare, but sacrificial military service is acknowledged as a major contribution to our present national well-being. The anniversary of the unforgettably tragic dawn landings by Australian and New Zealand Army Corps (ANZACs) on the Gallipoli Peninsula in Turkey during the WW1 is observed on April 25 each year. ANZAC Day was instituted to honour the ANZACs who served and died in their first engagement in WW1. Their historic sacrifices are now remembered as an annual public holiday as a significant part of our national character.

In order to capitalise on the groundswell of community support for the 100th anniversary of our ANZAC heroes, and to exalt the Name of Jesus, replica editions of Active Service WGs (War Gospels) were issued to soldiers on the Western Front during WW1. They were produced for distribution prior to and during the ANZAC centenary celebrations and Remembrance Day observances. Further copies of the War Gospels and other Christian literature is obtainable from SGM Lifewords, PO Box 677, Baulkham Hills NSW 1755.

A good quality ANZAC Day Commemoration brochure issued from the office of the Hon. Kevin Andrews MP, Federal Member for Menzies and then Minister for Defense, was hand delivered to our letter box. In keeping with many ANZAC publications, no reference to the magnificent role of the military chaplains and the effect of Christian literature at Gallipoli and the Western Front in WW1 was made. A letter, including a War Gospel was forwarded to the honourable gentleman drawing his attention to this oversight. No reply was received.

Bishop John Taylor Smith, Chaplain General of the WW1 British forces who was responsible for the issue of the above-mentioned War Gospels, had two major ministry thrusts – to ensure that every soldier entered the trenches with a Gospel to help in his hour of great danger, and in preparing his prospective chaplains for ministry on the front line. His prime question was – "*What would you say to a man fatally wounded but conscious with only ten minutes to live?*"

Around forty-three million items of scripture were distributed during WW1. Each WG included a decision form based on John 1:12.

The final thoughts of fallen soldiers were often recorded in their last letters home. Thousands were killed. As their simple belongings were returned to loved ones, it was discovered that many had written their name on the decision form on the last page of the War Gospels with the date - in some cases only a few days, or even hours before their death. The above verse was used by chaplains as a particularly telling verse when ministering to men on active service.

Many families received a signed WG from a loved one who had never shown interest in the Christian faith. In some instances, bodies were recovered that could only be identified by a signed Gospel in his pocket. For others, the Gospels were treasured as keepsakes and handed down, testifying to the memory of family members who served in WW1.

An extract from SGM Lifewords archives illustrated this: 'A soldier was sent a small Bible book (WG) at the front. With time on his hands, he read and reread it. Despite never showing interest in spiritual things, the words sunk in, and he became a changed man known up and down the trenches as 'Singing Jim'. During a reconnaissance mission, a young soldier from his company was wounded between the trenches. A volunteer was asked to bring him in, and 'Singing Jim' stepped forward. He reached the man under cover of darkness and began crawling home with his friend on his back. Then a flare burst overhead, revealing their position. A single sniper shot rang out and 'Singing Jim' was killed outright. In his pocket was a long letter to his wife about how he had come to Christ, encouraging her to do the same. The wounded man offered to take the letter home to England and deliver it in person, telling this wife how her husband had laid down his life for him. He did indeed deliver it, but his company had one further request. While in England could he pick up more copies of the book 'Singing Jim' had been reading!

Bishop Taylor Smith once had a conversation with a young soldier that went something like this: Bishop: "When you think about the Cross of Christ, what do you see?"

Soldier: "I see Christ and two thieves crucified either side of him."

Bishop: "What else do you see?"

Soldier: "I see the soldiers gambling."

Bishop: "If that is all you see, I think you will have trouble with the Christian life. When I see the Cross with all that – I see old Bishop Taylor Smith. I was crucified with Christ!" (Galatians 2:20*).

It is hoped that this 100th anniversary edition will remind many of the Gallipoli landings, the epic battles of the Western Front and, more particularly, of the sacrificial Crucifixion of the Lord Jesus Christ. The battle with sin was won in a magnificent victory at the Cross. Resurrection is the proclamation of that victory. Should you desire to take your place in this victory march, the following 'Decision Form' included on the last page of the WG's are reproduced here for you to sign as your record of commitment to follow the Lord Jesus. 'Lest we forget.'

DECISION FORM

Being convinced that I am a sinner, and believing that Christ died for me, I now receive Him as my personal Saviour, and with His help I intend to confess Him before men.

"Yet to all who did receive Him, to those who believe in His name, He gave the right to become children of God." John 1:12

Name……………………………………

Address ……………………………………………

If you desire further spiritual guidance, please apply to your local Minister or the Secretary, Scripture Gift Mission.

Opportunities for War Gospels on Public Transport/Cafes

A retired lady from Sydney in Federation Square (Melbourne CBD) read aloud Taylor Smith's question and thoughtfully commented to her husband, "That's some question. I'll read this (WG) tonight." I emphasized the significance of Taylor Smith's reply:

"Yet to all who did receive Him, to those who believe in His name,
He gave the right to become the children of God"
(John 1:12).

Later, the lady's husband asked more questions about my ministry. Their Methodist heritage and good old-fashioned Aussie patriotism shone through.

On the train, a female studying prosthetics at university was interested in limbless soldiers and the ANZAC Centenary. She read John 8:12 and Lord Robert's message on God's guidance for health, comfort, and strength in sickness and adversity on the Gospel flyleaf.

A retiree, interested in ANZAC, accepted the WG. His father once attended a Baptist Church, but my contact admitted, "I'm the black sheep of the family."

On the bus, a pleasant Sudanese student known to me and who lived nearby, chatted freely saying, "I'll read this (WG). It will help me understand." A WG was mailed to a good friend in rural Victoria. She used it in conjunction with a talk to some fifty residents in a Senior Citizens home. It evoked memories and generated good discussion. The War Gospels were forwarded to a faithful praying friend in Naracoorte, SA. He reported in a phone call, that they were used to good effect at the crowded local ANZAC Day commemoration.

At a shopping centre café, a retired military policeman (with his wife) when told of my Police service record, disclosed a long list of war stories. He was familiar with the famous and victorious WW1 Charge of the Aussie Light Brigade in Beersheba. He accepted testimony and a WG.

An old soldier, selling red poppies in support of legatees at the Box Hill transit station, had never heard of the (WG) ministry. At an East Ringwood Cafe, the proprietor permitted me to issue Gospels in his facility and introduced me to a patron who accepted a War Gospel. An elderly retiree in East Ringwood and another on the nearby railway platform, both known to me, accepted them. Also at this cafe, a retired elderly charge nurse and hospital administrator was relaxing over coffee after tutoring local primary school pupils in reading skills. She informed me her grandfather was a Light Horseman in the famous Australian charge that liberated Israel from a long-standing, superior militarily occupation force. She was thrilled to receive a WG.

On the bus, a structural engineer, with Cretan heritage, was open to conversation. Passengers were getting agitated - the bus driver had inadvertently taken a wrong turn. No matter - we had more time to talk. My contact was steeped in firsthand WW2 heritage passed down by his parents, involving German and Allied warfare in his father-land. He took part in discussion on ANZAC Day and readily accepted a WG.

To a returned services volunteer guide at the Darling Harbour Maritime Museum, I said, "We owe our soldiers a huge debt of gratitude for their efforts on our behalf in war time." He was familiar with the details of the WW2 conflict but knew nothing of the role of WW1 military chaplains in distributing 1000's of the WG's to active servicemen at Gallipoli and the Western Front. He accepted one with thanks.

At the Manly Ferry Terminal, a likeable, elderly, bearded, long haired 'Issues' salesman, with whom I chat occasionally when visiting Sydney, accepted a WG. He said, "Ah Ha! A Holy Roller eh! I'll read this tonight. I once attended a Baptist Church."

ANZAC Day Outreach to Neighbours

In 2020 ANZAC Day commemorations during the coronavirus lockdown were different. No public celebrations were permitted. How to utilise the lockdown for the Gospel was the big question? After prayer, a pilot program consisting of several small packages specially designed for neighbours, were prepared. Each package contained a replica WG, an explanatory brochure, and some home cooked Anzac biscuits.

Seven neighbours accepted these hand delivered packages. Two packages were placed in letterboxes. One was posted interstate to relatives. Another was mailed to a married daughter in the UK. A neighbouring English engineer and his Venezuelan wife expressed gratitude. A Greek/Italian business couple were impressed. A senior retiree said, "Wonderful!" An elderly gentleman resident living opposite us for some thirty years, who we'd never met, visited during my ankle injury recovery. His goodwill gesture of a gift of mandarins grown in his backyard was appreciated.

Recently arrived tenants living opposite, expressed thanks with a return gift of a small ornamental pot plant and a note in our letter box inviting us to participate in a 'lockdown get to know you facetime call'. An elderly neighbour called as we walked past her home. She said, "My husband died of a heart attack yesterday. We were married sixty-nine years." He was an ex-serviceman. She accepted condolences and a WG and invited us for a return visit. Other opportunities arose to distribute packs in our local shopping centre. We met more neighbours during the Covid-19 lockdown than in all the forty-seven years we lived in this street. We prayed that each WG would be read, understood, and acted on by those who might not otherwise read a Gospel.

Remembrance Day – Lest We Forget

A similar outreach was conducted on Remembrance Day. On this day two minutes silence is always observed and dedicated to the memory of 102,800 Australian military personnel who died fighting to protect our nation in war and conflict. It is commemorated at the precise time WW1 ended at 11am on the 11th day of the 11th month in 1918.

Sixteen packs, each containing a WW1 replica WG, explanatory brochure, a sprig of rosemary and a 'Blessings' card, were distributed in our street and local shopping centre among those not previously contacted in the earlier ANZAC Day outreach. An encouraging note left two days later in our letterbox read thus: 'This comes with sincere appreciation. Thank you for your gift. Remembrance Day is special' (Signed by a neighbour).

Golden Wedding Anniversary

Jan spent her early years as a farmer's daughter in a farming district of Rannock near Coolamon in the Riverina District of NSW where we planned to celebrate our Golden Wedding Anniversary with friends, relatives, and neighbours.

Shops in towns and townships along the route from Melbourne to Coolamon displayed ANZAC memorabilia. War memorials erected in towns we travelled through hold greater interest for us now. We arrived at 'Avondale', a Bed and Breakfast farm stay near Coolamon for our celebrations. In a local café we caught up with family members and friends for a Saturday morning coffee.

In the evening, thirty-eight guests gathered at 'Avondale' for a BBQ. It was special to have our three adult children, their spouses, and grandchildren present. We closed the evening with a devotional, using an ANZAC theme to illustrate the value of scriptures in many years of marriage.

The focal point of our celebration was held on a sunny Sunday morning service in the local Uniting Church on Sunday 19th April - our actual wedding date. Jan learned her moral compass under the teachings of her parents and the Godly men and women at this church. Over the years she transferred these teachings into our marriage and family life. These beneficial teachings were acknowledged with gratitude to the church on our special occasion. The theme was 'Miracles Follow the Plough'. Church attendance for the occasion was swelled thrice above usual. Some twenty WGs were accepted. A country style morning tea after church followed. More WGs were accepted.

The following encouraging email was received from a religious education teacher friend from the southwest slopes' region of NSW, who attended our Golden Wedding Anniversary service. She said, "Greetings and hope your travels are going well. Just wanted to thank you for a lovely day at Rannock and hope you also enjoyed your weekend sharing with your family and friends. Bruce, I showed your replica Gospel of John (WG) at my two schools this week, and shared about ANZAC Day, and my lesson was, 'Who is Jesus, and did they know they could talk to Jesus at any time of day and in any place'. I used that thought from soldiers in WW1 and that they could talk to Jesus on the battlefield or wherever they were in need and they were not alone because Jesus was there with them. Also, about them carrying a Gospel in their pocket and if they believed they could sign their prayer of confession on the back, and how that would have comforted relatives when their effects were returned to them. So, thank you, and may it encourage them to trust Him too. Blessings'."

Our NewHope Baptist Church in North Blackburn promoted the story of the activities of the military WW1 chaplains in their services - 150 War Gospels were snapped up like hot cakes. They were issued on condition they would be passed on to people who might not otherwise read them. Good reports followed.

Hay, Hell, and Booligal

On our homeward journey, Jan and I were reminded of some colourfully local Australian history. Banjo Paterson, a celebrated early Australian bush poet, wrote many famous poems with an Australian flavor. My soft spot for outback Australia was fueled as a kid by some of Paterson's poems. I always hoped to travel to those remote outback localities he enshrined through poetry and prose in early Australian folklore. One of my favorite 'Banjo' poems is entitled, 'Hay, Hell and Booligal.' Hay is a pleasant, remote, prosperous outback NSW town. 'Hell' may refer to a sheep station property once called 'Hell's Gate', or the abandoned nearby 'One Tree Hotel'. Today my lengthy ambition to visit Booligal was fulfilled. We travelled an eighty kilometres section of the Cobb Highway (once a stock route) between Hay on the Murrumbidgee River and Booligal on the Lachlan River, across the flattest terrain on earth with a 360degree unimpeded view of the horizon. Kangaroos and emus grazed in lovely sunset hues painted by the roadside.

Booligal's population numbered twenty-eight. The local school had eight pupils. A young mother drove her three kids twenty kilometres to this school daily. She called in to the pub, and the local community centre while we were there, to pick up a loaf of frozen bread and icy poles for the kids. Comments from three local identities colourfully adorned our conversation. Jan pretended not to hear the blue language. ANZAC Day is big in this place. People from Sydney and Melbourne swell the population to over 100. They adjourn to the local pub for drinks afterwards. Imagine the war stories! The lady publican accepted two WGs and volunteered to give one copy to the local RSL President. Getting this leaflet into his hands made the long drive and a couple of pub squashes worthwhile!

The tiny hamlet of Booligal was compared somewhat humorously by Paterson with the western Riverina town of Hay NSW – modern, prosperous, and active. Conversely, Booligal with its pub, post office and very little else remained sparsely populated, remote, and isolated. Patterson lists Booligal's problems in his poem to include heat, sand, dust, flies, rabbits, mosquitoes, snakes, and drought. I enjoyed strolling along the banks of the nearby shady Lachlan River and viewing sunlit plains. We chatted with colourful locals, while reclining on the cool pub verandah, brushing away flies, sipping ale (Jan and I are non-drinkers) and sharing experiences. Reading poems and stories on the pub notice board extolling and immortalising 'Gun' shearers of long ago and pioneer settlers, was an educational experience. This is my kind of country. I always wanted to live somewhere like that, but it never happened.

Some seventy years ago, as an Echuca Technical College student, I travelled on a school tour to the NSW side of the Murray River opposite Swan Hill, where we visited the massive Murray Downs shearing shed operational between 1920 to 1998 when it closed. On our return from Booligal, we visited the Hay Shearers Hall of Fame. It was a genuine shearing shed constructed of red gum, Oregon, and corrugated iron. I discovered, to my surprise, that this shed was the old Murray Downs shearing shed, dismantled, and reassembled in Hay and renamed 'the Australian Shearers Hall of Fame'. A local identity, with two red kelpie dogs, gave us a shearing demonstration. Shades of many years ago. A nostalgic interlude for me!

To the Hay Tourist Information Centre receptionist, I asked, "Ever been to Hell?"

She replied, "No! I don't want to, either."

I explained to her, "The ANZACs went to Hell and back. Let me share a story, the media never talk about."

She accepted the War Gospel and said, "That's interesting, my daughter has to do a talk at school on ANZAC. She doesn't know where to start. This might help her. My boss is a Baptist. He's not a bad bloke either."

A female employee at the Hall of Fame still grieved her husband's death two years previously. I asked, "Have you heard Paterson's poem about Hay, Hell and Booligal?"

She said, "There's no such place as Hell" Regarding her bereavement she went on to say, "I've been to Hell and back."

I said, "Saturday was ANZAC Day. Soldiers at Gallipoli and the Western Front went to hell and back too. Let me give you something that helped them in their hour of great need." She gratefully accepted a War Gospel with explanation and thanked us for our interest. At the Hay Caravan Park, a discrepant West Australian couple in a derelict van with a mean and mangy Queensland healer (cattle dog), and a refined older lady from Sydney, accepted War Gospels.

Conclusion - Personal Reflections and Memories of WW2

I said to an old digger, (returned serviceman) "I was too young to fight in WW2, but I appreciate what you guys did for us."

He smiled and gently replied, "It was a long time ago." Another extolled the selfless service of our virtuous veterans.

I stated, "Many veterans believed in God. We must never forget them, and neither must we forget God." He accepted literature.

A plainly dressed, grey haired old lady with steady gaze and strength of character quietly said, "I was sewing trousers for soldiers in a clothing factory in Flinders Lane (CBD) on VP Day. The boss came in and said, 'It's over! You can all have two days off'."

My parents were farmers by the Murray Valley Highway near Kyabram. This little boy (me) dimly recollected watching in awe as convoys of military vehicles rumbled past our road gate. A platoon of armed and uniformed soldiers, with one weary, limping soldier yards behind in full battle dress route, marched past. As a little boy a car bumped along the corrugated gravel highway toward us, leaving a trail of dust. The driver powered up our lane, leapt out of his car, shouting, "It's over!" and quickly drove off. In more recent times Vietnam diggers wearing medals and ribbons, celebrate Long Tan Day.

Every Day is a School Day

Transitioning from life on a farm in a remote country district to street evangelising in the central business district of Melbourne, with all that happened between times, has been a huge and beneficial learning experience. We are now living in a multicultural society. An insight from an article in the September/December 2022 issue of 'Billions' was insightful. "Jesus was once asked, 'Who is my neighbour?' His answer reminds us that we are to look beyond appearances and circumstances and cast aside prejudices and stereotypes. We are called to welcome the stranger with generosity, care, and compassion'."

The Lord has peeled away my somewhat racist attitudes I learned in childhood. Ironically, my mother, who was prejudiced against certain nationalities, was born in Scotland. The practical follow-on from my various ministries has resulted in some lasting wonderfully warm-hearted friendships with people of different countries, cultures, and religions. They have contributed much to my understanding of Biblical doctrines, international relationships, and myself. I pray that all who read this book will be encouraged to reach out with Good News of the Gospel. I praise God that He has thus far led me.

> "Amazing grace, how sweet the sound
> That saved a wretch like me
> I once was lost, but now am found
> Was blind, but now I see.
> 'Twas grace that taught my heart to fear
> And grace, my fears relieved
> How precious did that grace appear
> The hour I first believed.
> When we've been there ten thousand years

Bright shining as the sun
We've no less days to sing God's praise
Than when we've first begun.
Amazing grace, how sweet the sound
That saved a wretch like me
I once was lost, but now am found
Was blind, but now I see."
(Songwriters: Paul Udouj, Gregory P. Cook.
For non-commercial use only.)

Taking it to heart:

1. Consider the almost unlimited opportunities of Gospel sharing in Australia.
2. Discuss some ways of evangelising in your locality.
3. Pray that God would reveal Gospel sharing opportunities in your daily activities.

References:

Galatians 2:20 – I have been crucified with Christ; it is no longer I that live, but Christ lives in me: and the life which I now live in the flesh I live by faith in the Son of God, who loved me and gave Himself for me.

Chapter 36

COVID-19 Lockdown (2020-2021)

> "He shall call upon Me, and I will answer him;
> I will be with him in trouble; I will deliver him and honour him,
> With long life I will satisfy him, and show
> him My salvation." (Psalm 91:15)

In 2020-2021 we found ourselves in an international crisis of massive proportions. The ongoing COVID-19 (Coronavirus) pandemic caused unprecedented disruption to individuals, families, businesses, churches, and nations. Lockdown in Melbourne commenced on 22nd March 2020 and concluded on 21st October 2021. Ensuing lockdown restrictions during this period lasted a total of 263 days. At various times during the lockdown these restrictions included:

- Masks and hand sanitising mandated.
- 1.5 metres social distancing.
- One hour of exercise per day.

- Driving within a radius of five kms of home.
- No visitors to your property, hospitals, or aged care.
- Sharing of food and drinks forbidden.
- Schools, restaurants, and cafes closed (take away coffee only!).
- Church services cancelled – online services permitted.
- Attendance at funerals limited to ten people and weddings cancelled.
- Many office staff and schoolteachers worked from home.

Melbourne's harshest lockdown restrictions in the world, led to an acute shortage of toilet paper! Hoarders came to blows, competing for last remaining toilet rolls on almost empty supermarkets shelves.

Despite all these restrictions, barriers were broken down, neighbours looked out for each other. We ended up getting to know more residents in our street during Covid than in all the fifty years we have lived here. Our family regularly checked on us. Our grandson kindly collected groceries each week and left them on the front porch.

In times like these, reflection on some historical perspectives helped. In the 1840's Spurgeon, Prince of Preachers, was pastoring a large church when London was gripped by an outbreak of Asiatic cholera. His congregation was decimated. Every day he visited bedsides and conducted funerals. Weary in body and sick in heart the burden was more than he could bear. One day, when returning from yet another funeral, Spurgeon saw in a shoemaker's shop front window this notice: 'Because you have made the LORD your defender, the Most High your protector, no disaster (coronavirus?) will strike you, no violence will come near your home.' (Psalm 91:9-10. TEV). Spurgeon immediately felt secure, refreshed, and clothed with immortality. He said, "I went on with my visitation of the dying in a calm and peaceful spirit. I felt no fear of evil and suffered no harm."

Generations have found protection from plagues, wars, dangers, evils, doubts, and depressions because they trusted God. The COVID-19 crisis was an opportune moment in history to appropriate God's promises. There is protection and security under the cover of God's wings (Psalm 91:4-6). Here there is no ill, but only good in mysterious forms, losses enrich us, sickness is our medicine, reproach our honour, and death our gain. 'God strengthens His people through His Word in times of plenty and need'. 'Bruises and Blessings' work together for good to them that love God and are called according to His purpose during mandatory lockdowns, safe distancing and wearing of masks.

May God bless, comfort, and strengthen you to serve Him. Your circumstances are not barriers to ministry, they are the ministry. God said, "I WILL save those who love me and protect those who acknowledge me as Lord. When they call to me, I WILL answer them; when they are in trouble, I WILL be with them. I WILL rescue them and honour them. I WILL reward them with long life; I WILL save them" (Psalm 91:15). Jan and I have found comfort in this Psalm. When uncertainty grips cling to Him who is steadfast. Our God is unstoppable.

Prayer:

"Father, help us to love You more than anything else and to share our faith in Jesus with everyone we can. Amen." (Prayer by Warren Hardig MFMG).

Chapter 37

Conclusion

My heritage is farming. Our properties bordered on what was then known as the 'Three Chain Road', an old stock route, connecting Echuca with Nathalia. This road later became the Murray Valley Highway. From time to time a drover in his battered old horse drawn van, slowly rumbled by with his flock of maybe 500 sheep feeding on roadside herbage in times of drought. Occasionally, as he travelled by, Dad let him overnight his sheep in a small paddock beside our home. The old drover was a returned WWI Gallipoli veteran. The sacrificial efforts of our soldiers in that war are remembered in our annual ANZAC Day commemorations.

My uncle, a pint-sized Scotsman, fought in three theatres of war during WW2 and was promoted to Sergeant in charge of a gun emplacement on the front line of a war zone. Another neighbour, who fought nearby, walked by this emplacement. He later mentioned to Dad in my presence, that while my uncle's crew were lying dead in the gun pit beside him, he alone with face barely recognisable beneath layers of black cordite, stayed at his post for three days firing his howitzer. After the war he was allotted a Soldier Settlers block, which he successfully developed into a profitable farming enterprise. Uncle never once discussed his war experience but suffered nightmares and severe attacks of malaria till the day he died. I visited him in the Heidelberg Repatriation Hospital on the eve of his death. He recognised me but couldn't or wouldn't communicate. Though I never once recalled being taught our military heritage in school, I had somehow developed a deep respect for the sacrificial service of our fighting men who defended at great cost, the freedoms we enjoy today.

Well documented stories of the victorious WW1 Light Brigade consisting of 800 mounted volunteer Aussie horsemen and their brilliant victory over 5,000 entrenched, battle hardened, mechanised, and seemingly invincible Turkish troops and their German commanders in the Middle East, moved me emotionally.

The Light Horse Brigade was comprised of the cream of young Australian manhood. Many from Christian homes had attended church and Sunday school. On the front line, a significant percentage of them participated in small groups, read Bible stories, prayed, and sang hymns. Christian faith carried them through to an incredible victory against huge odds. "Their weapons of warfare were not carnal but mighty in God for pulling down strongholds, casting down arguments and every high thing that exalted itself against the knowledge of God, bringing every thought into captivity to the obedience of Christ." (2 Corinthians 10:4). An old hymn puts it this way. 'Onward Christian soldiers marching as to war with the Cross of Jesus going on before.'

Paul said, "Be watchful in all things, endure afflictions, do the work of evangelism, fulfill your ministry" (2 Timothy 4:5). You may not be a Billy Graham, but all Christians are called to battle the world, the flesh, and the devil according to their giftedness and circumstances of their lives. Christians in sacrificial service are God's 'Light Horsemen' in today's world.

Perhaps God has valuable lessons to teach us on prayer when opportunities disappear. Do lack of opportunities intensify our prayer life or cause it to wither and die? There never was a better time for God's 'Light Horsemen' to battle sacrificially for the church being consigned to the outer perimeter of insignificance by a powerful enemy. The Bible reminds and assures us that gates of Hell shall never prevail against the church. Evangelism is rooted in Isaiah 22:22: "The key of the house of David I will lay on His shoulder; So, He shall open, and no one shall shut; and He shall shut, and none shall open." You may be the only Christian your contact ever meets. Lay aside the weights that easily hinder. Be God's 'Light Horseman' fighting injustice, corruption, rebellion, prejudice wherever you meet it.'

A frequently asked question with no easy answer is, 'If God loves us, why does He allow so much suffering, injustice and oppression?' Smith Wigglesworth, a prayerful evangelist of yesteryear answered this way: "Great faith is product of great fights. Great testimonies are the outcome of great tests. Great triumphs can only come out of great trials." Christians who survive the greatest suffering, often have the strongest faith. Betsie Ten Boon as she lay dying in the Ravensbruck Concentration Camp in WW2, turning to her sister Corrie, said, "We must tell them there is no pit so deep that He is not deeper still. They will listen to us Corrie because we have been here."

The history of the 'Light Brigade' clarifies and reinforces pride in our incredible Australian military history. However, the destructive, banner waving, bottle throwing violence of unruly mobs punching up Police Officers, disrupting cities and desecrating our sacred Melbourne Shrine of Remembrance with no regard for our hard-won historic past, troubles me deeply. But notwithstanding, a wide-open door exists for Christians to 'diligently add faith, virtue, knowledge, self-control, perseverance, godliness, brotherly kindness, and love to their community' (2 Peter 1:5-7). If these gifts are yours and abound, you will never be barren or unfruitful in good works. Don't let the world shut you down.

Prayer walking neighbourhood streets changes the spiritual climate of streets, cities, and nations. Prayer walking is on the scene without making one. It is praying in places where you expect God to answer. Extending prayers for the needs of our neighbours clarifies our praying. A friend and I have 'prayer walked' hundreds of streets in the previous five years (at the time of writing this book). Since COVID-19 Jan and I have regularly prayer walked our street, the nearby park and local shopping centre. Supporting this ministry is my prayer walking compatriot.

The Spirit exhorted the church in Smyrna to 'Be fearless Overcomers!' (Revelation 2:11*). The Christians' calling sometimes includes persecution, suffering, injustice, humiliation, and bitterness. It's a path trod by millions. It is sometimes called the 'The King's Highway'. One holy soul said, "There is no other way to life and inward peace but the way of the Cross." Nothing brings out so much of the love and help of Jesus as suffering. Trials and sorrows reveal new phases of God's wonderful plan and purpose for our world. We may go even further and say that often God allows our helplessness and failure to become so extraordinarily acute that His grace may have larger opportunities. 'Only as we reach our greatest extremity do we begin to fully realise what Jesus is prepared to be and do.' (Herald of Hope – Jan/Feb 2021).

We all hunger and thirst for a feast that satisfies our spiritual appetites. Jesus, on the night He was betrayed, at the institution of the Communion Feast, took bread and said, "Take eat this is my body broken for you." In the same manner, He took the cup saying, "This cup is the new covenant in my blood, drink in remembrance of me" (1 Corinthians 11:25).

The Cross is the Lord's table. Jesus, God's Spotless Lamb is our great supper. Feed on Him through faith for He made Him who knew no sin to be sin for us, that we might become the righteousness of God in Him. (2 Corinthians 5:21*). His eternal joy is our medicine. Burdened with sin? God forgives in Jesus' name and acquits our guilt. Not good enough to stand before God? Jesus puts us in a right legal standing before our Creator. Need strength and comfort? God is our strength and comfort. Sooner or later, the divine messenger will say, "All things are ready. Come to My supper." Then, if we believe Him, we'll close our eyes on earth, and open them in the heavenly mansion (John 14:2-3*). We will be like Him for we will see Him as He is. No matter how deep our need, if we have faith, God's supply will meet it. Jesus the great sacrifice, was slain. His Holy Bible is in our hands. The Holy Spirit illuminates that Word. The feast was never better. It never can be better. It is offered without money and without price. Make no excuses. Do not hesitate. Don't delay. Accept this invitation. Receive the grace of God in Jesus Christ. Spend eternity with Him. Come, for all things are ready. Jesus is waiting for you.

Vale Rev Joel Edwards

Rev Edwards, fellow traveller, one-time General Secretary of the Evangelical Alliance, International Director of Micah Challenge, and a senior figure in the UK Church, uniquely challenged evangelical Christians to unify. Prior to his death as a result of cancer, he left the following inspiring letter published in 'Eternity News.' I have neither heard of nor met Rev Edwards but the concluding line in his last letter summed it up for me:

He wrote: "Dear Friends, this is to say a final goodbye. First my incredible thanks for your prayers, love and holding on with me to that fingernail miracle. Words cannot express the depth, breadth, and height of my gratitude, but I have gone home. My earnest prayer is that your faith and tenacity on my behalf will not be considered a pointless religious exercise, but that it will have strengthened your faith in a God who is marvelous, mysterious, and majestic in all that He does: The Faithful One. I commend my family to you. I know you will watch over them in the months and years ahead. And I commend you to God and to the Word of His grace that is able to build us up and give us an inheritance among those that are being saved. **I wait to welcome you…** "

Soft Hearts and Hard feet

A twenty-one-year-old music student took the cheapest ship she could find and prayed to God to show her where to disembark. She disembarked in Hong Kong in 1966 and visited the Walled City - a small densely populated, high-rise slum for drug addicts, gangs, and sex workers. She loved that place, hated what was happening there, but wanted to be nowhere else. She envisaged it as a city ablaze with light, no more crying, pain or death, where sick people were healed, addicts set free, hungry filled, orphanages, homes for homeless and new dignity for those living in shame. She had no idea how to bring this about but with visionary zeal, imagined introducing the Walled City people to the one who could change it all - Jesus. Jackie Pullinger spent over fifty years working with heroin addicts, and sex workers. She once gave a talk entitled: 'Soft Hearts and Hard Feet.'

As with Jackie, I loved our city environment but hated things I saw happen there. Her soft heart and hard feet message inspired me in discouraging moments. Lord give us soft hearts for the suffering and hard feet to do something about it! Paul said:

> "Now then, we are ambassadors for Christ, as
> though God were pleading through us:
> we implore you on Christ's behalf, be reconciled to God."
> (2 Corinthians 5:20)

I began my Christian life at age fifteen. Now I am old. My years have passed in a flash. Every human heart feels the weight of sin. I am no exception, but Jesus takes our sin to the Cross and carries us safely to that eternal shore. Faith alone in the shed blood of Jesus cleans away my sin and guilt. The older I get the more I feel the need to cling to that foundation. The Bible says, "All have sinned and fallen short of God's glory." Trying to rid oneself of the weight of fear and shame of sin, transgressions and iniquity by religious rule keeping is impossible, but Jesus said, "Come to me, all you who labour and are heavy laden, and I will give you rest" (Matthew 11:28). That's why I'm a Christian. Apart from a few Christians, none of my street evangelism contacts offered a Divine Saviour like Jesus.

This humble and incomplete record of sharing the good news with thousands who embraced different faiths or none at all, resulted in spiritual growth in my personal journey. Through engaging with both believers and non-believers on the streets, I learned valuable lessons about the great doctrines of the Christian faith and cross-cultural communication. Jesus said, "If anyone thirsts let him come to me and drink. He who believes in Me, as scripture says, out of his heart shall flow rivers of living waters."

A significant prayer for my readers is that older Christians will become more proactive in downloading their experiences of Great Commission activities to younger Christians. We have a wealth of experience and knowledge to share. Why not help them as they develop their ministries? "What is the most important question in all the world for you?"

By dying to self and receiving Him as Lord and Saviour, we can offer the water of life to a world filled with false doctrine, anger, anxieties, and hatred. Let's not forget that we are the hands and feet of Jesus. Our most important task is sharing the love of Jesus with the lost and desperately needy. Sectarianism, eastern philosophies and the New Age influence is creeping into our Christian values and church life unawares. The challenge for Christianity is to stand firmly 'in front of them all' with the Crucified, Resurrected living Lord Jesus Christ (1 Corinthians 2:5*).

For eleven years, Richard Johnson, referred to in the introduction of this book, endured insults from convicts and opposition from authorities as he laboured for spiritual revival among his flock. He faithfully proclaimed the Gospel until the day he and his wife departed again for England. When the population grew beyond his ability to shepherd them, Johnson published a letter to be circulated among the colonists urging them to turn from their sin and embrace Christ. It concludes:

"This will be my daily prayers to God for you. I shall pray for your eternal salvation, for your present welfare, for the preservation, peace and prosperity of this colony: and especially for the more abundant and manifest success of the Redeemer's cause and kingdom, and for the effusion and out-pouring of His Holy Spirit, not only here but in every part of the habitable globe. Longing, hoping and waiting for the dawn of that happy day when the heathen shall be given to the Lord Jesus for His inheritance, and the uttermost parts of the earth for his possession and when all the ends of the earth shall see, believe and rejoice in the salvation of God." (p124 "Great Southland Revival' by Mahlburg and Marsh).

If your desire is to serve Jesus with all your heart you might pray the following prayer:

"Dear Lord Jesus, I have given my life to you, but I repent right now, because I have done very little that is constructive for your Kingdom. Forgive me! From today I offer myself for full time service. Time is short. The Kingdom of God is at hand. People need to hear the Gospel and repent. There are so few preaching the good news of Christ. Many perish because they have never heard. I want to reach my neighbour, and Lord, if you should call me overseas, give me faith and courage to follow through, in Jesus precious name. Amen."

This book invites you to join a world changing movement with an unfinished agenda. There is always much more to hope for, much more to be done. The Christians calling is to finish what Jesus began in Jerusalem. His power and authority is ours.

I am your affectionate Friend and Servant in the Gospel of Christ, for the sake of the Great Commission

Bruce R. Kelly.

Taking it to Heart:

1. How are you challenged to be more proactive in your 'Great Commission' activities?
2. How might you encourage younger Christians in their spiritual growth?
3. Describe some ways you might undertake a mentoring ministry.

References:

John 14:2-3 – In my Father's house are many mansions, if it were not so I would have told you. I go to prepare a place for you. And if I go and prepare a place for you, I will come again and receive you to myself that where I am you may be also.

1 Corinthians 2:5 – That your faith should not be in the wisdom of men but in the power of God.

2 Corinthians 5:21 – For He made Him who knew no sin to be sin for us, that we might become the righteousness of God in Him.

Revelation 2:11 – He who has an ear, let him hear what the Spirit says to the churches. He who overcomes shall not be hurt by the second death.

Timeline

1936	Born at Kyabram Bush Nursing Hospitable. Resided twenty-five years with family on a farm at Wyuna Vic.
1943	Attended Wyuna South Primary School, Wyuna West Primary School, Tongala consolidated Primary School and Echuca Technical College.
1952	Spiritual experience triggered long lasting lifestyle changes.
19-10-1962	Commenced Police service at Russell Street HQ.
19-04-1965	Married at St Andrews Presbyterian Church, Wagga Wagga NSW to Janice Moncrieff.
1965-1966	Transferred to West Heidelberg Police Station and attended Heidelberg Presbyterian Church.
1966	Transferred to Geelong Police Station. Attended Drysdale Methodist Church.
	Two children born in Geelong Hospital.
1972	Transferred back to Russell Street Police Headquarters and promoted to Senior Constable. Membership at North Blackburn Baptist Church (Now NewHope Baptist).
1973	Third child born at Box Hill Hospital.

1974	Transferred to Doncaster Police Station.
1978-1979	Completed Bethel Bible course and taught courses next four years.
1977-1981	Law Instructor at the Victoria Police Academy.
1982-87	Balwyn Police Station.
1-2-1987	Inducted as Wandin Baptist Fellowship's first Pastor.
1-4-1987	Retired at early age with rank of Sergeant, having received the National Medal.
4-12-1987	Graduated successfully from a BUV Frontline Training Course and appointed a Baptist Home Missionary.
11-2-1990	Inducted as first Pastor of Altona Meadows Baptist Fellowship (now Point Cook Baptist Church).
8-8-1992	United with the Spanish Speaking Baptist Church in ministry/worship at Altona Meadows.
28-7-1996	Inducted as first Pastor of the Kununurra (NW Australia) Baptist Fellowship.
June 1999	Kununurra ministry concluded.
2000-2002	Interims (three to four months each) pastorates at Temora Baptist Church NSW, and twice at Newman Baptist Church WA.
2003-2016	City Street ministry adventure began in Box Hill and extended to Melbourne CBD.
28-2-2016	Membership transferred from NewHope Baptist Church (NBC) to Light Community Baptist Church, East Ringwood (LCBC).
2016-2020	Street ministry in East Ringwood and in our local area.
23-03-2020	First of six COVID-19 lockdowns (263 days in lockdown over two years).

TIMELINE

18-12-2020	Broken ankle (three surgeries and three weeks in respite care).
2020-2023	Street ministry continues in our local street, park, and shopping centre.
2021-2023	Writing this book a significant challenge!

Clockwise from top left: LCBC plaque; Family; Constable Kelly.

*Above: Induction by Rev John Simpson at Wandin Fellowship;
Below:. Baptism at Wandin Fellowship.*

Left: Bruce the preacher at Altona Meadows; Below: Baptism at Altona Meadows.

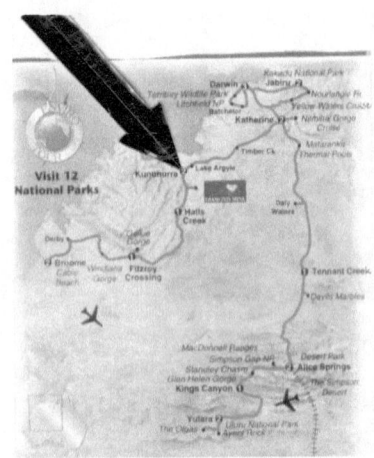

Clockwise from top: Altona Meadows English & Spanish congregations; Bruce & Jan, Kununurra WA; A map of Kununurra WA.

Clockwise from top: Kununurra Fellowship 1997; Martu kids at Newman WA; Paddy McGinty Kununurra WA.

Above: Flinders Street Railway Station, Melbourne VIC; Below: Federation Square, Melbourne VIC.

Indian Students at my 70th Birthday.

Japanese and Korean students in our home.

Samuel's baptism at NewHope.

Left: Vishnu and family 2018; Below: Sharing in McDonalds.

Above: Blessed by two Christians in HJ's; Below: Asian couple baptised, NewHope Church.

Above: Bruce with Brazilians; Below: Korean contact, Orleigh Park QLD.

Above: Delightful German contact & son, Litchfield NT; Below: Witnessing on a railway platform.

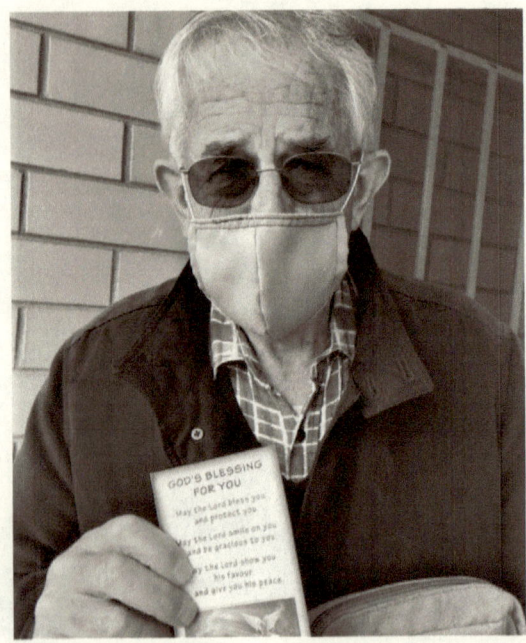

Above: Prayer walking; Bruce during Covid.

Above: Delightful German contact & son, Litchfield NT; Below: Witnessing on a railway platform.

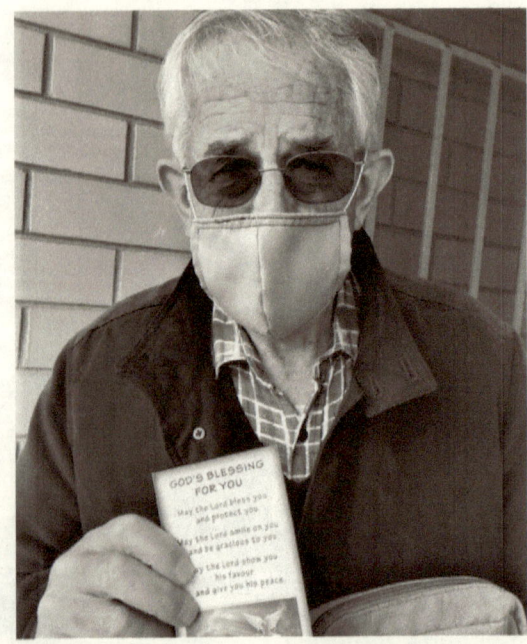

Above: Prayer walking; Bruce during Covid.

Above: Bill Pomery Naracoorte SA; Below: Bruce and Jan with Wesley Duewel at MFM.

A flower seller in Sri Lanka.

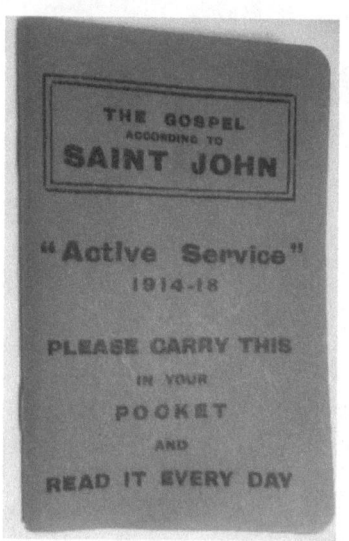

Clockwise from top left: Blessings card; WW1 Gospel; Site of first Christian Church Service in Australia.

Sergeant Kelly 1987

www.ingramcontent.com/pod-product-compliance
Lightning Source LLC
Chambersburg PA
CBHW021756220426
43662CB00006B/73